Housing as Commons

Housing as Commons

*Housing Alternatives as Response
to the Current Urban Crisis*

Edited by
Stavros Stavrides and Penny Travlou

BLOOMSBURY ACADEMIC
LONDON • NEW YORK • OXFORD • NEW DELHI • SYDNEY

BLOOMSBURY ACADEMIC
Bloomsbury Publishing Plc
50 Bedford Square, London, WC1B 3DP, UK
1385 Broadway, New York, NY 10018, USA
29 Earlsfort Terrace, Dublin 2, Ireland

BLOOMSBURY, BLOOMSBURY ACADEMIC and the Diana logo are trademarks
of Bloomsbury Publishing Plc

First published in Great Britain 2022

Cover design by Adriana Brioso

ISBN: HB: 978-1-7869-9998-6
PB: 978-1-7869-9997-9
ePDF: 978-1-7869-9999-3
eBook: 978-1-9134-4101-2

Series: In Common

Typeset by Deanta Global Publishing Services, Chennai, India
Printed and bound in Great Britain

To find out more about our authors and books visit www.bloomsbury.com and
sign up for our newsletters.

Contents

Figures

Acknowledgements

We planned this book before the recent COVID-19 pandemic and we feel very happy that it has now become a reality in spite of the huge problems we all had to face due to this global health crisis. We hoped that more opportunities for collective in-person work between the contributors would have been available, since the idea of exploring aspects of a potential commoning culture needs to be based on practices of knowledge commoning and the sharing of thoughts between those involved. Unfortunately, this did not become possible. We want to thank, however, all the contributors for their support, their enthusiasm and their work that often transcended the difficulties of this period. With most of them, we have collaborated in various occasions in the past, so, this collection is the mature result, we hope, of many intersecting research trajectories.

We both like to thank our students as they have offered us very often interesting thoughts and critical appraisal of our research endeavours as well as of our theoretical work. Although we are affiliated to different academic environments, bridges between them have proven very productive and inspiring.

We would also like to thank the editors of Bloomsbury for offering us the opportunity to publish this book. We are especially thankful to our editors Tomasz Hoskins and Nayiri Kendir for their support and understanding in these challenging times to publish our book. We are thankful to our proof reader Nivethitha Tamilselvan for her detailed editorial work on the manuscript. We are indebted to the invaluable support, constructive feedback and comments we have received by the Commons Series Editor, Professor Massimo de Angelis. His own work on the commons has inspired us and offered us the right space to publish this collection of in-depth studies on housing as commons.

We would like to dedicate this book to all the communities, initiatives, groups and projects that our contributors have presented in their individual chapters. Their example of commoning practices is inspirational and makes it possible for us to envision a global tapestry of housing as commons.

Contributors

Himanshu Burte is an architect and urbanist. He is Associate Professor at the Centre for Urban Science and Engineering (CUSE), Indian Institute of Technology Bombay (IIT Bombay). He is also the coeditor, with Amita Bhide, of the book *Urban Parallax: Policy and the City in Contemporary India* (2018). His research focuses on infrastructural space, subaltern placemaking and a range of practices related to the pursuit of a more just and sustainable urbanism in India.

Angus Cameron is an architect currently studying for his master's in architecture in London School of Architecture. As an undergraduate student in the Edinburgh School of Architecture and Landscape Architecture, University of Edinburgh, he was awarded the Rogers Stirk Harbour + Partners Scholarship. While at BVN architecture office in Sydney, he collaborated with indigenous architects and projects that later informed his dissertation project in which he received a distinction.

Lucia Capanema Alvares is an architect and urban planner and holds a master's degree and PhD in regional planning from the University of Illinois at Urbana-Champaign. She is Associate Professor at the Graduate Programme in Architecture and Urban Planning, Fluminense Federal University. Her research interests focus on multidisciplinary and participatory planning – particularly their methods and techniques, urban public space, sustainability, social movements, mobility and the city as commons.

Claudio Cattaneo is researcher at Masaryk University and precarious professor at the Autonomous University of Barcelona (UAB). He is a member of the Can Masdeu social project in Barcelona. His present and past research is related to the squatter's movement, degrowth, and landscape agroecology. He is the coeditor of the book *The Squatters' Movement in Europe: Commons and Autonomy as Alternatives to Capitalism* (2014).

Irina Davidovici is a trained architect and the director of the GTA Archives, ETH Zurich (since 2022). Prior to her current position, she led the doctoral program at the GTA Institute and taught as guest professor at EPFL Lausanne.

Her areas of expertise are the history and ideology of urban housing, as well as transfers of professional knowledge in contemporary architecture, particularly in Switzerland and Britain. Among numerous publications, she is the author of *Forms of Practice: German-Swiss Architecture 1980–2000* (2012, 2018) and editor of *Colquhounery: Alan Colquhoun from Bricolage to Myth* (2015). Two more manuscripts are in production for 2022, *Common Grounds: A Comparative History of Early Housing Estates in Europe* and *The Autonomy of Theory: Ticinese Architecture as Tendenzen, 1965–1985*.

Purva Dewoolkar is a SEED-funded PhD researcher at the University of Manchester. She is a trained architect and holds a master's degree in Urban Design from Kamla Raheja Vidyanidhi Institute of Architecture, Mumbai. Previously, she worked as the programme coordinator for the Transforming M East Ward Project, an action research project of Tata Institute of Social Sciences (TISS) that seeks to create a model of inclusive urban development in M East Ward, the poorest municipal ward in Mumbai.

Ana Fernandes is a full Professor at the School of Architectures of the Federal University of Bahia and a senior researcher (1A) of the National Council of Technological and Scientific Development in Brazil, and collaborates with different universities abroad. She is an architect and urbanista with a PhD (1985) in Aménagement et Environnement, Institut d'Urbanisme de Paris, and a postdoctoral degree from Columbia University (1996–7) and École d'Architecture Paris Malaquais (2004). She coordinates the Common Place Research Group, while her main areas of research and publishing focus on urbanism history and memory, city production, public spaces, common spaces, politics, policies, and the right to the city.

Glória Cecília dos Santos Figueiredo is Professor at the School of Architecture of the Federal University of Bahia, in History, Theory and Criticism of Urbanism, Urban and Regional Planning and Landscaping – Brazil and Latin America (since 2015). She is an urban planner with a master's degree and a PhD from the Federal University of Bahia (2011 and 2015). She is a member of the Common Place Research Group, and her work about Real Estate and the Social Construction of the Value in the City won her, in 2013, the Best Master's Dissertation Award from the National Association of Postgraduate Studies in Urban and Regional Planning. Currently, she is member of the Research Council of the University.

João B. M. Tonucci Filho is Assistant Professor of Urban and Regional Economics at the Center for Development and Regional Planning at the

Faculty of Economic Sciences and a collaborating professor at the Graduate Program in Architecture and Urbanism, both at the Federal University of Minas Gerais (UFMG), Belo Horizonte, Brazil. He is also a research associate of the National Institute of Science and Technology Observatório das Metrópoles. He holds a bachelor's degree in Economics, a master's in Architecture and Urbanism, and a PhD in Geography. He was a visiting scholar at the City Institute, York University, Toronto, and is currently a visiting fellow at the Center for Urban Studies at the University of Amsterdam. As a critical urban scholar, his research lies at the intersection of urban political economy, economic geography, and urban planning, covering topics such as metropolitan planning, property markets, land and housing policy, popular economies, urban commons and the right to the city.

Marc Gavaldà is Associate Professor of ecological economics at the Autonomous University of Barcelona (UAB). He is a member of the squatted social center of Kan Pasqual and the filmmakers collective of Alerta Amazonica, where he has directed a number of documentaries. His research interests focus on extractivism, environmental conflicts, oil impacts, and indigenous resistances in Amazon basin. He is the author of the *books Bolivian Oil Stains* (1999) and *The Recolonization* (2003), and has made the documentaries *Vivir sobre el pozo* (2002), *Tentayapi* (2005) and *Patagonia petrolera* (2008).

Mohamed Magdi Hagras is an urban designer, planner, researcher and Assistant Lecturer at the American University in Cairo (AUC). His practice and research focus on the socio-economic impact assessment process over the past decade. He has worked with local and international organizations like UNESCO, UNDP and UNHCR, in different scales of urban development projects in Egypt. He also participated in many international academic and professional projects in the fields of architecture, urban design, and urban development with public participation. His ultimate goal is to improve the urban quality of life in the cities around the world.

Matthias Heyden is a carpenter, architect and a research associate at the TU Berlin. He is also a guest professor at the Academy of Fine Arts in Nuremberg and lecturer at the California Institute of the Arts. He has been the co-organizer and co-designer of the Berlin limited equity coop K 77. Exemplary works from within his Berlin office are the event series and book *Hier entsteht: Strategien partizipativer Architektur und räumlicher*

Aneignung; the exhibition, public talks and magazines *An Architektur 19 - 21: Community Design. Involvement and Architecture in the US since 1963*; and the research project *Where If Not Us? Participatory Design and Its Radical Approaches*. In 2018, he coordinated the *Experimentdays.18* and *urbanize! Internationales Festival für urbane Erkundungen*. Since 2020, he is employed in the cityhall Berlin Friedrichshain-Kreuzberg while focusing on cooperative and common good-oriented planning and building affairs in the district and the city as a whole. He is an activist for a Community Land Trust in Berlin.

Christian Hiller is a media scientist, curator and editor at ARCH+ Zeitschrift für Architektur und Stadtdiskurs (ARCH+ journal for architecture and urban discourse). He has been a member of the research group *Art as Research* (Junge Akademie, Berlin-Brandenburg Academy of Sciences and Humanities) and cofounder of the series *Salon Art + Science* (Akademie der Künste, Berlin). He has also worked as a researcher on the DFG-project *Urban Interventions* (HFBK University of Fine Arts Hamburg). From 2014 to 2016, he worked as cocurator at the Haus der Kulturen der Welt, Berlin, where he was head of research for the exhibition project *Wohnungsfrage*, and has edited the publication series *Wohnungsfrage*. Since 2016, he has been part of the curatorial team of *project bauhaus* and editor of *ARCH+* and has worked as a curatorial researcher for *bauhaus imaginista*.

Jelica Jovanović is an architect, architectural historian and a PhD student of architectural preservation at the University of Technology in Vienna. She collaborated on the projects *Unfinished Modernisations: Between Utopia and Pragmatism* (2010–12) and *(In)appropriate monuments* (2015–17), as well as the evaluation and protection of New Belgrade's Central Zone and Experimental Blocks 1 and 2. She was a curatorial assistant of the exhibition *Toward a Concrete Utopia: Architecture in Yugoslavia, 1948-1980* at the Museum of Modern Art in New York (2018–19). Within Docomomo Serbia, she edited the *Register of Modern Architecture and Urbanism in Serbia 1945-1990* (2018) and the *Typology Atlas: Housing. Residential Neighbourhoods, Blocks, Conglomerates, Sites 1945-1990* (2020), as well as coordinated the documentation of and coauthored the projects *Virtual Library* (from 2014) and *Arhiva modernizma* (from 2018). She organizes Summer Schools of Architecture in Bač and Rogljevo (from 2010). She has coauthored the book *Bogdan Bogdanović Biblioteka Beograd, an Architect's Library* (2019).

Lalitha Kamath is a trained urban planner and an urbanist. She is an associate professor at the Centre for Urban Policy and Governance, School of Habitat Studies, Tata Institute of Social Sciences, Mumbai. Her research interests focus on urbanization, local governance and planning, urban infrastructure, urban informality and public participation. She is particularly interested in learning from and theorizing everyday urbanisms and contributing to academic and practitioner networks within India and the Global South. Her first book, *Participolis: Consent and Contention in Neoliberal Urban Governance* (Routledge Cities and the Urban Imperative Series, 2013, coedited with K. Coelho and M. Vijayabaskar), focused on a critical exploration of emerging discourses and practices of 'citizen participation' in urban governance reforms in India. More recent work has focused on the violence of becoming urban in the Global South.

Nikolas Kanavaris is an architect and activist who lives and works in Athens. He holds an MA in Architecture, and he is now finishing his MSc in Architecture 'Space, Culture and Design' in NTUA. He works as a practising architect and a theatre stage designer. He has teaching experience in Housing Design courses in NTUA and has also worked in Greek translations of texts around the commons.

Tonia Katerini works as a freelance architect since 1982. She was a member of the team 'Participatory planning company' (1984–8) as well as a member of the initiative 'Solidarity for All', specializing on housing issues (2012–16). From 2015 to 2018, she was the elected president of the Greek Architects Association (SADAS-PEA). She is a member of the movement against foreclosure with systematic action and research on housing issues, political space, and social solidarity. She is also a member of the activist group STOP-AUCTIONS, which participates in the European Action Coalition for the Right to Housing and the City.

Joviano Maia Mayer is an art educator and popular lawyer working on human rights, the environment, communities, and territories in conflict. He holds a master's degree (2015) and a PhD (2020) in Architecture and Urbanism from the Universidade Federal de Minas Gerais (UFMG). He is a founding partner of the Margarida Alves Collective of People's Advice and a researcher at the 'Indisciplinary' Group of UFMG. His law practice and research focus on land conflicts, urban reform, urban right and urban law.

He is also a professional circus technician and a graduate from the Interscholastic Center for Culture, Art, Languages and Technologies

(CICALT). He is currently taking technical courses in agroecology at the Alternative Technology Service – Serta (Pernambuco Education Department, Brazil).

Anh-Linh Ngo is an architect, author and editor in chief of ARCH+ Zeitschrift für Architektur und Stadtdiskurs (ARCH+ journal for architecture and urban discourse). He is cofounder of the international initiative 'projekt Bauhaus'. Anh-Linh Ngo was on the advisory board of the Institut für Auslandsbeziehungen (ifa) from 2010 until 2016. During this time, he developed the touring exhibition *Post-Oil City*. He is the initiator and curator of *An Atlas of Commoning: Orte des Gemeinschaffens*, a worldwide touring ifa exhibition which premiered in Berlin in 2018.

Catalina Ortiz holds a PhD in Urban Planning and Policy from the University of Illinois at Chicago as Fulbright scholar. She is an Associate Professor in the Bartlett Development Planning Unit, University College London. Her research includes the negotiated coproduction of space in Global South cities around urban design, strategic spatial planning, and urban policy mobility practices. She uses decolonial and critical urban theory through urban knowledge coproduction methodologies to study the politics of space production to foster spatial and epistemic justice.

Gabriela Leandro Pereira is a Professor at the School of Architecture of the Federal University of Bahia, Salvador. She is a member of the Lugar Comum Research Group, where she develops research into narratives, histories and cartographies produced about the city and its erasures, intersected by the debate on racialities and gender. She is the author of the book *Body, Discourse and Territory: City in Dispute in the Folds of Carolina Maria de Jesus' Narrative*, an adaptation of her doctoral thesis for which she won the Best Thesis Award from the National Association of Postgraduate Studies in Urban and Regional Planning (2017). Her research interests focus on urban cultures, peripheries, popular cultures, gender, race, right to the city, urban and environmental planning, history of architecture, history of cities and urbanism in Brazil, Latin America and the African diaspora.

Ioanna Piniara is a Greek architect/researcher and holds a PhD in Architectural Design from the Architectural Association (AA). Since her postgraduate studies, she developed a research interest in privacy as a biopolitical device for the control of domesticity, which was supported by the

Greek State Scholarship Foundation. Her doctoral research further explored the instrumentalization of the 'private' by the neoliberal doctrine and its spatial ramifications in urban housing in Europe supported by the AA, the Onassis Foundation, and the A. G. Leventis Foundation. She is currently a design consultant at the 'Projective Cities' MPhil in Architecture and Urban Design program and a lecturer at History and Theory Studies at the AA.

AbdouMaliq Simone is an urbanist with an abiding interest in the spatial and social compositions of urban regions. He is Senior Professorial Fellow at the Urban Institute, University of Sheffield, and Visiting Professor of Urban Studies at the African Centre for Cities, University of Cape Town. His key publications include the following: *For the City Yet to Come: Urban Change in Four African Cities* (2004), *City Life from Jakarta to Dakar: Movements at the Crossroads* (2009), *Jakarta: Drawing the City Near* (2014), *New Urban Worlds: Inhabiting Dissonant Times* (with Edgar Pieterse, 2017), *Improvised Lives: Rhythms of Endurance for an Urban South* (2018), and *The Surrounds: Urban Life Within and Beyond Capture* (forthcoming).

Harry Smith is Professor and Deputy Director at the Urban Institute, Heriot-Watt University. His research interests focus on how people coproduce and comanage their built environment, ranging from institutional and governance issues in planning and housing to physical design. Much of his work has an international focus, collaborating with partners in Latin America, Europe and Africa, examining planning and housing issues, community empowerment, participatory processes and user involvement with a focus on low-income areas. In recent years, he has led transdisciplinary research on the coproduction of landslide risk management in self-built neighbourhoods in Latin America. He has published widely on planning and development in the Global South.

Stavros Stavrides is an architect, activist and Professor at the School of Architecture, National Technical University of Athens Greece. His research focuses on forms of emancipating spatial practices and urban commoning, characteristically developed in his last books *Common Space: The City as Commons* (2016 in English, in Greek 2018, in Turkish 2018 and in Portuguese, forthcoming) and *Common Spaces of Urban Emancipation* (forthcoming in English). He has published numerous articles on spatial theory and urban struggles, as well as the following books: *The Symbolic Relation to Space* (1990), *Advertising and the Meaning of Space* (1996), *The Texture of Things* (with E. Kotsou, 1996), *From the City-as-Screen to the City-as-Stage* (2002 National Book Award), *Suspended Spaces of Alterity* (2010), and *Towards the City of Thresholds* (in English, 2010, in Spanish, 2016 and in Turkish 2016).

Penny Travlou is Senior Lecturer in Cultural Geography and Theory at the Edinburgh School of Architecture and Landscape Architecture, University of Edinburgh. Her research focuses on social and spatial justice, the commons, collaborative practices, emerging networks, feminist methodologies, epistemologies of the South and ethnography. She has been involved in international research projects in Latin America and Europe funded by the EU and UK Research Councils. As an activist, she has been involved in grassroots and self-organized initiatives on housing and refugees' rights in Greece. She is Co-director of the *Feminist Autonomous Centre for Research* in Athens, a non-profit independent research organization that focuses on feminist and queer studies, participatory education and activism.

Introduction

Revisiting the housing question: The potentialities of urban commoning

Stavros Stavrides and Penny Travlou

Experiences of struggle for housing ignited by the lack of social and affordable housing and foreclosure evictions, as well as practices of establishing shared and self-managed housing areas, unfold in a world of harsh inequalities. In such a context, it becomes crucially important to think again about the need to define common urban worlds 'from below' (De Angelis 2012a, 2012b; Stavrides 2016). We need to trace contemporary practices of urban commoning through which people redefine what is to be shared and how (Hardt and Negri 2009), against and beyond the dominant model of the partitioned and exclusionary city. Commoning practices (Linebaugh 2008) importantly produce new relations between people:

> To speak of the commons as if it were a natural resource is misleading at best and dangerous at worst. The commons is an activity and, if anything, it expresses relationships in society that are inseparable from relations nature. It might be better to keep the word as a verb, an activity, rather than as a noun, a substantive. (Linebaugh 2008: 279)

Commoning practices encourage creative encounters and negotiations through which forms of sharing are organized and common life takes shape. They do not simply produce or distribute goods but essentially create new forms of life (Agamben 2000), forms of life in common.

Housing becomes one of the major focal points of urban commoning, especially for those who either are excluded from the official city or actively challenge dominant patterns of inhabiting (e.g. the suburban dream, the alienating housing blocks and the gated community). Reclaiming housing as commons is, thus, an active force for urban and social transformation that needs to be carefully studied by those and for those who seek ways to approach social emancipation (Stavrides 2019).

Friedrich Engels' seminal essay on the housing question (2012 [1872]) is well known as a polemic response to Pierre-Joseph Proudhon's suggestion that workers should become owners of their houses so as to avoid the constant threat of becoming homeless. Neither Engels nor Proudhon questions the fact that everyone should have a decent house to live in. What, however, separates them is the relation of relevant struggles for housing to the prospect of an emancipated society. Engels thinks that if workers are bound to a house, that they additionally have to work even harder in order to pay, they lose their power to negotiate their workforce. They cannot move to other places since the house keeps them chained to nearby jobs. Furthermore, Engels accuses Proudhon that in his suggestion he actually paves the way to workers becoming petit bourgeois individualists: in this way, they distance themselves from the collective experiences and interests of cooperation that essentially form the basis of class consciousness.

In this nineteenth-century controversy, one can already discern an important distinction that resurfaces today in a new socio-historical context: Is housing a good to be claimed and distributed in ways dependent upon the characteristics of the corresponding society (capitalism), or is it a set of spatiotemporal relations that crucially shapes social life itself and, therefore, directly affects any challenge to social and urban order?

According to the first approach, housing is one more good to be demanded by all in order to ensure a decent life. However, according to the second one, housing, depending on its form, legal status and relation to the city and to that considered as necessary social services, gives shape to living conditions and, thus, defines to a great extent the conditions of social life. Following the second approach, visionary architects, planners and politicians sought to imagine and implement different social relations by envisioning different ways to conceive a future society's houses.

More connected to the first approach, 'realist' politicians have sought to devise policies that would at times facilitate access to housing for those in need, while actually depoliticizing the demand for housing by disconnecting it from demands for social change. Such a definition of the housing problem has of course become a contested terrain: supporters of social reform have in many cases pushed what started as a distribution issue to the limits of structural changes. Social housing production, affordable housing policies and tenet's protection measures were explicit results of struggles that deeply affected geometries of power, without however destroying the pillars of capitalist (re)production.

What appears to lie beneath the surface of such a contested terrain is a question that challenges the dominant view according to which the house is, after all, a merchandise to be sold and bought. What if, however, the house is not a container that facilitates life but one of its most crucial preconditions? A focus on natural needs and, therefore, rights would include housing as prime right. A focus on citizen, culturally defined, needs and rights would consider housing as the right that essentially guarantees citizenship (Holston 2008). One way or another, housing is reclaimed from the unfettered action of market laws.

Rethinking housing by theorizing the commons

What the recent discussion about the commons may introduce to the housing question is its disentanglement from the legal economic and political approach that considers it as the locus of the private, the locus of privacy, private ownership and private aspirations. Once this naturalized view is challenged, we may see the central role of cohabitation, of inhabiting together, that has always been the defining force of housing. The housing question could, thus, be reformulated. Instead of asking in which way people may have access to housing (in just ways, in market regulated ways, in ways that reproduce patterns of approved behaviour, etc.), one should ask what kinds of coinhabiting need to be pursued in order to support specific social relations. Following this, one will then have to specify criteria concerning such social relations: egalitarian cohabitation differs, for example, from cohabitation based on social hierarchies (patriarchal, race based, income based, etc.).

If housing is to be reformulated through the lens of commons theory, then, of course, one has to take sides: Which commons theory? What is to be considered as the practice of commoning? Here we can specifically relate commoning with the processes of creating and nurturing communities (see Bollier and Helfrich 2014, 2015). This recognition is a critique of the limited view of the commons as (only) a pool of resources (see Ostrom 1990). As Julie Ristau (2011), codirector of *On the Commons*, suggests:

> the act of commoning draws on a network of relationships made under the expectation that we will each take care of one another and with a shared understanding that some things belong to all of us – which is the essence of the commons itself. The practice of commoning demonstrates a shift in thinking from the prevailing ethic of 'you're on your own' to 'we're in this together'. (On the Commons 2011 online)

From this perspective, the practice of commoning is an activity based on relationality where sharing and caring are integral parts of what Berlant calls 'affective infrastructures' (2016: 399). Berlant speaks specifically about the need to act collectively against a 'broken world' (Berlant 2016: 399) such as the current pandemic crisis.

To discuss housing under this theoretical prism of commoning, then, one needs to directly link the questioning of dominant social relations with an ecosystemic approach. By this, we mean that housing cannot be just defined in relation to tangible infrastructures, for example, buildings. Instead, we should look at a much wider perspective that includes the intangible and affective infrastructures of each specific socio-urban context: the community alliances and the shared spaces produced by those living there. This approach aligns close to what is referred to as 'habitat' in Latin American housing scholarship, an inclusive term that recognizes the participation of different actors in the making of shared spaces for living a life in common (a view explicitly developed in the interview with Catalina Ortiz, Harry Smith conducted by Penny Travlou and included in this volume).

If at the centre of the housing as commons approach lies a problematization of coinhabiting practices, we must explore the ways those practices are shaped. We may distinguish at least three levels of shaping factors: the first level refers to the conditions of production of housing, the second to the design and planning choices and the third to the legal status of housing.

The conditions of housing production that have created potentialities of commoning widely differ, even if we limit ourselves to cases from nineteenth century to today. It seems appropriate to recognize this historical limit since it is during the nineteenth century that we first observe the devastating results of the housing crisis in industrial societies as well as first witness the militant criticism of urban and social injustices which gave rise to many proposals and practices that questioned the housing conditions (usually as part of a broader criticism of society).

As it is well documented, the so-called utopian socialists proposed new ways of social organization, while explicitly connecting them with visions of different inhabitation arrangements. Robert Owen's *New Harmony* proposal may be considered as one of the first such attempts to envision an ideal community based on equality and sharing. His plans for building a multifamily housing scheme were expressed in the form of a huge rectangle of houses that had various common use buildings in the middle (including a huge square). Although his so-called ideal 'township' plans were not realized, it is important to note that his views can be compared to a commoning ethos. He explicitly favoured the establishment of community kitchens, collective childcare and the development of a communal education system aimed at supporting both the children and their parents. Followers of Owen managed to build a few model communities in the United States and explicitly supported equality between men and women in everyday tasks (including household jobs).

Departing from Owen's focus on a rational calculus of social harmony, Charles Fourier, the other great nineteenth-century utopian socialist, put an emphasis on passion and love. In his highly controversial first work, *Théorie de quatre mouvements et de destinées générales* (1808), he 'offered "glimpses" of a better world – a world organized according to the "dictates" of the passions' (Beecher 2012: 94). Fourier's vision was never really translated to an alternative housing community. Although the most famous Fourierist project, *Familistére*, was constructed by Jean-Baptiste André Godin, its main characteristics were more close to a housing association for workers (actually the workers of Godin's factory) with lots of available-to-all services (primarily related to health and education). Godin kept for himself the right to lead and manage the project, and although he was more or less well intended, he never resigned from a paternalist attitude towards the community (Kontaratos 2014). Fourier's call for a *Nouveau monde amoureaux* would have to wait to be rediscovered in the libertarian experiments at co-living of the 1960s.

We may consider as a crucial stage in the history of collective housing the relevant programmes of Weimar Republic (1919–33). The Social Democratic administration of this period has produced remarkable social housing projects that went beyond a mere set of welfare state policies. Although closely related to local state mechanisms, large housing complexes were meant to be part of a supported workers culture that was to transcend the limitations of capitalist urban life.

Weimar *Siedlungen*, those new housing neighbourhoods usually at the periphery of existing cities, were envisaged as pilot examples of a future urban society. According to M. Tafuri, such plans were intended to express the rationality of 'liberated work'. A 'utopian ethic' connects to 'the myth of the proletariat as standard-bearer of a "new world" and of a socialism founded on a society of *conscious producers*: the phantom of socialization is evoked by "images" of a possible alternative to the capitalist city as a whole' (1990: 214).

Weimar *Siedlungen* were conceived and constructed not simply as a solution to the problem of acute housing shortage but also as a means to create a different kind of sociality, based on the projected values of communal living. Facilities concerning child care and laundry as well as outdoor community spaces were designed as parts of an almost-autonomous urban milieu focused on developing habits of sharing and mutual help. Although Weimar architects especially linked to those projects, as Bruno Taut and Martin Wagner, were leading proponents of modernist functionalism and a rationalist planning culture that aimed at taming or replacing the chaos of industrial metropolis, their proposals and work had a visionary focus that may be compared to commoning aspirations. They did not mobilize people towards such a focus of social reform, but they definitely contributed to the reformulating of the problem of city life in the direction of an emancipated society. What was perhaps their major handicap is that, being Social Democrats or simply well-intended planning rationalists, they did not recognize the limitations of top-down decision making and of relying on public funding within a predominant market-oriented economy.

The communitarian, socialist or anarchist, ideal inspiring concrete Social Democratic central European housing projects had to confront the reality of the capital city. Tafuri insists that such projects were essentially based on an anti-urban ethos and a nostalgic longing for a non-alienated urban community (1976: 116–24). As in the case of numerous plans of nineteenth-century utopias of collective life, the historical city itself was to be reproduced by a new kind of urban spatiality developed from scratch – as if communal bonds could only be established by abandoning the alienating anonymity of existing big cities. The idea that planning rationality will ensure the functioning of shared life (based on cooperative relations of production as well as of social reproduction) is present in both those periods. What Owen tried to ensure through his paternalistic obsessions, Weimar architects and politicians tried to achieve through the exemplary establishment of a new urban order based on the calculated efficiency of cohabitation patterns that the modernist planning and architecture were supposed to guarantee.

An example that seems to depart from such a dead-end trajectory is the housing projects of Red Vienna (Blau 1999). Building on the pre-existing tradition of Viennese housing blocks arranged around a common use courtyard, the new projects were constructed not outside the city but around the city's historic nucleus. They were conceived in the form of building complexes that were to have at their centre a communal *Hof* (yard). The urban life that unfolded in those large shared yards came very near to an ethos of commoning, albeit supported by choices in which the inhabitants did not participate. Sharing facilities and the use of outdoor space in the yard promoted in those complexes a kind of class solidarity that has been proven present in a dramatic way when in such neighbourhoods workers had to barricade themselves against the Nazi coup attacks (Zednicek 2009).

Interesting experiments of collective inhabiting have unfolded in the first years after the Russian Revolution (Kopp 1970). The idea of *Dom Kommuna* (House Commune), a housing model meant to create cohabiting conditions with extensive shared facilities, was harshly criticized by the party authorities. The modernist rational and 'functional' new Soviet cities would replace such experiments on collectivization, further promoting a state-centred programmed city life to match a state-centred programmed economy. Departing from the mainstream Soviet housing policies were the Yugoslav plans for new housing areas. As is shown in one of this book's chapters (the contribution of Jelica Jovanovich), in the early days of Yugoslav socialism a possible way towards housing self-management was pursued that came close to a culture of house commoning.

Throughout the nineteenth and twentieth centuries, housing has been an important form of action and thought for visionaries and activists, because it was considered as a crucial means to develop an alternative urban life. As we have seen, at the centre of such alternative views about housing is a rethinking of urban community and urban society. There seems to have been at least two different ways to concretize such views. One way is based on the assumption that alternative housing communities will be established in new pilot urban arrangements (new cities or new city-like settlements) that prefigure a new development of urbanity. The other way is based on the idea that building – like structures of a different arrangement logic – may become condensers of a new sociality. Depending on the history and the choices made in each period, designed or realized utopias of a new collective ethos have been closer to aspirations for a new city or to aspirations for new housing building communities. The common characteristic which transverses this spectrum of actually pursued or possible options was the choice to develop facilities of common use through which habits of sharing would develop (or, even, be created). What, however, may become a criterion through which one may decide how close all those efforts came to an urban commoning culture is the level of participation of inhabitants themselves to practices that collectively define and develop a shared world.

The housing question and the problem of power distribution

Commons literature has focused on conditions of production and distribution as well as on conditions of legal right and property status. Such approaches may indeed help defining in each case the possibilities as well as the actualities of alternative housing projects.

What seems, however, to be at the root of the housing question (and thus of the answers to this question) is the problem of power: What kind of social relations develop in housing areas that establish sharing? Are these relations based on solidarity and equality? What kind of gender, class, age, race and so on hierarchies 'corrupt' the commoning potentialities? And, is the production of different kinds of housing spaces a way to ensure commoning in and through cohabiting?

This leads us to another way of rethinking the history of housing as commons. In line with an extensive literature on the latent everyday resistances to dominant patterns of urban life or to the idea that everydayness contains the seeds of a different urban future, we may explore city life in search of urban commoning practices that develop within existing housing conditions. Some of the chapters of this collection indeed focus on such an endeavour. Thus, Mohamed Magdi Hagras explores the commoning potentialities in informal housing areas in Cairo (and the failures of dominant policies to support them), Himanshu Burte focuses on the importance of commoning in subaltern placemaking in Mumbai, and Lalitha Kamath and Purva Dewoolkar observe the development of commoning-focused 'activist infrastructures' in the Mumbai informal settlement Cheetah Camp.

This approach may be connected to the reappraisal of modern city life in which elements of liberating promises are unearthed (as in the work of Georg Simmel, Walter Benjamin and Siegfried Kracauer). It may be also connected to the complex everydayness of contemporary big cities (as in the work of Henri Lefebvre or Michel de Certeau). But, it may transcend the limits of Western thought tradition, opening possibilities of connecting to different cultural and social worlds. The logic of *Buen Vivir*, for example, summarizes an indigenous Latin American perspective that is based on a view of cohabitation which includes humans, non-humans, more-than-humans and nature as a subject partner (Acosta 2012). Along these lines, *Buen Vivir* is a 'system of life' based on the process of becoming, and on learning how to live well: a way of life that is community-centric, ecologically balanced and culturally sensitive. What seems to quite well align with *Buen Vivir*, nevertheless, is 'commoning': the notion of making/becoming a common.

Although non-Western problematizations of housing as commons are not yet developed, it is extremely important to observe how experiences and examples coming from outside the so-called First World may deeply influence relevant research as well as produce new theoretical arguments. It is not by chance, for example, that the chapter on Salvador de Bahia explicitly shifts the meaning of housing to encompass the plurality of habitat. Likewise, the chapter on Medellin's social urbanism shifts towards the discussion on habitat offering examples of community participation such as *coinvite* and *mingas*, which both translate between communal work, a gathering and celebration. Habitat, thus, becomes an expanded space to include all these shared spaces of commoning practices by the inhabitants. One needs to be attentive, though, when using non-Western examples to avoid the fallacy of romanticizing them, but instead placing them within their actual sociocultural context. For example, in the case of Australian Aboriginal architecture, Western academia has described it as 'vernacular'. Cameron and Travlou, in their chapter, criticize this characterization as rather derogatory and an imprint of colononization. They question why Aboriginal housing practices do not have equal billing in the architectural discourse but are rather positioned within a very narrow framework. Their research, instead, seeks to situate housing as an important site of engagement for indigenous people and suggest a new reading of ethno-architecture based on decolonizing architectural discourse and practice.

We may also explore the potentialities of housing movements by focusing on the way they explicitly or implicitly make it possible for new subjects of cohabitation to emerge. As is also being shown in some of the following chapters, homeless movements develop in certain cases a commoning ethos shared by their members that is meant to define not only the conditions of struggle but also the future conditions of living together in a housing neighbourhood (provided they manage to be victorious in their struggle). Subjects of housing struggles, thus, may be shaped through their action and forms of deliberation to become commoners, subjects that create themselves as they collectively create the rules, processes and agreed-upon priorities of sharing (Stavrides 2019). Mathias Heyden, being also an activist and participant in the Berlin housing squats movement, reflects in an interview included in this book on the power of collective action and the potentialities of sharing as they unfolded in Berlin struggles for commoning the city. Stavros Stavrides explores the processes of dissident subjectivation that develop in Mexican 'autonomous neighbourhoods' and suggests that they may become exemplary cases of the emancipatory power of commoning. Lucia Capanema Alvares, João B. M. Tonucci Filho and Joviano Maia Mayer analyse the Dandara Community-Occupation in Belo Horizonte (Brazil) by focusing on the formation of countervailing powers, networks and connections, based on communication, cooperation and creativity.

In both ways of approaching the problem of power within urban commoning, issues of established asymmetries arise. We may learn a lot from the fact that many nineteenth-century visionaries questioned the predominance of family relations in housing schemes. For some, this meant detaching housing proposals from the idea of an agglomeration of individuality spaces within an overall communal arrangement with shared kitchens, kindergartens and, in some cases, rural or small handicraft production installations. And, for some, this meant abolishing the family altogether because it was taken to represent the molecule of power asymmetries and developing housing communes of various kinds.

As D. Hayden clearly shows it, radical feminists of the nineteenth century explicitly argued against dominant moralist views that 'proscribed conventional marriage and motherhood as the ideal for all women' (Hayden 1982: 94). Marie Stevens Case (Howland) was one of them. An admirer of the Fourierist Social Palace, *Familistére*, created by Godin at Guise (France), 'she was one of the first American women in active political life to challenge the nuclear family, sexual monogamy and private child care' (Hayden 1982: 112). Involved in many radical cooperative efforts to house communities based on sharing and mutuality, she actually emblematized an early confluence of feminist struggle for equality with a radical orientation towards collective life based on urban commoning. Explicitly referring to the experience and views of such nineteenth-century feminists, S. Federici suggests:

> If the house is the oikos on which the economy is built, then it is women, historically the houseworkers and house prisoners, who must take the initiative to reclaim the house as a center of collective life, one traversed by multiple people and forms of cooperation, providing safety without isolation and fixation, allowing for the sharing and circulation of community possessions, and, above all, providing the foundation for collective forms of reproduction. (2019: 112)

The ideas that sparked, motivated and sustained efforts of establishing communities of sharing, are many, both in the past and in the present. Researchers have correctly pointed out that religious communities have often produced interesting examples of communes of sharing. Faith and a common identity have been at the root of such endeavours that, nevertheless, often accepted the 'paternalistic' predominance of charismatic religious leaders (Rexroth 1975; Holloway 1966).

Efforts based on socialist or anarchist ideas were and are often envisaged as ways to prefigure a future society. As we see in some of the following chapters, prefigurative practices are not merely exemplary acts of dedicated militants. They are practices that deeply transform subjects of cohabiting and power relations within cohabiting. Not that those efforts are by definition equalitarian and non-hierarchic. Commoning ethos, as is shown, needs to continuously develop the means to establish and reproduce itself against the prevailing individualist values as well as against disputes and confrontations that arise concerning leadership and organization issues.

Focusing on the problem of power relations developed, encouraged or denied and reconfigured in cohabiting practices helps us navigate our way through a contradiction that seems to prevail in problematizing housing conditions: Where should the limits be established between the private and the shared realm, and the limits that define, or even connect while separating areas of common use and areas of privacy? Ioanna Piniara's chapter traces the roots of a dominant neoliberal approach to urban housing in post-war ideas for urban reconstruction in London. By appropriating the council housing legacy, this policy produced new urban enclosures in which exclusionary privacy may be experienced in the centre of a historic city. To consider housing as essentially an area of commoning means to rethink established boundaries, canonical design and legal directives and individualist as well as collectivist mentalities. And above all, it means to rethink the relation between commoning practices and practices (as well as organized patterns of action) supported by dominant institutions that mark areas of confrontation rather than indicate areas of coexistence. In many cases, the state (local, federal or national), considered as a historical formation of sovereign power, limits or openly opposes commoning perspectives. As we will see in some chapters, though, by negotiating with the state through struggle or 'invited participation' (Miraftab 2009), urban commoning may manage to establish counter-hegemonic conditions in the production and life of alternative housing schemes. Take, for example, the case of housing cooperatives in Zurich where the local municipal authorities play an operative role. Irina Davidovici asks in her chapter whether cooperative housing can be seen as a commons in isolation from state and market forces, and, if so, how we could reconcile the active involvement of official agencies and commercial developers at the various stages of this cooperative history.

The emancipatory prospects of each resulting case can be judged of course according to the stakes at issue in the specific historical period and to the level of mobilization of people themselves that will corroborate their power to affect decisions. Latin American movements, for example, have repeatedly emphasized the role struggles for housing have for reclaiming the 'right to the city'. Let us remember that Lefebvre considers the city as 'the perpetual *oeuvre* of the inhabitants, themselves mobile and mobilized for and by this *oeuvre*. . . . [T]his means that time-spaces become works of art' (Lefebvre 1996: 173–4). Thus, the right to the city is essentially the right to collectively create the city. Reclaiming the city as commons means reclaiming the power of collective creativity: reclaiming the city as oeuvre.

According to J. Holston, demands of marginalized or homeless people for housing represent a 'politicization of the *oikos*' since, in them, dispossessed people 'struggle for rights to have a daily life . . . worthy of a citizen's dignity' (Holston 2008: 313). Struggles that prioritize demands for decent housing (as the confluence point for demands concerning the right to decent living) often explicitly develop forms of popular power. A kind of power, that is, which is not only promoting sharing and equality but is perceived and enacted as an area of commoning too. Many of such struggles are being shaped by efforts to ensure horizontality in decision making, rotation in duties, openness to collaboration and mutual help and, of course, solidarity. Power, thus, is being shared instead of being accumulated. Such an example of sharing horizontal governance and enacting solidarity and mutual aid is the housing squats for refugees in Athens. City Plaza, a former abandoned hotel turned into a squat to house refugees, has operated for almost four years becoming, as Nicolas Kanavaris suggests in his contributing chapter, a paradigm of co-living where its residents collectively decided on the way they manage the space using assemblies as a tool for decision making. Beyond this, City Plaza has proven that solidarity as a care mechanism is responsible for the longevity of the squat. This is again a reference to 'affective infrastructures' where relations, associations and practices of resistance enable people to enact politics of care and solidarity (Berlant 2016). In the case of Cheetah Camp in Mumbai, affective infrastructures, as well as the solidarity relations developed between the urban poor, are seen indeed as the alternative of sovereignty and power through the prism of activism from below. In this example, the values of shared caring and mutual flourishing, rooted in common struggles, are to create a better place, lived in common.

In the context of neoliberal governance and capitalist economy, housing projects are treated as areas of social control and urban order, as well as opportunities for speculation and profit-making. Welfare state considerations have regressed in the current neoliberal 'state crafting', which, according to L. Wacquant, prioritizes a 'disciplinary social policy' (2017: 72). This amounts to the focusing of social policies on 'corrective workfare' that imposes 'specific behavioral mandates' while expanding, at the same time, penal policies (2017). In such a context, commoning may represent a set of actions and experiences that challenge the integration of housing to current market and governance priorities. Commoning may be expressed in conditions of cohabiting that promote the sharing of services and responsibilities. Depending on the specific socio-urban context, such ways of living in common may acquire an emblematic, paradigmatic or, even, prefigurative character. Can Masdeu and Kan Pasqual rurban squats in the outskirts of Barcelona offer a good example of inhabiting the commons where their governance model is based on self-institutionalization and autonomy. In their chapter, Marc Gavaldà and Claudio Cattaneo suggest that collective autonomy within these eco-squats does not only relate to cohabitation but also to 'the reproductive task of feeding themselves'.

Commoning may also be present in collective resistances to enclosure policies that privatize existing affordable or social housing building stock. S. Hodkinson names such struggles for housing 'strategic and tactical interventions' that develop housing commons as 'forms of protection against the market' (2012: 438). What seems to worry him, though, is the possibility of 'weakening the protective shield that strategic housing commons provide' when putting an emphasis on experiments of collective 'living in common' (2012: 439). Actually, both perspectives need to be explored and actively pursued. In an effort to study the potentialities of specific struggles to protect the right to housing, several chapters in this book trace the characteristics of relevant movements and implicitly or explicitly connect them to commoning actions. The anti-auction movement in Athens is one among such examples: it has managed to bring together a significant number of local collectives, initiatives and individual activists to successfully stop the auctions in many occasions. The right to housing is in the forefront of this movement as the anti-auction activist, Tonia Katerini, writes in her chapter. She suggests that the movement's activists must act on three levels: first, to provide knowledge to the public on the dimension of the housing issues in Athens; second, to assist and empower people who have been affected; and, finally, to stop any attempt of loss of home through auctions and evictions. Such struggles became exceedingly important especially during the recent economic (and social) crisis in Greece spanning the period roughly from 2008 to 2019. During this period, a country that has one of the highest percentages of home ownership in Europe was explicitly struck by the immense inability of people to pay for their housing loans as well as for the everyday bills and obligations. As Katerini's text explains, an advancing proletarianization struck the lower middle class and further deepened the vulnerability of the urban poor, including the refugees and the immigrants. In such a context, the owned house that has provided (especially from the last world war on) the most important safety net for the dominated classes is becoming less and less affordable. Precarity and the resulting fear for the future becomes the dominant experience for many people who used to consider their life conditions more or less guaranteed not by a welfare state (as in many European states) but by the ownership of a house: a stable locus of family life.

Especially in countries in which home ownership is common for lower and middle classes (including Greece and Spain in Europe), people are used to the idea that owning a house means for them having access to a good that makes them members of the society. Homelessness was the ultimate loss of this right to membership. It is in this way that house is for most a good that everybody should be able to use. Does this mean that house was understood as a common good? This is really debatable. What seems to be more accurate is that house ownership is considered by both the dominant and the dominated as the major proof of living well (with differing priorities depending on the class one belongs to). What possibly opens the path to thinking about housing as a common good or housing as the focus of commoning experience is perhaps the crisis itself and the ways it has shaken the status of home ownership. Can the – albeit still weak – housing movements of today ignite such collective explorations? And can the prolonged effects of the crisis (especially multiplied by the recent pandemic crisis) become the fertile ground for the emerging networks of cohabitation solidarity?

The only possible solution to Hodkinson's dilemma may come from the experiences of concrete struggles. In certain socio-urban contexts, the struggle of the urban poor for housing is forced to directly confront policies that consider parts of the population as expendable. In such a context, housing commons become both the means and the scope of struggle. The inherent potentiality of commoning in and through housing movement action is, thus, the outcome of the 'politicization of oikos' in the neoliberal cities of acute spatial and social injustices. In order to retain the transformative power of commoning, it is important to always combine experiences of commoning with forms of social organization that resist both the power of the market and the domination of the state.

Many and different ways to understand and protect housing as a decisive area of sharing and living in common have developed throughout the recent urban and social history. Daring experiments, imaginative utopias and fierce struggles have to teach us a lot. It remains to the potential today's commoners to mobilize this knowledge in efforts to restore the creative power of sharing in and through cohabiting.

A final note concerning the production of this book: For the purpose of collecting contributions on the topic of housing considered as an area of commoning, we, as editors, contacted people engaged with this topic not merely as researchers or theorists but also as active participants in efforts to promote and explore the potentialities of commoning. A crucial aspect of such efforts is, we believe, the sharing of knowledge and experiences which we explicitly tried to become a shaping factor of our collaborative project. This volume, thus, attempts to both express and promote a commoning ethos that should characterize any work on the commons. Clearly, beyond any dominant practice of enclosing knowledge or intellectual skills, this collective endeavour, then, is a modest contribution to a research on commoning that reflects the values of commoning.

References

Acosta, A. (2012), Buen Vivir: An Opportunity to Imagine Another World. In *Inside a Champion: An Analysis of the Brazilian Development Model.* Ed. Heinrich Böll Foundation. 192–210. https://www.boell.de/sites/default/files/Inside_A_Champion_Democracy.pdf#page=194.

Agamben, G. (2000), Form of Life. In *Means Without End*, Minneapolis: University of Minnesota Press. 3–12.

Beecher, J. (2012), Women's Rights and Women's Liberation in Charles Fourier's Early Writings. In *Utopian Moments: Reading Utopian Texts*. Ed. Miguel A. Ramiro Avilés and J. C. Davis. London: Bloomsbury Academic. 92–8.

Berlant, L. (2016), The Commons: Infrastructures for Troubling Times*. *Environment and Planning D: Society and Space* 34(3): 393–419. doi: https://doi.org/10.1177/0263775816645989

Blau, E. (1999), *The Architecture of Red Vienna 1919–1934*, Cambridge, MA: The MIT Press.

Bollier, D. and Helfrich, S. (Eds) (2014), *The Wealth of the Commons: A World Beyond Market & State*. Heinrich Böll Foundation. http://wealthofthecommons.org

Bollier, D. and Helfrich, S. (Eds) (2015), *Patterns of Commoning*. Amherst, MA: The Commons Strategy Group/Off the Commons Books.

De Angelis, M. (2012a), Crises, Movements and Commons. *Borderlands*, 11. http://www.borderlands.net.au/vol11no2_2012/deangelis_crises.htm (accessed September 20, 2014).

De Angelis, M. (2012b), Crises, Capital and Cooperation: Does Capital Need a Commons Fix? In *The Wealth of the Commons. A World beyond Market and State*, Ed. Bollier, D. and S. Helfrich. Amherst, MA: Levellers Press, 184–91.

Engels, Fr. ([1872] 2012), *The Housing Question*. London: Union Books

Federici, S. (2019), *Re-enchanting the World: Feminism and the Politics of the Common*. Oakland: PM Press.

Hardt, M. and Negri, A. (2009), *Commonwealth*. Cambridge, MA: Harvard University Press.

Hayden, D. (1982), *The Grand Domestic Revolution*. Cambridge: The MIT Press

Hodkinson, S. (2012), The Return of the Housing Question. *Ephemera* 12: 423–44.

Holloway, M. (1966), *Utopian Communities in America 1680–1880*. New York: Dover Publications

Holston, J. (2008), *Insurgent Citizenship: Disjunctions of Democracy and Modernity in Brazil*. Princeton: Princeton University Press.

Lefebvre, H. (1996), *Writings on Cities*, Oxford: Blackwell.

Linebaugh, P. (2008), *The Magna Carta Manifesto: Liberties and Commons for All*. Berkeley: California University Press.

Kopp, A. (1970), *Town and Revolution. Soviet Architecture and City Planning 1917–1935*. New York: George Braziller.

Kontaratos, S. (2014), *Utopia and Urban Planning* (In Greek). Athens: MIET.

Miraftab, F. (2009), Insurgent Planning: Situating Radical Planning in the Global South. *Planning Theory* 8(1): 32–50.

Ostrom, E. (1990), *Governing the Commons: The Evolution of Institutions for Collective Action*. Cambridge: Cambridge University Press.

Rexroth, K. (1975), *Communalism: From its Origins to the 20th Century*. London: Peter Owen Publishers

Ristau, J. (2011), What is Commoning, Anyway? Activating the Power of Social Cooperation to Get Things Done – and Bring Us Together. *On the Commons,* 3 March 2011. http://www.onthecommons.org/work/what-commoning -anyway#sthash.6oYDUwk8.dpbs

Stavrides, S. (2016), *Common Space. The City as Commons.* London: Zed Books.

Stavrides, S. (2019), *Common Spaces of Urban Emancipation.* Manchester: Manchester University Press

Tafuri, M. (1976), *Architecture and Utopia: Design and Capitalist Development.* Cambridge: The MIT Press

Tafuri, M (1990), *The Sphere and the Labyrinth. Avant-gardes and Architecture from Piranesi to the 1970's,* Cambridge, MA: MIT Press.

Wacquant, L. (2017), Three Steps to a Historical Anthropology of Actually Existing Neoliberalism. *Social Anthropology* 20(1): 66–79.

Zednicek, W. (2009), *Architektur des Roten Wien,* Wien: Verlag Walter Zednicek.

Part I

Informal housing, infrastructures and commoning practices

1

Weaving commons in Salvador (Bahia, Brazil)

Urgency, recognition, convergence

Ana Fernandes, Glória Cecília Figueiredo and
Gabriela Leandro Pereira

Introduction

Salvador – capital of Bahia, located in Brazil's Northeastern region – is the city where the groups involved in this city-common network are based. With an estimated population of around three million inhabitants (IBGE, 2021), composed mostly of Black people, Salvador is a complex city, as it accumulates processes that constitute the Latin American cities (Pirez, 2016). These processes are materialized by colonial inheritances, modernization, accelerated growth, as well as segregated and selective urbanization. The urban fabric that weaves itself over time is marked by the asymmetric power relations between the different political, economic, social and racial groups that inhabit, dispute, negotiate and daily formulate ways of living.

Unequal infrastructure and urban equipment provision, denied access to housing and land regularization, gangs and militia fights for territorial control are some of the problems resulting from conjuncted action between the public and the private spheres. Simultaneously, new dynamics and new socialization practices are created to challenge this unequal reality, shaping a powerful place to think Brazilian reality and the cities of the South – offering important contributions to the field of urban studies. This fact brings about a conceptual and theoretical re-elaboration of this reality, one that criticizes the conventional epistemologies that do not adhere properly to its ontology.

Under this perspective, this chapter shares experiences and lessons of a collaborative space provided by an exchange[1] between students,

---

[1] In 2015, reacting to a provocation by DPU-The Bartlett-UCL, the research group *Lugar Comum*, from UFBA's Faculty of Architecture, adheres to the idea of a four-

professors and researchers from the Federal University of Bahia mainly the *Lugar Comum* (Common Place) Research Group) and the Faculty of Architecture) and University College London (Bartlett Planning Development Unit), and associations, movements and urban collectives from Salvador, namely, *Acervo da Laje*; *Associação Amigos de Gegê e dos Moradores da Gamboa de Baixo* (Association Friends of Gegê and of Residents of Gamboa de Baixo); *Associação de Moradores e Amigos do Centro Histórico* (AMACH) (Association of Residents and Friends of the Historic Center); *Fórum de Entidades do Nordeste de Amaralina* (FOSERENA) (Neighbourhood Forum in Nordeste de Amaralina); through the project *Cine Maloca*; *Associação Nova República* (Association New Republic); *Paróquia Santo André* (Santo André Parish), the *Associação de Moradores do Nordeste de Amaralina* (Association of Residents of Nordeste de Amaralina); *Movimento de Luta nos Bairros, Vilas e Favelas* (Movement of Struggles in the Neighbourhoods, Villages and Slums) and the *Ocupação Luísa Mahin* (MLB) (Occupation Luísa Mahin); *Movimento Sem Teto da Bahia* (Homeless Worker's Movement); the *Ocupações IPAC II e III* (Occupations IPAC II and III), *Força e Luta Guerreira Maria* (MSTB) (Occupation Warrior Maria's Strength and Struggle); as well as *Rede de Associações de Saramandaia* (RAS) (Network of Associations from Saramandaia), through the cultural project *Arte Consciente* and *Balanço das Latas Brasil.*

   One way to approach this collaboration is through the weaving metaphor, for it refers to the processual, open and relational character imbued in the practice of defining a shared domain. As a common in process – or commoning – it is intertwined with the dimensions of scale, scope and relations involved in the collective action (Blaser & de la Cadena, 2017) as well as duration, permanently activated and permeating the entire process. This occasion of collaborative work – among universities and a variety of popular organizations, with different interests and historical build-ups interacting in the construction of this relation[2] – sought to develop a shared formation and learning process that would simultaneously engage ethical commitment with knowledge production, horizontality along the problem-defining process, and the construction of actions and reflections

year exchange (2016–19) with professors and students, involving both universities and various popular collectives operating in seven territories of the city of Salvador. Approximately 20 professors from both universities, 25 leaders of movements and collectives, 250 students – 100 of them from 34 countries other than Brazil – and countless locals – that contributed to the process on different occasions – have attended the programme.

2   An approach to the action of these movements in relation with universities is worked out in Walker, Carvalho, Diaconescu (eds) (2020).

deemed strategic for everyone involved. In the process, many intertwined themes arose to be addressed as urgencies of urban life in Salvador: housing, infrastructure, mobility, social equipment, collective spaces, economy, culture and memory.

It is from this interlacing of issues that urban dwelling, much more than *stricto sensu* housing unit, imposed itself as a perspective capable of aggregating the complex and multidimensional process that concerns irreducibly collective life, practised space and the common, in their multiple expressions and achievements in cities. Dwelling as initially conceived by Martin Heidegger (1971, p. 3), as one of his four simple onenesses 'belonging to men's being with one another', and taken up by Henri Lefebvre. For him, 'dwelling is an open place' (Lefebvre, 2003, p. 124) and comes together with lived experience of everyday life, with urban and social space as activity, as situation (Elder, 2004) and as potential conflict.

It follows that, understanding the whole city as dwelling – or as commons – reveals it as a promising space for insurgency. This is due to its essentially collective nature, constituted by systems of objects and systems of actions (Santos, 1996); due to the multiple and conflictive construction work, which derives from expanded cooperation and lively accumulated work; and finally, due to the accumulated and procedural surplus. Thus, a number of initiatives, counter-trends, experimentations, actions, confrontations and associations challenge the common making of cities with scales, durations and distinct political, social and cultural profiles. The urban common is, therefore, at the same time, a productive reason (Hardt & Negri, 2005) – expanded cooperation processes and sharing of subjectivities – and an alternative reason (Dardot & Laval, 2014) – which implies the practice of movements and logics of appropriation of cities and territories. In this permanently renewed process that always involves constitution and institution, the common supposes the assurance of a common advantage, which assumes a certain agreement between what is fair and what is necessary (Dardot & Laval, 2014).

Hence, although the collectives involve their own necessities and conditioning factors, when in group, they share a common perspective that is potentially fruitful for all. When referring to everyone as a group, we will use the word practitioners, due to its permanently active character. Therefore, we seek to build a workspace based on dialogue, with the goal to interactively and inter-pedagogically form students, professors and locals within a broad perspective on the right to the city. From the resulting (and presupposed) fight against social enclosure and invisibility, as well as against the political delegitimation of urban collectives, arose the search and the situated construction of necessary tools and productive actions towards a democratic enlargement of urban horizons.

Thus, arose and updated by decolonial perspectives and the politics of care (Puig de la Bellacasa, 2017), a space of 'interknowledge' (Santos, 2007) emerges. This space facilitates a kind of engagement that points beyond the fixed limit of opposition or denunciation of neoliberal urban policies of death. Collective care, abandonment of hierarchy and reparation enable us to glimpse and experience other imageries and realities, which are situated in and from everyday life, actual politics and actual cities. These attitudes also affect, effectively and potentially, in distinct ways, power relations and its constitutive subjects, by causing a shift in positions and relations.

The urgency of the common

The shared interest in the experience was defined upon two urgent circumstances: one originated in the city and the other in the university.

Urgency is a state of existence and crisis of the Brazilian cities. The blatant inequalities that structure them entail in continued and renewed situations of fragmentation, segregation, racism, precariousness, insecurity, risks and invisibility to large portions of the population and the territory, especially to the most vulnerable ones. The city in question, as most Brazilian cities, is ruthless and – despite the abundance of life and creation present in the so-called territories of poverty – demands enduring concentrated effort, struggles and mobilization as ordinary requirements for one to insert oneself in it.

The demands related to the expanded possibilities of reproduction in the city mobilized the urgencies of the associations, movements and collectives taking part in the exchange, directly problematizing the issue of the common city, in its various scales. The city inhabited by these collective subjects and revealed by their encounter with the university is marked by historical and renewed processes of subalternization, dispossession, impoverishment and vulnerabilization. Here, the so-called necropower (Mbembe, 2018) delineates the politics of death, bringing to the scene the production of zones or territories where the free right to kill would be confirmed.

The Latin American city's hegemonic articulation, symbolized here by the contemporary city of Salvador, materializes itself in massive, racialized and hypersexualized processes (Collins, 2015; Gonzales, 1984; Nascimento, 1978) of precarious urbanization (Oliveira, 1982), associated to low levels of popular integrativity, as well as non-modern worlds within these global and local orders (Chakravartty & Silva, 2012; Dirlik, 2007). The conflictive spheres resulting from city interventions and transformational processes reveal themselves as important spaces of interaction, opening a kind of crossroad between their uncommon worlds (Blaser & de la Cadena, 2018) and releasing a range of possibilities, disagreements and negotiations on ways, contents, senses and effects of urban transformations.

Based on this complex and vital encounter, the search for development of commons reveals a way of engagement that challenges the unitary logic of the state's public sphere, reopening and repoliticizing the discussion and (re) formulation of collective issues, through more autonomous and democratic spheres (Boullosa, 2013).

But urgency is also a state of existence and crisis in the university. Not only knowledge production implicates even more complex issues, but its social validation has also been constantly put in check. Issues concerning decoloniality and epistemic justice, for instance, cause the recognition of distinctive systems of thought, which – without any eccentricity or folklore – based themselves on other ontological and social structures. Therefore, they also bring about the necessity of challenging our own philosophical system. That means, how does one deal with otherness, in a reciprocal and legitimate way, one that is agreed and symmetrical?

The issue for universities, in their common and heterogeneous condition, would be that of building a composite space, in which the members (as Mouffe (2007) reminds us, in her agonistic democracy) are legitimized while building the power to speak, as well as the power to listen and their distinct reception conditions. A plural system of references is collectively legitimized. In this path, the co-implication of subjects of resistance and creation is quintessential, for it turns interaction into the politics in the act of the common's constitution itself.

Therefore, the point here, evidently, is neither the assistentialist extension nor the instrumental research that supports the neoliberal university. On the contrary, this encounter, born out of many urges, yearns for the abandonment of hierarchy in the relationships between the university and the marginalized territories, destabilizing and reformulating the terms and contents of the knowledge elaboration. The commitment with collective actions, in favour both of life and of confrontation with subalternization processes, calls us upon an ethics of social engagement in gestures of ontological and epistemological opening. That is to say, collaborations – such as this one – are opportunities for us to challenge the science's and the university's hegemonic practices, that, to this day, are still mostly guided by the colonial canons of modern science and their hierarchies of power knowledge.

Hence, the urgency to build a political and technical space of shared learning as a step towards a repositioning in the face of established interdictions to the right to the common city for most of its population.

At first, the experience was aimed at the activation of each territory. At this stage, the collectives' leaders had prominent roles. They worked mobilizing the residents while keeping contact with the university to establish which contents should be discussed according to what was urgent in each case. It was about constituting a still-fragile relationship network that, polarized by the university, connected the many collectives involved.

Recognition and the common in process

Recognition in the collaborative space within the exchange embraces the residents' very humanity in the territories involved, for its absence means death (Noguera, 2016). The associations, movements and collectives taking part in the exchange recognize themselves as located in territories of self-declared Black people majority. In this sense, both racial recognition and its implications are reciprocal in disputes for access to the city, as well as their interdiction or fragility and instability in the face of the public power, but not only.

Considering the asymmetrical process of full citizenship recognition experienced by multiracial and unequal societies with a past marked by slavery and colonialism such as the Brazilian society, it is a fact that the full access to plural and existential rights meets with operational obstacles that prevent its achievement. As stated by Frantz Fanon (2008), there is, in the movement of recognizing humanity, the action/condition of being recognized by the other as a person. Their value and human reality depend on this (Glissant, 2008; Nascimento, 1986). Being able to be perceived in one's own distinction, with no homogeneity nor substitution: that is, what can grant richness to humanity itself.

This challenge was present directly and continuously throughout the experience of the exchange. Thereby, both the reciprocal recognition among the practitioners and the recognition of a common agenda turned out to be central. This process, therefore, instead of being guided by the requirement for transparency as an acceptance and comparability condition, assumes that distinctive 'opacities can coexist and converge', entangling the senses of comprehension and configuring a warp that presupposes the displacement of any Other from the barbarian condition to that of citizen (Glissant, 2008). Therefore, differences would not establish autisms but would base the relation on freedoms, whose rule of ethical, individual or community action is set up on the very relation and its perspectives.

In this recognition, also produced by accumulation, positionalities in open conflict have been urging the construction of alliances involving universities and residents of marginalized territories in Salvador. Several are the matters in the agenda: violations, threats of removal, impacts and difficulties imposed on marginalized territories by public or private corporations; support to solidarity networks or to actions of propositional elaboration and creation of alternatives in response to the demands of collective life; participation on public debates regarding issues concerning the city or building dialogues within researches. In other words, the whole agenda aims to build solidarity and arenas, within different temporalities and contexts, in which confrontation, demands, negotiations, propositions, ruptures, alliances and conquests are made possible.

The experience of the exchange is one of these occasions in which, amid the general game of social antagonism and hegemonic versions of politics in the city, an encounter of distinctive subjects, knowledges and experiences becomes possible. This is an inflection in the usual fragmentation and indifference regarding otherness. The mutual recognition of these diverse practitioners is built through the cultivation of relationships of trust, based on previous engagement and/or to be confirmed over time, as well as through a common space of coexistence and action.

Among professors and students, the aim was understanding and integrating the references that were brought and problematized by the collectives involved. Initially, through a cognitive-political-ethical commitment, the goal of the collaboration was discussing, documenting and generating learning actions about collective practices of the right to the city in Salvador. Structured around a diverse field of methodologies, the process' basis were the collective meetings, walks and territorial displacements. In 2016, and part of 2017, the people involved in the exchange examined the recognition of the sensitive questions, of different ranges and scales, posed by the residents.

Professors, students and researchers attended the meetings (in)formed mostly through readings and theoretical-methodological questions. Nevertheless, meetings made us understand the provisionality of the starting schemes, constantly updated by the residents' knowledges and 'matters of concern' (Latour, 2005). Therefore, a dialogical and sensitive-practical space of discussion and exchanges is opened; if it does not erase the past experiences of both sides, it allows a reciprocal (re)cognition, as well as enables the elaboration of knowledges and uncommon in common-common practices.

The MSTB, a movement inspired by – but different than – the National Forum of Urban Reform (FNRU), congregated almost forty occupations formed mostly by Black women, who challenged and reclaimed propriety's social function, associated with the resistance against racial and gender inequalities. During the exchange's first year, in 2016, the university brought questions such as: What is the importance of MSTB to the city centre? Where are the current occupation residents from? What is the role of MSTB in accessing and guaranteeing the right to the city? These questions, made by two occupations of this Movement in the Salvador's Historic Centre, named IPAC II and IPAC III, with twenty-six families occupying two buildings, combined themselves with the residents' demand for a physical-architectonic register of the buildings, elaborating blueprints that could strengthen their struggle and negotiations for rights.

Through this encounter of expectations, the practitioners decided together to come up with a sort of social register, instead of only physical one. Its goal would be to collect the historical data about the occupations and their protagonists, from the motives they had to occupy the buildings at the Historic Centre to the information about how families divide and organize themselves inside the occupied buildings, and how they organize themselves as a movement. The intention of this social register amplifies the dimensions of the struggle and the negotiation to guarantee adequate housing, in accordance with their lifestyles and history.

As of 2017, the dialogue with the MSTB moved from Salvador's Historic Centre to one of its more recent occupations, in a vacant land, at a region of urban expansion very far from the Historic Centre, with a great demand for infrastructure. The group of seventy-eight residents from the *Ocupação Força e Luta Guerreira Maria*, associated with the MSTB, had then, as one of its main urgencies, to advance in the constitution of qualified conditions of permanence.

The *Gamboa de Baixo*, a community placed in the central and infrastructured area of the city, bordering the *Baía de Todos os Santos* (All Saints Bay), gathers around 260 families. Despite its geographic privilege, it is marked by intense dynamics of segregation, precarization and neglect by the public administration. It has a history of mobilization, resistance and struggle for permanence. The university brought a more abstract perception of such processes, similar to those that occur in other popular neighbourhoods. There is also the recognition of the patrimonial dimension of the place, given the presence of the *Forte de São Paulo da Gamboa* (Saint Paul's Gamboa Fortress), which goes back to the seventeenth century.

In this case, the group of students started the work questioning the relationship between a material asset protected by Brazilian heritage list and the residents' struggle for the right to the city. Preliminarily, they aimed to understand the perspectives of the neighbourhood's population about tangible and intangible heritage and how such perspectives related with the institutional one. In the cooperative work with the residents, such issues acquired density and unfolded in a movement of practical and conceptual approximation between *Gamboa de Baixo*'s daily reality and its issues of interest. After this unfolding, the recognition of this territory as an intangible cultural heritage became central: being a traditional fishing community, its location in the city, its history and its ways of living feed the discussion around permanence strategies.

The *Acervo da Laje* is another exceptional space located in the suburban and poor rail expansion of Salvador, called Subúrbio Ferroviário. Created to be an ambience of exchanges and artistic creation, it allows and strengthens ways to rearticulate life, which is often interdicted by violence and abandon in this context. *Acervo da Laje* is seen by its founders and by its network of collaborators as a place of popular art collection, memory and promotion of cultural and artistic initiatives within peripheral areas. By doing so, it challenges the praxis and, subjectively, the place of subalternity imposed to this kind of production and its subjects. Therefore, there is an emphasis on the re-elaboration of urban imaginaries and representations as active elements constructing reality, as the constituents of the space (Santillán, 2019). It is a mode of generative confrontation in the face of the reduction of this peripheral area to a dichotomous and negative pole (informal, irregular, illegal or scarce), and in the face of the naturalization of racial and power hierarchies in the city.

At first, students proposed to trace the repercussion of this collective space in the area, that is, in which ways it interfered in the community's comprehension of place, leading to its understanding of the right to the city. However, *Acervo da Laje*'s potential of action, experienced during the exchange, collapses any simplistic attempt of framing the space and the subjects around it in terms of manifestation of a mere cultural equipment within the city's informal space. The cultural and subjective multilayered interaction, more than the located one, imposed itself as a path for reflection.

The students had brought to AMACH – that gathers people who reside at the city's heritage centre's heart – the idea of working with the situation of social rent;[3] that was the situation of most of the 108 families that acquired the right to live there. The idea was to understand the conditions of the residents that were granted social housing, the most recent policy to be implemented and their relation to the achievement of the right to the city.

AMACH reacted to it, pointing out that this issue would not embrace the complexity and magnitude of the issues that were the residents' greatest concerns. Eleven years after the signature of a Conduct Adjustment

---

[3] A monthly benefit provided by the state for low-income families who have suffered property losses due to public calamity. It has an emergency and temporary purpose.

Declaration, a legal agreement that held the state accountable for the provision of social rights to these residents (included in the Seventh Stage of the Historic Centre of Salvador Recovery Program), they continued to suffer under a severe process of abandonment and precariousness. Thus, 25 of the 108 beneficiary families in the agreement did not have access to the renovated housing units, the community day-care had not been built, AMACH's headquarters was under eviction threat, the community kitchen was closed and the prosecutor's office did not monitor the compliance of the legal agreement. Above all, the managing committee, the main collective space to discuss all these issues and decide how to implement them, had been shut down.

With this inversion, the terms of the collaboration were re-elaborated. The common question was: How should public policies aimed at the support of the vulnerable population in the Historic Centre of Salvador ensure the right to the city?

As of 2017's exchange, three more territories joined this collaboration space, with which the university already had been working together: the *Ocupação Luísa Mahin*, located in Comércio, a central neighbourhood; the Nordeste de Amaralina; and Saramandaia. This inclusion broadened the network, as well as the process of mutual recognition between the participants and the territories involved.

The *Ocupação Luísa Mahin*, managed by MLB, in which twelve families lived, had a relatively short span of existence – one year. In this sense, it was in a situation that, although distinct, converged with that of MSTB's Ocupação Força e Luta Guerreira Maria, facing challenges to guarantee the permanence of its residents and of its initiatives of production of goods and community services. The struggle for the expansion of a sphere of rights that could qualify the collective conditions of life was also present.

The addition of *Nordeste de Amaralina* and *Saramandaia* emphasizes the complexity and the challenges involving clusters of large, heterogeneous and populous neighbourhoods submitted to historic processes of precarization and racism, but that are creatively confronted with vigorous community initiatives to enable collective life conditions in the mentioned territories.

The *Nordeste de Amaralina*, part of a cluster of neighbourhoods with around 200,000 people, houses approximately 22,000 residents (IBGE, 2012), with a wide variety of artistic and cultural manifestations, and copes with historic problems related to the lack both of infrastructure and public services (education, sports, leisure, health and sanitation). Its population also struggles daily against stigmatization processes, that authorize racism, violation of children's and youth's rights, police brutality and Black genocide, especially of Black youth.

Saramandaia, a neighbourhood with an estimated population of 12,000 people (IBGE, 2010), experiences similar issues to those of Nordeste de Amaralina. Currently, its residents face intense disputes, given its proximity to the city's financial centre. They also suffer from the impact of real estate developments and public and private mobility projects' constructions. Such interventions disrespect this territory's existence and threaten to dismantle it, not without facing resistance – the collective agency that has been organizing and enabling the life conditions of its population.

The encounter and the coexistence between the universities and the seven territories made reciprocal recognitions possible, weaving commons. From this encounter, a sense of collaboration emerged, with more or less intensity; we were no longer only one or another, nor a mere sum of all elements. We started to establish a shared common, born out of this interactive space, open to an attempt of epistemic redistribution, always incomplete, at the intersection between university and each one of the associations, movements and collectives that composed the exchange's alliance.

But it is important to ask ourselves: What, in fact, was being recognized? In this exchange, we experienced and elaborated an inter-recognition of subjects, collectives and individuals of the involved territories – including the university's itself – their relations and ways of life, and their problems, demands, politics and actions of public and private agents.

In all territories, there are recurring situations or threats of forced removals due to risk situations or to scaled urban interventions driven by the state or by private companies. But also, they are permeated by insufficient and low-quality supply of public services and infrastructure, by the lack of access to social rights, which would be formally guaranteed, or by intense surveillance and police brutality. These are processes closely linked to the dispossession anchored in racial issues, which indicate connections and interweavings between historical practices of racial banishment – as a form of legal-institutional violence – and contemporary ways of financial extractivism (Roy & Rolnik, 2020). However, these violent processes operate in dense territories, anchored in life forms that are entrenched and thriving in ancestry. That is, they do not only react to but also exceed these oppressions, constituting places of abundance and creation. From these places arise an incessant collective production of infrastructures as well as goods, services, values, sociabilities and imaginaries which sustain and constitute these spaces of common life. In the constitution and transformation of the city, a complex interrelationality is highlighted in the connections between mechanisms of dispossession and repositionings of Blackness, constantly redefining the territories' political ecologies.

That is why the recognition process was potentialized by encounters that took place in the territories. The collective itineraries made it possible for the practitioners to elaborate and inquire freely various issues of interest evoked by diverse dimensions, such as materialities, landscapes, subjectivities and life stories. Senses and socio-spatial logics also emerged from this coexistence in the territories, essential to this construction.

The initial dialogues in 2016 and 2017 took place mainly through different groups that gathered students, professors and residents from only one territory, although there were also meetings that would bring everyone together. The immersion in each one of them ended up being restrictive to its own interlocutors, that is, the residents, students and professors of each corresponding group. Although the general meetings allowed debates across realities and subjects from the seven territories, they took place mainly in the university, which meant the reduction of both the learning potential and the organization that was made possible by the physical presence in the territories.

The discussions advanced then towards a common understanding: it would be necessary to promote co-responsibility during the elaboration and articulation of readings and further problematization. This co-responsibility is based on the compromise that associations, movements and collectives, together with students and professors, would visit the seven territories involved in the project and would elaborate the methodology of the work. This goal of going beyond immersion and recognition concerning specific issues of each territory was more vigorously evidenced during the years of 2018 and 2019.

Then there was an important update in the collective approach of the exchange and its challenges. The experience and the knowledges gathered until this point were then potentialized through a convergence that was only possible due to the formation of groups that mixed residents of many territories. This group composition, for being more heterogeneous, consolidated a sense of a common space for learning and practising, enabling the collective formulation of transversal questions, both common and specific, based in a form of recognition that was both reciprocal and co-implicated. We all became practitioners of this common in process.

For this to happen, it was decisive to prepare in advance the methodological discussion that would guide 2018's experience. Through meetings that brought together the research group *Lugar Comum* and the associations, movements and collectives from all the seven territories. The group collectively decided to organize general themes that pointed to significant questions and dimensions evidenced in the process of recognition that had been built until this point. Housing, culture and memory, economy, violence, infrastructure and mobility, social equipment and collective spaces were the themes that became central.

By conducting the exchange's activities together, logistics appeared also as a central issue. Around 100 people took part in the exchange in 2018; so, it was necessary to develop an approach that would organize all people involved in a non-excluding way, emphasizing the multidimensionality of the priority issues. Thus, housing and economy, culture and memory, infrastructure and mobility, social equipment and collective spaces were all main issues that were approached transversely with the issue of violence.

Although we mobilized a nomenclature applied in different territorial readings, we moved towards its de-essentialization, by opening them to a collective (re)-formulation while dialoguing with the residents' issues of interest, as well as their knowledges and collective urban representations. Common issues, dimensions and reality conditions of urban life shared by the seven involved territories, but experienced differently, were recognized in their ontological pluralism and heterogeneity (Stengers, 2005).

Convergences of the common and expansions

Through the intense and fruitful process of recognition established among the territories, we aimed to imagine circumstances and spaces that, as previously stated, could point to common advantages to everyone, a deal between the just and the necessary, ordering the common (Dardot & Laval, 2014). From the knowledge construction's point of view, we aimed to understand it as an intervention in reality, through advisory activities, and not only its representation (Santos, 2007). A kind of activation of the common, collective by nature and by option, emerges, conditioned by its elaboration in politics, both as an act and as a potential (Dardot & Laval, 2014).

Three converging instances of experience, expansive to the common, are central for our thinking: the richness both of the agenda and the tools for action that were built collectively; the blossoming of connected territories; and the activation of the state towards its obligations and commitments.

The chosen agenda topics reflect the vitality and dramas of urban life in an unequal city. If it is true that they are inspired by the principles of an urban policy that, in a progressive perspective, point to the construction of a fairer and more plural city, their vitality consists precisely in the re-elaboration and concretization of their terms, directly from the living space.[4]

---

4   Absences are also part of this process. The issue of violence, for example, despite being recognized as relevant by practitioners, was not established as a theme to be freely

This brings to the centre of the scene a daily life flooded with specific, non-hegemonic – and usually delegitimized – modes and needs that end up disappearing in the implementation of general policies. These are realities refusing to give up their own existences by keeping their work with small-scale fishing, within peripheral cultures and intangible cultural assets, and within low centralities, community spaces, social recycling of spaces, among others. If 'residue proves to be the most precious' (Lefebvre, 1991, p. 110) to knowledge urban processes, by constantly interrogating and updating them, it also proves to be precious here as a means both to approach with respect and to update plural life and rights' forms, as well as a principle to implement public policies. Even more when this residual can turn out – under a much more detained and overall view, beyond the seven territories – exactly as its opposite, regarding the whole city of Salvador.

That is to say, the common is not stable. Through commoning, it is rather expansive (Stavrides, 2016). Therefore, it does not homogenize, but rather connects divergent and asymmetrical fields (Blaser & de la Cadena, 2017)

These divergences, interpreted as active differences, are not a fossilized expression of pre-existence, but rather implicate a continuous, open and negotiated process of change of the common's constitutive relations' quality. As Stavrides (2016, p. 32) states, 'worlds of commoning are worlds in movement'.

That is why the search for equality does not refer to 'uniformity, homogeneity or unity; on the contrary' (Hardt & Negri, 2016, p. 335). Plurality, heterogeneity and distinct opacities ground the institution of the common, which is, at one time, 'a quality of the action and what that same action establishes' (Dardot & Laval, 2014, p. 282). That is, 'an instituting praxis produces its own subject in the continuity of an exercise which is always to be renewed beyond the creative act' (Dardot & Laval, 2014, p. 445).

According to this perspective, it was possible to engage in the construction of the instruments for collective action, because it affords a movement of expansion towards the common, creating new resources through 'expansive circuits of encounter' (Hardt & Negri, 2016, p. 282).

Interpreted as collaborative methodologies between the university and the civil society for the achievement of the right to the city, these instruments sought to attain, at the same time, the principles and the ethics of shared learning and the elaboration of information, analyses and technical-political requests for the key issues defined by each territory individually

discussed, both because it constitutes itself as an extremely sensitive issue and because of the threat of death that is always present in the spheres of public and private security and in the sphere of drug trafficking itself.

and collectively by them all (Fernandes et al., 2017 and 2018). It was an opportunity to face the fragmentation and the indifference present in urban policies and also to open situated perspectives of negotiation for vulnerable populations.

The significant issues for the residents are not resolvable through the dominant urbanity regimes, especially if we take into account the conjuncture of great backslash and violence of the state actions, which would have, supposedly, the power to modify such conditions. This impasse showed us some important limits and challenges that needed to be taken into consideration in an action that could be capable, without capitulation, of transforming the city.

In this sense, we sought to broaden the process of urban action, opening the field of visibility from the territories to the city, through issues deemed strategic by the practitioners – particularly the movements, the associations and the collectives. In the exchange experience, there was the drafting of collective action instruments, such as the following: *Gamboa de Baixo's* multi-referential register; *Ocupação Força e Luta Guerreira Maria's* social register; a video production with *Acervo da Laje*; popular audit with *AMACH* and with *RAS*; the participatory cartography at Nordeste de Amaralina; and the detailed dossier and video testimonies about Luisa Mahin (MLB).

The experiences of elaboration of collective action instruments can be read as exercises for the construction of an experimental utopia (Lefebvre, 1991), in which the setting up of possibilities and the overcoming of problems require the transformation of reality's conditions and of society itself. This fictional experimentalism cannot be, however, interpreted as opposite to reality, but rather as a construction of another sense of reality (Rancière, 2012; Estévez-Vilariño & Figueiredo, 2019).

Possibilities anchored in other imaginations, when examined through the collective action instruments, indicated a movement from the recognition to the convergence and expansion in a politics of care (Puig de la Bellacasa, 2017). This means the commitment with the abandonment of hierarchy and the reparation of the relations in all seven territories, with respect, candour and loyalty, in a reciprocal system of alliances and of strengthening of the collective agencies that enable their lifestyles in the desired construction of another city.

The practices concerning housing, for instance, emerged in a very complex way, immediately related to its quality as dwelling, as common. First, it establishes itself as a collective problem, due to precariousness, whether in possession or in terms of access to goods and services. Second, far beyond the understanding of the house as a monofunctional place, this place of life is constantly entangled with the development of income generation activities for families, be it production of goods, commerce or services, involving other collective instances of articulation.

That is, dwelling in those territories points to imbricated issues such as updated practices of collective occupations of land and buildings in the city (MSTB and MLB) or the dynamism of popular circuits such as artisanal fishing, which associates specific forms of housing and practices of livelihood production (*Gamboa de Baixo*) (Figure 1.1). Or yet the struggling against precarious housing processes through both institutional strategies and daily transgressions (AMACH). Not to mention the role of artistic and cultural initiatives (as *Acervo da Laje* and those present in neighbourhoods such as Saramandaia and Nordeste de Amaralina) that becomes evident in the creation of 'positivity semantics'[5] (Evaristo, quoted in Martins & Cruz, 2020),

Figure 1.1 Common City Network Images Mosaic. (Copyright Lugar Comum Research Group.)

---

[5]   T.N.: In Brazilian Portuguese: 'semântica da positividade'.

which allied to an otherness politics, tension – practically and subjectively – the place of subalternity and the ontological disregard concerning Black territories. Last, but not least, both strongly collectives, there are also demands for the expansion of housing policies and the struggle for worthy permanence in the territories.

In this regard, the notion of territory always challenges, in this manifold and interactive way, the social relations making up the processes of social reproduction, both locally and as a network (Haesbaert, 2004). The connection between territories that was built throughout the exchange experience meant the drafting of a network, shaped by the shared interest, by the practitioners' autonomy and by common expectations. It is possible to oppose the segmentation of the city and its consequent concealment of both places for living and social agents with the cultivation of a space that recovered and re-elaborated stories, practices and specific aspirations and investigated, with convergences and divergences, possibilities of collective action. Everyone is transformed by their involvement in the common weaving, from which we highlight three dimensions. The first is a collective and engaging pedagogic process that combines reflection, learning and action. Second, by the flows it generates and the roles it plays, there is a simultaneous constitution of places of both welcoming and connection. This system of movements instigates constant reflections on the conditions of existence, the ways of being in public and the care with each one and with the other. Finally, the common weaving broadens the urban horizons, making the city less restricted and more open, rich and solidary in the experience's perspective, magnetizing, thus, its unfolding and continuity.

The heteronomous condition of popular strata shows – inevitably, though with great discredit – the state, in its many instances, as the main interlocutor, since it should be the leading ensurer of positive rights in the cities, providing basic conditions of existence.[6] In this sense, despite the proud development of autonomous practices in many territories, such practices bring with them many needs related to physical space, materials, specialized professionals and so on, and these needs can only be met through public action. Besides those needs, there were also those linked to collective and public systems, especially those related to network infrastructure, to equipment and to public spaces.

The addressing of these issues to the state, however, even with all the institutionalized mediation from the university, was done in an active and

---

[6] Among the Republic's fundamental objectives listed in the Constitution of the Federative Republic of Brazil's Article 3, one can find the following: 'to eradicate poverty and substandard living conditions and to reduce social and regional inequalities; [and] to promote the well-being of all, without prejudice as to origin, race, sex, colour, age and any other forms of discrimination'.

combative way, with the support of the collective's accumulated experiences and enduring struggles for their own existences, legitimacy and presence in the city. The dialogues with the City Hall and with the state government combined large experience with invented and invited spaces (Miraftab, 2016) and were understood as a necessary – but not sufficient – action to build a common city, where the validity and expansion of rights are unequivocally combined with the autonomy and solidarity of action, with different forms of full appropriation of the city and with freedom of expression of the various collective subjects of rights.

Two inversions were significant to its completion as a necessary instance of dialogue. First, the practitioners were the ones to decide collectively what would be the theme and which state agents should be invited. Second, most of the dialogues took place in the very territories that are often discredited or criminalized by the public administration and by society. The effective and latent junction between the place-territory[7] and the claims replaces the imperial definitions of initiatives and of the city's negotiation spaces, enabling the change of the terms in which they happen. On the one hand, there is a sort of effect demonstration of the demands that are impossible to ignore. On the other hand, there is the recognition of the place-territory as a legitimate space for the interaction between the public administration and the residents, reinstating it in the proper public sphere.

Facing the state's institutionality collectively and publicly demands a mediated passage between the abstraction and the anonymity of the machine and its embodiment in different public agents. Thus, at the beginning, there was a flagrant asymmetry. We had, from each place-territory, what was the most representative, historically and affectionately constitutive of the struggle and life in common, while the public hierarchies varied in positions and decision-making skills. Thus, it was a positive surprise that the majority of the organizations invited (twenty-two out of twenty-six) sent representatives to the dialogue circles, observing that only in two occasions someone with effective decision-making capacity was present. Even with these weak powers, the interaction with public agents inserted in this machine opened two horizons of possibilities: on the one hand, there was the raising of awareness and reactivation of these agents – mainly technicians who, once faced with such an intense situation and with such urgent demands, have committed to forward the demands; on the other hand, for the residents, such direct access

---

[7]   The union between the concepts of place and territory seems appropriate to this discussion, considering – as did Serpa (2017, p. 590) in his existentialist essay – that 'place has to do with love, commitment and a sense of responsibility' and 'territory has to do with possession and domination', creating thus a confluence between affection and politics and between the dimension of life and the dimension of power.

to public agents, getting to know their names and contacts, turned out to be a promise – perhaps a chimerical one – made on this meeting.[8]

There was also a third element: not only the state is opaque in its structure and action but also the communication and information channels are neglected and poorly functional. There are explicit significant barriers in this field, which are related both to the vocabulary and language that are used in it, which have no regard for comprehension whatsoever, and to the state's complex way of operating, tangled and fragmented in instances and sectors, legislations and competences, which become even harder to understand when combined with concessions or bestowals to the private sector.

Agenda, territory and the state's activation were, thus, the three instances of relations and systems of solidarity, among so many others, that pointed to the institution of a common among the collectives as praxis that confers to it meaning, vitality and horizons. Meaning derives from dwellers' real and pragmatic demands on lived space in its multiple dimensions, settled by themselves. Sharing and commoning those perspectives among all collectives involved in the exchange confer vitality and engagement to the experience, a kind of joy of acting, which delineates an expectation, an emulation of the future – which can be activated at any time – anchored in solidarity and hope.

By way of openings

The experience of the common in act and in potential requires a reflection, still in progress, about its character and constitution process.

There are many dimensions of the common organizing social life, even if latent: networks of cooperation, solidarity and affection, as well as networks of interest and of political action permeate the daily relations in the neighbourhoods, in the universities and among them. The common construction requires both the recognition of each and every one of these networks and relations and their coordination, through a permanent, delicate, ever-moving work, with mutant rules that are relationally structured.

It is a matter of accumulated overlapping distinct commons in constant transformation. They carry distinct temporalities and historicities within them, for they are constituted in social and political processes with diverse durations and ranges, from the secular institution of the people's common goods to the

---

[8] We systematized the six dialogue circles, reporting all the discussion process and listing the names and contact information from all the practitioners. We also wrote a commitment letter containing the demands that were discussed, which was then signed by everyone.

burst of revolts, contestations and insurgencies around a common horizon. The common action in the present activates latent commons, for it presupposes, uses, merges and transforms these different times and social experiences, creating ruptures and new forms of action and society perspectives.

The activation of various agents and the promotion of spaces for talking, listening and accessing the public sphere are still important common dimensions in progress that are translated in conducts and in a language that can be shared. Here is fully expressed the pedagogical and political construction of inter-knowledge, to which converge different knowledges in the active, ethical and committed quest for paths towards spatial and epistemic justice.

Among everything we learnt in the exchange experience, one of the most important things was that the vulnerable, Black and multiple city of Salvador confront the subalternization processes in a generative manner. The residents react to the constant instabilities with constant adaptations and improvisations (Simone, 2019) and transversal logics (Caldeira, 2017) that rearticulate life conditions and confront the subjugations. A multitude of life plans are performed in this city, whose ontological difference (Harney & Moten, 2013) makes it impossible to be approached by the conventional dichotomous concepts in urban studies, requiring thus not only new categories and concepts but also epistemic redistribution.

Our goal here is not to romanticize and idealize this mainly popular experience of the common, activated through the seven territories. We shall not forget that there are many restraints and adversities implicated in this experience. The persistent structural fragmentation of the city can be perceived in the difficulty of managing moments of connection among the territories beyond the events enabled by the exchange. Also emerges the lack of involvement of most of these territories' inhabitants, whose participation was almost always restricted to members previously engaged in urban collectives. Likewise, the latency period that most collective actions go through after the annual exchange period can be pointed out. Even if keeping the senses of cooperation and solidarity, there still remains the challenge of reflecting on the network support of this intense exchange even after the activity ended.

Anyhow, this incomplete and open experience of collective construction continues to refer to articulatory, contingent and co-constitutive practices of the social (Laclau, 1996), of common domains, of its subjects and of life itself, which ethically needs to be multidirectionally preserved. The city as a common brings this promise.[9]

---

[9]   Translated from Portuguese by Bruna Barros and Jess Oliveira.

References

Blaser, M. & de la Cadena, M. (2017). The Uncommons: An Introduction. *Anthropologica*, 59(2, October), 185–93.

Blaser, M. & de la Cadena, M. (2018). Introduction: Pluriverse: Proposals for a World of Many Worlds. In: de la Cadena, M. & Blaser, M. (ed.). *A World of Many Worlds*. Durham: Duke University Press, 1–22.

Boullosa, R. F. (2013). Mirando ao revés as políticas públicas: notas sobre um percurso de pesquisa. *Pensamento & Realidade*, 28, 68–86.

Caldeira, T. P. (2017). Peripheral Urbanization: Autoconstruction, Transversal Logics, and Politics in Cities of the Global South. *Environment and Planning D: Society and Space*, 35(1), 3–20. https://doi.org/10.1177/0263775816658479

Chakravartty, P. & Silva, D. F. (2012). Race, Empire, and the Crisis of the Subprime. *American Quarterly*, 64(3, September), 361–85.

Collins, John F. (2015). *Revolt of the Saints: Memory and Redemption in the Twilight of Brazilian Racial Democracy*. Durham, NC: Duke University Press. 480 pp.

Dardot, P. & Laval, C. (2014). *Commun. Essai sur la Révolution au XXIéme Siècle*. Paris: La Découverte.

Dirlik, A. (2007). *Global Modernity*. New York: Routledge. https://doi.org/10.4324/9781315634401

Elden, S. (2004). *Understanding Henri Lefebvre. Theory and the Possible*. London: A&C Black.

Estévez-Vilariño, B. & Figueiredo, G. C. S (2019). Perícia Popular no Centro Histórico de Salvador. Ficções políticas, desentendimentos radicais e encontros com cuidado. Trabalho apresentado no 2o Seminário Internacional Urbanismo Biopolítico, Universidade Federal de Minas Gerais, Belo Horizonte.

Faculdade de Arquitetura da Universidade Federal da Bahia (FAUFBA); The Bartlett Planning Development Unit at University College London (DPU) (2017). *Cadastro Multirreferencial da Comunidade Tradicional Pesqueira Urbana da Gamboa de Baixo*. Salvador.

Fanon, F. (2008). *Pele negra, máscaras brancas*. Bahia: Editora Edufba.

Fernandes, A., Figueiredo, G. C., Espinoza, J. C. H., Frediani, A. A., Rigon, A., Vermehren, I. O., Walker, J. & Monson, T. (2017). Introdução. In: Ana Fernandes, Glória Cecília Figueiredo & José Carlos Huapaya. (Org.). *Práticas Coletivas e o Direito à Cidade em Salvador, Bahia*. 1st edn.Salvador: UFBA.

Fernandes, A., Frediani, A. A. (Org.), Vermehren, I. O. (Org.), Mendoza, M. M. (Org.) & Risi, F. (Org.) (2018). *Collective Practices, Instruments for Collective Action and the Right to the City in Salvador, Bahia. Práticas Coletivas, Instrumentos para a Ação e o Direito à Cidade em Salvador, Bahia*. 1st edn. Londres: London: DPU/The Bartlett/UCL, 1–8.

Glissant, Édouard (2008). Pela Opacidade. *Revista Criação & Crítica*, 1, 53–5.

Gonzales, L. (1984). Racismo e Sexismo na Cultura Brasileira. *Revista Ciências Sociais Hoje, Anpocs*, 223–44.

Gorelik, A. (2003). Ciudad, Modernidad, Modernización. *Universitas Humanística [en linea]*, 56, 11–27 [fecha de Consulta 19 de Junio de 2020]. ISSN: 0120-4807. Disponible en: https://www.redalyc.org/articulo.oa?id =79105602

Haesbaert, Rogerio. (2004). *O Mito da Desterritorialização*. Rio de Janeiro: Bertrand Brasil

Hardt, Michael & Negri, Antonio (2005). *Multidão. Guerra e Democracia na era do Império*. Rio de Janeiro/São Paulo: Ed. Record.

Hardt, Michael & Negri, Antonio (2016). *Bem Estar Comum*. Rio de Janeiro/São Paulo: Ed. Record.

Harney, S. & Moten, F. (2013). *The Undercommons: Fugitive Planning and Black Study*. New York, NY: Autonomedia.

Heidegger, Martin (1971). Building Dwelling Thinking. In *Poetry, Language, Thought*. New York: Harper Colophon Books. HYPERLINK "http://acnet .pratt.edu/~arch543p/readings/Heidegger.html" http://acnet.pratt.edu/ ~arch543p/readings/Heidegger.html.

IBGE. (2012). *Censo Brasileiro de 2010 (Salvador)*. Rio de Janeiro: IBGE.

IBGE. (2021). *Cidades e Estados*. Salvador. Available at: https://www.ibge.gov.br/ cidades-e-estados/ba/salvador.html

Laclau, E. (1996). Poder e representação. *Estudos Sociedade e Agricultura*, 7(dez. 1996), 7–28. Disponível em: http://bibliotecavirtual.clacso.org.ar/ar/libros/ brasil/cpda/ estudos/sete/laclau7.htm (Accessed January 5, 2020).

Latour, B. (2005). *Reassembling the Social: An Introduction to Actor-Network Theory*. Oxford: Oxford University Press.

Lefebvre, H. (1991). *O Direito à Cidade*. São Paulo: Editora Moraes Ltda.

Lefebvre, Henri. (2003). *Key Writings*. London; New York: Continuum.

Martins, H. & Cruz, M. M. (2020). *Negro ou preto? Lideranças negras refletem sobre o uso dos termos ao longo da história*. Belo Horizonte: Jornal Estado de Minas Gerais. https://www.em.com.br/app/noticia/gerais/2020/11/20/ interna_gerais,1208016/negro-ou-preto-liderancas-negras-refletem-sobre-o -uso-dos-termos-ao-l.shtml (Accessed January 17, 2020).

Mbembe, A. (2018). *Necropolítica*. 3rd edn. São Paulo: n-1 edições.

Miraftab, F. (2016). Insurgência, planejamento e a perspectiva de um urbanismo humano. *Revista de Estudos Urbanos e Regionais*, ANPUR, 18(3, set–dez), 363–77.

Mouffe, C. (2007). *En Torno a lo Político*. Buenos Aires: Fondo de Cultura Económica.

Nascimento, A. (1978). *O Genocídio do Negro Brasileiro: processo de um racismo mascarado*. São Paulo: Editora Paz e Terra.

Nascimento, B. (1986). Sistemas sociais alternativos organizados pelos negros: dos quilombos às favelas. In: *Beatriz Nascimento: intelectual e quilombola. Possibilidade nos dias de destruição*.

Noguera, Renato. (2016). Dos condenados da terra à necropolítica: diálogos filosóficos entre Frantz Fanon e Achille Mbembe. *Revista Latino Americana do Colégio Internacional de Filosofia*, 3.

Oliveira, F. (1982). O Estado e o urbano no Brasil. *Revista Espaço e Debates*, 6, 37.

Pírez, P. (2016). Las heterogéneas formas de produción y consumo de la urbanización latinoamericana. *Quid 16*, 6, 131–67.

Puig de la Bellacasa, M. (2017). *Matters of Care. Speculative Ethics in More Than Human Worlds*. Minneapolis: University of Minnesota Press.

Ranciére, J. (2012). *O espectador emancipado*. São Paulo: Martins Fontes, 2012.

Roy, A. & Rolnik, R. (2020). Metodologias de pesquisa-ação para promover a justiça habitacional. In: F.A. Moreira, R. Rolnik & P. F. Santoro (eds). *Cartografias da produção, transitoriedade e despossessão dos territórios populares*. São Paulo: Observatório de Remoções, 17–30.

Santillán Cornejo, Alfredo (2019). *La construción imaginaria del Sur de Quito*. Quito: Flacso Ecuador.

Santos, B. S. (2007). *Para além do Pensamento Abissal: das Linhas Globais a uma Ecologia de Saberes*. São Paulo: Novos Estudos 79, Novembro.

Santos, M. (1996). *A Natureza do Espaço: técnica e tempo, razão e emoção*. São Paulo: Hucitec.

Serpa, A. (2017). Ser lugar e ser território como experiências do ser-no-mundo: um exercício de existencialismo geográfico. *GEO-USP. Espaço e Tempo*, 21(2). https://www.revistas.usp.br/geousp/article/view/125427

Simone, A. (2019). *Improvised Lives. Rhythms of Endurance in a Urban South*. Cambridge: Polity Press.

Stavrides, S. (2016). *Common Space. The City as Commons*. Chicago, IL: The University of Chicago Press Books.

Stengers, I. (2005). The Cosmopolitical Proposal. In: B. Latour & P. Weibel (ed.). *Making Things Public: Atmospheres of Democracy*. Cambridge, MA: MIT Press.

Walker, J., Carvalho, Marcos Bau & Diaconescu, I. (eds) (2020). *Urban Claims and the Right to the City. Grassroots Perspectives from Salvador da Bahia and London*. Londres: UCL Press.

2

Activists infrastructures and commoning 'from below'

The case of Cheetah Camp, Mumbai

Lalitha Kamath and Purva Dewoolkar

In the 1950s, when Morarji Desai was the Chief Minister [of Mahara-shtra], he evicted people from the footpath [especially in the areas around the Bombay port where daily wage labourers had settled] and we were shifted out to Janata Colony. They just dumped us there without any facilities. There was no light, bushes around, no road or water. We slowly developed the area. I was born in 1961. In 1965, Bhabha Atomic Research Centre (BARC) proposed to construct a residential colony for its staff where Janta colony was located. From 1967, they started telling us we had to leave and in 1970, they purchased land in Cheetah Camp to relocate us. . . . In 1975 the BMC [Brihanmumbai Municipal Corporation – BMC] started demolishing our houses. Emergency had been declared and my Daddy and 40 other activists were put in jail for resisting the eviction. I was in 7th standard then and all the kids were involved in the colony's movement. We barricaded the colony so the police couldn't come inside to break our houses but nothing stopped the demolition. We were relocated to Cheetah Camp. This was our second relocation.

(Interview, Javed Bhai 9/4/18)

Javed Bhai[1] was inculcated into social movements and community leadership by his father, who joined the Congress Party in 1967 on the threat of eviction of Janta Colony. When Mumbai's Municipal Corporation (BMC) refused to rehabilitate all 5,500 families of Janta Colony, stating that only those paying rent to the BMC were eligible for rehabilitation, the community fought this, as the aforementioned vignette illustrates. Javed Bhai's father filed the court

---

[1] Bhai, meaning brother, is a respectful and affectionate address for an older man.

case that went all the way to the Supreme Court demanding that all families should be relocated in the same place as they were all one community. In this way, the community resisted state efforts to divide them based on those who had paid rent. They succeeded in getting plots of 10 × 10 square feet allocated to the non-paying families too, on humanitarian grounds.

As Javed Bhai tells this story, his gentle demeanour and soft-spoken manner belie the indomitable spirit he has shown in leading Cheetah Camp's varied housing struggles. Together with a group of friends, who he has grown up with, they work to improve the neighbourhood. Javed Bhai describes his group as those coming from different social and religious backgrounds but who commonly initiate social activities in association with the local masjid (mosque). The strong foundation of this group's friendship has been co-created through processes of shared goals and struggles and of everyday collective living in place.

Among his friends is his mentor, Ehsan Bhai, a businessman who entered politics reluctantly – 'to do something for Cheetah Camp'. As a city corporator, he talked of strategically wielding his position as independent corporator in cross-party bargaining to support housing struggles in Cheetah Camp. Before entering politics, he had made a name for himself – from helping individuals (filling forms and collecting donations for those in need) to working on systemic issues (school, sewer lines and water connections) that served the community as a whole.

The life histories of community activists like Javed Bhai and Ehsan Bhai are integrally linked to each other, and with the life history of places like Cheetah Camp through housing struggles for creating a better, shared place and future. The interwoven web of knowledge practice and affective relations that activists bring to bear in this endeavour can be seen as a living infrastructure that underpins the process of making and sustaining informal places. Infrastructure is commonly associated with physical systems – pipelines, wires and roads. In important work, Simone (2004) has extended its usage to cover people's activities in the city. 'People as infrastructure' depends

> on the ability of residents to engage complex combinations of objects, spaces, persons, and practices. These conjunctions become an infrastructure – a platform providing for and reproducing life in the city. (p. 407)

We draw upon Simone's work to talk about one type of people infrastructure – community activists – which is of crucial importance in inspiring new forms of solidarity, shared caring, creative adjustments and common life.

Focusing on activist infrastructure makes us confront its relative invisibility, drawing it from the background to the foreground of research on informal housing. These infrastructures make a variety of things possible – social, institutional, material – from schools to creating refuge and from greater mobility for members to greater ability to remain rooted in the place they hold dear. If material infrastructures have long promised modernity and development to people everywhere, activist infrastructures symbolize the engines of agency that can transform places from below. Attention to activist infrastructures makes us see informal settlements as already structured (by the denial of formal and adequate housing and service provision) but also in formation – by participating in the collective labour of commoning to exert presence in the city and negotiating citizenship claims that run counter to the dominant pattern of housing and habitation. It is therefore important to understand the work that goes into creating and maintaining these living infrastructures, and consequently their possibilities and limits for transformation of settlement and city.

We develop the case of one informal settlement, Cheetah Camp, to illustrate how living infrastructures initiate three different counterprojects and the ensuing trajectory of place-in-process over a fifty-year period.

Methodology

Our understanding of the way activist infrastructures operate is based on a long-term engagement with Javed Bhai and M/East ward, the city administrative unit where Cheetah Camp is located, supplemented with conducting in-depth interviews with community activists. The second author's interactions with Javed Bhai have been ongoing since early 2014, particularly in her capacity as a member of the Transforming M Ward project of the Tata Institute of Social Sciences (TISS). This is an action research project that has initiated a forum of representatives from the slum communities in M/East Ward, called M Ward Convenor Forum. This forum, of which Javed Bhai is a convenor, informs the project on the concerns in the community that ought to be addressed. This chapter has greatly benefitted from the second author's nuanced insights on how activist infrastructures work through her own participation in roads and transport project struggles and relations with Javed Bhai.

Javed Bhai is a key community leader of Cheetah Camp, witness to previous evictions and crucial to the remaking of community life anew. Although Javed Bhai works with his group and is sustained by their 'caring friendships', to use Ramamurthy's evocative phrase (2019), we have seen him as central to the building and sustaining of activist infrastructures and have consciously chosen to tell the settlement story from his perspective. We draw on his narratives, practices and lived reality to reconstruct the process for commoning from below.

Brief background to Cheetah Camp

Cheetah Camp is located in M/East ward (one of twenty-four administrative wards of Mumbai). M/East ward is a site of multiple deprivations – insecure and inadequate housing, high environmental risks and the lowest human development parameters in the city. These deprivations have been exacerbated by an ongoing use of this peripheral suburb for locating polluting activities (waste-dumping ground and polluting industries) and vulnerable social groups (beggars, children in need of institutional care, and relocation of slums from central areas of the city).

Cheetah Camp is divided into 11 sectors and has a population of 78,674, according to a TISS survey done in 2011. Its population has a majority of Muslims (70 per cent) followed by Hindus (22 per cent). Despite forty-four years of incremental development, it still today lacks basic amenities like water and sanitation.

Commoning from below: Transformations of place

Creating public amenities: School-making in Cheetah Camp

Although state-provided Cheetah Camp wasn't a planned site, no space was allocated for gutters or proper passages in between plots. The only facilities provided prior to people being shifted there were a public school operating till seventh grade, a public standpost providing water at a common point, and common toilets. Due to the lack of educational options, prevailing sociocultural norms of not sending girls outside the community, and poverty, 80 per cent of students dropped out after seventh grade. Many children were employed in doing home-based work, their employment supplementing the family incomes. Javed Bhai was convinced that a public school should be a major focus of their struggle, perhaps influenced by his own personal experiences of school failure.

> After coming to Cheetah Camp, I failed twice. I failed in ninth and tenth class. Here the environment was not conducive for education because we

were staying with some other family. It was rainy season and we didn't construct the house in Cheetah camp for a while because it was marshy land with lot of mosquitoes. (Interview, Javed Bhai 14/12/16)

Javed Bhai saw school-making as a crucial goal for placemaking and securing the futures of Cheetah Camp's youth. Thus began the story of how his group was instrumental in the making of twelve private and one public school in Cheetah Camp to cater to the burgeoning population which aspired to study in Urdu-, Hindi- and Tamil-medium schools, and not the local language medium of Marathi.

Javed Bhai's first idea was to start a (religious) library as a way of building youth's liking for reading. Through this, he became friends with the founder of Ideal Trust, who was a member of the Jamaat-e-Islami Hind, Thane[2], and would ultimately become the trust which ran the first private school in Cheetah Camp – Ideal School. This also put Javed Bhai in touch with the Jamaat's network of well-heeled, Muslim professionals.

The next strategy was to search for a vacant plot of land on which they could apply to build the school. On finding a suitable plot, they discovered that the owner lived in America and verbally negotiated with him to donate it for the school. Absent the owner, some of this land had already been built up by local land mafias, and Javed Bhai's group had to break these 'encroachments'. The core issue was that vacant lands represented a commons in highly congested neighbourhoods like Cheetah Camp and thus a huge opportunity to control land and infrastructure development in the community. This meant Javed Bhai and other leaders had not only to overrule the opposition of slum mafias but also to sideline conflicting visions for this land by others in the community. Here, their past record of working for the community was important in building their legitimacy to displace other visions and build a compound wall and put up a board naming this as Ideal School. They simultaneously applied to the BMC to start Grades V and VIII. They secured approval because Javed Bhai's father was a good friend of the politician, Nagesh Patil, from their time in the Congress Party,[3] and Nagesh was the elder brother of Amarnath Patil, the then corporator from the Shiv Sena Party[4] who facilitated the permission.

---

[2] The Jamaat-e-Islami is the first Islamic reformist movement in the Indian subcontinent formed in 1941. After Partition, the Jamaat-e-Islami Hind formed in 1948. See http://jihmaharashtra.org/eng/about-jamaat/history/

[3] The Congress Party is commonly understood as a centre-left, secular, national party of India.

[4] Shiv Sena is a regional party known for its nativist and Hindutva politics. It has dominated Mumbai's city politics since the 1980s. In 1995, it formed a coalition with

The next focus was raising money for constructing the school. Javed Bhai remembers going door-to-door with his daddy to seek donations and tapping many of their networks to receive building materials on credit. Since they had no school infrastructure in place, students were hesitant to join; so, Javed Bhai's group hit upon the idea of targeting dropouts. This is how they started two classes – Grades V and VIII – with fourteen children in a four-room building in 1983. In the second year, they had 1,500 students seeking admission, evidence of the dire need for a school.

The next few years saw a number of private schools opening in succession by people from within Cheetah Camp. Javed Bhai described his role in these as a supporting one – from advising on how to claim land, to using his contacts with city corporators, to influencing people within the community to support these ventures. He explained this support as not based on the motivation of ownership or private gain but one that measured value by what was good for the community and the settlement.

In 1993, Javed Bhai shared why and how they started a second public school, the Trombay Public School, revealing another set of ingeniously assembled strategies (Figure 2.1). While private schools had the benefit of quality and fit to local needs, public schools are free – of great value to the poorest in Cheetah Camp. Additionally, a municipal school signified state recognition of Cheetah Camp's existence by virtue of the decision to locate a public amenity in the neighbourhood, something sorely lacking in that part of the city. This time, Javed Bhai and his group leveraged the school adoption scheme, through which the BMC leased out municipal schools to be operated by non-profit organizations. They approached their member of legislative assembly (MLA), asking him to set up a school in their neighbourhood under his educational trust that ran 200 schools in the city. They also drew on MLA funds for the first big structural overhaul of the school building. More recently, Javed Bhai has started relying on corporate social responsibility (CSR) funds from companies that support education – such partnerships have resulted in establishing a computer lab, supporting mid-day meals for students, and organizing scholarships for Grade XI and XII students. Today, the school has 3,000 students.

The arduous process of building and sustaining private and public schools to consolidate the community's future was made up of the collective labour of many people – a process of commoning from below. Activist infrastructures played a key role in assembling a new and thickened web of relations with politicians, government institutions, religious institutions, educational

the Bharatiya Janata Party (BJP), a Hindu national party, and till 2019 these two parties contested elections Maharashtra jointly.

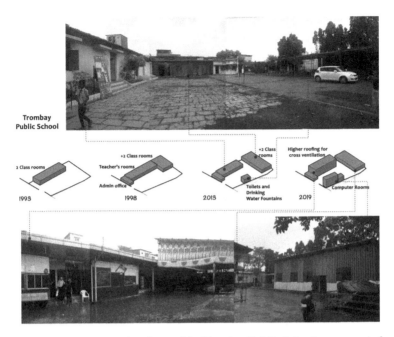

Figure 2.1 Incremental making of the Trombay Public School over a period of twenty-five years. Left to right shows the change in spatial configuration of the built form. (Source: Drawn by Author/Purva Dewoolkar.)

trusts, corporate firms and community members, channelling the collective knowledge, funds and contributions in-kind towards successful realization of thirteen schools. Figure 1 highlights this process for the Trombay Public School. By propagating schools as shared, self-managed and community spaces that were built through collective struggle and furthered relations of trust, friendship, reciprocity and agency, it actively challenged dominant modes of public amenities provision and placemaking in Mumbai.

Creating sanctuary

Cheetah Camp's housing struggles were focused not only on securing material housing and infrastructure but also on combating the stigma, discrimination and violence that the minority community was increasingly facing in Mumbai. The first such incident that seared Cheetah Camp's collective memory was one of police firing in 1984 that killed nine and led to the arrest of eighteen people who were confined in Yerwada Jail in Pune. Community leaders approached the Jamaat-e-Islami Hind for help, and they assisted with a lawyer and funds. Javed Bhai remembers travelling three hours each way to Pune for five to six days continuously to get everyone out of jail.

> In 1992 when the Babri Masjid[5] was demolished, we called different religious groups for a peace meeting and spoke about how we shouldn't allow 1984 to happen again. (Interview Javed Bhai, 9/4/18)

The Babri Mosque demolition raised existential questions about how activists could work to sustain the personhood, dignity and sense of belonging of Cheetah Camp, as a largely Muslim place, in the city. While this group of activists were successful in working for inter-religious peace, due to which they didn't face any violent incidents with the police, they recognized that combating communal violence wasn't enough. They decided to express their caring by creating a sanctuary for other families desperately fleeing the communal riots that had set much of the city ablaze. They mobilized funds and established a relief camp for a month.

> Muslims from places like Maharashtranagar, Mankhurd, Panjarapol, Ghatla and Punjabwadi where they were in minority, came to the camp. For a month we provided them everything including food, water, medicine and other essential things. . . . We helped them in getting relief money from the government. Construction of houses and providing material for construction was done by Tata Institute of Social Sciences. (Interview Javed Bhai, 9/4/18)

Year 1992 marked a landmark in Mumbai's history by substantially communalizing its politics and public sentiment. Cheetah Camp's image in the public sphere became cemented as a hotspot for crime, antisocial elements and terrorists. 'The Corporation never treated us equally, there were different laws for Cheetah Camp and different laws for other colonies,' Ayub shared (Interview, 24/01/17). Efforts to temper the (often-brutal) crackdowns on the community by local law enforcement have involved building good personal relations with police so that problems can be quickly resolved. Javed Bhai discusses how he pays weekly visits to the local police station to keep abreast with local arrests made and maintain goodwill. Navigating state agencies in times of growing discrimination has also meant strategically retreating from

---

5 The Babri Masjid is a mosque in Ayodhya that Hindus believe to be the birthplace of the Hindu God, Rama. It has been the site of a dispute between Hindus and Muslims since the eighteenth century. The Babri Masjid was demolished by Hindu devotees in 1992, which ignited communal riots nationwide.

sole dependence on the state and turning to funds and relations outside of the state – through religious, cultural or corporate organizations.

Sustaining communally harmonious politics within the community has been progressively more challenging. Looking back, Javed Bhai says:

> After coming here [Cheetah Camp] everything changed slowly. The Rashtriya Seva Sangh (RSS) [a mass cultural organisation affiliated to the Hindu nationalist BJP Party] started their camps in the area and they would entice Dalits to do something against Muslims. Growing polarization was also reflected among radical Muslims. So slowly the distance between communities increased. (Interview, 14/12/2016)

This politics was reflected in an overall hardening of party lines and affiliations – earlier, activists could collaborate with a Shiv Sena politician like Amarnath Patil, although deploring the party's nativist line, but this has now ceased. These community-level changes mirrored larger political economic shifts and tensions in the city and nation. But community activists continue to labour to assert a minority presence in a city that largely invisibilizes them and strive to do this inclusively.

People's plan as alternative to official development plan

Mumbai's development plan (DP) is a spatial land-use plan prepared by the BMC to plan for a twenty-year future. As a legal document, it shapes how space is allocated for different public amenities across the city. When preparing the third DP (2014–34), a process that began in 2009, the BMC for the first time included public consultations at the ward level (Kamath & Joseph, 2015). Many civil society groups, NGOs and academic institutions used this opportunity to come together to form a collective called Hamara Shehar Mumbai (HSM)[6] to understand the structural inequalities in the current distribution of public amenities locally, and move towards suggesting alternatives. In M/East ward, the Transforming M Ward project of TISS was working as part of HSM in taking the planning process to people. In intra-ward discussions, everyone fed off each other's knowledge and networks. Cheetah Camp's participation was unique in this effort because people in Cheetah Camp themselves made formal maps, using a technocratic, 'expert' language to challenge unjust ways of planning and propose their own alternative plan.

---

[6] See https://hamarasheharmumbai.org/

Javed Bhai's interest in mapping began once he recognized the DP's importance in influencing the future trajectory of Cheetah Camp, he said. He became very well versed with mapping, leading this process within the community. He formed a group of his friends into a core team that disseminated the DP to larger groups by conducting area-level meetings. Javed Bhai got involved in ground-truthing the existing land-use document the BMC published. For this he tried to find local resources. He enlisted the help of a young boy from the community, Salim, who was a draftsman at an architectural firm, for correcting errors in the official land-use maps. Salim drafted the plans on AutoCAD. The BMC had marked slums as brown patches in their plan since they were seen as 'illegal', and no planning was done or amenities marked for them. In Cheetah Camp, the community marked what they saw as amenities – existing schools and amenities, including religious structures and madrasas – in their map. Javed Bhai also helped organize large numbers of Cheetah Camp residents to come to the M ward project office in TISS campus to mark more amenities on Google Earth maps. The TISS name and this collective exercise helped to validate and build trust in mapping as a practice. Javed Bhai also approached maulanas requesting them to announce the mapping event after the Friday prayers to encourage people's participation. Javed Bhai's team didn't stop here but went on to make their own proposals for future land use for their community.

People of Cheetah Camp developed a People's Plan that proposed amenities the community needed, like a medical college, a civic training institute and a cultural centre. They presented this to the BMC as suggestions for what the community wanted in the DP. As with any people's movement, there were some who opposed this DP. That group approached TISS for information about the process and made their own plan that they submitted to BMC, although without dissemination in the public domain. Making a People's Plan was a way of staking a claim to land for public amenities which were deficient in the neighbourhood and ward. While the final DP accepted only 50 per cent of these demands, this campaign asserted the community's right to city-making by remaking the top-down planning process.

Javed Bhai continues to use the spatial learning he has acquired to pursue other projects. Mumbai's metro project is being formulated by the Mumbai Metropolitan Regional Development Agency (MMRDA). Overall, fourteen metro lines are being laid all over Mumbai. Metro line 2B passes from Andheri to Mankhurd but stops short of Cheetah Camp, although the metro car shed to service metro cars is proposed to be located in Cheetah Camp. Javed Bhai and his team demanded that the metro line be extended to Cheetah Camp so that its population of around 100,000, which had no direct connectivity to the local trains, could be serviced by the metro. Javed Bhai asked:

Why can't it [the extension] be done? The MP from Thane negotiated and took the metro line till his constituency Kasarbawadi so why can't we do the same here? I have corresponded with MMRDA regarding it. (Interview, 9/4/18)

Javed Bhai knew that they didn't have the support of their local member of parliament (MP), who was from the Shiv Sena, thus saying:

If we ask him [MP] to bring the metro to Cheetah camp, he will say it's a Muslim settlement, why give a metro to them? (Interview, 9/4/18)

Javed Bhai knew he had to assemble another strategy.

Javed Bhai found out that a survey was being done in Cheetah Camp to check how many houses were being affected by the road which led to the metro car shed. He also discovered that the survey was being done by Subhash, who was a friend of the TISS M ward project. Javed Bhai requested a 'friendly' meeting in which he and selected people from the community met the survey company and members from TISS to understand the situation. Javed Bhai learnt that approximately 550 houses would be demolished because of the upcoming approach road to the metro car shed passing through Cheetah Camp. He procured an 'unofficial' map from the surveyor, and an architect in MMRDA showed the proposed alignment of the road and the affected houses. After studying the situation, Javed Bhai's team proposed how the road could be realigned in such a manner that would save the 550 houses. If this realignment couldn't be accommodated, then they proposed that MMRDA should create an adequate livelihood rehabilitation plan with monetary compensation so that affected households could self-build new houses in-situ. Javed Bhai and his team astutely collected information from different contacts to understand how the community would be affected by the metro plan and propose alternatives that could be of mutual benefit to the community and city.

In all of this, Javed Bhai found out that the MMRDA chief was an alumnus of TISS, which greatly facilitated arranging a meeting where Javed Bhai powerfully put forth community demands, arguing that if self-redevelopment was an option, then additional sectors of Cheetah Camp could be accommodated. The MMRDA chief agreed to look through the self-redevelopment plan but unfortunately immediately thereafter Javed Bhai had to undergo a major heart surgery. In his absence, his team couldn't sustain this process. After four weeks, when Javed Bhai was back home, he restarted the meetings believing that there exists a possibility to negotiate a positive response from MMRDA, with the support of elected representatives.

How activist infrastructures transform place

Each of the three struggles highlights different journeys through which activists thickened and strengthened their collective infrastructure. At the heart of this activist work in informal settlements is building a local agency that rests on the relationship between knowledge and practice – building ways of knowing what works in different situations through experimenting with practice, where practice takes the form of assembling social relations and material objects in particular alignments in order to achieve situated change. Those practices that worked better than others sedimented into an operating knowledge that activists could use the next time round. This situated change is centred on the values of shared caring and mutual flourishing and rooted in their common struggles and lived experiences of creating a better place.

Learning from Cheetah Camp, two different kinds of knowing emerge as central. The first is knowing how the government system works in order to apply pressure at the right point so as to create an opening for change. The second is understanding how the community works so that systems of sharing, self-regulation and entrepreneurship could be developed to locally resolve problems. Both kinds of agency involved the practice of working in groups (Bhan et al., 2017) and understanding limits as much as possibilities. Together it represents a form of incremental learning best described as radical incrementalism (Pieterse, 2008), since it challenges the structures of inequality in the city.

Since the BMC was the predominant public agency that influenced Cheetah Camp's growth and possibilities till the 1990s, Cheetah Camp's activists spent time understanding this system. They realized that they needed to form partnerships with politicians and bureaucrats. Practising collaboration, as the previous section reveals, was informed by activists' knowing with whom they could forge successful relations: with politicians from the secular Congress Party (who were seen as sympathetic to the needs of minority communities), and those who shared religious and kinship ties with the community. Different activists also shared a strategy for targeting select bureaucrats, 'people-oriented bureaucrats', as Ayub described them, who were open to listening and willing to do work (Interview, 24/01/17). Collaborations centrally involved building social relations and utilizing them to enable infrastructural connections, as each of the housing struggles revealed. In each case, external help was sought at different points. The People's Plan story illuminated the thickened web of relations that activist infrastructures were able to draw from – including academic institutions like TISS, and larger city campaigns. A second equally important way of knowing, Ehsan Bhai shared, was studying the BMC's legal and regulatory frameworks – its notices and laws – so one wasn't 'misguided', and could speak with confidence in a 'formal' language to bureaucrats. This way activists could gain the respect of the administration and alter discursive meanings of 'slums' that structured officials' behaviour towards slum dwellers. A Third Way of knowing was to study the different sources and pathways of funds for infrastructure and housing purposes in the BMC that would help in leveraging those suitable for Cheetah Camp. Javed Bhai fluently cited examples for when central programme funds could be tapped, when MLA funds were appropriate, and when the BMC's 'contingency' funds could be used. This knowledge has been developed through long experience of doing – asking questions, filing right to information (RTI)[7] applications and studying government reports and records.

The second category of knowing was understanding how the community worked so as to elicit their trust, cooperation and mobilization in housing struggles. 'The community is not united on many issues for their development. I don't blame the community people for this, they don't have time,' said Javed Bhai. Given the difficulties of mobilizing and sustaining participation from larger collectives, Farooq shared his strategy for tapping the right people for particular jobs in terms of knowing and seeking two types of expertise. The first is people experts: those who know people – who have widespread networks based on *pehchaan* (who they know) and who know what happens in each house and how to negotiate with people and persuade them about the positive effects of a public good (such as the school) even if this involved inconvenience for some. Ehsan Bhai saw Javed Bhai as amply possessing this ability. The second type of expertise Farooq described as technical – a local carpenter who has technical knowledge of civil works or an architect from TISS who could be tapped to contribute through their specialized knowledge and practice. The key for activists was in being able to guide these 'talented' people towards achieving a larger community goal. Once success is achieved at a smaller scale – for example, in one sector of Cheetah Camp – this demonstration effect could be leveraged to convince people in other sectors to adopt similar practices.

Achieving change in a situated context required the ability to consistently follow up and be nimble – to anticipate larger political economic systemic changes that present opportunities or threats and quickly adapt. Ways of knowing had to be buttressed with practices of following up. The 'power of follow up', as Ehsan Bhai called it, was the process of following files through

---

[7] The Right to Information (RTI) is an act which sets out the rules and procedures regarding citizens' right to request public information in the interests of promoting transparency and accountability.

a labyrinthine government system till approvals were gained. Being nimble calls for a whole new set of ways of knowing and practising.

In the last fifty years, Mumbai has transformed and activist infrastructures have adapted in turn. Despite the period of Emergency when civil liberties were suspended, the 1970s were a golden period for NGO activism, and battles against forced demolitions in Cheetah Camp drew inspiration from others anti-eviction struggles that were being waged in cities across the country, describes Chaco, an employee of BUILD, an NGO that supported Cheetah Camp in its struggles against eviction from Janta Colony and rebuilding houses in Cheetah Camp. After the Emergency ended, people's organizations in Cheetah Camp united to negotiate with the state through the Janata Council, an all–political party movement. After 2000, with the consolidation of the Shiv Sena–BJP coalition in power at the state government, the situation changed substantially. The combination of nativist and Hindutva politics proved increasingly toxic for Cheetah Camp, and Javed Bhai described how they gradually withdrew from working with political parties:

> After 2000, we left the party line because the MLA wasn't ours, and also the larger situation changed – politicians now have become 'use and throw' only interested in their own growth, not like earlier where they used to listen and work for us. (Interview, 24/07/19)

Additionally, neoliberal changes in urban governance since the 1990s have led to greater entrepreneurialism among state agencies. The growing influence of the MMRDA – a non-elected parastatal – in shaping geographies of value in Mumbai through its ambitious transport infrastructure projects have meant that the BMC isn't the state institution that predominantly influences Cheetah Camp's growth and possibilities, unlike earlier. Cheetah Camp's activists, ever alert to the dynamic nature of the knowledge needed for neighbourhood improvement, have changed gears to begin negotiations and acquire expert knowledges around planning and land use more suited to the technocratic MMRDA. In the last few years, Javed Bhai refers more often to using CSR funds for various activities in Cheetah Camp, no doubt due to the withdrawal of responsibility by the state and its practice of increased outsourcing of services and projects to private and civil society agencies. This has required Cheetah Camp's activists to consciously reconfigure the way the government system works to include these new actors. Knowing how companies spend CSR funds and how this can be leveraged for Cheetah Camp is fast becoming a new way of knowing and practising.

Conclusion

Hazaaron khwahishen aisi ke har khwahish pe dam nikle
Bohat niklay mere armaan, lekin phir bhi kam nikle – Ghalib
[I have a thousand desires, each worth dying for
Many of my wishes were fulfilled – but still, few were fulfilled][8]

Javed Bhai quotes this famous couplet by the poet Mirza Ghalib to describe the endless human desires that exist in Cheetah Camp, given life by the harsh inequalities in Indian cities. While community activists have been successful in realizing some of these desires through continuous shared labour, care, resources and ingenuity, countless remain unfulfilled. While much of the chapter has focused on the potentials of activist infrastructures as the driver of places in the making, we end with some reflections on its limits.

Activists reveal the constant work involved in engaging people in commoning and the difficulties of sustaining this as a continuous effort within and outside the community. Javed Bhai acknowledges the difficulty of following up on court cases, with lawyers and other experts – who has the time and money for this work? Salim, for instance, doesn't come back to continue the spatial mapping work; he leaves to take up a job, get settled and look after his new family. Where earlier it was easier to tap social work students (many from nearby TISS) for working in the community, today social work graduates are more attuned to better-paying CSR jobs that are not embedded in communities. This epitomizes the ephemerality of (external) connections and the continuous improvisation that is required to grease the operation of activist infrastructures.

Community activists like Javed Bhai face the serious question of how to maintain living infrastructures which are vulnerable to different sustainability problems than physical infrastructures. This becomes increasingly relevant when no younger members of the community are consistently present in Cheetah Camp's struggles – most of the team have been part of struggles since the 1970s or 1980s and have built their collective agency and close bonds of friendship through these shared experiences. As these activists get older and increasingly prone to exhaustion of the body and the imagination in a fast-changing world, an increasingly fraught question is, who will take up the mantle of activism going forward? No records or blueprint exists for how

---

[8]   This is a loose interpretation of one of Mirza Ghalib's (1797–1869) most famous ghazals – 219, verse 1. Since translating these ghazals from Urdu to English is a complex task, multiple versions exist. For more details, see: http://www.columbia.edu/itc/mealac/pritchett/00ghalib/219/219_01.html?unicode

to do activism. Additionally, we cannot easily separate out ways of knowing and doing from the specificity of the person who knows and does – people and their social embeddedness deeply matter. Activist infrastructures of this sort seem doomed to decline in Cheetah Camp.

However, what is clear is that the activist infrastructures that we have discussed were assembled as a placemaking response suitable for the politics of a particular moment. In future times, it is possible that different forms of living infrastructures will emerge and inspire their own shared communities with new ways of claiming citizenship.

References

Bhan, G., Srinivas, S., Watson, V., & McFarlane, C. (2017). Learning From the City. In *The Routledge Companion to Planning in the Global South* (pp. 323–33). Routledge. https://doi.org/10.4324/9781317392842-27

Kamath, L., & Joseph, M. (2015). How a Participatory Process Can Matter in Planning the City. *Economic and Political Weekly*.

Pieterse, E. A. (2008). *City Futures: Confronting the Crisis of Urban Development* (pp. 271–6). Zed.

Ramamurthy, P. (2019). Sub-Plenary 3: '"Delhi" of Dostis (Friends): What Kind of Brotherhood?' RC21 annual conference, lecture notes, International Sociological Association Research Committee on Urban and Regional Development, RC21 annual conference, delivered September 16, 2019.

Simone, A. (2004). People as Infrastructure: Intersecting Fragments in Johannesburg. *Public Culture*, *16*(3), 407–29.

3

Subaltern place as an infrastructure of consolidation

Settling an informal neighbourhood in Mumbai

Himanshu Burte

Introduction

The literature around 'subaltern urbanism' has sought to valorize the life, communities, agency, economies, processes and spaces that urban subaltern populations in the Global South produce informally as the matrix of material and meaningful subsistence (Roy, 2011). I approach informal settlements in India as subaltern *places*, moments in a broader subaltern urbanism animating cities of the Global South and beyond (Schindler, 2014). Extending Simone's recasting of people themselves as infrastructure (2004), subaltern place-as-a-whole may be considered a critical infrastructure of survival and consolidation for its residents, with commoning being a key motive force. The implication is that commoned place is a means and basis of asserting a right to the city and to substantive citizenship.

The argument will be developed through a thematic case study of placemaking in an informal settlement in Mumbai over the second half of the twentieth century. I seek to delineate key contours of commoning in the making and maintenance of a subaltern place, by illuminating aspects of its settling as well as ongoing way of life. What this delineation tells us about the development of subaltern places and the substantive 'texture' of actually practised commoning is considered in the conclusion.

Subaltern place as infrastructure of consolidation

The informal settlement, or 'slum', is central to the discussion of housing and urban inequality in India. Simultaneously reviled by the elite and the state as a blot on the ideal of modern urban space, and grudgingly recognized as essential to the functioning of urban economies by them, it has been valorized in critical scholarship, though often problematically as a metonym for the crisis of Indian (and southern) urbanism (Roy, 2011). Meanwhile, the spatiality of slums has received inadequate attention that integrates diverse social, developmental and geographic considerations (Nijman, 2010), in spite of sophisticated and sympathetic conceptualizations like 'slum as achievement' (Fuchs, 2005) or 'occupancy urbanism' (Benjamin, 2007). Roy (2011) also argues that valorizing subaltern urbanism through ontological and topological approaches (focusing on the concrete spatial practices of the subaltern, for instance) could limit progress towards a more structurally critical and emancipatory discourse and practice. Thus, the spatial practices of urban subalternity bear closer scrutiny and appreciation but must also be analysed thematically in relation to broader arrangements and forces that produce and exploit this spatiality. This chapter consolidates subaltern urbanism's project in the concept of the social value that informal settlements concretize as places. Critically, this value (and place) is shown as being produced through a culture of commoning that opposes dominant statist as well as capitalist urban ideology.

Place is understood here to be a condition (or outcome) as well as a process which involves transformations of space, nature, institutions, norms and selves (Pred, 1984). It is located in the relationship between an 'empirical place' out there objectively (Auge, 1995) and its social and psychological construction by those 'attached' to it. That attachment, I suggest, is to the *value* that place concretizes (Tuan, 1977). The liberal planning theorist Kevin Lynch (1984, p. 116) acknowledges this 'value' in his description of a (good) settlement:

> A settlement is a valued arrangement, consciously changed and stabilized. Its elements are connected through an immense and intricate network, which can be understood only as a series of overlapping local systems, never rigidly or instantaneously linked, and yet part of a fabric without edge.

The diverse places that marginalized, voiceless, disempowered populations, social groups and individuals make out of found, 'given' or occupied sites can be understood as subaltern places.

Subalternity is understood here as an attribute of people as of their places, with the latter being usually, but not always, outside the norms of recognition by the state (Lloyd 2005). I suggest that subaltern place includes more than 'informal' place and its making. For instance, planned resettlement colonies, or urban villages in India, remain subaltern in the hierarchy of urban places. A minor but important point is that the lens of place – associated more consistently with urban spaces of the middle class and of substantive citizenship – when turned on spaces of the subaltern helps spotlight the value that they represent to their dwellers, thereby also challenging the 'ontological priority of dominant groups' (Chattopadhyay, 2012).

Place, as a moment in a broader urbanism, can be considered as commons. As (Gidwani & Baviskar, 2011) argue, 'the distinctive public culture of a city is perhaps the most generative yet unnoticed of urban commons.' Such a distinctive community culture of mutual assistance, solidarity and collective enjoyment has long been noted in settlements of the marginalized and vulnerable across the world and particularly in the Global South (Turner, 1976; Fullilove, 1996; Bayat, 2010; Benjamin, 2007), and has also been called 'informal placemaking' (Lombard, 2014).

Commons are different from 'public' (Gidwani & Baviskar, 2011). Public is limned definitively by state and law and therefore 'given' by them. Commons involve community, and occupy interstices of state and law (or may be their frontiers) and exceed the taxonomies of domination. More importantly, commons are made. They entail work – commoning (Gidwani & Baviskar, 2011). Stavrides (2016) argues that commoning goes beyond

> a process of production or appropriation of certain goods meant to be shared. Commoning is about complex and historically specific processes through which representations, practices and values intersect in circumscribing what is to be shared and how in a specific society.

For him, it necessarily involves the production of knowledge, personal orientations and collective capacity. The impulse of commoning emerges at least partly out of the privations imposed on marginalized populations by the broader capitalist structure of domination, and also as a struggle against it.

Commoning must necessarily negotiate contradictions of various kinds, and may be a dialectic between privatization and collectivization (Stavrides, 2016). In an urban informal settlement where strangers seeking subsistence and housing come from different places (within and outside the city) and cultural backgrounds, the dispute over 'what is considered as common' can have a sharp edge (Stavrides, 2016, p. 32). Where settlements start as non-collectives (Bayat, 2010) of strangers buying and moving into informal real estate developments – as in the case study at hand – or 'encroaching' private or public property quietly, that edge is likely to be sharper. In such contexts, the processes of commoning can be expected to be not consciously undertaken as a coherent project, to be always precarious and to be prone to failure, and thus requiring significant effort at maintaining the impulse for a collective life.

If, as the literature on housing suggests, commoned place is the very basis of consolidation of life and life chances for subaltern individuals, households and communities, can we think of it as a crucial infrastructure of the urban? Infrastructure is a relational concept. Something is infrastructure only in relation to something else it enables or provides a foundation for (Star, 1999, p. 380): in other words, infrastructure is legitimized as a social or quasi-social instrument to achieve a social purpose. In the second half of the twentieth century, transport, power, sanitation, data, etc. have been most commonly considered infrastructure because they facilitate large-scale, state-authorized accumulation. Interestingly, Simone (2004) asks us to think of people as infrastructure and expands the ambit of both the instrument and its object by, paradoxically, blurring the distinction between the two. In his account, social reproduction replaces economic accumulation as the object. And the very people whose social reproduction is thereby revalorized – along with their changeful, uncertain, unstable relationalities – are effectively recast as the instrument. The quasi-circularity of Simone's formulation simultaneously highlights the denial of the badly needed political and economic infrastructure to the subaltern, and the repressiveness of the conventional paradigm of actually existing infrastructures of domination. For our purposes here, it also allows us to get beyond parts of a city – road networks or public gardens and theatres, or indeed people's shared networks and knowledges – to think of place-as-a-whole as the most crucial infrastructure of urban life, especially for subaltern populations. The next section elucidates the making of subaltern place as an infrastructure of subsistence and consolidation through commoning, with the help of a case study of the settling of an informal settlement in Mumbai.

Pratap Nagar

Mumbai has been India's financial capital for long and a symbol of the country's urban inequalities, with the wretched and insecure living conditions of over half its population widely documented in policy, scholarship, popular culture and art. A city of colonial origin, it has a population of twelve million (twenty million in the metropolitan region) spread over 457 square kilometres, and has witnessed many waves of creation, expansion and demolition of informal settlements. Since Independence in 1947, the local and state government's attitude towards these settlements has involved different combinations of denial, tolerance, paternalism and predation (Bhide, 2009). Since liberalization in the 1990s, the state has directly demolished or caused the elimination of many settlements through policy action either to release land under them to the real estate market through redevelopment or to enable infrastructure construction and upgradation. The partial destruction of the particular settlement after the making of place discussed in the following text is part of the analytical context of this case study.

Pratap Nagar is a small community of about 5,000 households[1] within a large continuous expanse of informal settlements housing a few hundred thousand people in the 'suburb' of Jogeshwari (East), about 25 kilometres north of the CBD in south Mumbai. This self-identified settlement is not 'officially' demarcated within the larger informal fabric, though its boundaries are marked implicitly by changing addresses on shop-signs, and tacitly known to residents. The story of the making of Pratap Nagar as a valued place is important for its own subsequent trajectory, as well as being an instance of a fairly representative process of the socio-spatial consolidation of informal settlements in Mumbai and other Indian cities in the second half of the twentieth century.

Starting in the late 1950s, Pratap Nagar emerged as a cluster of unauthorized 'chawls' (barrack-like rows of rooms in a single ground storey structure) on a large stretch of private land, a long walk from the Jogeshwari suburban railway station. Most of the land under what later became Pratap Nagar was declared a No Development Zone (NDZ) in Mumbai's first DP (1967). By the 1980s, part of Pratap Nagar was already settled on the proposed 11.1 kilometre-long Jogeshwari Vikhroli Link Road (JVLR), which when built and widened later would come to be regarded as a crucial link between the city's two main north-south arterials, the Western and Eastern Express Highways, respectively. JVLR was completed as a two-lane road in the 1990s with the first round of displacement and resettlement. Another round followed the widening and alignment modifications between 2006 and 2011 under the World Bank-funded Mumbai Urban Transport Project (MUTP), to increase road capacity and speeds in the urban and metropolitan network. Under the funder's pressure, Maharashtra state drafted a pioneering Resettlement and Rehabilitation policy in 1997, the first of its kind for urban resettlement in India.[2] The policy aided local communities' struggle for a more just resettlement process, as well as relatively favourable location, design and construction characteristics of the resettlement colony for over 700 displaced households. Nevertheless, in spite

---

[1] A JVLR-related report counted 5,226 tenements in Pratap Nagar (Econ Pollution Control Consultants, 2002, p. 22). It must be noted that the report gathered together a number of other contiguous communities under the name of Pratap Nagar. I have followed that convention for convenience and readability.

[2] The state government's commitment to this progressive policy has been weak. MUIP, which followed MUTP, reverted to some less progressive aspects of previous policy.

of this relatively progressive resettlement policy, two things happened that provide important context for the argument here. The erasure of part of the settlement by the road 'maimed' the settlement as a place in important ways: by taking away important common spaces of gathering that happened to be in its path, by spatially dividing the community into two parts and by removing a chunk of the community to the resettlement colony a kilometre away. At the same time, the resettlement colony of largely seven-storey buildings (formally christened optimistically by residents later as Sukh Sagar, 'sea of happiness') has proved very difficult to turn into a supportive place in its first decade. As with such programmes and spaces, a large number of resettled families have illegally sold or rented out their tenements because of unaffordable maintenance costs and lack of essential community support, and been effectively displaced doubly. While I cannot elaborate on these two stories here, their significance rests on the argument that what was lost in displacement was the value of place as an infrastructure of private and social subsistence and consolidation. The construction of this value through commoning against a hostile socio-material context is the focus of this chapter. The case study develops a thematic argument drawing on a schematic oral history developed through oral history and qualitative interviews with twenty-three people, including with long-term residents and community leaders, and two focus group discussions with residents of Pratap Nagar as well as of the resettlement colony.

Two related 'levels' of commoning practices can be noted in the making of a viable subaltern place at Pratap Nagar. One, everyday practice implicating everybody in the pressures of everyday commoning in the face of urgencies and desires of private consolidation. Two, exceptional initiatives of commoning that emerge from the everyday (Lefebvre, 2002, p. 44) but transcend it in different ways, sometimes stopping at pleasures of sociability and solidarity, and at others going beyond towards deepening the lived experience and political practice of citizenship, relevant to claiming a right to the city. Both are visible in the three themes through which the story of subaltern placemaking in Pratap Nagar is told here: making everyday place, private and common; making place work; and making selves and citizenship in and out of place.[3]

Making place

Pratap Nagar was settled from the 1950s (when it lay outside Mumbai's city limits). The state then bore an attitude of denial and hostility towards

---

[3]   The two sections that follow are modified extracts from my unpublished dissertation (Burte, 2017)

slums that has been called a 'phase of negation' (Bhide, 2009). Labour in
fringe settlements of this kind was connected to jobs in the city through
the railway line nearby, but the settlements themselves lacked roads, water
supply and toilets. House construction was rudimentary. Many chawls were
built of mud-plastered masonry with fired clay tiles on cheap wooden roof
structures. Others had even cheaper wattle-and-daub (some still visible in the
1988 documentary *Jod Rasta Tod Rasta*[4]) construction. These had been built
and 'sold' by informal real estate entrepreneurs associated with the upper-
caste North Indian (mainly from Uttar Pradesh and Bihar) migrant dairy
entrepreneurs.[5] They had neither title to land nor building permission from
the gram panchayat (village local government); so, the constructions were
unauthorized from the very beginning. As housing need and Jogeshwari's
attractiveness (due to its railway station) burgeoned together, especially after
the city limits were extended to include the suburb in 1957, some stables were
slowly turned into rooms, possibly with the informal support of the land
owners' caretakers, local corporators and MCGM.[6] Early entrants moved
into a settlement surrounded by 'jungle' (mixed, low scrub forest). On payday
evenings in the early 1960s, people walked home from the railway station
in the dark worried about getting robbed.[7] Police presence was almost non-
existent, and the nearest police station was a few kilometres away at Andheri.

An unselfconscious, traditional habitus of collective inhabiting appears
to have driven the making of a viable place out of these sketchy beginnings
at Pratap Nagar. Its relatively limited diversity – the majority being Marathi-
speaking families from intermediate and backward castes – is likely to have
helped. In the 1950s, many young households moved in from different
places: from nearby settlements, the city to the south, displaced either by
development or by a lack of affordable housing, or from villages in the
hinterland looking for work. In the first couple of decades, homes and
households had to be consolidated physically and socioeconomically while
securing absent basic services through practices of negotiation with more
privileged groups nearby, and making claims politically through elected
representatives and local movements after 1957. Exceptional leadership
and everyday neighbourliness were equally important elements of the
consolidation of private and community life together, materially and socially.

<hr>

[4] Produced by an NGO called YUVA for awareness building, and directed by Nasreen
     Contractor and Alpa Vora. Available at: https://pad.ma/CGP/info
[5] Nitin Kubal, interview, 6 September 2015.
[6] An elderly resident even remembers a South Indian caretaker in the employ of the Parsi
     families who would regularly visit the land and whose 'permission', he believes, must
     have been taken for each chawl. Interview with Vithal Sawant, 24 August 2015.
[7] Interview Hanuman Kubal, 6 September 2015.

The physical consolidation of place involved ensuring durable physical security, shelter and basic comfort. When he bought his room in the early 1960s, 85-year-old Vithal Sawant's home was bare shelter made of wattle-and-daub with roughly levelled earth inside and out. Like many other residents, he takes in the house and the neighbourhood with a sweep of his arm and says, 'All this was made by us.'[8] The transformation of a hut into a painted masonry house like his – with polished stone flooring and aluminium windows inside, and narrow paved lanes with open or covered drains (carrying grey water from the indoor bathrooms without water closets, which most houses have built by now) leading to occasional gathering spaces – is indeed remarkable, even if cramped and more basic than 'formal' neighbourhoods in the city (Figure 3.1).

The lack of basic services was overcome through *practices,* by negotiating collectively with nearby stable owners who allowed women from the informal settlements to fill their pots at their municipal taps.[9] In other settlements, residents dug wells for water where they could, and women washed clothes at the many ponds in the landscape, thus drawing on common natural

Figure 3.1 A paved open space with benches in Pratap Nagar. (Photograph by Author/Himanshu Burte, November 2020.)

---

[8] Interview, 24 August 2015.
[9] The proximity and contact with both, the State Reserve Police Force (SRPF) and the stable owners and workers, would soon lead to conflict and violence.

resources. Most chawls had been built without a dedicated toilet block, so its residents went to defecate on a hillock nearby on undeveloped land owned by the State Reserve Police Force (SRPF). A part of the campus was also a large playground for young boys till its compound wall was repaired and completed in the 1990s. While in some chawls the owners built common toilets, in others many residents themselves pooled money to build them over time, typically by clearing a patch of scrub at the edge of the settlement.

Material challenges led ordinary residents to become community leaders who helped build greater security through various means over time, with women playing an important role. For instance, in the early decades, the flimsiness of house construction kept women acutely vulnerable to sexual harassment. The police would not ordinarily venture into the maze of narrow lanes, allowing wide latitude to the rule of violence. A once-fiery community leader who was in her seventies when I interviewed her, Kalpana Mahale, remembers that a gangster once forcibly entered a woman's house with a sword when her husband was away and threatened her, asking for her daughter to be sent to him.[10] The woman approached Mahale for help, who managed to complain to the police and successfully had the man externed. But the police themselves could be a menace. Mahale was herself harassed by a police inspector, when her husband was abroad for work, till she successfully engaged his superior in her support. Mahale ascribes her physical fearlessness and general confidence to growing up in a family of police and army men. It helped that she could twirl a thick bamboo menacingly and scare away any man in a confrontation!

At a more everyday level, leadership, community action and small-scale philanthropy were central to the struggle to acquire basic infrastructure from the city. Mahale recalls that her husband (who worked for a few years in the Middle East) personally paid for putting up streetlights decades ago in their lane.[11] Vithal Sawant once threatened the municipal corporation with an agitation and a roadblock on the arterial Western Express Highway next door, for a pump to push water up to the settlement from the nearby Andheri Pump House. Subsequently, the local councillor Rajeshwar Raginwar managed to get a pump house built nearby on a bridge over a natural water course to bring water to the area.[12] Sawant also lobbied a state government minister successfully in 1974 to sanction a Kamgar Kalyan Kendra (Workers' Welfare Centre) next to his home on an open patch of land that he is proud to have protected against privatization. This centre provides a range

---

[10] Interview, 27 August 2015. Mahale passed away recently.
[11] Interview, 27 August 2015.
[12] Interview, 24 August 2015.

of subsidized educational and vocational training to families of registered workers in private and public sector enterprises, and serves a large part of the city nearby. An upper storey built over the small building a few years ago is rented out to local residents for family events like christening or engagement ceremonies, and is an essential infrastructure of community life. Individual leadership and agency have thus been crucial in forging collective life and agency.

Leadership was important for fostering relationality and common purpose. Sawant recalls starting the Ganpati *mandal* (an association for community celebration of the Ganpati festival) in his neighbourhood in 1964 to gather newly arrived residents together and build community out of a Bayatian non-collective marked by anomie. Interestingly, the appropriate reproduction of traditional cultural form was a twinned motive: he found the existing tradition of celebration in the community graceless.

While 'exceptional' moments like agitations and festivals have been important, everyday processes and traditions like those around neighbourliness are at the core of collective life, and therefore of commoning, in Pratap Nagar. Neighbourliness is often imbued with the spirit of kinship reproducing inherited social and cultural forms. Though she is from the same cultural background as the neighbours she met on moving in after marriage, a woman in her fifties said, 'my neighbours taught me all about religious rituals.' She pointed in different directions to the homes of her sister, mother-in-law and sister-in-law, enumerating the different kinds of support she has received at different times of need. Of course, she quickly added that those women are not really her relatives – she just considers them to be that. 'My own relatives say, "she does not need relatives, she wants only her neighbours!"' she says, laughing at the mildly scandalous accusation she happily accepts.[13]

Making place work

A very particular form of collective agency of place – however protean, precarious, contradictory and even repressive in some respects – appears to have taken hold in the initial decades of Pratap Nagar's existence. This is the result of diverse small and big efforts including mechanisms of getting house lanes cleaned regularly, upgrading community toilets periodically and developing and protecting common open spaces from encroachment,

[13] Interview, 24 August 2015.

especially those like the main *maidan* (playground), where all community celebrations from Ganpati to festival dances would occur till it was lost to JVLR. The texture of this ensemble of practices and institutions of making the place work is complex, though the lived sense of community is palpable even today.

Formal governance and management structures have been sparse in Pratap Nagar, possibly because it is not a single, bounded property with centralized management of space and infrastructure.[14] Most households paid rent to chawl owners (who sometimes live in the settlement), and the maintenance of the house property was thus a matter between the two parties (though, in practice, the tenant's responsibility). Chawl committees or a larger federation have been the key forum of formal, everyday functional association and cooperative action. In spite of the culture of neighbourliness, the capacity for organized collective action, even if at a very small scale (of say ten to twenty houses in a chawl), is a challenge, especially in times of crisis, like when a municipal notice of demolition is served on the chawl owners because of repeated non-payment of taxes. Then, there are capital expenses on repair, reconstruction of the community toilets every few years, or the need to pave over or replace the lane paving. These can go up to a few hundred thousand rupees, well outside the reach of households subsisting, today, on anything between Rs 5 and 15,000 per month. In these cases, chawl committees collect what money they can from members, but also liaise with state- and central government-level political representatives for a good part of the expenses to be covered through the official Local Area Development funds at the latter's disposal. This dependence on political representatives clearly reinforces a contradictory impulse of clientelism, which some in the community believe has corroded traditions of collective life in the last fifteen or twenty years. This reveals a key limitation of everyday commoning culture, which cannot yet exceed bounds set by broader sociopolitical structures.

Yet, the everyday culture of commoning growing out of an ethic of neighbourliness has also partly overcome certain other structural impediments. One such potential barrier is historical prejudice on the axis of social difference and hierarchy. An important initiative of commoning through maintenance at Pratap Nagar continues to date with the Buddha Vihar, a religio-political community space of the Dalit (historically untouchable) community, which sought to reject the oppressive caste structure of Hinduism and embraced Buddhism under the leadership of Dr B.R. Ambedkar soon after India gained independence. Almost the entire

---

[14] This passage draws on a number of interviews and conversations with Nitin Kubal mainly over 2014–15.

group of Dalit households in Pratap Nagar happened to have settled on the alignment of the JVLR, and were displaced in 1990 and moved to an unsatisfactory resettlement colony a couple of kilometres up the same road. However, the Buddha Vihar they had built lay outside the road alignment and was spared. Though not living in Pratap Nagar any more, the displaced Dalit community continues to maintain the Buddha Vihar as their religious space, but also offers it as a gathering space for the rest of the local non-Dalit community. The space was a central meeting place for mobilization to resist JVLR's widening in the early 2000s.

Making selves in and out of place

All self is in place (Casey 2001, p. 684), so constantly (re)making place involves (re)making selves, as well as social structures (Pred 1984). At Pratap Nagar, the material production and maintenance of place has been accompanied by an intense culture of sociopolitical mobilization spanning the ideological spectrum. In the 1980s, a fledgling NGO called Youth for Unity and Voluntary Action (YUVA) had sought to empower youth in different ways in Jogeshwari. An important example of democratization this initiative led to is a youth collective called Prerna Mitra Mandal ('prerna' means inspiration in Marathi, and 'mitra mandal' means an association of friends).[15] Prerna was founded in 1994 and was active till recently, for about twenty-five years. The founders were a group of educated youth in their twenties marked by a critical curiosity about the world around them, searching for an appropriate ethical stance for personal and civic practice. While some of the founders went on to become full-time activists and NGO workers, others became professionals, teachers and biologists, among other things.

Prerna was a utopian project of forging both a new social, cultural and political consciousness and relations, and can be regarded as an 'institution of expanding commoning' (Stavrides, 2016). At its peak, it was a voluntary organization with about 200 young people as members (from poor and economically precarious families), drawn from Pratap Nagar and other nearby settlements. It was known in the wider neighbourhood

---

[15] '*Prerna*' means inspiration, and '*mitramandal*' is literally 'friends' association'. The latter phrase is very common in the names of such groups. It is particularly instructive because it combines the impersonal civil society form of the gathering of rational subjects for a defined purpose, with the informal, affective dynamic of friendship. The actual practice of such associations is clearly founded on the affective normativities of 'friendship' commonly accepted in the social group.

as a platform and a collective agent of critical social commentary. Boys and girls worked together in its activities, expanding the room for contact and interaction across the strictly policed gender barriers of a conservative community. Conceived as a collective enterprise materially rooted in the voluntary support from the community, it experimented with forms of internal governance. For instance, in the course of a five-year experiment in representative decision making for 'efficiency', the group learnt that concentration of power in the executive committee had led their own fellow travellers towards authoritarianism. Working through the resulting ill will and friction, Prerna adopted a mode of collective decision making, accepting losses of efficiency for a more democratic culture. The organization's public action used many channels. Street plays were a staple, as were occasional, and locally famous, street corner blackboards that carried commentary on current affairs and matters of community importance handwritten in chalk. Among its early initiatives was a community library stocked with books bought strictly out of contributions collected from the wider community. In a few years, the library received nominal recognition and annual funds from the state government. But these were never enough to secure a physical space for the library, and for years it kept moving from one rented or loaned space to another in the settlement. In spite of the precarity, Prerna remained committed to its community-funding model, rejecting the occasional offers of sponsorship by elected representatives so as to retain community control over the resource. Notably, the ethic of neighbourliness in Pratap Nagar provided a firm foundation for the organization's project of commoning, even in the support that full-time volunteers could take for granted. As a founding member recalled, 'we were always sure of a place to sleep and a meal at some friend's place.'[16] In less than a decade of its existence, Prerna had incubated a progressive sociopolitical subjectivity as a practice and an ideal that young people could shape themselves towards. One of its founders went on to become the state-level head of YUVA, a renowned NGO by the 2000s, and later an impactful water rights activist at city scale. Prerna also prepared another local youth for leading a sustained campaign of resistance against the spatial injustices associated with the demolition of community infrastructure and problems associated with displacement and resettlement that JVLR caused after 2006. He is now a respected local social activist, alongside being a social sector professional active in urban affairs.

[16] 'Interview with Sitaram Shelar, 5 February 2020'

Conclusion

The brief account of one case of subaltern placemaking mentioned earlier suggests a number of things. To begin with, place is more generally reaffirmed as a materially, and not just culturally, significant force for human life. Its value is embodied in an ensemble of: the material infrastructure of homes and shared infrastructure like open spaces; micro-governance systems and neighbourly solidarities; and emergent platforms and mechanisms for self-making and remaking, whether as workers (Kamgar Kalyan Kendra) or citizens (Prerna). Further, this value has clearly been created through commoning practices that take many forms. These include the impulse to take risks to help others, doing things (like fetching water) collectively for practical reasons, and consciously forging collective action either for festivals or self-making. It also includes protecting common spaces and amenities.

Important insights also emerge about commoning. Commoning must always negotiate internal and external limitations, contradictions and threats specific to subaltern place in a southern city like Mumbai. A traditional habitus of asserting and yielding to leadership has been central to Pratap Nagar, and contradicts Stavrides's ideas about collective decision making in an idealized commoning horizon, though Prerna upheld exactly that consciousness and practice. Commoning, though outside the law in one sense, is also constrained by structural limits set by the state and law as the dependence on political representatives for acquiring and funding basic infrastructure demonstrates. However, the commoning spirit is also seen overcoming structural barriers like caste to an extent, as with the displaced Dalit community's Buddha Vihar being opened for wider community mobilization.

Pratap Nagar's experience can reasonably be considered broadly representative of a large number of established informal settlements in Mumbai. Given that over half the population of the city lives in subaltern places, commoning place is a practice essential to survival for large sections of the urban population. Thus, the practice of commoning place may itself be an intangible and processual infrastructure of subsistence and consolidation, as much as the place that it produces. Commoning place also constitutes a quiet and pervasive everyday resistance to the expansion of state domination and the culture of privatization. We are thus led to a broader possibility. Given that formal, middle-class residential spaces in Mumbai and other Indian cities are highly privatized and relatively weakly commoned even within their property boundaries, can valued subaltern places be considered a potential infrastructure of expanding commoning in the city?

Acknowledgements

This chapter draws on my doctoral dissertation research. I am particularly grateful to Vidyadhar Phatak and Amita Bhide for important discussions, feedback and leads. I owe a great debt to Nitin Kubal for being my anchor in Pratap Nagar – his passion for justice and commitment to grassroots work is an inspiration. I am also grateful to all the respondents who spared their time, experiences and insights. The research was conducted as part of a project titled 'People Places and Infrastructure: Countering Urban Violence and Promoting Justice in Rio, Durban and Mumbai', funded under the Safe and Inclusive Cities programme by IDRC, Canada, over 2013–16.

References

Agier, M. (2010). Forced migration and asylum: Stateless citizens today. In C. Audebert and M. K. Dorai (ed.), *Migration in a Globalised World: New Research Issues and Prospects* (pp. 183–90). Amsterdam: Amsterdam University Press.

Agustín, Ó. G., & Jørgensen, M. B. (2019). Autonomous solidarity: Hotel City Plaza. In Ó. G. Agustín and M. B. Jørgensen (ed.), *Solidarity and the 'Refugee Crisis' in Europe* (pp. 49–72). London: Palgrave Macmillan.

Agustín, Ó. G., & Jørgensen, M. B. (2019). Conceptualizing solidarity: An analytical framework. In *Solidarity and the 'Refugee Crisis' in Europe* (pp. 23–47).

Auge, M. (1995). *Non-places: An Introduction to Supermodernity* (J. Howe, Trans.). London and New York: Verso.

Bayat, A. (2010). Introduction: The art of presence. In A. Bayat (ed.), *Life as Politics: How Ordinary People Change the Middle East* (pp. 1–26). Amsterdam: Amsterdam University Press.

Benjamin, S. (2007). Occupancy urbanism: Ten theses. In M. Narula, S. Sengupta, J. Bagchi and R. Sundaram (eds.), *Sarai Reader 2007: Frontiers* (pp. 538–563). Sarai.

Bhide, A. (2009). Shifting terrains of communities and community organization: Reflections on organizing for housing rights in Mumbai. *Community Development Journal*. doi: 10.1093/cdj/bsp026

Bollier, D. (2014). *Think Like a Commoner: A Short Introduction to the Life of the Commons*. New Society Publishers.

Borch, C., & Kornberger, M. (2015). *Urban Commons: Rethinking the City*. Routledge.

Bresnihan, P., & Byrne, M. (2014). Escape into the city: Everyday practices of commoning and the production of urban space in Dublin. *Antipode, 47*(1), 36–54.

Bulley, D. (2015). Ethics, power and space: International hospitality beyond Derrida. *Hospitality & Society, 5*(2), pp. 185–201.

Burte, H. (2017). *Trajectories of Place.* Doctoral dissertation, CEPT University.

Caffentzis, G. (2009). The future of 'the commons': Neoliberalism's 'plan B' or the original disaccumulation of capital? *New Formations, 69: Imperial Ecologies,* pp. 23–41.

Candea, M., & Col, G. (2012). The return to hospitality. *Journal of the Royal Anthropological Institute,* 18, pp. S1–S19.

Casey, E. S. (2001). Between geography and philosophy: What does it mean to be in the place-world? *Annals of the Association of American Geographers, 91*(4), pp. 683–93.

Chattopadhyay, S. (2012). *Unlearning the City: Infrastructure in a New Optical Field.* Minneapolis: University of Minnesota Press.

De Angelis, M. (2011). Η τραγωδία των καπιταλιστικών κοινών [The tragedy of the capitalist commons]. *Commons vs Crisis,* 94.

De Angelis, M. (2019). Migrants' inhabiting through commoning and state enclosures. A postface. *Citizenship Studies, 23*(6), pp. 627–36.

Derrida, J., & Dufourmante, A. (2006 [1996]). *Περί Φιλοξενίας (Of Hospitality)* (Μ. Βαγγέλης, Trans.) ΕΚΚΡΕΜΕΣ [ekkremes].

Econ Pollution Control Consultants. (2002). *Community Environmental for Environmental Management Plan (CEMP) at Permanent Resettlement Site at Plot No. CTS No. 190 (pt) Majas Village.* MMRDA, MUTP. Mumbai: MMRDA.

Fuchs, M. (2005). Slum as achievement: Governmentality and the agency of slum dwellers. In E. Hust, & M. Mann (ed.), *Urbanization and Governance in India* (pp. 102–23). New Delhi: Manohar.

Fullilove, M. T. (1996, December). Psychiatric implications of displacement: Contributions from the psychology of place. *American Journal of Psychiatry, 153*(12), pp. 1516–23.

Galgano, A. (2017). Tomorrow's neighbors: Strategies for temporary refugee integration in Athens, Greece. *NYU Abu Dhabi Journal of Social Sciences,* pp. 1–28.

Gidwani, V., & Baviskar, A. (2011). Urban commons. *Economic and Political Weekly, 46*(50), pp. 42–3.

Gutiérrez Sánchez, I. (2017). *Commoning Spaces of Social Reproduction. Citizen-led Welfare Infrastructures in Crisis-Ridden Athens.* UniFi, School of Architecture, Φλωρεντία [Florence].

Haddad, E. (2016, 2 May). Solidarity, squats and self-management assisting migrants in Greece. *Equal Times.*

Iliadi, A. (2016, Οκτώβριος 12). *Re.Framing Activism.* Retrieved from http://reframe.sussex.ac.uk/activistmedia/2016/10/the-radical-potential-of-media-publicity-the-case-of-city-plaza-refugee-squat-in-athens/

Kakoliris, G. (2015). Jacques Derrida on the ethics of hospitality. *The Ethics of Subjectivity,* pp. 144–56.

Kakoliris, G. (2019). Jacques Derrida and René Schérer on hospitality. *Dianoesis: A Journal of Philosophy,* pp. 23–42.

Kanavaris, N., & Makaronas, S. (2017). *Refugee Accommodation Squat City Plaza: A "Weird" Village.* Athens: Dspace NTUA Library.

Kanavaris, N., Makaronas, S., & Stellatou, D. (2018). *Bridging the Diverse – Social Center Jasmine.* Athens: Dspace NTUA Library.

Kapsali, M. (2019). *The Politics of Urban Commons: Participatory Urbanism In Thessaloniki During The 2010 Crisis.* Thessaloniki.

Karaliotas, L. (2017). Towards commoning institutions in, against and beyond the 'Greek crisis'. Retrieved from Eurozin: https://www.eurozine.com/towards-commoning-institutions-in-against-and-beyond-the-greek-crisis/

Karyotis, T. (2016). The eviction of three occupied refugee shelters in Thessaloniki marks another episode in the Greek government's war on grassroots solidarity efforts. *ROAR Magazine.*

Katrini, E. (2020). Spatial manifestations of collective refugee housing – the case of City Plaza. *Radical Housing Journal, 2*(1), pp. 29–53.

King, A., & Manoussaki-Adamopoulou, I. (2019, Αυγούστου 26). Greek police raid Athens squats and arrest migrants. *The Guardian.*

King, A., & Manoussaki-Adamopoulou, I. (2019, August 29). Inside exarcheia: The self-governing community Athens police want rid of. *The Guardian.*

Koptyaeva, A. (2017, June). Collective homemaking in transit. *Forced Migration Review: Shelter in Displacement, 55*, pp. 37–8.

Kotronaki, L. (2018). Outside the doors: Refugee accommodation squats and heterotopy politics. *The South Atlantic Quarterly, 117*(4), pp. 914–24.

Kotronaki, L., Lafazani, O., & Maniatis, G. (2018). Living resistance: Experiences from the refugee housing squat in Athens. *The South Atlantic Quarterly, 117*(4), pp. 892–95.

Lafazani, O. (2012). The border between theory and activism. *ACME An International Journal for Critical Geographies, 11*(2), pp. 189–93.

Lafazani, O. (2016). documenta14.

Lafazani, O. (2017). *1.5 Year City Plaza: A Project on the Antipodes of Bordering and Control Policies.* (Antipode, Editor) Retrieved from Antipode Online: https://antipodeonline.org/2017/11/13/intervention-city-plaza/

Lafazani, O. (2018a, June). Κρίση and Μετανάστευση in Greece: From illegal migrants to refugees. *Sociology, 52*(3), pp. 619–25.

Lafazani, O. (2018b, October). Homeplace plaza: Challenging the border between host and hosted. *The South Atlantic Quartery, 117*(4), pp. 896–904.

Lefebvre, H. (2002). *Critique of Everyday Life* (Vol. II). London; New York: Verso.

Lima Camargo, L. O. (2015). The Interstices of hospitality. *Research in Hospitality Management, 5*, pp. 19–27.

Linebaugh, P. (2010). Some principles of the commons. *Weekend Edition*, January 8–10.

Lloyd, D. (2005). The subaltern in motion: Subalternity, the popular and Irish working class history. *Postcolonial Studies, 8*(4), 421–37.

Lombard, M. (2014). Constructing ordinary places: Place-making in urban informal settlements in Mexico. *Progress in Planning*, pp. 1–53.

Lynch, K. (1984). *Good City Form*. Cambridge, MA: MIT Press.

Maniatis, G. (2018). From a crisis of management to humanitarian crisis management. *The South Atlantic Quarterly, 117*(4), pp. 905–13.

Martinez, M. A., Dadusc, D., & Grazioli, M. (2019). Introduction: Citizenship as inhabitance? Migrant housing squats versus institutional accommodation. *Citizenship Studies, 23*(6), pp. 521–539.

McGuirk, J. (2015, June 15). Urban commons have radical potential – it's not just about community gardens. *The Guardian*, International Edition.

Mezzadra, S. (2018). In the wake of the Greek spring and the summer of migration. *The South Atlantic Quarterly, 117*(4), pp. 925–33.

Montagna, N., & Grazioli, M. (2019). Urban commons and freedom of movement – The housing struggles of recently arrived migrants in Rome. *Citizenship Studies, 23*(9), pp. 577–92.

Nijman, J. (2010). A study of space in Mumbai's slums. *Tijdschrift voor Economische en Sociale Geografie, 101*, pp. 4–17.

Papataxiarchis, E. (2006a). Τα άχθη της ετερότητας, Διαστάσεις της πολιτισμικής διαφοροποίησης στην Ελλάδατου πρώιμου 21ου αιώνα [Burdens of alterity: Aspects of cultural differentiation in early 21th-century]. In Ε. Παπαταξιάρχης (ed.), *Περιπέτειες της ετερότητας: Η παραγωγή της πολιτισμικής διαφοράς στη σημερινή Ελλάδα [Adventures of Alterity: The Production of Cultural Difference in Contemporary Greece]*. Alexandria.

Papataxiarchis, E. (2006b). Το καθεστώς της διαφορετικότητας στην Ελληνική κοινωνία, Υποθέσεις εργασίας. In Ε. Παπαταξιάρχης (ed.), *Περιπέτειες της ετερότητας: Η παραγωγή της πολιτισμικής διαφοράς στη σημερινή Ελλάδα [Adventures of Alterity: The Production of Cultural Difference in Contemporary Greece]* (pp. 407–469). Alexandria.

Papataxiarchis, E. (2014). Ὁ αδιανόητος ρατσισμός: Η πολιτικοποίηση της 'φιλοξενίας' την εποχή της κρίσης' ['The inconceivable racism: The politicization of "hospitality" in the age of crisis']. *Synchrona, 127*, pp. 46–62.

Papataxiarchis, E. (2016a, April). Being 'there' at the front line of the 'European refugee crisis' – part 1. *Antropoly Today*, pp. 3–7.

Papataxiarchis, E. (2016b, June). Being 'there' at the front line of the 'European refugee crisis' – part 2. *Anthropology Today*, pp. 3–7.

Papataxiarchis, E. (2016c, May). Unwrapping solidarity? Society reborn in austerity. *Social Anthropology, 24*, pp. 205–10.

Papataxiarchis, E. (2016d, October). ΜΙΑ ΜΕΓΑΛΗ ΑΝΑΤΡΟΠΗ: Η ΕΥΡΩΠΑΪΚΗ ΠΡΟΣΦΥΓΙΚΗ ΚΡΙΣΗ ΚΑΙ Ο ΝΕΟΣ ΠΑΤΡΙΩΤΙΣΜΟΣ ΤΗΣ ΑΛΛΗΛΕΓΓΥΗΣ. *ΣΥΓΧΡΟΝΑ ΘΕΜΑΤΑ, 132-133*, pp. 7–28.

Pred, A. (1984, June). Place as historically contingent process: Structuration and the time- geography of becoming places. *Annals of the Association of American Geographers, 74*(2), pp. 279–97.

Raimondi, V. (2019). For 'common struggles of migrants and locals'. Migrant activism and squatting in Athens. *Citizenship Studies, 23*(6), pp. 559–76.

Rakopoulos, T. (2016, May). Solidarity: The egalitarian tensions of a bridge-concept. *Social Anthropology, 24*, pp. 142–51.

Roy, A. (2011). Slumdog cities: Rethinking subaltern urbanism. *International Journal of Urban and Regional Research, 35*(2), pp. 223–38.

Rozakou, K. (2012). The biopolitics of hospitality in Greece: Humanitarianism and the management of refugees. *American Ethnologist, 39*, pp. 562–77.

Rozakou, K. (2016). Crafting the volunteer: Voluntary associations and the reformation of sociality. *Journal of Modern Greek Studies, 34*, pp. 79–102.

Rozakou, K. (2016, May). Socialities of solidarity: Revisiting the gift taboo in times of crises: Socialities of solidarity. *Social Anthropology, 24*, pp. 185–99.

Schindler, S. (2014). Understanding urban processes in Flint, Michigan: Approaching 'subaltern urbanism' inductively. *International Journal of Urban and Regional Research, 38*(3), pp. 791–804.

Siapera, E. (2019, April). Refugee solidarity in Europe: Shifting the discourse. *European Journal of Cultural Studies, 22*, pp. 245–266.

Simone, A. (2004). People as infrastructure: Intersecting fragments in Johannesburg. *Public Culture, 16*(3), pp. 407–429.

Solidarity2Refugees. (n.d.). Retrieved from http://solidarity2refugees.gr /39-mines-city-plaza-oloklirosi-enos-kyklou-archi-enos-neou/?fbclid =IwAR21QYRNWLJvYwYGXzzF_01RiL3c-YmMYzqKs13zJuXfD -AlWcVCUwqok18.

Squire, V. (2018, July). Mobile solidarities and precariousness at City Plaza: Beyond vulnerable and disposable lives. *Studies in Social Justice, 12*(1), pp. 111–32.

Squire, V., & Darling, J. (2013). The "minor" politics of rightful presence: Justice and relationality in city of sanctuary. *International Political Sociology, 7*, pp. 59–74.

Star, S. L. (1999). The ethnography of infrastructure. *American Behavioral Scientist, 43*(3), pp. 377–91.

Stavrides, S. (2014). Emerging common spaces as a challenge to the city of crisis. *City, 18*, pp. 546–50.

Stavrides, S. (2015). Common space as threshold space: Urban commoning in struggles to reappropriate public space. *Footprint*, pp. 9–19.

Stavrides, S. (2016). *Common Space: The City as Commons*. London: Zed Books Ltd.

Tsavdaroglou, C. (2018). The newcomer's right to the common space: The case of Athens during the refugee crisis. *ACME An International Journal for Critical Geographies, 17*(2), pp. 376–401.

Tsavdaroglou, C. (2019). Reimagining a transnational right to the city: No border actions and commoning practices in Thessaloniki. *Social Inclusion, 7*(2), pp. 219–29.

Tsavdaroglou, C., Giannopoulou, C., Lafazani, O., Pistikos, I., & Petropoulou, C. (2018). De(constructing) the refugees' right to the city: State-run camps versus commoning practices in athens, thessaloniki and mytilene. Vol. Refugees and forced immigration '18 conference proceedings. Istanbul.

Tsavdaroglou, C., Giannopoulou, C., Petropoulou, C., & Pistikos, I. (2019). Acts for refugees' right to the city and commoning practices of care-tizenship in Athens, Mytilene and Thessaloniki. *Social Inclusion, 7*, pp. 119–30.

Tuan, Y.-F. (1977). *Space and Place: The Perspective of Experience.* Minneapolis: University of Minnesota Press.

Turner, J. F. (1976). *Housing by People: Towards Autonomy in Building Environments.* London: Marion Boyars.

Velegrakis, G., & Kosyfologou, A. (2018). The city plaza immigrants' housing project in Athens and the sosial solidarity medical center of Thessaloniki. In *Alternatives in a World of Crisis* (pp. 222–55). Rosa Luxemburg Stiftung.

4

Commoning Aboriginal
ethno-architecture

Indigenous housing experiences in Australia

Angus Cameron and Penny Travlou

Introduction

Architecture created and built by Indigenous people, adjusted as required to suit their own changing needs, and supportive of their own social organisation, belief system and lifestyle, all done by themselves using their own technologies, labour and skills, and drawing on the traditions of their pre-contact (or classical) Indigenous architecture.

(Memmott and Fantin 2005: 185)

Prior to colonial settlements, the dominant Indigenous architecture in Australia was domestic, in the form of traveller camps. This Aboriginal ethno-architecture was misconstrued as representing a primitive culture (Memmot and Fantin 2005; Memmot 2007). This racist misrepresentation ignores the intricate relationship between the physical and social environment that was enacted in indigenous architecture. A fundamental characteristic of ethno-architecture is that it is a material extension of environmental conditions and behavioural norms, defined by spatial and cognitive rules and behaviours in response to environmental (e.g. seasonal), social and ecological factors. It refers to the knowledge system of a community; therefore, it can be regarded as a type of 'descriptive epistemology' (Memmott 2007). Long, Memmott and Seelig suggested that Indigenous housing in Australia includes:

All aspects of the production, management, maintenance and occupation of Indigenous living environments [. . .] social, behavioural and physical properties of living environments. (2007: 110)

Ethno-architecture exists within a complex meshwork of environmental and social relationships and is framed by these relationships rather than by form and structure. As an expression of these relationships, ethno-architecture facilitates a high degree of congruence between the behavioural and the spatial environment (Memmott and GoSam 1999). Its meaning systems, styles and knowledge constitute the semiotics of indigenous architectural expression. In this chapter, we attempt to frame ethno-architectural space within the Indigenous Australian paradigm, as a process and an outcome: a process of 'doing' architecture by indigenous groups and an outcome whereby indigenous cultural values and principles materialize in spatial form. Australia's ethno-architecture is not stagnant and ahistorical: owing to its innate fluidity and responsiveness to change, it will continue to evolve, as it has done since Australia's colonization.

The chapter locates Indigenous ethno-architecture into the broader context of the discourse on the commons, threaded through Indigenous existence and its practices. Common space can be defined as a space created and recreated by a group – in this case, the Indigenous people of Australia – through practices of participation (Stavrides 2016). Commoning is, thus, the deployment of the multitude of (indigenous) practices, while ethno-architecture is a topological extension of these practices (Sohn et al. 2015: 52). The production of the condition of the commons is, therefore, integral to ethno-architecture. The space of the commons can be described as a set of spatial relations resulting from relations between people (Stavrides 2015). The incessant activities of commoning stem from the relationship between particular groups and from the struggle of these groups to exercise their own practices of inhabitation and realize their cultural identity.

Common space goes beyond the private and public: it is the 'commonwealth of all our natural and cultural milieus' (Stavrides 2015: 11), which everyone has equal right to access. This pool of resources, which contains a repertoire of Indigenous experiences and knowledge, is shared among the members of the community. The collective of indigenous camp inhabitants can share and utilize this commonwealth. The exchange of information and services this sharing entails weaves the fabric of a common sociality and allow knowledge, meanings and forms to emerge anew or be reinvented.

Furthermore, indigenous common spaces are not the enclaves of a fixed, isolated culture but hybrid collectives that continue to evolve. This chapter proposes that the practices of ethno-architectural commoning are not episodic forms, but processes improvised collectively through a dialectic of negotiation. Commoning practices generate a temporality founded on life habits and processes, 'both produced and productive, created and creative' (Sohn et al. 2015: 62). Commoning is not an aim, but the processes indigenous people engage with. If it allows itself to become enclosed in circumscribed rules of conduct, commoning will cancel itself.

Commoning also has a deconstructive capacity which enables marginalized Indigenous people to resist their assimilation in Australia's settler society. On these grounds, ethno-architecture realizes:

[a] right to common spaces, not as a demand from networks of authority, but as a self-initiated and self-sustained collective claim that starts by changing ourselves into the differential multitude so that we can unearth unpredictable experiences and symbiotic dreams and change the world without taking power. (Sohn et al. 2015: 72)

Commoning ethno-architecture: A historical definition

Walter Roth's 1897 publication *Ethnological Studies among the North-West-Central Queensland Aborigines* was the first cultural analysis of Aboriginal people in the region. Roth's ethnographic and anthropological study, the first to document the indigenous architecture on the Georgina River, remains one of the most significant publications on NW Australia to date (Long 2008).

Roth's (1897, 1910) ethnographic accounts document an emblematic Aboriginal architectural form: the travellers' camp, consisting of temporary and semi-permanent dwellings. Prior to colonial settlement, the dominant Aboriginal architecture was domestic: travelling camps built by hunter-gatherers. Aboriginal people travelling across the country would quickly build a camp consisting of domiciliary spaces that were used for as little as a few hours or overnight (Davidson and Memmott 2008). For centuries, Australia's indigenous people maintained a distinctive domiciliary architecture which utilized ubiquitous resources as building materials. Aboriginal dwellings were functional, with their architecture influenced mainly by the available materials and personal need (Wigley and Wigley in Memmott 2003).

The travellers' camp was also a space produced through commoning. Commoning is threaded through the multitude of the practices that constitute the Australian indigenous existence, and thus feeds into all aspects of indigenous architectural expression. The travellers' camp should not be interpreted as a space that merely 'unfolds' in the landscape. Instead, each Aboriginal person in the camp generates their own spatiality by moving and altering elements in the landscape. Renewed continuously in the context of the collective, these practices construct a common spatiality. The participatory self-organization of, and improvisation within, these traveller camps cultivate a morphological fluidity and the emergence of new potentialities. This lack of fixity is exemplified by the diverse architectural practices in the traveller camps, which prompted Thomson (1939) to suggest that the different types of camp architecture could be identified with different Aboriginal groups.

Ethno-architecture is enacted through the relationship between Indigenous people and their environment. Ethno-architectural practices, therefore, are not realized under a specific set of rules but through differential relations. The built environment should not be perceived as an assemblage of constructs consisting of lifeless parts but as a 'multiplicity of bodies: humans, animals and vegetation' (Sohn et al. 2015: 60). The inputs between these multiple bodies are reciprocal, as the physical components of the ecological assemblage influence behaviour. The spaces of commoning where the 'classical' Australian ethno-architecture is reproduced thus defy spatial codification. They are unpredictable.

Ethno-architecture and Western architecture do not have an equal billing in architectural discourse. Ethno-architecture has its own traditions, approaches, processes and reference points. Davidson and Memmott ask: 'Why is it that the Western concept of architecture is referred to as "high style"?' (Davidson and Memmott 2008: 51). Historian Alan Colquhoun distinguished 'modern' society from the 'primitive' world and suggested that Indigenous architecture exists in a 'vacuum of timelessness' (Tuhiwai Smith 2012: 20). This racist categorization of Indigenous architecture as 'primitive' reflects an inbuilt bias. By legitimizing the dismissal of Indigenous cultures, it may have stifled the development of Indigenous architecture. This preconception highlights the challenges of reconciling cultural differences; furthermore, it should prompt us to interrogate the wider assumptions that shape the non-Indigenous discourse on architecture itself (Memmott 2018: 90). How did Western architecture attain its elevated position? It appears that the Western architectural discourse has been reluctant to share its epistemological hegemony with Indigenous ethno-architectural principles and traditions. Instead, it has assigned Indigenous architectures to the realm of the 'vernacular' (Memmott 2018: 51) – a contemptuous term referring to the language of the 'commoner'.

In Australia, the foundations of 'classical', pre-contact ethno-architecture have persisted since colonization, despite the assimilation of Western materials in the ethno-architectural vocabulary. Colonization marked a new era of ethno-architecture: the development of an acculturated ethno-architecture, in the form of self-constructed fringe settlements. Displaced in mainly vacant Crown land, Aboriginal people had the autonomy to design and build their own domiciliary spaces. By determining the locations of, and spatial relations with, each other, Aboriginal people effectively became their own town planners (Memmott and GoSam 1999: 5).

White settlers disapproved of Aboriginal people taking up residence on the outskirts of newly established Western towns. Aboriginal people were ascribed with the social status of 'fringe dwellers', who did not conform to Western dwelling practices and standards of behaviour, and thus represented a threat (Memmott 2000: 40). Reynolds, an ethnographer, argues that the positioning of fringe settlements was not random, but reflected the 'socioeconomic dynamics of the complex relationship which developed between townspeople and fringe dwellers' (in Memmott and GoSam 1999: 50). Indigenous fringe settlements exhibited a porous economic relationship with the town, and often were a reservoir of cheap labour in return for goods and access to services. The social privacy and autonomy of the settlements were, nonetheless, maintained as a result of their distance from the towns. This allowed Indigenous activities, such as ceremonies, dancing and rituals, to continue, maintaining the complex socio-spatial behaviours of the Aboriginal society while generating regular complaints from white settlers about the drunkenness, noise, indecency and squalor of the fringe settlers. While some of these claims may be well founded, the divisive labelling was one of the strategies used to condone the containment and oppression of Australia's Indigenous people, and to justify the settlers' power to remove then (Memmott and GoSam 1999: 7).

Indigenous people are equipped with a memory of dwelling practices and a range of possible tactics that can be actualized in different circumstances. The commoning potential of Indigenous behaviours has enabled acculturated ethno-architecture to respond proactively to the some of the social effects of the colonization of Australia (Barcham 1998). The changing and adaptable nature of Indigenous Australian dwellings and spatial relationships demonstrates that culture is not a static recollection of the past. Meanings are often overwritten, revised, revitalized and contested. The borders of Indigenous identity are porous, allowing encounters with the Other. The knowledge generated through these encounters deconstructs the epistemological edge of the West.

Ethno-architecture hinges on socio-spatial structures. Ethno-architecture in Australia was characterized by modest physical structures and, at the same time, a 'highly structured use of space', as exemplified by Henry's Camp (Memmott and GoSam 1999: 7). The form, scale and life cycle of Australia's Indigenous architecture can only make sense if the domiciliary patterns of socio-spatial behaviour are taken into account. Camp activities and patterns realized the spatial and economic imperatives of its Indigenous occupants. Architectural elements were intrinsic in substantiating spatial behavioural patterns such as kinship, household structure, hearths, seasonality, external orientation, sleeping patterns, rules of avoidance, responses to death, to name a few. All these factors influenced the camp's physical variables (size, spatial structure, shelter type), and also the hunting methods and movement of the camp inhabitants (Memmott and GoSam 1999). Understanding how Aboriginal people perceived and ordered their landscape is also crucial. Socio-spatial structures were integral to the maintenance and flourishing of ethno-architecture in Aboriginal camps. They enabled groups to retain their residential location – spatial zones – in relation to each other, while continuing to maintain a common social identity (Memmott 2006).

Australian Aborigines were, and remain, materially and culturally oppressed. In the face of this oppression, their autonomous, distinct social lifestyle mobilized a collective strength to resist colonization, challenge assimilation and formulate practices of negotiation. In the course of their colonial struggles, Australia's Indigenous people had to devise new ways of survival and to adapt their social relations, which deviate from the dominant Western models. The colonial imperative of 'order' aimed at taming the highly variegated socio-spatial relations and culture of Australia's Indigenous communities. Ethno-architecture played a critical role in the rejection of this 'normalisation' and assimilation. The indigenous inhabitation of space and the behavioural practices through which this inhabitation is realized rupture the homogenizing colonial narrative. Aboriginal fringe settlements testify to the fact that, notwithstanding the challenges, parts of Australia's landscape continue to evade normalization.

At the same time, the fringe settlements break down the membranes of spatial separation. The location of these settlements vis-à-vis Australia's towns and cities positions their Indigenous inhabitants as 'proximal outsiders', while the practices of appropriation of space by these inhabitants place them outside the prevailing urban ethos. The fringe settlements facilitate the material encounters that weave the fabric of a diverse, porous landscape. In these settlements, commoning ethno-architecture makes it possible to share knowledge and experience and encourages a contestation that often transgresses Western norms.

The colonization of Australia forced its indigenous people into the condition of exiles. In the indigenous communities displaced into enclaves, the patterns of life were violently disrupted. In the long struggle of Indigenous Australians, this condition of exile often led to new experiences of interaction with, and evaluating Australia's colonial society. Evicted from their land, Indigenous people did not have the option of being open and receptive to the colonizing otherness they were forced to face. As Indigenous others, they were excluded from colonial society. Their position is reminiscent of Giorgio

Agamben's description of Nazi concentration camp inmates as 'stripped of every political status' (Agamben 1995: 101). Indigenous behaviours, including the maintenance of Aboriginal spatialities, were an affirmation of Indigenous values in the face of the trauma of displacement. Despite being subjected to highly discriminatory colonizing policies, fringe settlements continued to maintain and (re-)create distinct social bonds, realized in the everyday habits and behaviours within the settlement camps. James Scott describes such practices as low-profile resistance disguised behind gestures of conformity (in Stavrides 2018). Mundane, daily-life practices allow for a constant renegotiation of one's position in a hierarchical order. These practices should not, therefore, be viewed as fixed habits but as turning points which constantly evaluate past and present experiences. The camps are thus (also) the loci of a multitude of hermeneutic processes that generate new possibilities and affordances. They permit the cultivation and testing of indigenous ideas and ways of life, despite the enforced estrangement of Australia's Indigenous communities.

Henry's Camp, for instance underwent a ceaseless transformation. It was in a state of constant flux, constantly altered to meet its residents' various, and ever-changing, spatial needs (Long 2005). The repositioning and fluidity of the camp's material infrastructure was one of its most notable characteristics. Stephen Long (2005) describes people sitting by the fire, using vehicles as furniture and moving walls and cars to make shade. 'People did not simply "use" this yard space, they were continually interacting with it and modifying it', he comments (Long 2005: 223). There were no established rules of location for any objects: all objects could be moved or appropriated freely. Fringe settlement practices thus exemplify Dovey and Polakit's (2007: 113) 'slippages' – the shift between criteria, practices and meanings in indigenous discourse. Cars slip from vehicle to sunshade, caravans slip from transport to storage and garbage slips from rubbish to building material.

Deleuze and Guattari's (1988: 353) categories of 'smooth' and 'striated', in reference to something without boundaries and something strictly defined, respectively, provide a useful theoretical lens through which to view ethno-architectural commoning practices. Smoothness alludes to the slippage between opposites. Deleuze and Guattari postulate that every space encompasses both the 'smooth' and the 'striated', often 'enfolding' into each other (Deleuze and Guattari 1988: 353). The fringe settlements could thus be viewed as labyrinths of spatial folds, with each fold causing elements and meanings to lose their bearings of spatial order. In this light, Australia's fringe settlements care be understood as threshold spaces of negotiation where dialectical opposites fold into each other. Different tribes compose and arrange their camps in different ways that break down the striated (Long 2005). There is a plethora of minimal transformations and slippages in the ways of wall construction, firewood collection, moving of the caravans and shifting of the debris. This enfolding of opposites through slippages challenges all pre-established functional separations between things (Gutiérrez Sánchez 2017: 4).

Western construction techniques are often adopted in the fringe settlements in order to upgrade the structural and hygienic attributes of acculturated ethno-architecture. This adaptation, nevertheless, usually does not disrupt, or infringe in, the social and spatial fabric of the camp. To invoke semiotic theory, the syntax of the fringe settlement is Indigenous, but its semantic overlay is Western (Memmott and GoSam 1999: 7).

As a space of negotiation, the fringe settlement facilitates encounters, moments of serendipity and opportunities for appropriation (Mossman 2018). Its fluid spatiality is constituted in an indeterminate fashion, through the deployment of multiple agentive capacities. Camp spaces, therefore, cannot remain static. They are unstable and disputed, continuously transformed with the adoption of 'exogenous' elements (Gutiérrez Sánchez 2017). Indigenous practices demonstrate that it is possible to construct a commoning ethno-architecture (even) by appropriating Western economic methods and adapting them to Indigenous requirements. If anything, this appropriation has strengthened the camp residents' autonomous capacity to satisfy their needs (Altmann 2019). The Western elements are translated; upon this translation, they become co-opted in the collective reproduction of an indigenous common world. Ethno-architecture adopts elements of the hegemonic culture while maintaining its ambiguity, grounded on indigeneity. Due to this capacity for appropriation, the transformation of fringe settlements during the colonial struggle displays fragments of a different, emancipated life.

To completely seal off their behaviours, practices and identity would be very dangerous for Australia's Indigenous communities. This would precipitate the reduction of ethno-architecture into a romanticized, imagined 'state of innocence'. The Indigenous practitioners of ethno-architecture choose not to become a sealed enclave of otherness, fenced behind rigid boundaries and accessed under specific use rules, but a threshold (cf., Stavrides 2018).

Commoning ethno-architecture: Boundaries and thresholds

Boundaries and thresholds are of utmost importance in Indigenous ethno-architecture. Thresholds belong to both sides of a boundary, at once separating and connecting these sides in a tension that holds open their difference. In the colonial project, boundaries have been deployed as tools to contain Indigenous people – the severing and gridding of the land that displaced Indigenous communities and created settlements. When acted upon through movement, however, these boundaries can become converted into crossings (Stavrides 2018). Despite the distance that separates different Indigenous camps, movement and social interaction between them break down camp taxonomy and impart a dialectical quality. Constant crossings render the boundary between camps dubious, even undefined.

> Groups of people establish distance between themselves yet cross that distance physically, visually, or socially. People are regularly in-between camps although the various camps are distinct and distant there is movement and interaction between them. (Long 2005: 239)

The liminal spatiality of the camps promotes interrelationships between people, camps and places. The freedom to define socio-spatial arrangements through continuous 'movement and interaction' creates a social intensity:

> Others joined the camp for a feed and a yarn. Some people stayed out by the fire; others sat under the tree and some used cars at the periphery of the space as 'furniture'. (Long 2005: 201)

Australian ethno-architecture acquires a liminal quality by accommodating and expressing socio-spatial behaviours that can be transient and easy to move to another place. Opening the camp to outsiders expresses the potentiality of sharing and allows for diverse uses of the camp space and materials.

This discussion alludes to the spatiality of passages, with its congruent conditions of entry and exit, which permit cultures to communicate without cancelling each other out. Had non-Indigenous and Indigenous Australians met thresholds rather than boundaries, would each other's otherness been be so harshly oppositional? The white settlers tried to ensure that the socio-spatial practices of the fringe settlements remained confined within the settlement borders. The settlements were often treated as spatial and social enclaves. Yet, as the porous nature of the fringe settlement borders manifests, Indigenous people and their architecture dwelt on the threshold connecting the two cultures. A liminal spatiality also characterizes the relationship between the camps and the external world, as Aboriginal people often cross into the white settlements for resources, or to offer themselves as cheap labour.

The modes and protocols of how architecture mediates intercultural encounters are hard to document. Such encounters, however, generate ethno-architectural responses, which can often be unpredictable (Losckhe

2019). These encounters take place at thresholds, where spatial practices become palpable. Forced to inhabit otherness, indigenous people find ways to perforate the perimeter of their enclave. Continuous inventive negotiation enables Indigenous socio-spatial behaviours to break out from the constraints of imposed habits. Indigenous people utilize practices of socio-spatial commoning in a way that destabilizes discriminatory taxonomies and allows new cultural enunciations of hybridity. The ethno-architectural processes of invention and improvisation, and negotiation and appropriation, transform camp settlements into liminal spaces.

Commoning ethno-architecture: Porosity

The pores on our skin are passages that permit communication between our body and the surrounding environment (Stavrides 2018). Similarly, porous borders enable constant transformation and the emergence of new ideas (Sohn et al. 2015). In Australia's indigenous settlements, transformations – a caravan becoming a wall or storage – are invariably mediated through porous boundaries. This mediation translates foreign categories in the terms of the local, Indigenous logic (Barcham 1998: 307). Natural or architectural elements – caravans, corrugated iron, fires, sand – are moveable and/or malleable; they become appropriated through porous borders (Long 2005).

Elements conventionally intended for a predetermined function (e.g. vehicles) can thus become transported into a new relationship of ambiguity: 'such de-familiarization of space promotes loose and playful responses, a re-discovery of spaces' (Franck and Stevens 2007: 10). By allowing the manipulation of Western architectural forms, porous conditions can challenge architectural phenotypes. Since many assumed opposites are culturally coded, the recoding of these opposites in their new, Indigenous people-place context is crucial. On a macrolevel, porous boundaries are, therefore, essential for the suspension of the binaries of indigeneity/non-indigeneity. For its residents, the fringe settlement is not a fixed taxonomy of procedures but a porous place of interaction with the non-Indigenous other.

Commoning ethno-architecture: Encountering 'otherness'

In the name of progress, the colonial West unleashed exclusionary imperialist ideologies of the self and the Other (see Bhabha 2004). Indigenous ethno-architecture is not simply a circumscribed enclave of otherness that has to be defended, but it is a manifestation of dynamic social practices of counteraction. The Indigenous/non-Indigenous dichotomy is a discourse of thresholds, where differences meet. Stavrides (2018) discusses how to deal with otherness in a way that continues to produce encounters and exchanges, without effacing differences. Stephen Long's (2005) study explores how Indigenous Australians encounter the non-Indigenous Other through materials, and how they adapt these materials to fit Indigenous auditory and visual requirements. Inventiveness and commoning practices of everyday life help Indigenous communities to build a bridge to the Other. The inhabitants of the fringe settlements do not simply reject the materials coming from outside but find ways to incorporate them in the settlement's life. A corrugated iron wall, for instance, will be adapted to the height most appropriate for Aboriginal socio-spatial behaviour. This process of adaptation leads to dynamic transformations.

Despite seeking correspondences between cultures, Indigenous adaptation does not create an unobstructed mirroring of cultures. Importantly, the passage through the settlement threshold does not permit full and unlimited access without gestures of mutual recognition and tokens of negotiation. As Indigenous history makes evident, unlimited access could result in complete assimilation and extinction of indigeneity. Passages to otherness are, therefore, formalized.

Just as tree barks were formerly used to protect from the wind, cars are nowadays used in fringe settlements as windbreaks. It is important to contest the singularities of difference – in this case, exemplified by the function of a car. Aboriginal people choose to 'articulate the diverse subjects of differentiation' (Bhabha 2004: 108), for example, by repurposing the car as furniture or a windbreak. Through a continuous negation – a process and not an accomplished state – Australia's Indigenous spatialities thus mould alternative cultural values. It is only through this – often precarious – appropriation of otherness that counter-paradigms to colonial normality can emerge.

In the face of oppression, this commoning ethno-architecture can emblematize a community in motion. In the way it reappropriates, recomposes and decomposes spaces in response to the dominant culture that engulfs and threatens Indigenous communities, ethno-architecture consistently exhibits a 'virus like existence' (Sohn, Kousoulas and Bruyns 2015: 3). It is a conduit though which Indigenous communities invent forms of organization that match their implicit political aims. While change has been forced upon Australia's Indigenous people, they choose to engage with this change actively, deploying their ethno-architectural inventiveness to construct thresholds and negotiate social relations.

It is critical to recognize the dynamic processual nature of commoning ethno-architecture. Ethno-architecture should be understood in terms of change. This change is Indigenous-defined and controlled, distinct from that imposed by the colonizing regime. Indigenous ethno-architecture can be seen to construct social artefacts that continuously adapt and create new social bonds. Indigenous commoning practices have enabled acculturated ethno-architecture to flourish by remaining osmotic, porous and adaptable, proactively responding to social change. By appropriating colonial architectural forms while resisting assimilation, acculturated ethno-architecture culminates to a markedly progressive typology.

Commoning ethno-architecture: Fringe settlements

The bulldozers of the Australian governmental have often threatened fringe settlements – a testament to ethno-architecture's viral presence. By the 1980s, most fringe settlements were destroyed. In 1969, housing was provided to Aboriginal people as part of the State Commonwealth Housing Agreement. This housing was administered by the Department of Aboriginal Islander Affairs (DAIA) as an instrument of Aboriginal assimilation. The Housing Agreement aimed to juxtapose 'whites' and 'blacks' and creating a 'scatterization effect' (Memmott 1996), which would break down Aboriginal cultural values and ultimately efface any possible resistance. Aboriginal people were forcibly moved into DAIA housing settlements, which were based on an Anglo-Australian family model. A gradual sedentism was thus implemented, as the colonial state tried to infiltrate all capillaries of Indigenous society to ensure cultural assimilation. Architecture was thus complicit in this colonizing onslaught on Australia's Indigenous societies.

The spatial syntax of the DAIA housing, however, was markedly unsuitable for the needs of its Indigenous occupants, forcing them to adapt their behaviour. Some aspects of Aboriginal behaviour (but not all) were translated into the conventional house form. That such a transition was required reveals the incongruence between Aboriginal domestic activities and patterns, and the Anglo-Australian house form. The primary functional requirements of Aboriginal communities and the subtleties of Indigenous domestic life – kinship laws, avoidance behaviour, sharing – struggled to conform with the conventional typology of the DAIA house. As the unsuitability of the DAIA houses became evident, their spaces were promptly transformed to fit the needs of their occupants. Functional spaces would often be used in ways that differed radically from those designated by the architectural plan: instead of sleeping in beds, for instance, the DAIA house occupants slept on the floor. By means of the creation of hybrid housing spaces through unpredictable practices of inhabitation, a non-Indigenous architecture was thus transformed into an Indigenous one.

DAIA housing exhibited the characteristics of enclosed enclaves, with clearly demarcated borders between inside and outside and a strict taxonomy of rooms that effaced the connection to the land. To compensate for the lack of space, and reconcile their new environment with Indigenous traditions of inhabitation, DAIA residents also built temporary huts and shanties reminiscent of fringe settlements. This type of ethno-architecture thus emerged from Indigenous communities seeking to reconstitute Aboriginal meanings in an alien built environment (Greenop 2011).

A lack of understanding of Aboriginal values and practices of inhabitation pervades the Western architectural profession. Indigenous cultural imperatives would be indeed difficult to reconcile with DAIA housing (Fantin and Greenop 2011). Indigenous people inhabit space through repetition that links the past and present. They redefine the present by reinscribing lessons from 'classical' ethno-architecture onto present spatiality. They refuse to follow the script that the DAIA houses would impose on their domiciliary behaviour. By adapting DAIA housing to the various functions of commoning, they assert their distinctive socio-spatial pattern over non-Indigenous physical space (Long, Memmott and Seelig 2007). They interrogate Western housing in distinct, yet multifarious ways, continually 'tailoring' it to fit the norms of Aboriginal domiciliarity.

Distance

The idea of Indigenous difference from the West is deeply entrenched. Inherent within ethnographic studies is the notion of 'researching' others who are different. This notion of Indigenous otherness, which feeds into a hegemonic Western identity, is a product of distance. Yet, a sufficient distance is crucial not just for Western ethnographers but also for the colonized 'others', as it enables the latter to question the taxonomies within relationships and the subconscious hierarchies within identities. Indigenous people do not simply submit to these taxonomies; they actively establish a sufficient intermediate distance (also) by interrogating and adapting their inhabited space. If this distance is too large, a relationship between Indigenous and non-Indigenous is impossible. No distance, on the other hand, amounts to a condition of absolute coincidence, whereby the other is recognized as the same as us. For (aspects of) otherness to be accepted, therefore, it is important to preserve some distance as a precondition for, and a critical – albeit dubious, measure of the encounter between Indigenous and non-Indigenous.

A sufficient distance will permit the crossing of boundaries while the dominions on each side of the boundary are preserved as distinct. This distance will thus be the vector of a communication founded on (supposedly) 'equal' terms that permit the distribution of power between Indigenous and non-Indigenous to be negotiated. In Australia, as elsewhere, the Indigenous–non-Indigenous relationship has not been conducted on equal terms. One-hundred and fifty years of colonial domination would cast doubt on the feasibility of such a sufficient distance. This design of the DAIA houses, aiming eliminate all distance between Indigenous and non-indigenous Australians by forcing the latter to inhabit spaces codified by Anglo-Australian design, illustrates this condition.

As noted earlier, Aboriginal people in Australia resisted both their assimilation and their transformation into a fixed, romanticized 'Other' with no option of negotiation. The Aboriginal inhabitants of DAIA housing did not simply destroy their houses, but tried to construct sufficient distance by adapting them. But what distance is 'sufficient'? What is the distance that would support crossings, a field of exchange and negotiation, while preventing the assimilation and expropriation of the Indigenous Other? The answer to these questions hinges on the perception and position of Indigenous people in Australian society and in the academic paradigm.

These questions are also constantly addressed to, and answered, by Indigenous people, in Australia and elsewhere in the world. David Harvey (2013) illustrates the importance for Indigenous communities to not simply reject otherness and its consequences (the formation of secluded, defensive enclaves) but, instead, to explore this condition as (also) an opportunity: 'Enclosure is a temporary political means to pursue a common political end' (2013: 79). In response to the expanding colonial frontier, ethno-architecture occupies a constantly shifting landscape. It often appropriates Western capitalist values and deploys them as tools for maintaining distance. This distance enables it to thrive and defeat assimilation.

Conclusion

Australia's Indigenous communities have maintained a border that enables them to engage with the colonial condition – a major rupture in Australia's long historical continuum. In Australia's ethno-architecture, the Aboriginal housing precedents are not simply rendered as a romantic tradition but become reappropriated; they are part of necessity, not of nostalgia. This chapter calls for Australia's Indigenous ethno-architecture to be understood as a dynamic, cyclical and evolving process of commoning that facilitates contention, negotiation, conflict and contribution. This commoning ethno-architecture serves as a tool to translate – and question – Western assumptions, negotiate cultural differences and, through this negotiation, articulate new meanings in architecture.

Ethno-architecture enables its Indigenous practitioners to construct threshold zones where differences can meet and interact at a sufficient distance. This is an unsettling, disruptive process which holds otherness open and allows for the marginalized Indigenous to symbolize themselves. The precedence of this commoning ethno-architecture may provide insights in how to 'reinstall a lost equilibration' (Stavrides 2016: 254) that colonization disrupted. For this to become possible, it is important that the translation of ethno-architectural practices does not efface the struggle that motivated them, nor does it reduce its practitioners to discursive raw material. To maintain its emancipatory potential in the face of capitalist-colonial expansion, ethno-architecture must be practised by political actors, in the context of a social and political movement. As a response to colonization, ethno-architecture enables Indigenous communities to step out of the enforced epistemic boundaries, become the arbiter of their own typology and reformulate and envision an indigenous conception of the world.

Acknowledgements

This chapter has been proofread by Dr Nikos Kourampas, University of Edinburgh.

References

Agamben, G. (1995). *Homo Sacer: Sovereign Power and Bare Life*. California: Stanford University Press.

Altmann, P. (2019). 'The Commons as Colonisation – The Well-Intentioned Appropriation of Buen Vivir'. *Bulletin of Latin American Research Society for Latin American Studies*. https://doi.org/10.1111/blar.12941.

Barcham, M. (1998). 'The Challenge of Urban Maori: Reconciling Conceptions of Indigeneity and Social Change'. *Asia Pacific Viewpoint*, 39(3): 303–14.

Bhabha, H. K. (2004). *The Location of Culture*. London: Taylor and Francis.

Davidson, J. and Memmott, P. (2008). 'Exploring a Cross-Cultural Theory of Architecture'. *Traditional Dwellings and Settlements Review* 19(2): 51–68.

Deleuze, G. and Guattari, F. (1988). *A Thousand Plateaus Capitalism and Schizophrenia*. London: Continuum.

Dovey, K. and Polakit, K. (2007). 'Urban Slippage Smooth and Striated Streetscapes in Bangkok'. In K. A. Franck and Q. Stevens, eds., *Loose Space Possibility and Diversity in Urban Life*, London: Routledge, 113–31.

Fantin, S. and Greenop, K. (2011). *Sorcery and Spirits: Intercultural Housing and Place in Aboriginal Australia*. University of Queensland, Australia: Aboriginal Environments Research Centre School of Geography, Planning and Architecture. University of Queensland.

Franck, K. A., and Q. Stevens. eds., (2007). *Loose Space: Possibility and Diversity in Urban Life*. Edited by Karen A. Franck and Quentin Stevens. USA: Routledge.

Greenop, K. (2009). 'Housing and identity in the urban indigenous community: Initial findings in Inala, Queensland'. In *Society of Architectural Historians, Australia and New Zealand (SAHANZ) Annual Conference*. Auckland, New Zealand, 2-5 July 2009. Auckland, New Zealand: University of Auckland.

Harvey, D. (2013). *Rebel Cities: From the Right to the City to the Urban Revolution*. London: Verso.

Long, S. (2005). *Gidyea Fire: A Study of the Transformation and Maintenance of Aboriginal Place Properties on the Georgina River*. Australia: University of Queensland.

Long, S. (2008). 'Transformation of Railway Along Georgina River'. In A. Leach, A. Moulis and N. Sully, eds., *Shifting Views: Selected Essays on the Architectural History of Australia and New Zealand*, St Lucia, Qld: University of Queensland Press.

Long, S., Memmott, P. and Seelig, T. (2007). *An audit and review of Australian Indigenous housing research*, Australian AHURI Final Report No. 102, Australian Housing and Urban Research Institute Limited, Melbourne, https://www.ahuri.edu.au/research/final-reports/102.

Loschke, S. K. (2019). *Non Standard Architectural Productions: Between Aestethic Experience and Social Action*. Vol. 1. London: Routledge.

Memmott, P. (1996). 'From the Curry to the Weal: Aboriginal Town Camps and Compounds of the Western Back-Blocks'. *Fabrications : The Journal of the Society of Architectural Historians, Australia and New Zealand* 7, 1–50.

Memmott, P. C. (2000). The way it was: Customary camps and houses in the southern Gulf of Carpentaria. In P. Read, ed., *Settlement: A History of Australian Indigenous Housing*. Canberra: Aboriginal Studies Press. pp. 15–39.

Memmott, P. (2002). 'Sociospatial Structures of Australian Aboriginal Settlements'. *Australian Aboriginal Studies* 1: 67–86.

Memmott, P. (2003). 'Customary Aboriginal Behaviour Patterns and Housing Design'. *TAKE 2: Housing Design in Indigenous Australia*, 26–39.

Memmott, P. (2004). 'Aboriginal Housing: Has the State of Art Improved?'. *Architecture Australia* 93(1): 46–8.

Memmott, P. (2007). *Gunyah, Goodie & Wurley*. Queensland, Australia: University of Queensland Press.

Memmott, P. (2008). 'Indigenous Culture and Architecture in the South Pacific Region'. *Fabrications*,18(1) https://doi.org/https://www.tandfonline.com/action/showCitFormats?doi=10.1080/10331867.2008.10539623.

Memmott, P. (2018). The Re-invention of the 'Behaviour Setting' in the New Indigenous Architecture. In E. Grant et al. (eds) *The Handbook of Contemporary Indigenous Architecture*. Singapore: Springer, pp. 831–68.

Memmott, P. and Fantin, S. (2005). 'The study of indigenous ethno-architecture in Australia'. In B. Rigsby and D. N. Peterson (eds.), *Thomson: the man and scholar*. Canberra, ACT, Australia: The Academy of the Social Sciences in Australiapp. 185–210.

Memmott, P. and GoSam, C. (1999). 'Australian Indigenous Architecture – Its Forms and Evolution'. *Thresholds, Papers of the Sixteenth Annual Conference of the Society of Architectural Historians Australia and New Zealand*. Aboriginal Environments Research Centre.

Mossman, M. (2018). 'Third Space in Architecture'. In: Chap. 22 R. Kiddle, L. P. Stewart and K. O'Brien, eds., *Our Voices: Indigeneity and Architecture*. Novato, CA: ORO Editions. pp. 198–209.

Roth, W. E. (1897). *Ethnological Studies among the North-West-Central Queensland Aborigines*. USA: Cambridge University Press.

Roth, W. F. (1910). *North Queensland Ethnography. Bulletin No. 16. Huts and Shelters*. Sydney: Records of the Australian Museum. doi:10.385 3/j.0067-1975.8.1910.934

Sánchez, I. Gutiérrez. (2017). 'Commoning Spaces of Social Reproduction Citizen-Led Welfare Infrastructures in Crisis-Ridden Athens'. *Infrastructures of Caring Citizenship*.

Smith, L. Tuhiwai. (2012). *Decolonizing Methodologies: Research and Indigenous Peoples*. London: Zed Books Ltd.

Sohn, H., Kousoulas, S. and Bruyns, G. (2015). 'Commoning as Differentiated Publicness'. *Footprint* 16: 1–8.

Stavrides, S. (2015). 'Common Space as Threshold Space: Urban Commoning in Struggles to Re-Appropriate Public Space'. *Footprint* 16: 9–19.

Stavrides, S. (2016). *Common Space: The City as Commons*. London: Zed Books.

Stavrides, S. (2018). *Towards the City of Thresholds*. Brooklyn, NY: Common Notions.

Stavrides, S. and de Angelis, M. (2010). 'On the Commons: A Public Interview with Massimo De Angelis and Stavros Stavrides'. In *An Architektur*.

Thomson, D. F. (1939). *The Seasonal Factor in Human Culture Illustrated from the Life of a Contemporary Nomadic Group*. Vol. 5. Cambridge University Press.

Wigley, J. and Wigley, B. (2003). 'Remote Conundrums: The Changing Role of Housing in Aboriginal Communities'. In P. Memmott, ed., *TAKE 2: Housing Design in Indigenous Australia*. Brisbane: The Royal Australian Institute of Architects.

5

Feeding together

The revolution starts in the kitchen

Marc Gavaldà and Claudio Cattaneo

Introduction

This chapter focuses on food as a fundamental aspect within two squatted housing commons (*rurban* communities) on the hills of Barcelona. The rationale of the chapter is conceiving housing as a common and, nested within it, the perspective of food as a common, which is important because, particularly in Mediterranean countries, the kitchen and the food culture is a fundamental element of inhabiting. Moreover, it can be considered as intangible cultural heritage, where autonomous self-organized practices can also be included (Travlou, 2020). When joined together, the everyday commoning practices of habitation and of alimentation integrate each other into an enhanced dimension of communal living.

Politically speaking, the rationale of the chapter stands where the right to housing meets reclaims for food sovereignty and for agroecology. Housing and alimentation are also central elements of capitalism and contribute heavily to environmental degradation, economic crises and rising inequalities. Neither market nor state capitalism can be the sole institutions providing for these two basic universal needs. For instance, when left unchecked to the expansion of capitalism, housing has turned into a lucrative business, the negative outcomes for the benefit of only a few are visible, at best, in growing gentrification, land-use change and degradation, urban-sprawl and undesired infrastructure development. At worst, they are responsible of the economic crisis, skyrocketing unemployment, increased inequalities, home evictions, rising public debt and an unprecedented sense of urban injustice.

Similarly, alimentation turned into a capitalist business has led to the rise of agro-industrial intensification, which is responsible for the loss of traditional farming practices, loss of bio-cultural landscapes (Tello and Gonzalez de Molina, 2017; Font et al., 2020; Cattaneo et al., 2018). Also, the widespread use of pesticides which is responsible also for biodiversity loss (Geiger et al., 2010), while the increase in animal products is promoting climate change – with methane emissions (a greenhouse gas which is twenty-five times more powerful than CO_2) (Padrò et al., 2017). In addition, capitalist food production creates social problems related to the expansion of the agrofuel industry (necessary in agricultural machines), land-grabbing, globalization of the markets and speculation with primary commodities, which, in turn, have been an explanatory factor of the 2008 drought crisis ("World Food Price Crisis", Wikipedia, 2007), river eutrophication, groundwater pollution, soil erosion and nutrient loss (Foley et al., 2011; Wada et al., 2010; Millennium Ecosystem Assessment, 2005). The state version of growth capitalism is no good either. Expansion in the agriculture frontier and changes in agro-industrial practices have left, in ex-communist countries, similar environmental disasters, pollution, further exhaustion of natural resources and social problems (see, for example, Edelstein et al., 2012; Siciliano, 2013).

Finally, in a country like Spain – that can be representative of all South and Eastern Europe – the state has approached the housing question by colluding with the interests of neoliberal capitalism, turning itself into a social enemy. Some collectives have started to self-organize into commons, in order to defend themselves against this enemy.

Context: Commoners as squatters with high diversity and contradictions

Conceiving food as a common does not necessarily require that the 'commoners' are also squatters. This idea – that we argue is a desirable one – can be fostered within any housing collective – be it a housing cooperative, a cohousing experience or even a shared flat – that is interested in putting alimentation at the centre of their everyday commoning practices.

The cases at hand represent a specific situation in which the housing collectives take the form of squatter communities that have explicit political interests towards collectivization and self-organization and in which the food element is one area where these ideals can be realized, often with evident contradictions and limitations. Our aim is to explain how they do so, what similarities and what differences arise, and what are their implications.

Even if they might appear very similar – both are squats, with a housing community, in a *rurban* environment – they are not. We aim at highlighting differences in order to understand that commoning, far from being an insignificant and rather homogeneous alternative beyond the state and capitalism, represents instead a window of opportunities that commoners can explore and experiment in a self-institutionalized and autonomous way. Diversity and contradictions within these apparently similar cases of housing as commons are therefore what we want to highlight in order to inform and hopefully invite more people to start new and more diverse experiences of housing as common.

On a methodological level, the authors of this chapter are inhabitants of these communities. We represent here our own visions as insiders, first-hand contributions that can be richer and better 'lived' than those from external researchers; however, these visions do not represent the common vision of our own communities, which in both cases is not only much more complex and enriched but also undefined and constantly evolving.

Presentation of the projects

Both squats – Kan Pasqual (KP) and Can Masdeu (CMD) – are large rural houses located in the mountain/hilly rural environment of the Collserola range – a stunning natural park that is like a balcony at the centre of the Barcelona Metropolitan Area and which has historically been, at large, agricultural land. The original interest of the collectives was, like most squatters, to squat a place that would allow them to self-organize – as most squatters look for; however, beyond the provision of a rooftop and some physical space for offering social activities, the collectives sought for access to land as a source of food and fuel – something that, in the European squatters tradition, was a novelty.

Kan Pasqual, close to the highest peak, is an old farmhouse in the north face of the hills of Collserola, at 450 m.s.m (Meters above sea level). This property, owned by the Collserola Park authority, was abandoned since the mid-1980s, until it was squatted at the end of 1996, with eight to ten inhabitants. Inspired by the Zapatista autonomy and social ecology (Bookchin, 1982), KP has recovered a property of 30 hectares (ha) of forest and abandoned fields to implement a collective project and move towards self-sufficiency as a way of breaking with the society of consumption and empowering from below. Politically, the group is involved in the Rural Occupation Network (Red de Okupación Rural) where mutual support is practised to consolidate projects for the liberation of abandoned lands. It is also linked to environmental movements, anarchists and urban squatting in Barcelona.

Its location, in the heart of the forests of the Collserola Natural Park but only one hour from Barcelona, allows the combination of rural activities with labour, political and cultural activities in the city.

Since its inception, this group has chosen to build and appropriate tools that allow them to cut off some dependencies on the state and the market. In particular, in their twenty-three years of life, they have not connected to the conventional electricity grid. Energy autonomy is therefore one of the foundational values which the collective have developed with the installation of an electrical system powered by photovoltaic and wind energy.

The lands that surround the house are conceived as a source of resources (firewood, wood, medicinal plants) and food production in its five vegetable gardens, about 0.4 hectares. Rainwater collection is carried out, and gray waters are purified and recycled for irrigation. Heating is exclusively with dead biomass from the nearby forest. Economically, a combination of individual and collective economy is practised. With the weekly sale of the bread, the expenses of feeding and infrastructures of the collective are managed. In addition, the space is conceived as an Occupied Social Centre (CSO) promoting activities and offering space for use by social movements

Can Masdeu, located at the north end of the Collserola Park and facing the city of Barcelona, stands at a ten-minute walking distance from the working-class neighbourhood of Nou Barris. The building, which is at least 500 years old, is a former leprossarium, which the owner, Sant Pau Hospital, notwithstanding its official value as a historical heritage, abandoned in the 1960s; hence, when the squatters occupied it in late 2001, they found the building in a derelict state.

Since then a community of between twenty and thirty people have inhabited the place (thirty in 2019), starting two political projects: the creation of a housing commons and the start of a large social centre. This included transforming it into a home, restoring the derelict parts, refurbishing its inside, installing new water, electric and grey water infrastructure, a few thermal solar panels, several wooden stoves, gas kitchens, dry-compost toilets and even building two new self-contained houses in the place of totally derelict buildings.

The community also began a social centre, located in a few large rooms on one side of the building and outside: restoring the old water irrigation and collection infrastructure – water comes from wells and mines in the mountain and is stored in large tanks – and the agricultural terraces, 3,000 square metre of garden have been opened for the local community. Moreover, the social centre is active on Thursdays – when outsiders can volunteer in garden tasks and on most Sundays, when a tour of the project is offered (part of the environmental education project), and activities and workshops take place inside the social centre and in the outdoor gardens.

Although the social centre with its activities and community gardens is an interesting example of managing a commons, the focus of the chapter goes towards the political project of housing as a commons.

The social metabolism of diets

Here we analyse food of the two commons from the material perspective: where food comes from, how it is prepared, consumed and disposed of. Food is a vital element, and it is important that it is managed in the most environmentally sustainable way – that is, according to agroecological and permaculture principles. Agroecology is the study of ecological processes applied to agricultural production systems (https://en.wikipedia.org/wiki /Agroecology), since ecological processes end up being a circular flow of matter and energy – in the sense that the output of a process is the input of the next one – here we are going to explain how in these communities agricultural production systems are connected to distribution consumption and disposal process – which in turn are the input of agricultural production. To this extent, we can say that a permaculture approach inspires the metabolism of food and diets in KP and CMD. Having said this, we are going to acknowledge also the limitations and contradictions that appear in the day-to-day food practices of these communities that are in contrast with the agroecological and permaculture ideals of their members. We will argue that these contradictions, rather than limitations, are reinforcing the case for commoning.

Diet composition: Gardens, farmed animals and purchases

In KP there are some gardens at distances of 50 to 200 metres from the kitchen and a chicken yard. These provide the following: potatoes 30 per cent of the yearly need; lettuce, 80 per cent; onions 10 per cent; tomatoes 30 per cent; eggs 50 per cent; and most part of the insignificant amount of meat eaten. Other cropped vegetables are cabbage, leeks, garlic, peas in winter, and beans and cucurbitaceae (pumpkin family) for the summer garden. The main limitations are the collection and storage of rainwater and the low availability of winter sun. Fruit trees like cherry trees, blackberries and prunes are processed for making marmalades and alcohol distillation. They also produce beer for auto-consumption and to generate money for the collective

The rest of the diet consists of cereals – mainly rice and pasta, non-organic, from the Iberian peninsula; local organic flour for baking bread; legumes directly bought from Iberian organic farmers; sporadically fish; quinoa, coffee, mate, soy products and some nuts come from outside Europe. All these items are purchased in supermarkets and greengrocers in neighbouring towns (7 kilometres). The food expense is approximately €1.25/person/day or €4,000/year for the entire collective. This cash is in turn generated by collective financial activities, mainly the baking, distribution and sale of organic wood-oven bread.

In CMD there are four main garden plots, separated 50 to 100 metres from the kitchen, with similar crops to KP – no potatoes or onions but more cabbage, carrot, beetroot pepper, aubergine and cucumbers. Chickens – owned by a group – play a minor role and are not managed by the collective. Wild pigs from the forest have been hunted with traps but only when they have invaded the gardens: in the dry summers of 2015 and 2016 – when even some of the few oak trees of the forest died – they were the main 'harvest'. Food produced in the gardens supplies 30–40 per cent of vegetables and 5 per cent of fruits eaten at home (apples, pears, oranges, lemons, prunes, caqui). Eggs are an insignificant amount.

The collective food expenditure is about €2.5/person/day – that is, twice as much as in KP – or €26,000/year for the entire collective. Ninety per cent of the purchased food is organic and home delivered; approximately 10 per cent is food either bought in local supermarkets (for a value of €1,000/year) or fish bought at the local street market (for a value of €700/year), at the local market. Organic suppliers are as follows: for fresh fruits and vegetables (€7,100/year), one local cooperative, one agroecological cooperative and a self-employed person; for eggs (€1,100/year), cheese (€1,900/year), olive oil (500 litres, €3,600/year) and meat (30 kilograms €300/year), suppliers are small enterprises or self-employed persons. This is to highlight that sustainable agriculture is more than simply organic: being seasonal, locally sourced and sold by non-profit/small enterprises are also important aspects. For cereals, flours, legumes (€8,000/year), herbs (€500/year), tea and coffee (€1,000/year), suppliers are local retailers, possibly cooperatives. This cash is generated by collective financial activities – mainly the outdoor spring festival in the CMD outdoor – and by individual contributions (€80/month).

Organization of gardens and purchase of collective (and personal) food

In KP the organization of the work of the vegetable gardens is distributed in four production plots, with a dedication of about ten to twenty hours per week per garden during the summer months and less in the winter. Work is done in a spontaneous voluntary basis. The buying of cereals, seeds and legumes in bulk is decided each time in the assembly. Suppliers are independent food distributors, cooperatives and family businesses. The rest of the products is purchased on a weekly basis in supermarkets and greengrocers in a spontaneous way, mainly by those members who regularly use the car. The collective decided not to become a member of a local consumers cooperative of organic products because the prices of the products normally sold are considered too expensive. On the other hand, dumpster diving and food recycling from local shops is regularly practised.

In CMD with a formal organization in well-structured tasks and responsibilities, including financial accounting, one person is in charge of buying food gas bottles and cleaning products and four more are in charge of the house gardens (approximately 500 square metres). Work, mostly done on the open garden day, lasting four to six hours, requires two to three house persons per week and is attended by an average of eight to ten volunteers, throughout the year.

Dedication is therefore forty to sixty hours per week in total. The open day is a successful scheme by which outsiders learn gardening and spend a nice day in nature, and commoners receive much-needed help. A protocol for sustainable and healthy food purchase has been defined over the years by the assembly process and executed by the person in charge of purchasing food. Among the tasks, the search for new suppliers is a constant one. In this way, a broader variety of products is now collectively purchased. Note that originally the purchase of collective food was limited to vegan products. At the very beginning, food skipping in local markets and supermarkets was done daily, and often some fruits were collected directly in farms (olive harvesting for oil, apples and once pears for marmalade and grapes for wine). With the passing of time, recycling and direct recollection in field have disappeared, while purchase of food from animal origins has been included, always keeping in mind agroecological and nutritional criteria. In turn, products considered expensive – such as tahini – or from farmed animals – such as eggs and cheese – are distributed equally to each individual for personal consumption. The 10 per cent of food purchased in local supermarkets – including non-organic foods – is done so in a spontaneous way. Moreover, almost every member has food purchased on an individual basis, such as alcoholic beverages and breakfast and children's supplies.

Organization of cooking and cleaning

In KP, a formal non-organization of kitchen and cleaning shifts has been established. Being a small group (less than ten people), it works based on trust and mutual commitments between users. There are unwritten rules based on 'uses and customs' that suggest that all members of the collective cook for the entire group, meals being the meeting point for the collective. In addition, two external kitchens have been enabled to meet the needs of family units. Note that this system of working without shifts is periodically questioned by some members who express inequalities in the distribution of the kitchen tasks. These differences do not necessarily respond to gender differences, although women tend to clean the kitchen more often than the average. Finally, bread – part of which is sold and constitutes the main source of income for collective expenditures – is baked every week with people working in a less non-organized system; during the weekly assembly, people voluntarily sign up for doing the different bread-making and selling tasks.

In CMD a calendar is displayed in the kitchen in which each member is assumed to sign in for two cooking and cleaning shifts per month. With twenty to twenty-five adults in the group, almost all meals are communally provided – note that on Thursday morning, the open working and gardening day, cooking is one of the tasks assigned to the inhabitants who are attending the day. In the past years, a specific WhatsApp group has been created so that the cook can know how many people will eat. At the end of the year a recount of how many times people have signed in is made public. At the beginning of 2020, a proposal to refine even more the duty has been implemented, according to which the cook must note down how many hours the shift has lasted.[1] Bread is also baked, but lately on a very irregular basis – every two to three weeks, some of it being frozen and defrosted upon need. This implies more purchases of bread from the local supermarket, mainly on an individual basis (Figure 5.1).

Energy

In KP butane is normally used for cooking; about twenty-five gas bottles are used per year (at €1/kilogram, and with each bottle weighing 12 kilograms, it makes approximately 300 kilograms/year), which are complemented in winter by a wood stove that serves the triple function of heating the space, heating water and cooking food. Firewood is obtained from the surrounding forest, which is an important source of provisioning services: oak trees, holm oaks and pines provide most of the heating needs of the community, which, in turn, dedicates an average of fifteen hours of work per month during

---

[1] At the time of writing – February 2020 – this agreement has not been implemented due to a feeling of excessive home bureaucratization.

Figure 5.1 Can Masdeu kitchen. (Photograph by Claudio Cattaneo.)

winter for the collection, cutting and transportation of firewood, and for the lighting of stoves collected only from fallen trees.

In CMD approximately ninety gas bottles of butane are consumed for cooking (1,100 kilograms/year), a lot of electricity for electric stoves and some wood for baking bread. Electricity is freely taken from the grid, while wood comes from the local forest – collected from fallen trees during storms (which are becoming more frequent due to climate change) or from the olive pruning of one of the inhabitants' farm.

Waste and recycling

In KP, plastic waste is usually generated from the packaging of food purchased such as milk, cheeses and vegetables; this is normally disposed of in plastic containers. Glass bottles are also thrown in glass containers. Paper and cardboard instead are burnt in lighting stoves. Recycled food is another source of waste but, this being already waste in the first place, it does not add to the environmental impact of the community. Organic waste from the kitchen is separated into two parts. The edible parts are for the chickens – which are fed mainly from these leftovers and in part from recycled bread and vegetables – the rest is put in the compost heap that will end up in the vegetable gardens, so closing two material loops. A self-built dry toilet is used so that humanure and urine are also remaining in the place – a triple win as, with respect to a WC, this saves water, does not pollute water and keeps nutrients in place.

In CMD garbage disposal is also collectively organized during the Thursday working day, with plastic, glass and paper going to the correspondent containers (about 30 kilograms/week, or 1 kilogram/person/ week). Glass and plastic come almost entirely from the food system. Boxes from the supplier of vegetables are given back. Organic residues are treated as in KP, and dry toilets are also in place.

Discussion

There are many ways to inhabit commons. In other contexts, we have presented as similar cases (Cattaneo and Gavaldà, 2010), KP and CMD can be framed as homogeneous cases – both are rurban squats on the hills of Barcelona with similar longevity and ideals – but on taking a closer look from 'inside', amazing differences are unveiled.

This is because the horizontal decision-making processes and self-organization that characterize the management of commons can result in very different outcomes in the way the commons are organized. We go on to discuss how and why CMD and KP have arrived where they are with respect to how the need for alimentation is satisfied in a material and organizational way.

The main elements are the following: the origin of food; related to it, the broader approach to the collective versus individual income generation debate; and, finally, formal organization versus non-organization.

As per the origin of food, the explanation of why KP does not join one of the main cooperatives of ecological consumption is due to certain consumption inertias that have been perpetuated over the years and that are based on sort of unquestionable myths.

One of them is the expensive price of organic products. Since the collective is based on a very demonetized economy, the collective income generated from bread sale – which is by the way sold mainly to those consumer cooperatives – would not be enough to cover such expenses. This situation could be resolved by either increasing work in the bread business or introducing contributions as in CMD. For the moment, there is no consensus on either solution, leaving the collective stuck in the contradictory practice of unsustainable consumption and waste disposal. Another reason is related to the formal non-organization of any task in KP, including household chores such as cooking or the purchase of food: what is observed is that the car is often used in the displacements of some of the KP members who, in turn, are those who more likely to purchase food as they encounter supermarkets on their drives and then easily transport what was bought to KP. However, the low importance that the collective gives towards a food policy coherent with its ideals diminishes the strength of the emancipatory social project that KP aims to be. This is a reoccurring and still unresolved debate.

On the one hand, the explicit politics of non-organization, which spans across all tasks of the KP collective, from any of the household chores – including garden activities and wood collection – passes through the maintenance and improvement of the community's infrastructure. In addition, the work related to collective income generation is – now and over the twenty-three years of the project's existence – a remarkable accomplishment with respect to successful commons governance. Not controlling people and believing that generosity, personal freedom, spontaneity, mutual trust and tolerance are the most valued dimensions of everyday life has been proven to work over the long term.

On the other hand, in CMD there has been an increase in formal organization over its eighteen years of life. Feeding-related tasks are rotative (two cooking shifts per person per month) or assigned as responsibilities (three to four persons in charge of gardening, one of food purchases, one of accounting) or done on the working day (cleaning of the storeroom, throwing rubbish, maintenance and improvement of tools and equipment). The result is a higher living standard – that is, the benefits of having meals ready and on time almost every day and good working conditions for the cook in a clean and well-equipped kitchen – at the cost of more hours dedicated to collective work than in KP. This is due to the formation of consensus on this type of shift organization and the shared obligations and commitments. This organization, which is marked by shared obligations, not only in the kitchen but also in the compartmentalization of tasks in shifts and work commissions, nevertheless feeds a certain tendency to bureaucratization of daily tasks that has also been evidenced as a source of conflicts. If a sense of constant comparison and control over housemates is the price for an equitable distribution of work, conflicts and discussions are always present. Since the early stages of the CMD project – where no formal organization system had yet been established, – there have been evident inequalities in work distribution. The problem is that differently from the early history of KP, CMD had a troubled beginning, with constant eviction attempts putting a lot of pressure on having to work to save the project: organizing assemblies, legal work, media work and logistic work for the physical defence had to be carried out while having to set up living infrastructure. The house was empty when squatted, with no water or electricity connections – while having to repair it structurally; it was found in a semi-derelict state with partly fallen roofs and rain leaking in because it had suffered from a negligent abandonment over forty years. And all of this while having to do day-to-day task and set up a community of twenty-five inhabitants, largely unknown to each other, who answered the call to join the project launched by the initiator group made up of only eight persons. It was a crazy time with extraordinary activity that frequently resulted in activist burnout or hyper-stress for some and which was not helped by the disinterest of other people towards the fate of the project. Many people left, new ones joined with more motivation, but, still, organizational structure was urgently needed, at least for the feeding tasks. The first year, the rotation system for cooking was established together with one for dumpster diving. In fact, gardens were not yet established, and the collective economy had such a small income from individual contributions that it could only cover the bulk purchase of non-organic grains.

However, we can argue that this much-needed organization continued and even increased even when external pressure declined and dedication to the community start-up became less demanding. Probably it is due to the size of the group: not only does CMD have more than double the inhabitants of KP, but the number of potential conflicts increases even more. In a group of 10 there can be 45 one-to-one relationships (and potential conflicts); in a group of 25, there are 300.

Moreover, even if 'sustainability' or 'social transformation' are important values for both communities, the ways these ideals have been realized are different: CMD has focused more on a sustainable food policy, but in energy consumption terms – including space heating and sanitation – its performance has become much less sustainable than it used to be, while KP is self-sufficient in electricity needs.

From a monetary perspective, CMD is more monetized than KP – and not only in food-related needs – and the individual quota (back then of €1/day) was the first solution established for generating collective income. Collective ways to generate collective income arrived later – by opening a social centre that on Sunday catered for the attenders of the activities organized by the house residents and by organizing one or two big parties per year. But the individual quota always remained, and even increased as the expenditure on more good-quality organic food increased. CMD's food policy has a beneficial impact for the social transformation that is being pursued in the present; as seen, the extra cost per person per day is just above €1, which, from the KP demonetized perspective, is not a negligible cost that would require each individual to generate money outside the community, as self-employed workers or in the labour market.

On the other hand, in KP food not generated in the garden comes from commercial distribution chains and recycling. In the long run, this consumption does not provide a social or productive transformation. However, by the fact of subsisting economically with community work generated from the benefits of the sale of bread, a social project has been built that demonstrates that one can live in this world without working for labour exploitation networks, which is considered an important fact in KP more than in CMD. To conclude, we have seen that in both projects the way alimentation is managed offers useful insights that highlight where the best and worst characteristics of each organizational system are reflected.

The approximation to this issue from a metabolic (energy, material and financial) perspective is extremely relevant with respect to the social and environmental impact of everyday life. Decisions about what and how we feed ourselves are politically relevant in social emancipation movements. In particular, the squatting movement in Barcelona should not separate political decisions from everyday ones, because the construction of a different world must undoubtedly go through the revision of the origin, production and transport of food, as well as the roles and the organization of the kitchen in communal spaces. Another world is possible only if we also change our kitchens (Figure 5.2).

Figure 5.2 A convivial gathering in Kan Pasqual. (Photograph by Marc Galvada.)

References

Bookchin, M. (1982). *The Ecology of Freedom: The Emergence and Dissolution of Hierarchy*. Palo Alto, CA: Cheshire Books. Spanish translation: Bookchin, M. (1999). *La Ecología de la Libertad. La emergencia y la disolución de las jerarquías*. Madrid: Nossa y Jara Editores.

Cattaneo, C., Marull, J. and Tello, E. (2018). Landscape agroecology. The dysfunctionalities of industrial agriculture and the loss of the circular bioeconomy in the Barcelona Region, 1956–2009. *Sustainability*, 10(12), 4722.

Edelstein, M., Cerny, A. and Gadeav, A., eds. (2012). *Disaster by Design: The Aral Sea and Its Lessons for Sustainability*. Bingley: Emerald Publishing.

Foley, et al. (2011). Solutions for a cultivated planet. *Nature*, 478, 337–342.

Font, C., Padró, R., Cattaneo, C., Marull, J. and Tello, E. (2020). How farmers shape cultural landscapes. Dealing with information in farm systems (Vallès County, Catalonia, 1860). *Ecological Indicators*, 112, 106104.

Geiger, F., Bengtsson, J., Berendse, F., Weisser, W., Emmerson, M., Morales, M., Ceryngier, P., Liira. J., Tscharntke. T., Winqvist, C., Eggers, S., Bommarco, R., Pärt, T., Bretagnolle, V., Plantegenest. M., Clement. L., Dennis, C., Palmer. C., Oñate, J. J., Guerrero, I., Hawro, V., Aavik, T., Thies, C., Flohre, A., Haenke, S., Fischer, C., Goedhart, P., Inchausti, P. (2010). Persistent negative effects of pesticides on biodiversity and biological control potential on European farmland. *Basic and Applied Ecology*, 11, 97–105.

Millennium Ecosystem Assessment (2005). *Ecosystems and Human Well-being: Synthesis*. Washington, DC: Island Press.

Padró, R., Marco, I., Cattaneo, C., Caravaca, J. and Tello, E. (2017). Does your landscape mirror what you eat? A long-term socio-metabolic analysis of a local food system in Vallès County (Spain, 1860–1956–1999). In Frankova, E. et al., eds., *Socio-Metabolic Perspectives on the Sustainability of Local Food Systems*, New York: Springer, 133–164.

Siciliano, G., 2013. Rural-urban migration and domestic land grabbing in China. *Population Space and Place*, 20(4), 333–351.

Tello, E and Gonzalez de Molina, M. (2017). Methodological challenges and general criteria for assessing and designing local sustainable Agri-food systems: A socio-ecological approach at landscape level. In Frankova, E. et al., eds., *Socio-Metabolic Perspectives on the Sustainability of Local Food Systems*, Springer, 133–164.

Travlou, P. (2020). From cooking to commoning: the making of intangible cultural heritage in OneLoveKitchen, Athens. In Lekakis, S., ed., *Cultural Heritage in the Realm of the Commons: Conversations on the Case of Greece*. London: Ubiquity Press, 159–182. DOI: https://doi.org/10.5334/bcj.j. License: CC-BY.

Wada, et al. (2010). Global depletion of groundwater resources. *Geophysical Research Letters*, 37. doi:10.1029/2010GL044571

Part II

Cooperatives, squats and housing struggles

6

Hybrid commons

Housing cooperatives in Zurich

Irina Davidovici

Introduction

If we were to compare cooperative housing initiatives across the globe, besides the generalized, perennial 'housing question' which they seek to address, several common themes emerge.[1] Defined by the common principle of alliance of interests, housing cooperatives often result from local grassroots initiatives, and greatly depend on specific constellations of people and historical circumstances. As an alternative to market housing, their existence runs counter to mainstream political, administrative and economic logics. Their long-term survival depends not only upon the resourcefulness, solidarity and resilience of members but also upon the political will of external parties. Some of the most substantial cooperative movements are located in Central and Northern Europe, in prosperous countries with established rental cultures, whereas they are less likely to occur in those where welfare structures have eroded and homeownership ideologies have a greater hold (Kemeny, 2005). Their historical evolution also displays common patterns, whereby initially progressive agendas are gradually translated into legal and economic frameworks to aid the growth of cooperatives, while diluting much of their original ideological subtext. The trajectory of cooperatives in Nordic countries illustrates how, once grown beyond a certain scale, cooperatives can cease representing an alternative minority model. Their gradual adoption of

---

[1] Such an overview was provided by the International Conference Tackling the global housing challenges Housing cooperatives' role in the provision of affordable housing, organized by the Zurich Association of Swiss Housing Cooperatives (WBG) and the ETH Centre for Research on Architecture, Society and the Built Environment (ETH CASE WOHNFORUM), ZAZ – Zentrum Architektur Zürich, 6 December 2019. The following discussion on collective traits is derived from the presentations of speakers from Europe, Asia, Africa and Latin America.

social landlord characteristics and behaviours, competing and increasingly entering the market, results in tensions between the original idealism and their pragmatic institutionalization. By contrast, fledgling initiatives, such as currently emerging in developing economies, are positively precarious without the support of political and financial frameworks for growth.

Sociopolitical and ethical agendas, while being the common fundaments of many cooperatives, are not, however, a prerequisite for their long-term functioning. Legally, cooperatives operate as registered companies – albeit collectively owned ones, and subject to different (re)generative principles than capitalist enterprises. They must ensure not only their members' well-being but also their own continued economic existence. While this double binding principle makes the model viable, it is also the source of its inner contradictions. As businesses, cooperatives have to mediate between utopian principles of equality and common property on the one hand and survival in the market culture on the other. The resulting sense of negotiation and eventually compromise raises the question: To which extent may housing cooperatives be considered a commons?

Often, housing cooperatives only prosper with the explicit support of state or market agencies. Contrary to expectations, they do not develop in a void, but in reaction to a problematic status quo, such as scarcity of housing or of tenant rights. Cooperatives can be viewed as niche enterprises, guided by principles other than short-term profit. In order to achieve a substantial amount of built stock, they tend to rely on legal and financial mechanisms (incentives, subsidies, land leases etc.) for gaining access to suitable sites and for building on them. They can hardly expand or survive in the long-term without the explicit support of political governance. In theory at least, highly efficient top-down welfare structures would meet the demand for affordable housing just enough to thwart motivation of citizens to self-organize their own. The durability of cooperatives is therefore largely dependent on their complementarity with centralized welfare structures. Thus, for a housing sector often described as a 'third-way' common between market and state welfare models, the cooperative sector operates less as an alternative than as a hybrid sharing characteristics with both.

Zurich Cooperatives: A functioning commons?

The case of housing cooperatives in Zurich offers fertile ground for the examination of a highly functional connection to state (in this case municipal) authority. In Switzerland as a whole, the cooperative model is long established and widely accepted in food production and light manufacturing sectors even more than in housing. This popularity is subject to an entrenched cultural mindset that values collectivity and strategic alliances over individual interest. The cooperative principles are favoured by the federal political structure, which empowers local authorities, and the liberal economy, in which welfare structures are decentralized. The principles of participatory democracy protect citizens' interests and render municipalities more responsive to the localized needs of their constituents. Politically, Swiss cooperatives are not subsidiaries, but partners of local government, the terms of this partnership varying with the locality (Durban, 2007, p. 3). Since the commune (or municipality) is the 'autonomous cell' of Swiss democracy, its political leanings, which can differ from those of the canton, are crucial in determining the extent of this collaboration.[2]

In the residential sector too, cooperatives play a central role. At 5 per cent of the total housing stock, they represent the third most established stakeholder, albeit trailing a long way behind market rental (57 per cent) and private ownership (38 per cent) (Wohnen Schweiz, 2018, p. 20). Zurich is the largest cooperative hub, concentrating more than 50,000 of the 150,000 cooperative dwellings currently across Switzerland (Wohnbaugenossenschaften Schweiz, 2020). As much as a quarter of the city's total housing stock is non-profit, a ratio which, following a referendum in 2011, is set up to increase to 30 per cent by 2040 (Stadt Zürich, 2011, pp. 11–14). In a housing culture dominated by rentals, with a 99 per cent occupancy rate and a saturated market that limits home ownership, cooperatives have long offered an effective complement to the meagre provisions for fully subsidized social housing.

The current flourishing of Zurich housing cooperatives is rooted in more than 100 years of political developments and ideological shifts. The model is highly specific, based upon a historical partnership between cooperatives and the traditionally left-leaning municipality. While the city of Zurich counts as only 1 among 162 municipalities in the eponymous canton – albeit the largest and densest among them – its autonomy has allowed it a specific flexibility.

---

[2] An important concept in the formation of cooperatives is that of self-help: they are sometimes and only partially subsidized by the state, upon accepting certain quotas for residents of given income and demographic profiles. However, the existence of cooperatives is enabled by state legislation. In referendums pertaining to cooperative legislation, popular opinion is normally supportive. From 1910 cooperatives with a seed capital of 10 per cent became eligible for federal support, figure further lowered in 1924 to 6 per cent, in a popular vote with 87 per cent in favour. Local government becomes increasingly a partner in cooperative developments as developable land becomes more difficult to obtain. The city grants the so-called *Baurecht*, which allows cooperatives to develop on land owned by local authorities without the considerable cost of purchasing it. The *Baurecht* (right to build) is the most important instrument for ground acquisition in housing development, accounting for 40 per cent of current cooperative housing stock, a higher percentage in more recent schemes.

Switzerland's largest industrial and metropolitan centre had every interest to actively assist the ascendancy of cooperatives in order to cater for the large influx of workers and organize new settlements at various stage of its territorial growth. Thus, the success of its cooperatives has been dependent not only on the impetus and scope of citizen initiatives but more so on the symbiotic relationship established over time with the city and its policies. The resulting system is so widespread as to allow significant variations in the size, structure and ideology of cooperatives. It is also not infallible: demand far outweighs the offer, membership is restricted by too high or too low levels of income, and some of the conditions for access to cooperative housing can be perceived by many as intrusive. And yet, this model's capacity to absorb and respond to periodic critiques and revisions throughout its venerable history is a mark of its resilience.

Viewing the history of Zurich's cooperatives through the lens of housing commons allows us to consider their contribution in a holistic manner, shifting attention from housing as resource to the actors and processes governing its use. In theory, commons comprise three interdependent components: the resource being shared, the community of users and the rules according to which the sharing takes place (De Angelis and Stavrides, 2010, p. 4). This chapter loosely follows these notions through the history of Zurich's cooperatives, tracing the transformation of the common resources, commoners and commoning practices at different stages. It will focus in greater detail on the new generation of cooperatives that has emerged in the last quarter century, signalling how ideological shifts have had an effect not only on the architectural and urban expression of cooperatives but also on their structural composition as housing commons. The investigation is based on a double hypothesis: firstly, that housing cooperatives follow a repeatable pattern, from progressive, even utopian, prototype to institutionalization; and secondly, that as commons they operate not in isolation from, but as hybrids with state and market components.

From defensive gesture to people's housing: 1890s–1950s

Privately organized, the historical precursors to Zurich's cooperatives were animated by the paternalistic logic of industrialists. The Fierzhäuser in Zurich's Industriequartier (1873–80), built by textile entrepreneur and politician Johann Heinrich Fierz, are widely considered to be the earliest action to ease the city's affordable housing crisis. Modelled on the 'cité ouvrière' in Mulhouse and the Rieter settlement in Winterthur (1865–70), the settlement of semi-detached houses with gardens was conceived as a corrective to the dense, speculative tenements close to factory areas and the railways. Fierz founded an Aktienbauverein to fund the settlement and offer workers access to fresh air, light and green areas (Kälin, 2013).

Zurich's first housing cooperative, Zürcher Bau und Spargennossenschaft, was founded in 1892 by a group of middle-class tenants, who pooled up resources to 'save up and build' – as per the cooperative's name – their own apartment blocks in Sonneggstrasse. This first cooperative was motivated less by a social agenda than by a defensive strategy to create a protected resource safe from speculation (Kurz, 2014). Despite other early examples, the cooperative solution was restricted by the required 34 per cent equity, which placed it out of reach for the majority of the population. In 1907, the fledgling cooperative movement received a crucial boost with the city authorities' legal commitment to promote healthy affordable housing – a motion that marks the beginnings of the alliance between city and cooperatives. Limmat I, a pilot housing estate designed by city architect W. Fissler, was conceived as a prototype for improved and hygienic affordable housing.

The turning point for the future of cooperatives came, however, in 1910, when the city voted into law the 'Principles Regarding the Promotion of Public-Interest Building Cooperatives'. The new legislation allowed the city to provide affordable land plots, and allowed cooperatives to seek mortgage loans to cover 90 per cent of the construction investment. Of the remaining 10 per cent equity, the local authority would cover a further 1 per cent, which meant that from the point the city became a shareholder in its cooperatives. This move, and particularly the reduction of the necessary seed funding to 9 per cent, opened the possibility of housing cooperatives to be organized by and for the working classes. In conditions where Zurich's population tripled between 1880 and 1920, and through the economic crisis following the First World War, the high demand for affordable housing and the motivation to self-organize peaked. The railway workers' cooperative Baugenossenschaft des eidgenössischen Personals (BEP) was founded in 1910, followed by Allgemeine Baugenossenschaft Zurich (ABZ) in 1916. These were popular bottom-up initiatives, fuelled by door-to-door recruitment, with low monthly membership rates accessible even for poor families, and their membership grew in their thousands. In 1924, a popular referendum saw the adoption of an improved housing policy that decreased the equity further to 5.6 per cent – a rate that still applies to cooperative development. The local government incentivized construction with capital loans and investments, in exchange for the inclusion of one municipal representative on the board of cooperatives. The 1924 statute also provided, for each development, the option of municipal subsidies for lower-income households. Strictly regulated by the local authorities, this social housing provision is not overly popular with cooperatives and the percentage of subsidized flats remains to date relatively low – circa 13 per cent of the cooperative stock.

Throughout the 1920s, the supportive housing policies led to large-scale developments in Zurich's new working-class districts in Aussersihl and Industriequartier. Characteristically decorated with frescoes and sculptural motifs, these rather monumental developments impacted visibly on the urban fabric. Instead of bitty plots of earlier speculative tenements, further densified by productive workshops in the inner yards, the new cooperative 'colonies' were planned as large-scale, well-lit and ventilated quadrangles, enclosing generous gardens and even parks for play and recreation (Figure 6.1).

These inner-city perimeter blocks with an internal planted courtyard, popular with the workers' communities of the so-called Rotes Zürich (Red Zurich), were typologically complemented by suburban Siedlungen on the city periphery, which took the form of Garden Cities of cottages or low

Figure 6.1 The perimeter block Industrie II, better known as Roter Block (the Red Block), was designed by Peter Giumini for the cooperative Baugenossenschaft des Eidgenössischen Personals Zürich (BEP) in 1920. Its massing, dwelling typology and decorative scheme are representative of the heroic stage of Zurich's early working-class cooperatives. (Photograph by Irina Davidovici).

blocks with generous gardens. These cooperatives provided nuclear family flats, with or without gardens, and with a limited set of collective facilities usually intended for the residents – childcare, launderettes, social clubs, in close vicinity to primary schools (Durban, 2007; Rieger, 1975).

Temporarily stymied by the Great Depression, the construction of cooperative estates gained again momentum in the 1940s and 1950s. At this time, the city as a whole was experiencing a building boom: 10,000 new dwellings, including more than half of Zurich's current cooperative stock, were built between 1942 and 1957. The lands amassed by the annexation of peripheral communes in 1934 were developed to masterplans drawn by city architect Albert H. Steiner. Once the large inner-city sites had been built up, the design of monumental perimeter blocks of the 1920s and 1930s was replaced by Garden City ensembles of family cottages and three- to four-storey-high blocks of flats with gabled roofs, so prevalent as to express a collective mindset (Figure 6.2).

Figure 6.2 The Goldacker Estate, designed by Karl Egender and Wilhelm Müller in 1947–8 for the Cooperative Sonnengarten (BGS). In the 1940s and 1950s, Zurich's production of cooperative housing reached an all-time high with Garden City ensembles of family cottages and low blocks of flats on the city's periphery. (Photograph by Irina Davidovici.)

As Caspar Schärer noted, this residential architecture denoted 'comfortable orderliness with nothing conspicuous, a moderate modernism and constrained individualization', expressing in turn the implicit demand that citizens 'subordinate themselves to a greater whole that would save them from iniquity and ensure that life would be tolerably good' (Schärer and Caspar, 2017, p. 25). This prevalent mentality illustrated an erosion of workers' cooperatives' initial ideological substrate. By the mid-1950s, little had remained of their early social programme, which, as formulated by ABZ founding member Dora Staudinger, aimed at 'building a new and better human community, in which . . . each person helps and assist the others hand in hand' (Kurz and Daniel, 2017, p. 190).

By this stage, cooperatives acted as little more than social landlords. The critical mass they had reached and the administrative role they had assumed made it more financially attractive to purchase ready-built housing estates built by private developers, in a dramatic reversal of the original agenda. In turn, the top-down management also allowed the residents' communities to become more passive, less likely to undertake the democratic participative practices to which they were still, technically, entitled (Balmer and Bernet, 2015, p. 190). This wearing down of the reformative and participative agendas of cooperatives resulted in a commercialization that represented a point of ideological surrender. In the 1960s, the traditional cooperative model, which had relentlessly provided for the working-class nuclear family, had reached a moment of crisis.[3]

An ideological reset: 1980–2020

In the early 1990s, an innovative perspective on collective living emerged in Zurich from the unlikely confluence of the cooperative tradition with the youth movements of the 1980s (Stahel and Voegeli, 2006). The new generation of housing cooperatives that resulted distinguished itself from the established cooperative model in its renewed insistence on self-governance and participation, placing sustainability at the centre of its building and operational activities. From shared resources and collective spaces, this sustainability agenda extended to stringent performance credentials in construction and inhabitation, and to the efficient use of inhabitable

---

[3] Between 1962 and 1990, the urban population dwindled by a fifth (Statistik Stadt Zürich, *Statistisches Jahrbuch Der Stadt Zürich* 2015, p. 30). The open drugs scene during the 1980s and early 1990s was a symptom of a deeper social malaise, the despondency of a younger generation pressured to conform.

space (Wohnen Schweiz, 2018, p. 21). The environmental commitment results in a new level of engagement with the urban realm in the concern with densification, reuse and mixed use. At the same time, societal change has dictated a shift in strategy from providing family-oriented dwellings to more complex mixtures of flats. Cooperatives have become a field of experimentation with multiple scenarios for collective living, including informal communes, patchwork or multigeneration families and collective accommodations for singles and the elderly (Hofer, 2011). The provision of a wide range of apartment types and sizes, with generous collective spaces, is tied in with the principles of space efficiency. The great majority of cooperative flats in Zurich constrain the rentable flat size according to the household size, which has incentivized cooperatives to consider the most efficient flat sizes in their housing stock. By voluntarily reducing the living surface per inhabitant, cooperatives seek to reduce both costs and environmental impact.

The newer generation of cooperatives is grounded in the utopian and environmentalist proposals of the 1980s youth movement in Zurich.[4] Amalgamating anti-bourgeois, anti-imperialist, New Age and feminist principles, the social unrest at the time gave rise to parallel citizen actions, which eventually found their most productive outlet in adopting cooperative formats. The Wogeno cooperative, established in 1981, purchased properties that were then run jointly by their residents, reviving the cooperative practice of self-organization. Each property was the responsibility of a household association, whose tenants collectively managed shared spaces and facilities, planned works of repair and maintenance, and chose new members and flatmates (WOGENO, 2018).[5] The Stauffacher squat, which occupied a

---

[4]   In May 1980, the city authority's decision to fund the refurbishment of the Opera House, while rejecting proposals for an autonomous youth centre, sparked the so-called *Opernhauskrawalle*. The Opera House riots set in motion a set of street demonstrations and were singularly responsible for the politicization of a new generation. In the last two decades, the decommissioning of industrial areas, especially along the railway (Zurich West, Oerlikon, etc.) has provided ample opportunities for the new construction. Prior to being redeveloped, several dormant postindustrial sites were occupied by squatters and became temporary centres of alternative culture (Wohlgroth Areal 1991–3, Kalkbreite 2003–8, Binz Areal 2006–13).

[5]   'Wogeno calculates the rents according to the principle of cost rent. This means that residents are exposed only slightly to market developments. Tenants must contribute up to 10 per cent of the investment costs in the form of equity capital, for which corresponding share certificates are issued. A small portion of the monthly rent is paid into a solidarity fund. Wogeno tenants are obliged to organize themselves in an association and to manage their house largely by themselves. This house association is also responsible to the Wogeno for the observance of contracts, the administration and the maintenance of the property. Budget, upcoming maintenance of the house, the common use of facilities such as garden, terrace, laundry room, lounges and other common matters are discussed by the tenants in their meetings as needed. Another

cluster of old townhouses threatened by a speculative commercial centre, was the reason for long-drawn, and sporadically violent, conflicts between resident activists and successive developers (Stahel and Voegeli, 2006, pp. 430–3). After its forceful clearance by police in January 1984, a third of the original occupants regrouped as the collective Karthago am Stauffacher, which advocated the creation of an autonomous, countercultural residential enclave (P. M., 1983, 1985).[6] Karthago eventually registered as a cooperative in 1991, establishing a fifty-strong, multigenerational collective household with shared accommodation, catering arrangements and communal duties.

The third and last example was the cooperative Dreieck, also the result of a citizen mobilization to protect an original triangular perimeter block in Aussersihl threatened with demolition. Initially constituted as neighbourhood association intending to preserve the communal, socially mixed, character of the area, Dreieck became a cooperative with some 200 members in 1996. The preserved houses were refurbished to high environmental standards, their roofs decked with solar panels, and the existing gaps in the street frontage filled with two new buildings, resulting in a heterogeneous piecemeal urban environment, at once intimate and lively. Small in scale and integrated to the point of invisibility in their residential locations, these pioneering new cooperatives have used the existing city fabric in an unostentatious way. While continuing to operate in much the same way, without drawing attention to their alternative lifestyle propositions, these collective actors have been at the centre of a network of like-minded initiatives, willing to share savoir faire and experience while competing for new opportunities for development.

A further step with regard to scale and architectural presence of the new cooperatives was breached by the cooperatives Kraftwerk1 and Kalkbreite. Kraftwerk1 represents the case apart of a bottom-up initiative, operating within and along the top-down planning strategies of the city as a way to reach its construction target.[7] It originated in an informal grouping of activists, sociologists, architects and planners who, under the banner Konzeptgruppe Städtebau (Conceptual Planning Group), discussed Zurich's development scenarios in the late 1980s. The group later split into two: the

---

    important difference to traditional cooperatives: the choice of new flatmates is the responsibility of the house association.'

6 This programme was theoretically underpinned by the utopian pamphlet Bolo'Bolo, published in 1983 by Stauffacher activist Hans Widmer under the pseudonym PM. Under this title, P.M. envisaged a global network of non-hierarchical, self-sufficient communes called bolos, conceived as 'extended households' of between 300 and 1,000 people.

7 The author in indebted to Andreas Hofer, architect, former squatter, activist and founding member of the Kraftwerk1 cooperative, who provided the details of this case study during a series of discussions and correspondence in 2016–18.

theoretical faction continued as the independent urban research centre INURA Zurich Institute, whereas the activist faction, headed by architect Andreas Hofer, concentrated on establishing a live-work community in the still active industrial district of Zurich West. It based its proposals upon the Sulzer-Escher-Wyss-Gestaltungsplan, which sought to keep inner-city industry viable by selling peripheral plots for offices and housing, concentrate production to core areas, and invest profits in future industries. This topic was put to vote in the 1992 referendum on the revision of zoning law, Bau- und Zonenordnung (Hofer, 2004). Produced as a collaboration between squatting activist Hans Widmer (under the pseudonym P.M.), Hofer and artist Martin Blum, the brochure *Kraftwerk1* (1993) served to recruit like-minded citizens interested in planning and social issues, mixed use, and new forms of living in Zurich's industrial district (Blum et al., 1993). This instigated a public consultation that detailed a live-work cooperative settlement with a wide variety of living arrangements, from conventional flats to larger units with shared kitchens and living areas, based on the WG (Wohngemeinschaft) model. Reconstituted in 1995 as cooperative, Kraftwerk1 negotiated the use of a site owned by corporate developer Oerlikon-Bührle, which resulted in its first development at Hardturm (1998-2001), designed by architects Bünzli Courvoisier to a revised masterplan by commercial architectural practice Stücheli. The completed Kraftwerk1 Hardturm offered ninety-one apartments, a kindergarten, workshops, live-work units, a room for guests, a communal hall and public roof terrace, bar and canteen, launderette and food shop, with a commercial block with offices and a public restaurant facing the main road.[8]

While the development was one of the first to adopt Minergie standards in its construction and environmental performance, its most experimental aspect lies in the layout and variation of apartment types, ranging in size from studios and conventional two- to four-bedroom apartments to larger dwellings for collective living. Kraftwerk1 became the prototypical application of the communitarian and environmentalist ideas of the squatting movement. The income-proportional rents resulted in a socially mixed resident community, including, besides the mostly middle-class professionals involved in the consultation process, a mixture of less privileged families, disabled groups, migrants and refugees.

---

[8] Even though the creation of speculative rental spaces went against cooperative principles, it helped attract investors and rents out workspace to several inhabitants. For Kraftwerk1 the combination of living and working was a fundamental part of the concept. The office spaces are rented out following adapted conditions of cooperative renting schemes; for instance, the rents are calculated on a non-speculative Kostenmiete.

The Cooperative Kalkbreite originated from its eponymous location in the heart of Aussersihl, on a contested site earmarked for affordable housing redevelopment since 1978. In the early 2000s, the site was used as a city tram depot with several ancillary buildings occupied by a squatting community. This formed the basis of a steering group, Kalkbreite Association, which secured in competition the lease for the site in 2006, with the cooperative concept of 'Neues Stück Stadt' (new part of the city). The association registered as cooperative one year later and agreed, in negotiations with the city of Zurich and its subsidiary, the public transport company VBZ, to develop the site by juxtaposing residential and public functions and the tram depot (Wolf et al., 2015, pp. 26–31). The architectural competition that followed in 2009, organized in collaboration with the city, was won by architects Müller Sigrist with the proposal of polygonal perimeter superblock raised above the covered tram depot. Located close to Karthago and Dreieck, this multistorey commercial, cultural and residential complex sets itself apart from these modest beacons of radical living in its monumental-scale and complex public programme, including an arthouse cinema, a restaurant, a bar, stores and offices. The residential block above these is accessed through a raised, landscaped inner courtyard, organized around a skylit *rue intérieure*. This internal itinerary connects residential, live-work, work and open functions into one continuous circuit, which integrates public and semi-public roof terraces. Typologically, the apartment range is extremely wide, comprising apartments, varying from studios and live-work units to large flat shares of up to fifteen inhabitants, including three cluster apartments of ten units each (Hofer, 2011).[9]

Neither Kraftwerk1 nor Kalkbreite were part of an established system for housing procurement. They resulted from specific windows of opportunity, dependent on the bottom-up actions of individuals on the one hand and involving negotiations and partnerships with various political and commercial partners on the other. Both scenarios show how grassroots initiatives reached their aim through alliances with commercial and political actors, making full use of the top-down planning and political tools at their disposal. Both were steered by groups of ideologically motivated, educated, middle-class activists who were able to articulate their demands and secure productive negotiations with market and state partners. Both illustrated an interest in housing innovation, combining flat-sharing housing typologies for collective living with more conventional family dwellings types in a large

9 A flat share (Wohngemeinschaft, or WG) is configured as individual bedrooms grouped around a common room and common kitchen, whereas in the cluster apartment similar common areas are shared among the inhabitants of small studios, each with its own kitchenette and bathroom.

variety of sizes as to attract a mixed community of users across social and income divides, and used open renting strategies to make use of available financial incentives. Both cooperatives expressed their interest in animating the urban areas of which they were part, by offering public and mixed-use facilities open to the surrounding communities. They were built to high standards of sustainability and adhered to low-energy strategies, such as the efficient reduction of living area per capita and actively discouraging the use of cars. Yet their target audience remains predominantly middle class, with a limited proportion of subsidized rents.

While animated by alternative, anti-capitalist aims, both exemplify an imperative to expand further, which puts them on a level of equivalence with traditional cooperatives, if not with speculative developers. Both have, since their inception, added to their portfolios new projects run along the same programmatic basis. After Hardturm, Kraftwerk1 developed the multigenerational collective Heizenholz (designed by Adrian Streich, completed 2012) and, on a decommissioned industrial site considered too remote by conventional developers, the superblock Zwicky Süd (Schneider Studer Primas, completed 2016). Based on the success of their original scheme, the Cooperative Kalkbreite was granted by the city the lease of a prominent site near the main railway station, Zollhaus, which opened in 2021 (won in competition in 2015 and designed by Enzmann Fischer Architects).

These projects continued to use architecture to explicitly signify their alternative ideologies through a variety of typological and iconographic motifs (from cluster apartments to wide, covered, communal terraces and walkways). These motifs have increasingly been adopted by traditional cooperatives and even by commercial developers keen to project a greener, more socially inclusive image, albeit without the underlying commoning procedures that ensure their long-term functioning.

Despite competing against each other when applying for the lease of available sites, the old and new cooperatives are willing to collaborate, share knowledge and involve external parties – of which, the local authority is the most active and constant partner. The flagship of this spirit of alliance was the cooperative Mehr als Wohnen, established in 2007 at the centenary of the partnership between the cooperative movement and the city, and subject to an architectural competition in 2008 (Hugentobler et al., 2016). The resulting Hunziker Areal, on another former industrial site in the north of Zurich, was developed according to the collaborative masterplan of Duplex and futurafrosch, won in competition in 2008. The ensemble, completed in 2015 after several years of public consultations. comprises thirteen blocks designed by several architectural practices (futurafrosch, Duplex, Müller Sigrist, Miroslav Sik, pool architekten). It is home to 1,200 living and

150 work tenants in a large variety of living and live-work typologies. Its residential programme is mixed with a variety of shops and businesses on the ground floor of most buildings, and its environmental credentials are signalled discreetly by the solar panels on their roofs and the communal vegetable garden.

Zurich cooperatives as housing commons

As shown earlier, all commons comprise a three-partite structure of a clearly defined body of resources, be they finite or infinite, material or immaterial; a set of rules, regulatory institutions and social practices determining the shared use of these resources (commoning practices); and a defined community of users, or commoners (Ostrom, 1990; De Angelis et al., 2010; Harvey, 2013). Transferred to housing, this three-pronged definition tends to denote residential and communal spaces as the common resource, although some significant additional resources are immaterial: security, sociability, time economy, convenience and urbanity. Balmer and Bernet defined housing commons through the extent to which housing is decommodified, that is, removed from the market, and self-organized, that is, subject to own rules, set up and adhered to by its resident commoners (Balmer and Bernet, 2015, p. 179). Tenants and cooperative members, as well as political enablers and economic sponsors, are considered as the extended community of (direct or indirect) users. Finally, commoning practices involve not only the sum of cohabitation activities but also practices pertaining to the acquisition, design and distribution of cooperative housing, including those circumscribed by property rights and housing policies. On these two accounts, Zurich cooperatives offer an exemplary application of the notion of housing commons, albeit one reliant on highly particular, advantageous statutory and economic frameworks. From a commons' perspective, Zurich cooperatives can be seen to represent a hybrid commons, coupled to the state agendas and market instruments that have rendered them possible.

Fluctuations in the three categories of the commons – resources, commoners and commoning processes – during the emergence and evolution of the cooperative model can help us throw light upon its nature as housing commons. In the 1890s and 1900s, the earliest cooperatives, driven by a defensive impulse to de-commodify homes, were set up by members of the lower middle classes that felt vulnerable to the vagaries of the rental market, such as office clerks, teachers and artisans. Despite their lower incomes, they were sufficiently prosperous to be able to secure substantial equities and sufficiently educated to self-organize and articulate their requirements.

The shared resource that resulted from their efforts was mostly a material commons: the housing stock, with a minimum of ancillary common spaces, laundries and courtyards for supervised safe play. An additional immaterial good would have been the resulting security and, perhaps, a sense of commonality among members. Architecturally, at this stage cooperative housing did not differ markedly from other residential multifamily housing types in the city; indeed, in the first cases the cooperative bought existing housing before developing their own. Commoning processes would have been limited to the pooling of resources necessary for the self-financing of each initiative, the buildings' purchase or construction and, finally, collective decisions regarding maintenance, new ventures and new members.

With the penetration of socialist values in the years around the First World War, the cooperative movement gained footing among the working classes, and became marked by a characteristic combination of ideology and pragmatism. This stage in the history of cooperatives represents a unique convergence of political and social agendas, using direct democracy as vehicle for consolidation of the model. Through a succession of referendums, Zurich voters elected officials sympathetic to their cause and adhered to supportive municipal housing policies, lobbied and voted in favour of advantageous financing structures, which in turn rendered the cooperative model affordable to larger swathes of the working population. The commoners at this stage were the newly empowered working-class, cooperative activists, founders and members, as well as politicians. Emil Klöti, the socialist city councillor and later mayor of Zurich, remained an active supporter throughout his long years in office, from 1907 to 1942 (Kurz, 2008, p. 32). While cooperatives grew in terms of member numbers or buildings size, so did their urban impact. The shared resources thus unlocked were the housing commons: the complementary typologies of inner-city 'colony' and suburban garden city, both equipped with natural light, fresh air and varying access to shared recreational spaces, gardens, transport, etc. Commoning practices also grew in complexity at this stage, ranging from strategic voting to self-organizational strategies: grassroots initiatives, acquisition of members by door-to-door recruitment, the drawing up of cooperative charters, citizen participation, etc.

In the years around and following the Second World War, the production of cooperative housing grew to the largest number of units achieved to date, albeit at the expense of self-organizational and participative strategies which were, by then, largely formalized. The material commons became satellite towns and multifamily blocks spread in green Siedlungen in the vicinity of active industrial areas. Commoners mostly subscribed to a nuclear family lifestyle, with the separation of tasks according to gender (productive/non-productive, work and child-rearing). With cooperative run as large social landlords, at this stage commoning practices would have been reduced to largely passive, conventional neighbourhood activities, without a great degree of self-determination or participation in decision-making processes.

The new generation of post-1980 cooperatives oversaw the next great change in the nature of the housing commons at hand, as the cooperative model became the vehicle for different ideological content. If we are to consider their activist origins in the social unrests of the 1980s, underscored by the experimental collectivism of countercultural living, then commons, commoners and commoning processes equally underwent processes of transformation. In the early stages of this revision, the commons were contested properties (empty townhouses, disused industrial buildings) removed from the market, subversively and almost always temporarily, by squatting or neighbourhood activism. These precarious commons were adapted to collective living practices in improvised and provisional ways: roof terraces were inhabited and planted, and facades and balconies were covered in graffiti and inscriptions, meant to mark them visibly and thus differentiate them from the speculative building stock. Notably, this specific iconography was shunned by the first radical co-ops that adhered to a more anonymous urban presence, even though it would be later re-evoked in newly built developments. At this stage, the commoners were represented by a mix of interested actors: squatters and activists belonging to a politicized, youthful middle class; neighbourhood associations and independent professional organizations, such as INURA and Konzeptgruppe Städtebau. Their commoning involved a wide variety of practices, from political protest and occupations to the production of posters and publications, organization of participative events and consultations, to practices of collective living such as communal eating, the organization of communal areas, gardening, childcare, etc.

Since the late 1990s, as the radical cooperatives have grown in size and stature as non-profit developers, the material resources thus unlocked have become increasingly visible: prominent housing blocks with a mix of collective and public programmes, innovative and experimental residential typologies (WG, cluster, etc.). The impact on the fabric of the city has become more clearly and permanently defined, as evidenced by large-scale developments such as Kalkbreite, Zwicky Süd, Hunziker Areal and the recently completed Zollhaus. This stage has been characterized by the institutionalization, under the statutory framework of cooperatives, of the collectivist ideologies that characterized the earlier social movements. The effect of this institutionalization is that commoning practices have grown increasingly specialized, with the creation of consultation processes and focus groups, the formalization of cooperative city alliances, the organization of concept and architectural competitions. Once the resources have been unlocked, they remain distinguishable from market housing by the adoption of communal practices and duties such as food preparation and communal eating, the management and maintenance of shared work and leisure areas, gardening activities, etc. Another difference from market housing lies in the adoption of demanding sustainable policies, both for the buildings which adopt high Minergie standards and for the cooperative members who agree to abide by no-car policies, 2,000 Watt society standards, etc. as conditions of their membership. It is clear that the mode of life thus prescribed is not for general living standards. It requires substantial time investment for self-governance and a greater that usual degree of interaction with neighbours.

The alternative modes of collective living promoted by the newer Zurich cooperatives have been formulated during consultation processes, by focus groups mainly made of middle-class participants. Membership, moreover, is conditional upon adhering to the norms and practices thus established, whether involving administrative meetings, rotating communal duties (cooking, gardening), the energy consumption controls or car ownership. On the basis of their communing practices, these cooperatives constitute a contested common, treading a fine line between collectivism and exclusivity: 'plainly put, this type of collective project, involving hours of voluntary work, thus requiring a rather specific lifestyle and cultural capital of a certain kind, is not for everyone' (Balmer and Bernet, 2015, p. 192).

Contested commons

As housing commons, the Zurich cooperatives appear to access the resources of shelter, communality and urbanity in highly specific, perhaps unique ways. Not only do they build up upon a historically established set of instruments for the decommodification of housing, but they demand commitment, time for self-organization and governance, an increased sense of personal responsibility and tolerance towards others, and the curtailment of some individual liberties, such as car ownership. The sharing of communal spaces, particularly in cluster apartments, makes additional demands upon the sense of privacy and individual entitlement that has become largely acceptable in current developed societies, and can be more readily accepted by people with similar backgrounds, norms and values. These conditions also prescribe the make-up of the commoners, who often comprise a mixture of middle-class families and less privileged groups or individuals, and for whom the alternative living models veer imperceptibly between lifestyle choice and necessary imposition.

In these conditions, how inclusive are these commons? What is their role, as built figures and hubs of urbanity in the city fabric, or as tightly knit communities in an urban, multicultural, diverse society? To probe this latest question, it is useful to consider the distinction between 'community' and 'public' proposed by architect and commons theoretician Stavros Stavrides:

> The community refers to an entity, mainly of a homogeneous group of people, whereas the idea of the public puts an emphasis on the relation between different communities. The public realm can be considered as the actual or virtual space where strangers and different people or groups with diverging forms of life can meet. The notion of the public urges our thinking about the commons to become more complex. The possibility of encounter in the realm of the public has an effect on how we conceptualize commoning and sharing. We have to acknowledge the difficulties of sharing as well as the contests and negotiations that are necessarily connected with the prospect of sharing. This is why I favour the idea of providing ground to build a public realm and give opportunities for discussing and negotiating what is good for all, rather than the idea of strengthening communities in their struggle to define their own commons. Relating commons to groups of similar people bears the danger of eventually creating closed communities. People thus may define themselves as commoners by excluding others from their milieu, from their own privileged commons. Conceptualizing commons on the basis of the public, however, does not focus on similarities or commonalities but on the very differences between people that can possibly meet on a purposefully instituted common ground. (De Angelis and Stavrides, 2010, p. 12)

It is significant in this respect that the newer generation of Zurich cooperatives has insisted on providing 'more than living' (Hugentobler et al., 2016). Translated into commons logic, this highlights the importance of the immaterial commons promoted besides the housing itself: commonality, convenience, safety, urbanity. One of the core concepts of the new cooperatives is a claim to the 'right to the city', reciprocally articulated as holding a responsibility towards the urban realm. Their programmatic porosity and mixed programming represent a gesture oriented outwards, towards the city and its inhabitants. The concept with which the Kalkbreite cooperative won the bid for the site was 'eine Stück Stadt' (a piece of the city), accepting the encounters and juxtapositions of interests specific to urban public life. And yet, its base of public venues, shops and restaurants, do not fully counter the inwardness articulated by the architecture. As an urban proposition, Kalkbreite and its equivalents cannot fully counter the suspicion that Stavrides harbours towards 'the idea that we can build our own small enclaves of otherness, our own liberated strongholds that could protect us from the power of the state' (De Angelis and Stavrides, 2010, p. 18). This leaves an open question addressed to the collective architectural and societal proposition of the new Zurich cooperatives. As housing commons, they do not (cannot) offer a simple, universal or mainstream solution to a general lack of affordable housing. This is because they are tied in with a collectivist cultural mentality that ultimately rejects libertarianism. The idea of cooperatives alleviates the larger problem of affordable housing by bringing into question the right to unlimited freedoms, by acknowledging that the nature of citizenship entails responsibilities and duties that forego private interest. It is in this additional sense that 'de-commodification' may be understood: not merely as the removal of the housing from the market and the rejection of short-term profit but also as the voluntary relinquishing of a few individual freedoms for the benefit of many.

References

Balmer, I. & Bernet, T. (2015) 'Housing as a Common Resource? Decommodification and Self–organization in Housing–Examples from Germany and Switzerland', in Mary Dellenbaugh (ed.) *Urban Commons: Moving Beyond State and Market*. Bauwelt Fundamente. Gütersloh; Basel: Bauverlag; Birkhäuser, 178–195.

Blum, M., Hofer, A. & P. M. (1993) *Kraftwerk1: Projekt für das Sulzer-Escher Wyss Areal*. Zürich: Paranoia-City.

De Angelis, M. & Stavrides, S. (2010) Beyond Markets or States: Commoning as Collective Practice. Public Interview with Massimo de Angelis (Political Economist, University of East London) and Stavros Stavrides (Architect, National Technical University of Athens). *AN Architektur: Produktion und Gebrauch gebauter Umwelt*, 23, 1–26.

De Angelis, M. & Stavrides, Stavros (2010) On the Commons: A Public Interview with Massimo De Angelis and Stavros Stavrides. *e-flux Journal*, 17. [online]. Available from: http://www.e-flux.com/journal/17/67351/on -the-commons-a-public-interview-with-massimo-de-angelis-and-stavros -stavrides/.

Durban, C., ed. (2007) *Mehr als Wohnen: gemeinnütziger Wohnungsbau in Zürich, 1907–2007: Bauten und Siedlungen*. Zürich: Stadt Zürich; gta-Verlag.

Harvey, D. (2013) *Rebel Cities: From the Right to the City to the Urban Revolution*. Paperback ed. London: Verso.

Hofer, A. (2004) 'Postindustrial Zurich −15 Years in Search for a New Paradigm of Public Planning', in Raffaele Paloscia & INURA (Org.) (eds.) *The Contested Metropolis: Six Cities at the Beginning of the 21st Century.* Basel; Boston: Birkhäuser, 247–52.

Hofer, A. (2011) Von der Familienwohnung zum Cluster-Grundriss. *Tec21* 23(7), 23–32.

Hugentobler, M. et al., eds. (2016) *More than Housing: Cooperative Planning – A Case Study in Zürich.* Edition Wohnen. Basel: Birkhäuser.

Kälin, A. (2013) *Die Fierz-Häuser als Vorläufer genossenschaftlichen Bauens* | *NZZ* [online]. Available from: https://www.nzz.ch/zuerich/die-fierz-haeuser-als-vorlaeufer-genossenschaftlichen-bauens-1.17991325 (Accessed 18 July 2020).

Kemeny, J. (2005) "The Really Big Trade-Off" between Home Ownership and Welfare: Castles' Evaluation of the 1980 Thesis, and a Reformulation 25 Years on. Housing, Theory and Society. [Online] 22(2), 59–75. [online]. Available from: http://www.tandfonline.com/doi/abs/10.1080/14036090510032727 (Accessed 3 September 2018).

Kurz, D. (2008) *Die Disziplinierung der Stadt: moderner Städtebau in Zürich ; 1900 bis 1940.* Zürich: gta Verl.

Kurz, D. (2014) *Die Genossenschaft baut mit an einer besseren Menschengemeinschaft. Wurzeln und Entwicklungslinien des gemeinnützigen Wohnens* [online]. Available from: http://www.wbg-h.ch/wp-content/uploads/2012/04/Geschichte-des-genossenschaftlichen- Wohnungsbaus-in-Z.%C3%BCrich.pdf (Accessed 1 February 2016).

Kurz, Daniel (2017) 'City and Cooperatives, a Housing Policy Symbiosis', in Dominique Boudet (ed.) *New Housing in Zurich. Typologies for a Changing Society.* Zurich: Park Book. pp. 31–7.

Ostrom, E. (1990) *Governing the* Commons: The *Evolution of* Institutions *for* Collective Action. *The Political Economy of Institutions and Decisions.* Cambridge; New York: Cambridge University Press.

P. M. (1983) *Bolo'bolo.* Zürich: Verlag Paranoia City.

P. M. (1985) *Stauffacher, Aussersihl über die inventiven Kräfte der neuen Weltgesellschaft.* Zürich: Verlag der Inventiven Kräfte.

Rieger, H. J. (1975) Farbige Genossenschaftskolonien in Zürich 1913–1933/ Colonies coopératives d'habitations colorées à Zurich, de 1913 à 1933. *Werk (Bern, Switzerland).* [Online] 62(3), 253–9.

Schärer, Caspar (2017) 'From the Disciplining of the City to the Urban Archipelago', in Dominique Boudet (ed.) *New Housing in Zurich. Typologies for a Changing Society.* Zurich: Park Book. pp. 23–7.

Stadt Zürich (2011) *Zürich stimmt ab 27.11.2011. Wohnpolitischer Grundsatzartikel in der Gemeinde ordnung: 'Bezahlbare Wohnungen für Zürich'* [online]. Available from: https://www.stadt-zuerich.ch/portal/de/index/politik_u_recht/abstimmungen_u_wahlen/archiv_abstimmungen/vergangene_termine/111127.html (Accessed 24 January 2021).

Stahel, T. & Voegeli, J. (2006) *Wo-Wo-Wonige: Stadt- und wohnpolitische Bewegungen in Zürich nach 1968. 1. Aufl.* Zürich: Paranoia City Verlag.

WOGENO (2018) *Geschichte und Grundgedanke* [online]. Available
    from: https://www.wogeno-zuerich.ch/genossenschaft/geschichte-und
    -grundgedanke/ (Accessed 24 January 2021).
Wohnbaugenossenschaften Schweiz (2020) *Wohnbaugenossenschaften Schweiz –
    Verband der gemeinnützigen Wohnbauträger* [online]. Available from: https://
    www.wbg-schweiz.ch/information/wohnbaugenossenschaften_schweiz
    (Accessed 16 February 2020).
WOHNEN SCHWEIZ (Org.) & Wohnbaugenossenschaften Schweiz. (Org.),
    (2018) *Der gemeinnützige Wohnungsbau in der Schweiz*. Bern: Stämpfli
    Publikationen.
Wolf, S. et al. (2015) *Kalkbreite: ein neues Stück Stadt*. Zürich: Genossenschaft
    Kalkbreite.

7

Urban commoning and popular power[1]

The 'autonomous neighbourhoods' in Mexico City

Stavros Stavrides

Self-managed housing and emancipating inventiveness

The housing question in Mexico (and in most Latin American metropolizes) is directly connected to major challenges to the dominant urban order. Socially marginalized or excluded populations face not only chronic joblessness but also extremely precarious housing conditions. Usually expelled to the peripheries of megacities, such populations either are depending upon ruthless landlords, who charge extreme rents for miserable apartments, or have to improvise in building a shelter in illegal or semi-illegal settlements (*favelas, villas miserias*, etc.)

In such a context, practices of cooperation and collective work are very important for the urban poor. As G. Esteva remarks, the poor can only survive if they combine their efforts, and if they devise ways to share scarce recourses and even scarcer means to use those recourses, whereas the middle classes or the rich can still reproduce themselves by being obstinately clinked to individualism (Esteva 2015).

Sharing and urban commoning, thus, are not practices chosen out of ideological preferences but, rather, essential ways to ensure a somewhat-bearable life for those people. However, through those practices and by evaluating the experiences linked to them, the urban poor probably learn how to take their lives in their hands and how to organize their communities as shared words. Commoning implicitly or explicitly politicizes the excluded populations: it shows them ways to different social relations, ways to different

---

[1] This text is a reworked form of the chapter *Commoning Neighbourhoods: Building Autonomy in Mexico City* included in Stavrides 2019.

economic relations and ways to different forms of common life that depart from dominant individualist principles.

Important experiments of urban commoning and collective self-management have unfolded in the peripheries of one of the largest cities in the world, Mexico City.

Autonomous neighbourhoods, organized by the direct participation of their inhabitants and through explicitly politicized movements, have developed as concrete examples of a different form of social organization based on equality and sharing. Space, territory, plays a crucial role not only in giving ground to those collective experiences but also in shaping them. Such neighbourhoods not only depart from dominant organizational forms of social relations but also explicitly challenge the prevailing characteristics of urban order and urban governance policies meant to sustain it.

One such neighbourhood on the eastern outskirts of the enormous metropolitan agglomeration of Mexico City is located in the Acapatzingo area. The neighbourhood is often referred to as *La Polvorilla*. It is part of an initiative by a movement called *Los Panchos,* which has already established a network of about ten similar neighbourhoods in Mexico City (Velázquez 2014: 103). *La Polvorilla* already has about 3,000 people involved in its development (Figure 7.1).

'In 1995, Cooperativa Acapatzingo, encompassing 596 families of informally employed people purchased in installments an abandoned mine used as a rubble depot to build their homes on the premises' (UN Habitat 2004). The value of land was very low and the area was situated at the periphery of the city amid an amorphous urban sprawl characterized by lack of urban installations and very poor housing conditions. Being a politically oriented initiative based on collective self-management and solidarity, the Cooperativa struggled to stay on the land by establishing an informal camp on the site and kept on demanding the economic support of the local and state urban authorities. Local politicians don't dare to create conflicts that they can't control. So, the Cooperativa finally gained access to a collective loan from the state's *Instituto de Vivienda del Distrito Federal* (Zibechi 2014: 55), a public sector institution established by the Mexican Constitution, which explicitly refers to the right to housing. This loan was based on a thirty-year credit and was meant to be used for the full payment of the land and the design and construction of the housing settlement.

They call this a project of autonomy; in organizing their own community, people manage to create their own spaces, their own forms of publicness. They are working towards energy self-sufficiency by placing solar panels in common spaces. They don't pay for water, but have installed a common

Figure 7.1 La Polvorilla: The semiprivate family yards. (Photograph by Stavros Stavrides.)

water purification installation. They have their own community gardens, a community radio station and other shared infrastructure.

They don't allow the police to enter, but maintain their own justice system – to create conditions of conviviality based on equality. This is an attempt to create a form of social organization independent of the state, free from state surveillance and control. However, they do this not to isolate themselves in an enclave of otherness. Cooperativa Acapatzingo is part of a network of similar initiatives, which advance the political effort of Los Panchos to construct popular power while fighting today for a better life in a huge capitalist metropolis. Cooperativism of such a kind has strong roots in Latin America and is an especially powerful tradition in housing movements (Nahoum 2015)

The second example in Mexico City is also a self-managed neighbourhood created by the *Brújula Roja* (meaning Red Compass) movement.

This neighbourhood is generally based on the Zapatista movement's values and modes of establishing self-governance – the main streets are named for the most important demands and principles of the Zapatista movement, *Democracia, Dignidad, Educación, Información, Salud*, etc. One of the founding members of the neighbourhood describes the beginning of this initiative thus:

Some of us in search for alternatives founded something half anarchist, half *principista* [a view that is against existing political parties and in support of the constitutional guaranties of liberty], half communist. Something in between a party and a brotherhood which aimed to educate without ceasing to fight, to act in solidarity, to help other groups, and to walk with the EZLN [the Zapatista Liberation Army] and the CNI [National Indigenous Congress]. (Pacheco, unpublished text)

The neighbourhood's name, *Tlanezi Calli*, in the Indigenous language of Nahuatl, means *House of the Dawn*. Approximately 1,150 people practice urban autonomy in relation to everyday needs for food, healthcare, education and work in community projects, for example, the construction of an autonomous sewage system. They even have a workshop to make their own clothes. During the recent pandemic crisis initiatives to support the most vulnerable by distributing food, hygienic masks, etc. were developed not only for the members of the community but also for the poor people in the surrounding neglected by the state areas (Figure 7.2).

Tlanezi co-inhabitants established their neighbourhood on a territory at first occupied by their movement and then bought through a collective

Figure 7.2 Tlanezi Calli: Preparing food packets in support of the most vulnerable during the Covid-19 pandemic. (Courtesy Tlanezi Calli archive.)

loan after long negotiations with the local state. They explicitly decided to maintain a collective ownership of land and to build their houses and shared spaces according to agreed-upon rules developed in their assembly. Those who wanted to support individual ownership had to leave the neighbourhood since they did not manage to convince the majority.

As both G. Esteva and R. Zibechi (among many Latin American thinkers) insist, Latin American anti-systemic movements are very much focused on the control, appropriation and transformation of urban (and rural) territory (Escobar 2018; Reyes and Kaufman 2011; Olson 2011). It is through the emergence of 'territories in resistance' (Zibechi 2012) that those 'from below' manage to effectively organize practices and forms of everydayness which shape and promote resistance to dominant life models. Autonomous neighbourhoods are such territories of resistance, and, as in every case in the history of dissident mobilizations, their spaces become not only safe shelters for those who struggle against everyday exploitation, misery and repression but also one of the most necessary means through which new subjects of action emerge.

As Gerardo, an Acpatzingo activist, explains:

> We have decided to create not only housing projects but also communities. For us to create a community means to be able to control our territory, to be able to establish our chosen habits and rules and our ways of solving the problems of living together, and thus, to be able to create our own history. Our own process of constructing autonomy.
>
> We have decided to pass from the project of creating dignified housing conditions to the project of creating a dignified life. This means that we have decided to improve life conditions in our communities by ensuring health, justice and security, as well as a different work logic for all by reconstructing the social fabric (*tejido social*) which is destroyed. The logic of the system is to progress as individuals against the others. Our principles in our organization emerge naturally as a respect for others no matter what color is their skin or what language they speak. What we all have in common is that they are fucking us, that we are poor. (interviewed by the author)

A crucial defining aspect of those autonomous urban communities is that their cohesion is not based on pre-existing and long-established shared identities as is the case of indigenous communities. Clarifying this difference, Gerardo says,

> Here we belong to different cultures. But we all meet in everyday praxis. Voluntary or community work is something common in indigenous

communities. But in cities, too, a similar tradition exists, so comrades are used to it. Instead of allowing a culture to dominate all the others we combine them: e.g. in common feasts many different cultures coexist (mainly of those who come from south Mexico). This is how to create a shared culture; we don't think any culture represents absolute truth. Knowledge is produced collectively and through combinations and synthesis. The feeling of belonging to a community is deeply rooted. (Zibechi 2012)

Zibechi too refers to the 'communitarian nature of Mexican *colonias* [urban housing areas]' (Zibechi 2014: 57). From this value system, a counter-dominant approach to cultural difference and individual particularity springs. This may be clearly shown in the ways such communities deal with pressing everyday social problems.

We are part of the society so we have difficulties with intra-family violence, addictions, everything. The difference is in how we deal with these problems. It would be very simple when we identify someone as alcoholic or drug addict to expel him from our communities but we would not differ from what the system does to us: the system does not want us because we dress in a certain way or speak in a certain way, it does not want us because we are poor. We don't intend or want to reproduce this logic of the system. What we try to do, in direct confrontation with this logic, is to create our own forms [of living together]. (Gerardo interview Zibechi 2014)

Accommodating otherness, then, is an essential constituent of autonomous neighbourhoods' commoning culture. A shared experience of being the potential (or, often, actual) outcasts of the system not only unites those people but also teaches them. This is not a struggle of brave and 'uncontaminated' idealists. 'We are not pure', say the Zapatistas (Esteva 2015: 90). 'All of us are crippled – some physically, some mentally, some emotionally' (Illich et al. in Esteva 2015). Realizing that striving to create a different community does not immediately release you from the devastating behaviour control imposed by dominant rules and values is an important lesson being learnt collectively in those neighbourhoods. So, space and community rules are always developed in a process of expanding the emancipating potentialities of commoning and self-management.

In Acapatzingo community, space production and maintenance are highly indicative of an ongoing struggle to create shared spaces, which, however, host the differentiated needs of different inhabitant groups.

Grouped around nine open squares with trees and ample open space, houses form smaller neighbourhoods of twenty to thirty individual two-story units. The square for the elderly is different from the square for the young people but both offer opportunities for mixed uses and creative encounters. Street pavements in which rich everyday socialization experiences unfold (including inventive children play) are wide and safe. The main street named Pancho Villa after the leader of Mexican Revolution (who is the central inspiring figure for Los Panchos) is a friendly outdoor space with few cars passing in very low speed. A community garden not only develops in the direction of establishing food sovereignty for the neighbourhood but also gives opportunities for collective creative work and for cultivating a different approach to nature:

> One of the main objectives of our urban agriculture commission is [to promote] the rescue of the earth, the love of the earth. . . . I don't know how it is in Greece, but here when we ask a child where does the food come from, it will answer from the market or from the Wallmart [American supermarket chain]. We have lost our rural origins, our farming descent. (Gerardo interview Esteva 2015)

While observing architectural elements, which usually regulate a clear and decisively marked transition from outside public space to inside private space, one can recognize in autonomous neighbourhoods an effort to shape different spatial relations based on different levels and forms of sharing. Thus, in Acapatzingo the outside is truly common space, while the inside, although it is family space (including spaces of family privacy), it is also part of a chain of spaces that characterizes house groups which have a distinct colour so as to indicate that they belong to the same group of collective work, a *brigada*. Small family courtyards, which are used especially by the women in their everyday house work, are separated from outside space by a perforated wall. This kind of outside border, a choice made by the general assembly, becomes an active threshold that both ensures and expresses in architectural form the precarious and precious connection of family life to outdoor activities (both common and 'private'). Pursuing similar aims, the *El Molino* autonomous neighbourhood assembly decided to plan and construct houses that have kitchens located in the house front so that mothers may see the children playing outside (Zibechi 2014: 52). It was the women's knowledge and active participation in the planning assemblies that provided such crucial insights to the design of the settlements (Gerardo interview Zibechi 2014). Juarez-Galeana explicitly refers to a relevant participatory planning workshop which took place in *La Polvorilla* (2006: 192)

In *Tlanezi Calli*, in front of each house's central door there is a threshold space, a small courtyard which is open but also clearly marked as distinct from the pedestrian streets that shape the settlement's circulation network (no cars are allowed in this housing area). This space becomes an area of family identity expression: each household has different ways to project such a shared collective identity (flower ports, decorative elements, mundane objects indicating everyday habits, etc.), although this may not always be the result of a conscious 'popular design' choice. The fact that those entrances are organized in pairs by the overall plan creates interesting juxtapositions and comparisons. A peculiar window opening connects those adjacent threshold areas giving to neighbouring families the opportunity to further develop or regulate the sharing of space.

Space commoning in autonomous metastatic communities

Autonomous neighbourhoods constitute experiments in community organization, collective efforts to create shared worlds in which the urban poor organize to protect themselves from the devastating exploitation conditions that prevail in the city. It is important to understand how those shared worlds are being shaped through practices of collaboration and rules that establish equality. And it is the community as a generator and a protector of these shared worlds that defines both the relevant practices and the spaces to house and promote them.

> The prime essence (*instancia superior*) of our communities is the general assembly (every week, every 15 days or every month depending on the rules of the corresponding neighbourhood), and then is the everyday work which is realized through seven different commissions of our organization: the economic commission, the maintenance commission (responsible for the water and electricity supply as well as for square and garden management), the vigilance commission (which guards our community – police is not allowed to enter – and which solves 'social situations' that arise in our community), . . . the education and culture commission,. . . . the communication commission (also responsible for our community radio station), . . . the urban agriculture commission and the health commission (including volunteers for health services – *promotores de salud*). (Gerardo interview *La Polvorilla* 2006)

The social organization of the autonomous community, then, is deeply rooted on a collective care for the goods and services, which are considered as common. These are to be shared equally with an extra attention for those members who are in most need. Community, thus, is not focused on a technical resource management but develops, instead, a participative form of government which encourages solidarity and builds popular power 'from below'. A constituent part of this model is the creation of everyday social bonds through organized groups of collaboration.

'In our communities we are organized in brigades. Each brigade has 20-25 persons and 7 of them are responsible for connecting the brigade with each one of the seven community commissions' (*La Polvorilla* 2006). Members of the brigade alternate in various duties and, through this procedure, they not only share the burdens of everydayness but also learn how to do things useful for themselves and to the community (like how to organize a radio programme, or how to make a blanket or maintain a garden). As already mentioned, the houses of those who belong to the same brigade have the same colour that is different from the colour of the others.

In *Acapatzingo* autonomous neighbourhood, the inhabitants' community established different shared spaces, spaces that can be considered not only as communal spaces but also as common spaces. This distinction becomes crucial if we aim at tracing the commoning potentialities which grow in such socio-spatial arrangements.

Within the perimeter of the neighbourhood, shared spaces are spaces of public use predominately for the members of the community. Those include streets, squares, meeting open spaces in which assemblies may take palace (including a football field), urban gardens and community facilities areas (a water tank, a community radio office, a preparatory school and a pharmacy). We can call those spaces communal spaces, recognizing that commoning practices develop in them under rules established by the community assembly. Community members may use those spaces and are also responsible for their construction, maintenance and protection. Commoning, thus, is especially limited to community members who participate equally in the various commoning practices. However, as Enrique Reynoso, an Acapatzingo activist, explains in an interview with R. Zibechi, 'We are a utopia that is not an island, but rather an open space that can have a contagious effect on society' (Zibechi 2014: 58). Acapatzingo community establishes multiple links with its surrounding neighbourhoods, 'training them [the inhabitants of those neighbourhoods] in the creation of base-level committees and community security; they also provide advice about how to respond to evictions, which recipients repay in food' (Zibechi 2014).

Following a similar path of osmotic relations with their urban surrounding, *Tlanezi Calli* has developed a community centre, which is located at the perimeter of the neighbourhood and has its own distinct entrance. Neighbours and people in need may enter the building and ask for help and support by the community's services (including a pharmacy, a common kitchen, a small preparatory class for school students, etc.).

This centre is more like an osmotic urban threshold that not only separates but also connects the heart of the autonomous neighbourhood with the nearby urban housing areas.

We can then guess that in their contagious relations with the rest of the city autonomous communities actually develop practices of expanding commoning (Stavrides 2016). People from outside the neighbourhood are not simply allowed to use certain of the community facilities (the preparatory school, the pharmacy or the community building during organized open feasts), but they are invited to be part of a process that attempts to metastasize throughout the city. Can we not then consider the corresponding communal spaces as common spaces in the making? Can we not see such spaces as potential catalysts in a commoning chain reaction?

Explicitly referring to the prospect of transplanting the urban commoning momentum developed in autonomous neighbourhoods to other urban self-management efforts, Enrique Reynoso says in another interview: 'Rather than grow the scale of our assemblies, we want the assemblies to multiply in other places, in whatever ways are appropriate' (Barrington-Bush 2016). Interestingly, this approach has created similar experiments of autonomous neighbourhoods in Mexico City. One of them, called *Xochitlanezi* (the Flower of the Dawn in Nahuatl), was born out of a group of young activists who had their assemblies in Tlanezi while preparing to occupy and claim an empty unused plot in a nearby area. Developing the values and aspirations of the urban community that hosted them, Xochitlanezi activists plan a neighbourhood of advanced collective facilities and organized common life.

Autonomous neighbourhoods actually participate actively in the promotion of collective resistance initiatives by becoming part of urban struggles, of campaigns and of movement networks. As Sergio, a member of *Tlanezi Calli*, remembers, the neighbourhood actively mobilized in support of the major struggle of Atenco farmers in 2006 when the neighbourhood was at the first phase of its construction. Atenco farmers were clashing with state forces at that time in an effort to keep their flower growing lands against a devastating compulsory expropriation order issued by the Mexican state in order to promote a Pharaonic construction project connected to the development of the city's airport. Tlanezi people decided to block those streets near their neighbourhood which were to be used by police to attack the

Atenco movement. Of course, they too had to confront the police riot squads because of their resistance, but they have managed to make it substantially more difficult for the harsh suppression of the struggle to become effective (as Sergio remarks while interviewed by the author). Blocking the suppressive mechanisms of the state is as much part of the community's struggle for a more just society as it is its members' effort to organize alternative forms of living together, of sharing a common world in the making.

A shared territory

The definition of a shared territory became crucial for the autonomous urban communities of Tlanezi Calli and Acapatzingo. By observing the forms through which this definition is materialized, one may further understand the ways those communities are connected to their territories.

Obviously, a gate explicitly marks an 'inside' and an 'outside'. And, of course, this impression is enhanced by the presence of guardians. A gate regulates and controls a passage. We can then talk about an explicitly circumscribed territory, belonging to a community that is determined to keep it and protect it from tresspassers. In both neighbourhoods, there exist explicit gates guarded by the inhabitants. In Acapatzingo, gates are marked by a recognizable symbol: a big red star denotes the community's shared ideology. Are we witnessing the presence of a gated community, albeit a collectively created one?

Actually, things are more complicated than they may seem. To understand the conditions of such an urban territory definition, we must connect it – and compare it – to another peculiar case of autonomous territory definition, that of the Zapatista *municipios*: One often observes in the Zapatista areas a sign that declares: '*Esta usted en territorio Zapatista en rebeldia. Aqui manda el pueblo y el gobierno obedece*' ('You are in Zapatista territory in rebellion. Here the people dictate and the government obeys'). What, however, is the exact meaning of this 'here'? Where exactly is this area? Does it have clearly demarcated borders? Usually, if not always, it doesn't. Villages in the *municipios* may have inhabitants that are not supporters of Zapatistas. And Zapatista *territorios* are scattered in a vast area, in Chiapas, with lots of non-Zapatista villages in between. The meaning and status quo of the Zapatista area is not based, then, on the existence of a strict borderline that separates it from the rest of the country. In an ongoing contestation with state and paramilitary forces, Zapatista territory is being defined through use and appropriation. Zapatistas have reclaimed vast areas for cultivation which used to belong to local feudal lords. State-defined property limits were and keep on being challenged. And there is a constant pressure from the government to re-establish in the area the rules and regulations of the state. So, Zapatista territory is a way of collectively defining through use and through community-decided rules a kind of shared space (Reyes 2015). Space commoning is based on practices of space appropriation rather than on community-guarded borderlines.

Compared to such a process of defining community space, the gate that clearly marks the area of administration buildings of the so-called *Junta de Buen Gobierno* in Oventic (a Zapatista autonomous small city) seems to belong to a different spatial logic. In this case, the 'here' seems to be clearly marked. However, one can observe that the area has actually rather vague and unprotected limits once one walks away from the buildings and immerses oneself in the surrounding forest. Is it, then, that this gate was not meant exactly to control access to the area but was rather constructed as an emblematic structure that tries to express the stark sociopolitical difference which this form of government explicitly establishes with dominant forms of governance? Is this gate, which hardly defines a closed limited territory, a declaration of difference rather than the imposition of a separation?

Returning back to Tlanezi and Acapatzingo, to those autonomous urban areas explicitly influenced by the Zapatista project of autonomy, one can observe similar characteristics in the definition of shared space. True, the conditions in a city, and, especially in a huge and differentiated city as the city of Mexico, are quite different from the Chiapas *altos* and the Lacandona rain forest villages. Defining space in a city is always an act that has to do with strict property regulations. However, people in the reclaimed land of those autonomous neighbourhoods do not aspire to create their 'own' safe havens in the middle of highly dangerous urban *periferias*. They rather attempt to construct shared housing areas to live in, which may be considered as materialized examples of a different kind of urban cohabitation. So, their gates do not only try to keep outside the threats that come from state or paramilitary forces. This attempt, anyhow, would be as meaningless as it is to barricade an autonomous area in Lacandona. Military or paramilitary forces can't be warded off by the efficiency of gates or borderline constructions but may only be countered by efficient community mobilizations and solidarity networks. So, these neighbourhood gates are more like declarations of autonomy, the way the Oventic gate is. It is not by chance that in Acapatzingo the emblems of the community's values are on the gates to express a meaningful difference. And, of course, in spite of the everyday mundane rituals of gate crossing, those who would want to enter with malignant intentions could almost effortlessly do so from less guarded areas that surround both neighbourhoods.

The fact of controlling a gate through the everyday presence of community members, who rotate in this duty, creates a ceremoniously established feeling of belonging to an autonomous territory. To understand this, it would suffice to observe the determination and even perhaps pride radiating from an old woman standing as a guard in one of the gates of Acapatzingo. She is surely defending something which is more than a territory. She is protecting a way of life which is in stark contrast to the surrounding poor and drug-governed neighbourhood.

Maybe there is a lesson here to be learnt. Space commoning as a crucial aspect of urban autonomy is not necessarily connected to a spatially defined community sovereignty or to the protection of a common property. Space commoning may radiate as a counterexample through territorial relations that are more complex. These relations are being performed in explicit acts of self-governance by and through commoning. And they may be understood only in the context of networks of cooperation and solidarity. Zapatista communities draw their power to exist from the relations of cooperation and mutual support between villages as regulated by the Juntas de Buen Gobierno. And the autonomous urban communities are equally able to establish their presence in the city because they proliferate through networks of mutual help and expanding empowerment. Their strength, symbolically expressed in their gates, is really depended upon those expanding networks. And one of their more powerful means to protect themselves and to flourish is to disconnect the collective imaginary of their inhabitants from the image of a closed growing enclave of otherness.

They are different, and they know it. But they struggle to make this difference important for the lives of those who share with them the same problems of mass expulsion: the urban poor.

The gate considered as an architectural element that shapes spatial relations may seem to be necessarily connected to the definition of controlled passages. However, the experience of the autonomous communities shows that gates can be not only organizational architectural forms but, importantly, expressive elements of a different understanding of territory. A recognizable architectural form, in such a context, becomes the concrete expressive materialization of the values connected to the shared spaces it gives access to. Throughout history, gates have often been connected to dominating values ceremonially expressed. Let us not forget that the triumphal arcs, erected as memorials of an emperor's successful war, were at the beginning only temporary constructions which had the form of gates through which the victorious leader entered the city. So, to reshape the meaning of gates in autonomous Mexican neighbourhoods is part of a process of redefining the public uses and meanings of shared space as common space.

Autonomous neighbourhoods in Mexico City directly challenge the dominant rules of urban governance. Producing in action elements of a popular self-management, they indeed shape a form of social organization in which commoning rather than capitalist command becomes the predominant characteristic.

As we have seen, commoning in such neighbourhoods is not simply a set of sharing practices that assists the urban poor to survive in precarious urban communities, although its importance in collective urban survival is of outmost importance. Commoning becomes the propelling force for the building of different, counter-dominant relations of collaboration and decision making. Urban self-management, considered as a specific counter-dominant model of urban governance, emerges through a set of practices and collective rule-making decisions that establish what participants themselves call autonomy (*autonomias* – in the plural).

Autonomy as a project and as unfolding collective experience does not develop, however, in the form of self-sustained and barricaded enclaves of 'otherness'. It is a metastatic virus-like form of social organization which attempts to establish networks or urban resistance in the process of building potentially emancipative relations of cohabitation. The prefigurative and exemplary elements of these urban practices are firmly based on experiences that people in need develop in their struggle for a decent life. Autonomous neighbourhoods, thus, may be at times tolerated by the dominant urban order, since they appear as a lesser evil compared to the possibility of urban unrest caused by desperate populations. However, they are actually a constant threat to dominant urban governance since they constitute organized shelters for the 'dangerous classes'. Choosing not to be satisfied by their small safe havens in the midst of an urban archipelago of violent clashes and rigid power geometries based on exploitation and segregation, autonomous neighbourhoods actively politicize their existence. They become condensers, catalysts and often igniters of urban struggles. And they show in practice that a different form of urban governance based on sharing, equality and solidarity is not only possible but also urgently needed. Against the highly discriminatory policies of the Mexican state, which is becoming more and more the arena of rivalling elites, and against the local mafias (connected in various ways with the economic and political elites), which impose harsh rules in the neighbourhoods of the poor, *autonomias* build a structure of self-government based on the sharing of power. If urban commoning may acquire the power to challenge capitalist urban governance, it will be through such organized struggles for building metastatic shared worlds, in and against the dominant urban order.

References

Barrington-Bush, L. (2016) 'Defeating Fear. Lessons from Mexico's Housing Movement'. Available at https://roarmag.org/essays/defeating-fear-lessons-mexicos-housing-movement/

Escobar, A. (2018) *Designs for the Pluriverse*. Durham, NC: Duke University Press.

Esteva, G. (2012) 'Hope From the Margins'. In D. Bollier and S. Helfrich (eds.) *The Wealth of the Commons. A World beyond Market and State*. Amherst, MA: Levellers Press. pp. 192–8.

Esteva, G. (2015) 'Enclosing the Enclosers: Autonomous Experiences from the Grassroots – beyond Development, Globalization and Postmodernity'. In F. Luisetti, J. Pickles and W. Kaiser (eds.) *The Anomie of the Earth. Philosophy, Politics, and Autonomy in Europe and the Americas*. Durham: Duke University Press. pp. 71–92.

Juarez-Galeana, L. G. (2006) 'Collaborative Public Open Space Design in Self-help Housing: Minas-Polvorilla, Mexico City'. In Roger Zetter and Georgia Butina Watson (eds.) *Designing Sustainable Cities in the Developing World*. Aldershot: Ashgate. pp. 179–96.

Nahoum, B. (2015) 'El Movimiento Cooperativista del Uruguay. autogestion, ayuda mutua, aporte proprio, propiedad collectiva'. In A. del Castillo and R. Valles (eds.) *Cooperativas de Vivienda en Uruguay*. Montevideo: Facultad de Architectura. pp. 36–47.

Olsson, J. (ed.) (2011) *El Camino Posible. Produccion del Habitat en America Latina*. Montevideo: Trilce.

Pacheco, S. (unpublished text). De donde venimos.

Reyes, A. (2015) 'Zapatismo: Other Geographies circa "The End of the World"'. *Environment and Planning D: Society and Space*, 33, pp. 408–24.

Reyes, A. and Kaufman, M. (2011) 'Sovereignty, Indigeneity, Territory: Zapatista Autonomy and the New Practices of Decolonization'. *The South Atlantic Quarterly*, 110(2), pp. 505–25.

Stavrides, S. (2016) *Common Space. The City as Commons*. London: Zed Books.

Stavrides, S. (2019) *Common Spaces of Urban Emancipation*. Manchester: Manchester University Press.

Torres Velazquez, E. (2014) 'A Pancho Villa no lo enterramos, lo sembramos. FPFVI-UNOPII, Comunidad de comunidades en la Ciudad de México'. *El Canelazo de la Ciudad*, 3 pp. 100–11.

UN Habitat (2004) 'Architecture and Urban Design Including Landscape and Cultural Recovery in the Housing Project "Minas Polvorilla"'. Available at http://mirror.unhabitat.org/bp/bp.list.details.aspx?bp_id=501

Zibechi, R. (2012) *Territories in Resistance. A Cartography of Latin American Movements*. Oakland: AK Press.

Zibechi, R. (2014) 'Mexico: Challenges and Difficulties of Urban Territories in Resistance'. In R. Stahler-Sholk, H. E. Vanden and M. Becker (eds.) *Rethinking Latin American Social Movements*. Lanham: Rowman and Littlefield. pp. 49–65.

8 .

Berlin and the city as commons

Christian Hiller, Anh-Linh Ngo and Max Kaldenhoff

(The conversation took place within the context of the project *An Atlas of Commoning: Places of Collective Production*, a touring exhibition developed by ARCH+ and the Carnegie Mellon University School of Architecture, presented by the Institut für Auslandsbeziehungen (ifa), and edited for and published in *ARCH+ 232, An Atlas of Commoning: Places of Collective Production*, 2018.)

Reprinted here by the kind permission of Anh-Linh Ngo, Herausgeber/ Editor-in-Chief ARCH+.

Interview

Anh-Linh Ngo: Mathias, you arrived at the theme of the 'commons' via the East Berlin squatters' movement in the immediate post-unification years, and also the more recent right to the city movement. Can you describe your journey to this topic from your practice as an architect who teaches and researches, and is also an activist. What is 'commoning' for you?

Mathias Heyden: Though the English terms 'commoning' or 'commons' are widely used in Germany, I prefer the German terms of *Gemeinschaffen* [literally accomplishing things in common] or *Gemeingüter* [literally common goods] because they are more explicit. Both terms raise the question of how goods are understood and dealt with in common. This category includes material and immaterial goods, both natural resources and commonly (re)produced goods. These are neither public nor private; they belong to everyone and no one. The idea provokes fundamental emotions, thoughts and actions that require, on an individual and collective level, a debate about principles, rather than about ideology or party politics.

To answer your question, I have to speak about my experience of Berlin's urban development from a top-down perspective as well as a bottom-up one.

I came to West Berlin in the autumn of 1987, and so for two years before the fall of the Wall, I had the chance to get an impression of the collective do-it-yourself urban culture back then, above all in Kreuzberg and Schöneberg. By that point, more than half of the around 200 squatted buildings which existed in the early 1980s had already been evicted. However, many squatted buildings, as well as other grassroots initiatives at a wide range of Berlin locations, could be kept going due to substantial resources, which the 'careful urban renewal' carried out under the auspices of the Internationale Bauausstellung 1984–7, above all the IBA-Alt, directed towards the restoration and modernization of late nineteenth-century properties. This context brought together a wide variety of protagonists, including activists, scholars, planners, non-profit economists and politicians who addressed themes like participation and environmental protection. It was also in this context that the 'Third Way' was frequently invoked as a strategy for societal policy when it came to questions like self-empowerment, self-organization and self-management.

ALN: What were your hopes with regard to the 'Third Way', which has a long tradition in twentieth-century political theory in looking for an alternative between capitalism and communism?

MH: The opening of the Berlin Wall meant that, literally overnight, thousands of properties in the centre of East Berlin became available for an alternative development: empty apartments, commercial premises, buildings and vacant lots. But from a political point of view, no choice was made to make progressive use of this situation: while in the East, 'actually existing socialism' had become obsolete, the capitalist West was dominated by the inert Helmut Kohl era. Given the experiences of the East German civil rights movement, which had played a fundamental role in the central roundtable discussions after the fall of the Wall, one of the demands raised was the development of a new constitution for the reunited Germany in grassroots processes. But in early 1990, the eastern version of the Christian Democrats won the first and last East German parliamentary elections. That, and the introduction of the Deutschmark in East Germany that summer, made it clear there would be no large-scale reorientation of society along a Third Way. Nonetheless, many people active in Berlin hoped that some kind of a Third Way could be implemented at least in urban development. It felt like all this urban space was at our feet; people had the knowhow and the means to carry out bottom-up processes of occupation and design. So, looking back, I would say that the fights for the free spaces of West and East Berlin were also about a desire for the city as commons.

ALN: In *The Property Issue*, Marija Maric describes one possible Third Way: socialized property in the former Yugoslavia. This was a kind of property based on self-management, neither publicly nor privately owned.[1] In terms of socio-spatial practices, what were the characteristics of Berlin's Third Way?

MH: From the middle of the 1980s onwards, after the crushing of the West Berlin squatters' movement – a campaign driven by the media and carried out by the police – it was less about socio-spatial alternatives, and more and more about finding alternative legal and economic frameworks. People living in buildings that were squatted between 1979 and 1984 in West Berlin either had to find individual contractual solutions, or else faced eviction. In addition, a long tenancy contract was needed in order to get public funding to restore and modernize the buildings. This was often urgently necessary.

Some of them bought the buildings they had occupied and created civil law associations [*GbR, Gesellschaft bürgerlichen Rechts*], which today is a very customary form of legal and economic association for *Baugruppen* [self-initiated co-housing projects in form of privately owned condominium associations]. Others formed non-profit associations, and concluded leasehold agreements, with church congregations or with foundations specially created for that purpose, for example.

Another possibility was collaboration with long-established housing cooperatives or with new ones, so as to keep the occupied building off the market. The idea was to establish decentralized legal and economic frameworks that were based on local participation in order to help related forms of socio-spatial practices to survive in the long term.

Christian Hiller: I find it remarkable that those kinds of processes had such broad support back then, including politicians and local administrators showing real engagement (even if it was extracted under pressure) in rethinking urban development; today, there are very few initiatives and projects which have that kind of intensive debate with politicians and local administrators. What was the dominant sociopolitical mood at the time?

[1]   Marija Maric, 'Property is a Verb: On Social Ownership in Yugoslavia', *The Property Issue* (Aachen: ARCH+, March 2018), 70ff.

MH: I'd like to come back to the period after 1989, above all because
from 1992 on I closely followed the development of the area around
Kastanienallee in Prenzlauer Berg. For many residents of Prenzlauer
Berg, both long-standing and newly arrived, questions of the Third
Way were still very much alive, whether through ideas of democratic
socialism, ecological municipalism, or some other bottom-up models
of society.

At the same time, the second wave of the squatting movement – which
emerged between the end of 1989 and the summer of 1990 in the centre
of what was East Berlin – faced the same 'Eat or Die' principle that West
Berlin activists had to confront in the 1980s. Around 130 buildings were
squatted in East Berlin: of these, about 100 went for an individual contract.
The remaining buildings were evicted, eventually. Frequently, the legalized
squatters encountered institutions, organizations, networks, groups and
individuals who had been involved in the 1980s and who had tried to translate
the spirit of grassroots democracy into their own particular practice.

CH: Which experiences stay with you from that time?
MH: In 1992, I took part in the action *Besetzn – Kunst – 1. Hilfe*
[Squatting – Art – First aid]: the occupation of Kastanienallee 77
[K 77], one of the oldest residential and commercial developments
in Prenzlauer Berg, originally from the mid-nineteenth century,
which had been sitting vacant for many years. Later, the
neighbourhood was declared the 'Teutoburger Platz Redevelopment
Area' and assigned to the S·T·E·R·N Gesellschaft der behutsamen
Stadterneuerung mbH [S·T·E·R·N Society for Careful Urban
Renewal], the successor organization to the IBA-Alt. We met with
alternative-minded planners, who explained their thinking for
the area around K 77. One suggestion was to cooperate with other
buildings in creating a combined heat and power plant, so as to
move away from coal heating, which was very common at the time.
Another suggestion was to cut passages through the very long block,
passing through our inner courtyard and the neighbouring ones. It
may sound banal, but I mention it because our communication was
on an urban planning level, not an architectural one. The planners
tried to make us understand that our ideas for K 77 would not
work if applied citywide, but that some aspects of our agenda were
very much of interest. We were exchanging views about the bigger
picture, about how people working with individual buildings could
contribute to the neighbourhood's collective development. Finally, it

Figure 8.1 K 77 studio, Berlin. (Photograph by Stavros Stavrides.

was also a matter of integrating us into the careful urban renewal of the eastern parts of Berlin. Some activists in Prenzlauer Berg rightly criticized this as a kind of pacification. However, just as crucial for that culture of discussion was the existence of the *Runder Tisch Instandbesetzung* ['Restoration squatting' roundtable] in Prenzlauer Berg (Figure 8.1).

ALN: What was the significance of this roundtable?

MH: Concerning the K 77, this roundtable met regularly for two years, from the action *Besetzn – Kunst – 1. Hilfe* until shortly before the agreement of a leasehold with *Umverteilen! Stiftung für eine, solidarische Welt* [Redistribute! Foundation for One Solidary World]. Looking back, I would say it was a crucial tool for creating urban development from bottom-up, and it can be regarded as a form of urban commoning. To sum up the mixture of factors:

1. Highly energized feelings, thoughts and actions within civil society
2. Unbureaucratic and/or affordable access to spaces
3. Left-alternative protagonists, both experienced and new, within the political and administrative spheres, in planning and architecture,

project development and project management, who were serious
about participation
4. Substantial public funds, which made the development of a
neighbourhood in the sense of the city as commons not only
imaginable but also in some places even a reality.

CH: In 2004, a key moment of historical transition, you and Jesko
Fezer together published the book *Hier entsteht. Strategien
partizipativer Architektur und räumlicher Aneignung* [Under
Construction: Strategies of Participatory Architecture and Spatial
Appropriation]. The book offers wide-ranging insights into
theories and practices of participation and self-empowerment
in planning and building since the 1960s, including experts
from Berlin's bottom-up scene, like raumlabor Berlin and Urban
Catalyst. This publication can be seen as a counter-position to Hans
Stimmann who, as the city-governments building director, had
dominated Berlin's urban development since the 1990s. Stimmann's
masterplan, the *Planwerk Innenstadt* [Inner City Plan], aimed at
dismantling the modernist heritage through what is known as
'critical reconstruction'.[2] Seen from today, the plan's failure was not
the result of the many voices which were raised in opposition to its
middle-class-driven neoconservatism. What was far more decisive
was the 'shortage' of wealthy Berliners who Stimmann and others
imagined as the developers of their market-conformist 'European
city'. The sites in question were filled and still mostly are being
filled by real estate consortia and other speculators. What does
that mean for the protagonists you have named, who had certainly
tried out many different concepts and models, but whose promising
toolbox could only make marginal inroads with politicians and
administrators?
MH: In my opinion, at least since the end of 1990s, as far as the
eastern inner city is concerned, it's been like: *OK, the fun's
over now.* Actually, even at the beginning of that decade it was
clear that a Third Way was not going to be feasible, despite the
aforementioned successful cooperations. Obviously, what was fatal
for any form of urban development driven by civil society was,
first, the over-hasty introduction of West German currency in
the summer of 1990 and, second, the decision to put roughly the
entirety of the East German public property up for sale on the open

2   See ARCH+ 122, *Von Berlin nach Neuteutonia* (April 1994).

market. The maxim 'restitution takes priority over compensation' basically destroyed most of East Germany's urbanistic achievements. Of course, in 2001, there was some hope that Berlin's first ruling coalition between the Social Democrats (SPD) and the PDS,[3] the left-wing successor to the East German ruling party, would result in at least a partial change of course. Instead, the sell-off of the city, begun under the leadership of the Christian Democrats in the previous decade, began to pick up speed.

CH: I had to deal with the consequences of this policy in the context of the project *Wohnungsfrage* [Housing Question], which took place at the Haus der Kulturen der Welt in 2015. What would you say is the current state of the housing question in Berlin?

MH: In recent years, housing has again become a subject of general public discussion. But the issue did not come out of nowhere. To mention a few key factors in its emergence: first, in the 1950s, the incorporation of private economic interests into the West German social housing system. Then there was the abolition of non-profit status for housing in the 1980s, then the capitalist takeover of East German public property.[4] What I should stress here is that of the approximately 600,000 publicly owned housing units that Berlin had in the 1990s, today fewer than 300,000 are part of the provision of affordable homes. To put it another way: in the early 1990s, around one-third of all Berliners lived in public housing, but since then, the figure has shrunk by half. The stock of affordable homes shrank even more due to the requirement that city-owned housing associations break even on their remaining portfolios, as well as the lifting of rent control restrictions on thousands of publicly funded but privately developed and managed housing units.

The first term of the SPD-PDS coalition also saw the founding of Berlin's 'Liegenschaftsfonds', whose purpose was to sell off city-owned property at the highest possible price, if it could not be demonstrated to be essential for the public interests. About the exact same time, you had the reduction of the city's districts from twenty-three to twelve. This made it much harder to maintain the previous closeness between local civil society and district politicians and administrators.

[3]   In 2007, the PDS—the Party of Democratic Socialism – merged with WASG [Labour and Social Justice – The Electoral Alternative] to form a new party, Die Linke.
[4]   See, for example, Andrej Holm, Ulrike Hamann, Sandy Kaltenborn (eds.), *Die Legende vom Sozialen Wohnungsbau, Berliner Hefte zu Geschichte und Gegenwart der Stadt*, no. 2, (Berlin, 2016).

So, the city's housing woes began long before the publication you mentioned earlier. In addition, cheap money flooding the real estate market in the wake of the global banking and economic crisis exacerbated the problem by exponentially intensifying investment in Berlin's 'concrete gold', a process which continues to this day. One of the results of these federal and municipal policies is the gentrification process that threatens to devastate not only individual neighbourhoods but the social fabric of the entire city.

ALN: Many current projects and initiatives that focus on urban development policies seem to be trying to reactivate experiences and tools from the past – the idea of housing cooperatives, for example. Of these ideas, which ones do you think are still significant, which should be taken forward or transformed?

MH: I think it is urgent – and very promising – to look at the urban planning agendas and instruments, in particular those strategies and methods that negotiate a building with its surroundings. In other words, how you take on a housing block, in terms of urban planning, morphology and social space, and how you seriously support participation and affordable living within a neighbourhood as a whole. Of course, you have to know that back then there were substantial public funds available for the equivalent work done by organizations like S·T·E·R·N and other intermediary agents. These resources weren't just for participatory planning processes: they also helped in implementing the building solutions that the processes came up with.

ALN: How do you judge recent developments like *Baugruppen* [self-initiated co-housing projects], which urban activists tend to look at with ambivalence?

MH: I have always looked at this form of private ownership – which self-initiated co-housing projects in form of condominium associations are, in the end – with a critical eye. Still, in my view, the experiences of such city-makers have to be included into our discussion. After all, their practices have been part of a collective do-it-yourself Berlin development since the mid-2000s. The projects have generally been executed without public subsidy, but often with serious ambitions in terms of architectural design and ecological sustainability. Of course, in most cases these ventures do not follow the principles of commoning but of private property. Nonetheless, I think even such self-initiated co-housing projects can be regarded as a possible approach towards urban participation. Their experiences of joint liability and collaboration during the planning and construction phase, can lead, in the best-case scenario, to a form of commonality, which can foster social relations and cooperation within the building and, ideally, also on the level of the neighbourhood.

ALN: In *The Property Issue*, which addresses the question of landownership, we discussed the need to go beyond small-scale solutions and to address large-scale land reforms. Land reform has not been seriously debated since the 1970s.

MH: That's right, along with a carefully thought-out development of the agendas and instruments we've already discussed, we have to fight for a land policy that takes Article 14, paragraph 2, of the German constitution seriously: 'Property entails obligations. Its use shall also serve the public good'. This comes down to the ways in which land values are benchmarked and market values are determined in the interest of the common good. It also would mean increased taxation of land and all other real estate profits. In addition, we would need an immediate halt to sales of publicly owned real estate, whether by federal, state or local authorities. Public ownership of land and buildings in the eastern part of the city, as well as substantial public holdings in West Berlin, were essential for the different forms of socially oriented urban development in the two halves of the city. We must emphatically promote the (re-)introduction of these agendas and instruments for asserting the right to the city. No more privatization; instead, accelerated re-communalization and permanent acquisitions of properties by the public sector in order to permanently achieve a spatial provision as public service.

However, in Berlin as commons, essential spatial resources like these cannot be handled from the top-down. To the best of my knowledge, right now the city-owned housing associations are favoured beneficiaries of the distribution of Berlin's remaining public properties. That is understandable, because since recently they have the task of building thousands of affordable housing units. But there are widespread doubts as to how democratic, genuinely transparent and participatory that process actually is. However, I believe that commoning in Berlin – ideally along with complete (self-)empowerment of tenants in public housing stock – should also mean access to public properties and to personal and financial resources for stakeholders like common good-minded co-housing projects, housing cooperatives, non-profit associations and projects within the framework of the *Mietshäuser Syndikat* [tenements' syndicate]. The (re)production of the city should be reflected in a grassroots and diverse landscape of protagonists. Anti-speculative legal and economic models for such practices have been tested for years: we just have to implement and massively multiply them. In addition, there are other models, which are common practice in other countries and could be very promising for Berlin.

ALN: What exactly do you have in mind?

MH: One particularly promising model for Berlin is the Community Land Trust (CLT), which has been practised in the United States since the 1970s. Briefly: CLTs function in a similar way to leasehold contracts, inasmuch as property owners make long-term transfer agreements with users, which guarantee them wide-ranging rights in terms of design, organization and administration. Buildings which have been renovated or developed by users – whether residential, commercial, or other typologies – can be sold on by the user-owners, but with anti-speculative restrictions. One of the decisive differences between CLTs and leasehold contracts is that CLTs are generally not limited to particular parcels of land, they can occupy a whole block or sites distributed around a neighbourhood, or be spread across the entire city. In addition, a CLT can involve very different organizational forms, including single-family homes, apartment buildings and housing cooperatives. Another difference is their pluralistic-democratic character: as a general rule, operations are determined by a democratically elected committee, with one-third of its members made up of users, one-third of activists from the local neighbourhood and one-third of outside experts who support the CLT. The spatial scope and the social framework encourage CLT members to get involved beyond their own community. Another comparably wide-ranging topic is land funds, which have increasingly become a subject of debate, and not just in Berlin.[5]

CH: Earlier, you spoke about 'real' participation. What does that mean for you?

MH: For me, real participation is given when, from beginning to end, people are part of the decision-making process and share responsibility.

ALN: How would you define the difference between participation and commoning?

MH: As I said at the outset, commoning is based on the premise that there are material and immaterial goods – both natural resources and commonly (re)produced goods – which are neither public nor

---

5   See also *The Property Issue* (Aachen: ARCH+, March 2018).

private, and which belong to everyone and no one. Whether it is
about water or fields, meadows or forests, digital resources or the
city itself, at the heart of this idea is always a radical and imaginative
debate about the 'We'. It concerns both individual and collective
ways of feeling, thinking and acting about how we, together,
maintain or establish, develop, design and care for a commons. On
the other hand, for me, participation literally means to have a part in
something specific, some part of the city, for example.

Of course, if it is a question of participation in political and economic power,
it is obvious that you can better achieve things together. But here, the creative
aspect of how the 'We' is formed is secondary. To put it another way, it makes
a difference whether it is about participating in power or about commoning
of power. In this context, Gustavo Esteva, the Mexican philosopher and
activist, uses the idea of *comunalidad*.[6] He says, it 'defines both a collection of
practices formed as creative adaptations of old traditions to resist old and new
colonialisms, and a mental space, a horizon of intelligibility: how you see and
experience the world as a We'. For this reason, participation and commoning
are not identical, but they are interwoven. So, they are both essential aspects
in achieving the right to the city.

ALN: Can you be more specific about that, with reference to current
    initiatives and projects? One of the most compelling concepts for us is
    the *Mietshäuser Syndikat*, which has managed to exert very promising
    leverage against the commodification of living space. It did so
    through a clever interpretation of existing structures: the exemplary
    free-market legal form – the GmbH, or limited liability company – in
    combination with the structure of an association.
MH: In my opinion, because of its political economy, the Mietshäuser
    Syndikat should be regarded as an exponent of urban commoning.
    The property titles for each of the 128 syndicate projects across
    Germany are not held by the individual non-profit association
    [*Hausverein*], made up by the tenants of each building, but by the
    limited liability company associated with the individual building
    [*HausGmbH*]. This limited company has two shareholders: the
    individual *Hausverein* and the Mietshäuser Syndikat GmbH, the
    syndicate as limited liability company formed by all individual

---

[6] 'The foundation and core of comunalidad are: 1) the communal territory, in which 2)
    authority fulfills an organizational function beginning with 3) communal work and 4)
    fiestas, creating a world through 5) the vernacular language,' Gustavo Estava, 'Hope
    from the Margins', wealthofthecommons.org/ essay/hope-margins.

HausGmbHs. Because the syndicate has a say in proceedings, its job is to permanently prevent the sale of the buildings, the conversion of the apartments into private properties, and other, similar attempts in privatizing the real estate assets. Even if an individual *Hausverein* were to cancel its participation in the individual *HausGmbH*, the property title would remain with the syndicate. Apart from the question of ownership, it is the tenants who decide about the everyday matters concerning their house. So, you could speak of a network of urban commons or of a housing commons that is permanently communicating on a national scale, both in terms of political economy and of day-to-day project practice. Resonating within those structures is the 'We' that Esteva talks about.

ALN: Compared to that, the 'We' question worked out somewhat differently in the ExRotaprint project in the Wedding district of Berlin. The site is characterized by heterogeneous usage, with one-third of the area devoted to work, one-third to art and one-third to social projects. In this way, they attempted to find space for the diversity of urban society. That brings us to the questions of rules, which have to be agreed upon to allow urban commoning to take place. ExRotaprint's rules are very simple, which allow for great openness within the project.

MH: Like the Mietshäuser Syndikat, ExRotaprint makes a contribution towards the city as commons by combining leasehold and non-profit status. The land on the site is owned by two foundations which have dedicated themselves to anti-speculative approaches to real estate. The buildings are administered through ExRotaprint gGmbH, the non-profit lease-holding tenant. Regarding the openness question, it is essential that the project secured long-term affordable commercial spaces: this allows local independent workers, engaged cultural workers and those working in the social sphere to make a long-term contribution to the neighbourhood and beyond. Or to put it another way: in assigning these spaces, the more attention the non-profit management pays to achieving a successful mixture of users, the more an urban commons can develop. In my opinion, that is very much the case, partly because the protagonists see the undertaking as a kind of social sculpture.

CH: Kotti & Co. is another Berlin initiative where the negotiation of a 'We' goes beyond the relationship between the individual and the community, in order to have an impact on society as a whole.

In this case, it becomes clear how these three levels intermesh: residents' individual concern that they might lose their apartments at Kottbusser Tor led to the formation of a group, which then developed an impressive bandwidth of agendas and instruments, had an effect beyond its specific location and absolutely had an impact on local politicians and administrators. In demanding the re-communalization of privatized housing stock, they are also thinking of a Weconstellation, which stretches right across society.

MH: I would agree with that. Kotti & Co symbolizes the struggle of all Berliners for the right to the city. They are fighting on their own behalf, but also, as it were, on behalf of all tenants, according to the credo that Berlin belongs to us all, because we all (re-) produce it on a daily basis, whether in a material or an immaterial sense. This became clear, for example, through their engagement in a citywide initiative for a referendum on rent control, funding for publicly subsidized restoration and modernization, as well as new affordable housing projects, among others [*Mietenvolksentscheid*]. They also practise a local urban commoning, in particular with their *gecekondu*. With no obligation, you can sit down in front of it and observe the comings and goings in the square, or you can go in, drink some tea, find out information, have a discussion, or just check out the latest posters, flyers and printed texts. The place is inviting for newcomers and is characterized by the kind of openness which Athenian architect-activist Stavros Stavrides has described as essential for the success of the city as commons.[7]

In the meantime, some of the former social housing around Kottbusser Tor has been re-communalized, and more may follow. But what remains unclear is the extent to which the subsequent public housing organization is ready to allow tenants to really participate in decision-making processes. As with, for example, the former inner-city airport Berlin-Tempelhof, the Tempelhofer Feld and adjacent airport buildings, city-owned companies do not see their responsibility to care for urban commons in terms of urban commoning. We can really only begin to talk about a society-wide We-formation when the public housing stock is put under grassroots management, so as to achieve long-term affordability. Only in this way can the right to the city become a reality for all.

---

[7] See pp. 14–19, as well as Stavros Stavrides and Mathias Heyden (eds.), *Gemeingut Stadt, Berliner Hefte zu Geschichte und Gegenwart der Stadt*, no. 4, (Berlin, 2017). English version as ePub and PDF: *City as Commons* (May 2018), eeclectic.de/ produkt/city-as-commons

CH: Which other bottom-up practices do you find important with regard to urban commoning?

MH: Spreefeld eG has been one successful project within the recent housing-cooperative scene.[8] In this case, it is important to know that the scheme began in the mid-2000s, when there was basically no support for cooperatives from public funds. You had to tackle these things using private resources. For this reason, there is always the possibility that cooperative shares might be turned into privately owned apartments. Nonetheless, there are practices here which point in the direction of urban commoning. As well as the many different forms of living and the different floor plans corresponding to them – above all the cluster apartments – I think the way they deal with open space is remarkable. The way the three buildings are positioned individually, but also in relation to each other, means the location is made accessible to very different groups of users. This becomes especially clear by the mix of functions on the ground floor – offices, workshops for handicraft, and cultural and social uses – and by the free, unfenced access from the public riverbank nearby, and from the street. In my opinion, these spatial and programmatic elements are how the project makes an important contribution to discussion about the city as commons, in particular within the context of the broader privatization of riverbanks in central Berlin.

ALN: What general contributions can cooperative living make to the city as commons?

MH: In cooperatives, you are a tenant and an owner at the same time, bound into cooperative principles of solidarity and democracy. Everyone has a voice in decisions that are important for everyone. In addition, you normally have lifelong tenancy rights, which can be passed on, with rents remaining stable or only slightly increasing. But there is a danger that a cooperative can have an exclusionary function, if it has paid off its debt and does not use its accumulating reserves to expand and thus enable other people to also enjoy cooperative living. So, it has to be stipulated: housing cooperatives must remain open to newcomers, if they want to be urban commoners. A distinction must be made here between long-established cooperatives, some of which manage several thousand apartments, and more recent ones, which often have only a few buildings. The former must be shaken out of their complacency, so

---

8   See pp. 62–9.

they can become contemporary protagonists in the struggle for the right to the city. The latter must be energetically supported with public resources.

Max Kaldenhoff: As well as the politics of housing, many people are also active in campaigning for urban open spaces, including the Prinzessinnengarten, for example. What significance do these initiatives and projects have for commoning?

MH: The assertion of the city as commons appears to be more frequent among campaigners for green spaces than among housing activists. One prominent example of this is the community garden Allmende-Kontor on Tempelhofer Feld. The Prinzessinnengarten also regards itself as commons, in particular by virtue of the Laube, a multistory open-air timber structure, which was built in 2017 for non-commercial, neighbourly and public service uses.[9] The fact that this property is publicly owned marks another level of urban commoning, but only the actions of Nomadisch Grün gGmbH, the non-profit limited liability company that is leasing the site, made the place open for the kind of diverse appropriation we know today. Alongside the professional and voluntary garden work, there is educational and cultural labour around fair and ecological agriculture, and so the project should also be read in the context of discourses on production and reproduction.[10] Another reason why the Prinzessinnengarten has become a point of reference regarding the city as commons is because it remains open to newcomers. You could say that the 'We' formulated by Esteva is constantly in a state of becoming here.

In closing, I would like to point out that the initiatives and projects discussed here offer promising practices for Berlin as commons. However, what remains an open question is whether the currently increasing cooperation with local politicians and administrators can succeed in this respect. For this reason, the theme of the city as commons should go hand-in-hand with debates on perspectives for municipalism here in Berlin. But that would be another conversation.

---

[9] See pp. 88–96.
[10] See also 'Feminism and the Politics of the Commons' by the social scientist and activist Silvia Federici, www.commoner.org.uk/?p=113, and Federici's contribution in *The Property Issue* (Aachen: ARCH+, March 2018), 142ff

Refugee housing squats as shared heterotopias

The case of City Plaza Athens squat

Nikolas Kanavaris

Introduction

The management of the incoming refugee 'flows' in Greece has emerged as a matter of great concern. After the 'long summer of migration' in 2015 (Lafazani, 2018a), when the proliferation of arriving refugees took place, a myriad of different politics concerning refugees emerged both from institutions and from informal groups. At the same time, after the general election in January 2015, a coalition government formed with Syriza and Anel political parties. Syriza was elected as a political party with left origins, grounded in social movements (anti-austerity movements) and struggles for social and political rights (Velegrakis & Kosyfologou, 2018). The re-election of Syriza after the referendum in the general election during September 2015 formed the political context in which the refugee 'crisis' was managed. The alignment of the Syriza government with the neoliberal politics of the EU and the continuation of the austerity measures – even if engaging a more 'fair' rhetoric – forced the party to deal with the refugee 'crisis' which was transforming into a humanitarian crisis (Maniatis, 2018). As part of a variant legislation regarding refugees, the EU-Turkey statement played a crucial role in the survival of refugees (Mezzadra, 2018). In this context, Syriza tried to maintain the façade of a 'left' government. This was reflected in the attempt to manage the refugee and humanitarian crisis in a 'humane' way. However, the core of the state's policy centred on the seclusion and the confinement of the refugee population. Power was given to many different organizations, from UNHCR to bigger and smaller NGOs which operate in the camps, providing apartments for rent and support with rental expenses (Galgano, 2017). As is already known, the complexity of the migration issue led the Syriza government to adopt a tolerant policy vis-à-vis the informal solidarity initiatives that were created among locals and internationals. A significant number of refugee squats began to operate following the EU-Turkey statement in the spring of 2016. The closure of borders and the insufficiency of the state to address the needs engendered an environment in which alternative forms of struggle and solidarity emerged to address the fact that refugees were no longer permitted to pass through Greece and along the Balkan Route but were to remain in Greece (Papataxiarchis, 2016δ),

The big solidarity movement presented a gradual decline as the years went by. In the summer of 2016 (Velegrakis & Kosyfologou, 2018; Karyotis, 2016), two refugee squats in Thessaloniki were evicted by the Syriza-Anel government including some in Athens. The elections during the summer of 2019 ushered in a government with Nea Dimokratia (New Democracy) in power which, from the first moment, attacked the refugee housing projects (King & Manoussaki-Adamopoulou, 2019). Since the hostile policy was a certainty, City Plaza squat had already decided to close (Solidarity2Refugees, n.d.), and the majority of the remaining squats were evicted in September 2019 (King & Manoussaki-Adamopoulou, 2019). These events marked the end of a network of struggles that had taken places mostly in Athens (and in Thessaloniki). The housing projects that emerged in the centre of the cities must be understood and interpreted in order to foster future attempts inspired from these struggles.

In this chapter, I aim to connect the refugee housing projects in Athens with the theory of the commons. The goal is to propose a conceptual framework through which these phenomena could be perceived and, subsequently, reintegrated into the discourse on urban commons. Refugee housing squats in the centre of Athens put forth a complexity in terms of concepts, practices, identities and spaces. However, the comparison of self-organized squats to state-run camps reduces this complexity: it crafts dichotomies that, on the one hand, criticize camps (as the archetype of hospitality), and, on the other hand, it 'romanticizes' refugee squats. The eviction of the majority of the housing projects, as mentioned earlier, prioritizes a subsequent and progressive round of struggles.

The refugee housing squats operated more or less for three years, and, at the same time, the programmatic targeting of these initiatives established presence and functioning. The focus of this argument is the potential of these spaces as urban commons. The questions raised were regarding their ability to be open to newcomers, to be expanded in the city and to attempt to 'diffuse the virus of change' (Stavrides, 2016 p. 73). The first part of the chapter concerns the way the conceptual framework of commons is perceived. In this context, refugee housing squats are perceived as shared heterotopias (Stavrides,2016), where boundaries are firm but penetrable the same time. The second part connects the notion of commoning with the anthropological concepts of hospitality and solidarity. The third part proposes a hermeneutic schema in which refugee housing squats form shared heterotopias through the praxis of autonomous solidarity between hosts and guests. The space of the squats is a spectrum of threshold spatialities where encounters between selfness and otherness take place. The limit between the liquid and unstable identities of the 'hosts' and 'guests' that are performed 'inside' the squat can be traced as a process of constantly remaking thresholds. In the fourth part, the ethnographic work from the 'refugee housing accommodation space, City Plaza'[1] is presented in order to illustrate the micro-social relations and conflicts between inhabitants, between inhabitants and outsiders, the channels of communication, and the limits throughout a constant effort of transformation.

Talking on the commons

The discourse around commons varies as commons is a concept which can take several, even contradicting, interpretations. Elinor Ostrom's work gave an analytical framework and examples that challenge the concept of 'the tragedy of the commons' and the problems relating to collective action (Bollier, 2014, p. 15). From this point of view, there are two different ways that commons can be perceived (Montagna & Grazioli, 2019; Tsavdaroglou, 2018; De Angelis, 2019). The first focuses on the shared recourses within a community, an approach closer to Ostrom's work. The other approach (Caffentzis, 2009; De Angelis, 2011; Bresnihan & Byrne, 2014) perceives commons as relational practices, which are invented in order to constitute a resource in common. The focus of this approach, which is going to be used in this chapter, is on the issue of the internal codes and power dispersion. The set of notions used to describe the commons are the

---

[1]   The fieldwork took place from the beginning of the squat and continued for 1.5 years due to my participation in the project. Parts of this section of the chapter (especially diagrams) are thoughts included in my thesis for the NTUA School of Architecture (Kanavaris and Makaronas, 2017).

division between the commoners and their community, the common pool of resources and the process of commoning. The concept of commoning, which is going to be followed in this chapter (Linebaugh, 2010), is one that stimulates action in the 'here and now' of the procedural formation of the commons. Commoning is a relational praxis which brings intimacy to the community, reshaping them into a group of commoners. It can be defined both as the set of rules and behaviours and as a new ethics sculpted in/through the community.

> The commons asks us to consider a different paradigm of social and moral order. It asks us to embrace social rules that are compatible with a more cooperative, civic-minded and inclusive set of values, norms and practices. (Bollier, 2014, p. 59)

Commons as natural resources are difficult to trace in the urban context (Borch et al., 2015). The discussion on urban commons mainly focuses on the multiplicity and heterogeneity of the contemporary metropolis. The phenomenon of market enclosures of public spaces is a constant process in cities all around the world, and the 'new-extractivism' policies have affected people's lives while many social movements struggle to counteract this. The movement of the 'squares', factory occupations and self-management initiatives, and urban gardens can be seen under the scope of urban commons. And, as Stavrides (2014, p. 95) questions, 'Do social movements [. . .] channel the redistribution claims of different social groups, or is it perhaps that in social movements the seeds of a different society find fertile ground?'

Refugee housing squats as shared heterotopias

> The specific socio spatial struggles of migrants' squats as practices of urban commoning and inhabitance (. . .) situate themselves outside and against forms of control of the state and of humanitarian forms of assistance.
>
> (Martinez et al., 2019 p. 3)

Although the discourse around commons is very active (Tsavdaroglou, 2018; Agustín, 2019), there is lack of references in the relation to commons and the current migration 'crisis'. Tsavdaroglou (2018), in his chapter, 'The Newcomers' Right to the Common Space: The Case of Athens during the Refugee Crisis', correlates the theory around urban commons with the refugee housing projects and considers them as an expression of the 'right to the city'. The occupation of buildings in the centre of the city and their transformation into co-housing units that enable common struggles between locals and refugees is a contradictory and complex process of sharing in the urban environment in terms of both resources (buildings, food supplies, etc.) and knowledge. As Kapsali (2019, p. 351) states:

> extraordinary politics of urban commons lie at their ability to advance universalizing political claims, grounded on the everyday lived experience of care, equality and empowerment [. . .] disrupt the existing order and point towards the creation of spaces of emancipator commoning outside and against the institutionalized urban taxonomy.

Even the action of squatting as an outlawed action produces, from the first moment, a totally different context of everyday life. There is a complex encounter of migrants, refugees, networks of local anti-racist collectivities, activists of the extra-parliamentary left and autonomous groups. This is the relational environment in which practices, codes of communication and ways of deciding are created in/through the co-living. These processes that are enabled in the squats have already been the focal point of different researchers in order to trace the common characteristics of these spaces (Haddad, 2016; Raimondi, 2019; Koptyaeva, 2017; Agustín, 2019, 2018).

> contemporary refugee housing common spaces could be seen as open communities of commoners, which through their spatial practices of commoning destabilize the State-led policies as well as the multiply and intersected power relations and seek to (re)claim both the physical and the social space producing unique collective common spaces. (Tsavdaroglou, Giannopoulou, Lafazani, Pistikos, & Petropoulou, 2018b, p. 9)

In this chapter, the phenomenon is approached with the term 'shared heterotopias'. The main concept of heterotopias for Stavrides is their relational power, the fact that they exist 'inside' an environment. The activist's collectivities who first occupied the building and the refugees who tried to find opportunities for better living conditions form an area where cultures and identities interact and new subjectivities can potentially emerge.

The majority of the occupied buildings are located in the centre of the city. The way these initiatives propose the co-living of a heterogeneous group of people cannot be perceived as 'normal'. Heterotopias as a concept are not about a secluded region and community that is placed at distance from the urban normality. Heterotopias define a specific entity, a territory that establishes limits while enabling passages and pass-through actions. These buildings encapsulate the everyday life of their inhabitants, but at the same time they are networked by the everyday life of the city. Shopping, cleaning clothes and bed sheets and visiting state offices are practices that shape these networks (Kotronaki, 2018; Tsavdaroglou, Giannopoulou, Petropoulou, & Pistikos, 2019; Kapsali, 2019). Even the simplest actions of refugees and migrants can be seen as political actions in the view of legality and illegality in the urban context. These relations and the transparency of interface between heterotopias and the 'normal' produce thresholds. The proximity of the 'interior' and the 'exterior', and of the 'normal' and the 'alter', shapes a liquid spatiality. Squatted buildings can be perceived as a continuum of thresholds through the fact that their existence is based on difference and comparison.

> Common space that is developed through such movement action is in-between space, threshold space [. . .] common space tends to be constantly redefined: common space happens and common space is shaped through collective action. (Stavrides, 2016, pp. 106–7)

The concept of 'shared heterotopias' can be useful in the interpretation of the inner space of the refugee housing squats. Those interior spaces are always connected with the 'outside'. Outside, here, could mean the urban environment, the legal system and the dominant social relations. The fundamental difference of these urban commons can be identified in the fact that there is not an agreed set of rules or values on which sharing actions are based. In reverse, the commonality of the inhabitants is formed through the process of the commoning and the ideas of commoning as such. Commoning in this case has a potentially unifying aspect. What each 'commoner' brings from the 'outside' provides the fertile soil or the burdens of the common project. In this chapter, it is argued that the refugee housing squats can potentially widen the framework of understanding the commons through the concept of 'shared heterotopias':

> City Plaza is very different from other political social centers or squats as it is not composed of a more or less homogeneous group that has

actively decided to participate in a self-organized and collective project. [. . .] What for other projects would be the ground agreement, such as anti-racism or anti-sexism, in City Plaza is part of the everyday struggle. (Lafazani, 2017)

As described earlier, there is a strong threshold quality in the spaces of these buildings, as a space in constant negotiation. Shared heterotopias are exposed to the danger of this fundamental contradiction. Thresholds can appear in two ways: as a potential bridge of difference and as a weak point of conflicts. Thresholds can enable a process towards openness and sharing, the 'mutual-infection' from the viral expansion of sharing practices; but, on the other hand, 'corrupted thresholds' can be the battlefields of reinforced difference, in which case these spaces can be transformed into enclaves for 'professionals of commons'. 'Corrupted thresholds' aim to expand sharing practices only among 'those who are similar to us', they oppose the 'different', and, as a result, they turn introspectively in search of the 'inner difference' as threat. Shared heterotopias create multiple thresholds that are related with the society (outside) across different levels: local, national and transnational. Heterotopias trace the dynamic relation with the broader context and reveal processes of constant recontextualization:

the emerging housing communities of the migrating populations can be seen as potential hybrid territorial thresholds as open communities in motion that constantly negotiate the various social identities and collectively seek and re-invent the culture of togetherness and coexistence. (Tsavdaroglou et al., 2018b, p. 16)

Commoning shaped in the border of the 'host/guest' relation

the boundaries of the migrants-commons are the result of a daily struggle, just from the 'non-citizen' perspective, they are formed through the commoning that involve inhabiting these spaces and social relationships, and open up spaces against and beyond the 'micropolitics of the border' and borderscapes.

(De Angelis, 2019, p. 4)

Common space is related with a community which is not clearly defined; in contrast, it is constantly open to difference. Instead of perceiving the arrival of a stranger as a threat, common space welcomes any newcomer to whom it projects the promise of revitalization. From this perspective, crucial aspect about commons is that commoners who are involved with the processes are equal (Stavrides, 2016, p. 107). This condition is approached not as an established reality, but rather as a potential outcome of collective effort. In the case of refugee housing projects, this condition takes a crucial role. The multiple differences presented in a refugee squat in regards to class, culture, language, gender and sexual orientation make the intention of equality complex and contradictory. Commons theory provides common principles, which may be really simple but still give shape to the commoning processes. In the case of the refugee squats, there are not such foundational principles; in contrast, the anticipations and aspirations of different groups inside the squats (local activists, international solidarians, refugees, migrants and several different subgroups under these main categories) are often inconsistent and even conflicting.

In order to analyse the way commoning is formed in refugee squats, the concept of hospitality is used. Refugee housing squats can be perceived as commons under the precondition that are created from very different intentions. As a result, their existence is based on the idea of equal sharing as a 'functioning' method of dealing with everyday life. The majority of the squats were the outcome of the action of local leftist, autonomous, anarchist and anti-racist collectivities: these local groups 'opened' the abandoned buildings in Athens, and thus they attained the privilege of having been there first. The action of squatting is usually the outcome of an organized collective discussion that questioned the intentions, goals and potentials. These local groups also – at least at the very beginning – were practically able to support their initiative and the durability of the squats through their pre-existing solidarity networks (Kapsali, 2019, p. 364). The main principles of equality, horizontality, participation and direct democracy are as programmatic starting points and targets. Those principles are to be respected, and thus everyday decisions have to be enmeshed with them.

The anarchist highlights the tensions that exist within the occupations, between migrants and activists themselves. In fact, all the effort aimed at creating communities that include migrants, teaching them how to collaborate in an 'anarchist way', betrays a logic of us/them, and imply a vaguely pedagogical approach that in some cases proves necessary for the success of self-management. Even in supposedly non-hierarchical contexts, power asymmetries are difficult to totally eliminate, especially in a situation characterised by temporal precarity and where the subjectivities involved belong to completely different cultural and political contexts. (Raimondi, 2019, p. 10)

Some scholars mention that there is an 'us-them' division in refugee housing squats (Rozakou, 2012; Lafazani, 2018b; Raimondi, 2019) that problematizes the power relation issues at a molecular interpersonal level. As Stavrides (2016, p. 272) mentions: 'We cannot avoid power since even contingent circumstances may always give advantages to some individuals over the others.' So, there is a crucial confrontation which happens in the encounter with the 'different', and the effort is to reshape the current power relations. This is a strenuous oeuvre with dead ends, coming backs, throughout the cohabitation process. This effort is, at the same time, revealed in the 'small scale' of everyday life and simultaneously in the 'big' decisions, wishes, etc. Refugee housing squats constitute a co-living of absolutely different subjects: the very practices of co-living and co-deciding are those on which the common is based. Sharing is the fundamental principle/practice through and in which different intentions, ideas and goals are negotiated.

> Encounters reveal some inherit contradictions, and the project overall entails many difficulties because it demands a highly scaled organization that often conflicts with the basic principles and values of the solidarity movement (...) prevailing ways of managing migration and the tendency to romanticize both solidarity projects and the migrants themselves. (Lafazani, 2018b, p. 897)

Lafazani (2018b), in her paper 'Homeplace Plaza: Challenging the Border between Host and Hosted', tries – from her own involvement in the project – to show how everyday life in City Plaza could challenge, through every moment, the existing power relations. The 'us-them' division is perceived as different groupings between hosts and guests. The main goal for Lafazani is the process of replacing the borders to create liquid groups of hosts and guests. Thus, the concept of hospitality emerges. Hospitality as a concept is described by Derrida (Περί Φιλοξενίας (Of Hospitality), 2006 [1996]) in the text 'Of hospitality' as a cultural practice linked with 'ethos'. Hospitality takes place in a bounded space with its borders having a variable permeability: these borders cannot be eliminated; they exist as there is the entity of 'self' in contrast to the 'other'. They can be physical or symbolic, but in any case they form the reflection of the violence incorporated in the encounter of selfness and otherness: 'a certain violence, or even "perjury" towards the absolute law of hospitality, begins immediately, from the threshold of the right to hospitality' (Kakoliris, 2015, p. 149). Hospitality as an ethos of the reception of the other becomes a practice through an action of traversal and the destabilization, which is related to this act and is the potential field in which difference could take a more flexible character.

Except for the more abstract approach on the concept of hospitality, anthropologists (Candea & Col, 2012; Lima Camargo, 2015; Rozakou, 2012; Papataxiarchis, 2006a) deal with hospitality as it 'happens' in ceremonies, interpersonal relations and exchanges in and through cultures. Bulley (2015) tries to expand the context of understanding hospitality as a spectrum of power relations, special proximity and affection. The spatial aspect of traversal, the pass-through of the threshold, is a practice that enables the expansion of the time/space of interaction. Encounters, crossing or deviated trajectories resignify the self/other relation and potentially 'make(s) the space your space rather than my space' (Bulley, 2015, p. 188).

> including spaces such as 'self-organized' camps, [. . .] demonstrate[s] the continuing agency of displaced people to disturb and unsettle the host/ guest binary by themselves constructing temporary, dangerous 'homes'. (Bulley, 2015, p. 193)

Hospitality as a practice in the micro-social level depends on the cultural context; thus, it is historically and socially defined. 'Greek hospitality' as it is perceived by Papaxiarchis (2006a) is a process whereby the guest is forced to become like the host, to imitate their gestures and behaviours. Becoming similar is the precondition of acceptance. During the refugee 'crisis' of 2015, there was a politicization of hospitality through the term 'solidarity' (Papataxiarchis, 2014). The notion of 'Unwrapping solidarity' (Papataxiarchis, 2016c) had emerged and was set as crucial elements of the Greek identity through the practice of solidarity to refugees alongside empathy and support for the displaced populations. Solidarity networks, which were established during the economic crisis (Rozakou, 2016; Karaliotas, 2017), were reactivated, addressing the different not as a local marginalized social group but as a refugee. Solidarity is a controversial process produced through conflicts and collaborations and opens potential channels of communication (Agustín & Jørgensen, 2019). Autonomous solidarity especially (Agustín Ó.G., 2019) can describe the case of refugee housing squats and can be distinguished from the humanistic solidarity of the NGO professionals, the state employees or the church.

Autonomous solidarity for the local activist groups is an attempt to reverse the fact that they are the dominant identity group and to spread the ideals of horizontality and equality throughout the projects. Solidarity groups become hosts but in a way that, in fact, they sabotage their role through the constant reflection on the power asymmetry issue. Autonomous solidarity forms a procedural spatial entity in which given power relations are liquid and always vulnerable in interaction. Space appropriates and incorporates a quality of transition where different kinds of spatial elements symbolize limits and where a common language between guests and hosts is created. As Tsavdaroglou argues:

in the emerging 'common spaces' the refugees shape the sense of belonging, security, and personal wellbeing, and along with the support of volunteers they have access to food, health care, education and employment. For this to occur the mode of communication, the characteristics and identities of the participants, both locals and refugees, are confronted with their limits, modified and troubled. The process of setting up the housing common spaces is based on collective practices, mutual aid and respect, horizontal organization, and emotional, communicative and aesthetic interactions. (Tsavdaroglou, 2018, p. 388)

In the majority of squats in Athens, there were a set of common practices (not in the same way or intensity) developed. They had to do with the everyday life of the residents and their involvement in shifts for security, cooking, eating, cleaning, entertainment, education, medical assistance, etc. Commoning in refugee housing squats is the interaction, conflict and the reflection on how these are reorganized under new circumstances. Squire (2018, p. 127) notes that

the uneven experience [. . .] between 'helper' and 'helped' [. . .] is the sharing of precarious lives through a solidaristic ethos; moreover, she suggests that this ethos is grounded not in family or relationships of kinship and cultural uniformity, but in a shared struggle that builds what we might call 'community' through presence and participation.

Commoning in the case of refugee housing squats has a lot to do with the praxis of autonomous solidarity. As it is described, autonomous solidarity is an emancipative hospitality that can potentially exist as a constant reflection on the everyday practices, reflection which argues whether the programmatic principles of each project (equality, horizontality) are traced into the micro-level of inhabitant's actions. Commoning is shaped by a division which deepens or softens depending on the circumstances. The division of hosts and guests in this case is not a strict emic division, but, rather, a flexible variation of groups. Hosts can potentially become guests and the opposite: it is a balance between two unfixed groupings always in the process of change. Host/guest division can also be seen as a more solid group of commoners, the group that forms each squat's community. This division is a vital and sometimes conflicting relationship, a relationship of difference which composes these urban commons. It can be argued that the conflicting relation between the multiple groups of hosts and guests according to the ethos of autonomous solidarity trace the tension that everyday commoning embodies.

Shared heterotopias beyond the host/guest division (?)

Is it possible to go beyond the host/guest division? The discourse on hospitality in a more abstract way prioritizes ethics because it points out the primitive violence that is embedded in the process. As presented earlier, hospitality at the micro-level of everyday practice can reveal the power relations created in the encounter with the 'other'. Concepts such as hospitality and solidarity can be traced across different social scales: at the EU level, the nation, the NGOs, in the neighbourhood and the antagonistic movement. There are multiple conceptualizations of the terms which can reveal, in each social formation, the 'state of hospitality-solidarity' referring to the 'state of difference' proposed by Papataxiarchis (2006b). Thus, refugee housing squats must be interpreted through this complex context of the 'state of Hospitality-Solidarity' and not as 'niches of freedom'. Shared heterotopias do not exist at the exterior of societies but in their limits; they evolved as boundary practices which are undermined and constantly under threat.

Shared heterotopias can be interrelated with the 'state of difference', and, at the same time, they can be understood as autonomous dynamic phenomena. They can develop strategies that contest and pressure state and dominant institutions. 'Rightful presence' (Squire et al., 2013), as a concept, gives meaning in the sharing practices under the idea of re-subjectification. Host/guest divisions 'invade' the squats as a viral outcome of the 'state of hospitality' by which commoning in the shared heterotopias hacks this division. Hosts/guests are not fixed groups, complete identities waiting to be performed; they are more liquid and easily reshaped groupings as people involved change (in political, social, affective terms). Hospitality is appropriated 'inside' the refugee housing squats in a negotiation with hospitality-solidarity as it happens in the neighbourhood, in the city, in the state. As such, commoning as a praxis of autonomous solidarity between hosts and guests is an alternative everyday life which overrides the rigid relation with the 'other'.

Squats are shaped by this boundary situation. They do not appear in a 'laboratory condition' totally independent from the state's mechanisms. The main issue that emerges from this approach is the necessity of openness towards the 'other'. Squats have the potential as shared heterotopias: to exist outside of the homogenous normality of the city not as seclusions but posed as challenge to this normality. Refugee housing squats have a potential to survive through spreading the virus of heterogeneity, and in the ability to infect and to be infected at the same time. This is the edgy existence of shared heterotopias which creates their procedural character. Refugee housing squats are 'alive' in their constant process of movement and transformation and in the ability to be open and to digest alterity through their flexible institutions. This approach offers an equalizing potentiality: the acceptance of the common goals of mutual participation and of non-hierarchical democracy is achieved through persistent reflection on the decisions and dilemmas (Tsavdaroglou, 2019).

Refugee housing squats as threshold spatialities produced by hosts and guests

> A kind of equalising potentiality seems to dwell on thresholds. Liminality, the spatiotemporal quality of threshold experience, is a condition that gives people the opportunity to share a commonworld-in-the-making.
>
> (Stavrides S., 2015, p. 12)

Shared heterotopias are composed by/through a continuum of thresholds. These thresholds, though they may refer to the 'inside', are simultaneously interrelated to the 'outside'. Commoning as a praxis bridges the difference through negotiations and conflicts. It is 'outside' of the squats where the origin of divisions, antagonisms and rivalries can be traced. However, 'inside' subjectivities that are shaped by the dominant relations of different societies interact in a different space where their identity is reappropriated. Squats as the definition of a space of heterogeneity digest this contradiction by forming porous spatialities. Difference must not be normalized; in contrast, a new community emerges which is not based on similarity and the host/ guest division, is enabled 'inside' a squat, and is a multiple dichotomy that is reflected through threshold spatialities. Space is interpreted in different ways, and it is transformed prescribing/inscribing the balance of this host/ guest relation. This process should not be perceived as linear and peaceful but, rather, as conflicting, difficult and tiring (Figure 9.1).

Despite the inner character, thresholds gain meaning through the relation with the 'outside'. As described earlier, there is a relation with the neighbourhood around squats, the city and the social media networks around the world. Therefore, 'inner' borders are infected by the outer context in the same way that they infect it. This struggling community, since it is open to the 'other', should always attempt to disrupt homogeneity by which is surrounded. The intention of infection, the attempt of a viral spreading of heterogeneity, as a milestone of community, can be addressed with hostility, hope or scepticism. This forms a relation between different groups of society which can be local or international; for example, envisaged common spaces emerge online through appropriating the spatial imaginary both for residents and the 'outsiders'.

Most of the refugee housing squats in Athens and Thessaloniki (Tsavdaroglou, Giannopoulou, Petropoulou, & Pistikos, 2019; Kapsali, 2019; Katrini, 2020) appear to have a similar way of organizing everyday life: there is a house assembly where decisions are taken, and there are more specialized meetings of groups related to cooking and food distribution, security and cleaning; in some squats, there were medical support groups, women's empowerment groups, children's activity groups and spaces related to these practices. In most of the cases, refugees, locals and international activists take part. These groups and their negotiation shape these fields of interaction which are going to be examined as thresholds.

This chapter takes as a case study the refugee housing Space City Plaza in Athens. City Plaza, a former hotel, is appropriated by the struggling mixed community, and space is organized in three units: entrance and management spaces, everyday life spaces, dormitory and protected sociality spaces (Figure 9.2).

Refugee housing squats as shared heterotopias produced by the praxis of autonomous solidarity between the liquid host/guest groupings create three types of thresholds. Firstly, the security threshold defines the outer limits of the squat in relation to the broader city context: it produces the conditions for an 'interior' common space by the fact that filters the newcomers. Secondly, the equalizing threshold in the everyday life spaces mostly concerns the issue of participation in the collective life of the co-housing project: the involvement in the various shifts is the primary attempt to undermine the

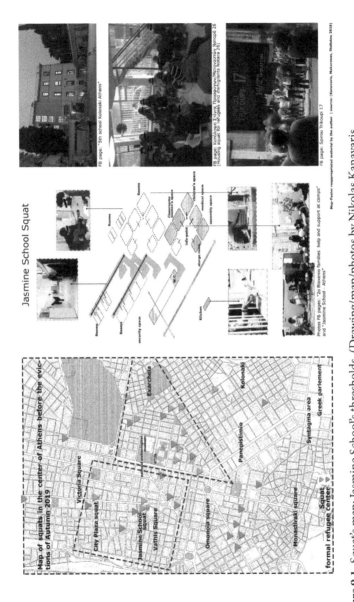

Figure 9.1 Squat's map: Jasmine School's thresholds. (Drawing/map/photos by Nikolas Kanavaris.)

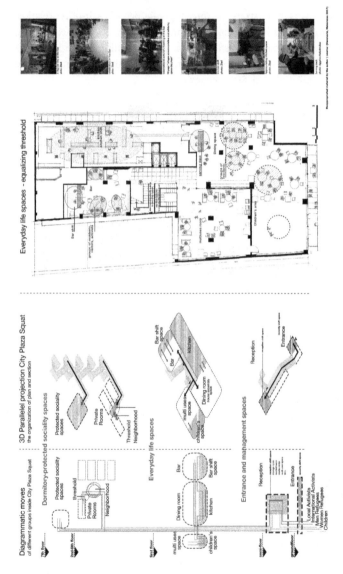

Figure 9.2 City Plaza diagrams. (Drawing/photos by Nikolas Kanavaris.)

host/guest binary. Thirdly, the privacy threshold is invented so as to facilitate the 'passages' between collective life and the core of the individual or family space.

The main goal is to illustrate the in/out, public/private, self/other relation as a condition of successive thresholds. In the case study of the refugee housing squat City Plaza, the spatial transformations and the multiple interpretations of the common space will be interrelated to the potential community of the squat. As Maniatis (2018, p. 893) suggests,

> the City Plaza community believed that the reappropriation of rights and freedoms could not be accomplished within one or several 'niches of freedom' beyond state and market control [. . .] small struggles and victories can shape social coalitions.

Entrance and management spaces

Entrance: Security threshold

City Plaza's entrance is a liminal space; it is the passage from the street, the neighbourhood and the city into the squat. It is a limit where negotiations and conflicts constantly took place. There were many different people seeking access: refugees looking for shelter, friends of inhabitants, international solidarians, police officers, the legal owners of the hotel and media, among others.

The multiple demands for traversal had to be filtered by the special group placed in the entrance which was the security shift. There were different arrangements of furniture responding to the need for variation over time. For example, in the first months following the opening of the squat, a huge number of refugees were outside of the entrance asking for shelter. The very first arrangement of the entrance had to deal with this issue in a way that was decided by the local activists. The political decision was not to overpopulate the building so as to provide spaces of dignity in contrast to the camps (Lafazani, 2018b).

The strictness of the security shift in the beginning (which was mostly crewed by local activists) was transformed by the interaction of the community. Mixed groups of local and international activists and refugees took over the security shift and helped to maintain a sense of security while at the same time enabling traversals. The table of the shift was the main element kept in the space from the first till the last moment, and inhabitants had to show their 'card', a piece of paper including their name and room number, in order to enter. The three different arrangements presented exemplify the different forms that this threshold space could take. The fact that this table symbolized a certain 'authority' was simultaneously softened by the fact that this space became a space of socialization. The sense of safety achieved by a deceleration of the traversal provided the opportunity for the members of the shift to become familiar with the inhabitants and their friends while also being aware of the potential threats that they should deal with.

The entrance as the actual threshold of the squat functioned not only as a protective mechanism but also as a booster of the sociality between the squat and the city. As is described by Kotronaki (2018), the entire neighbourhood around City Plaza was affected by the function of the squat and also by the external events organized by the community. The festivals (in Victoria Square or in Pedion Areos – a nearby park) and, most importantly, the network of people connected with the residents and their everyday life demonstrated the sociality expanding outside the limits of the common; the small street outside of the squat was, especially during spring and summer, full of people.

Reception: Organization threshold

The hotel's former reception space is in direct connection with the entrance. In this space, there was a new reception group appointed whose responsibility was the management of the project. The reception was where the newcomers were informed about the character of the project and its goals by the reception shift. The reception shift group was mostly crewed by local activists and some international activists. In order to be part of the reception shift, one needed to live or support the project for a long time. In this space the host/guest division is more apparent than in any other space of the squat; and that was a decision taken because refugee inhabitants changed over time because of their final goal to reach a northern European country. It was an attempt to maintain the political characteristics of the space. Host/guest relations exist, as Lafazani (2018b) explains, due to the fact that concepts and words (as squat, self-organization) are unknown to some of the residents. Some of them have never taken part in a practice of the antagonistic movement; they tend to look for 'experts' and 'managers'. Thus, crucial concepts of the project gain their meaning for refugees through the very actual practice in the space.

The reception space was close to crucial spaces like the food storage room, the medical room and the media centre. Local activists, drawing on their pre-existing networks were able to handle the food supplies issue, the medical assistance and the legal advices; and this was a critical factor that highlighted a certain dominance they attained as hosts. It was mostly the reception shift's role to direct the refugee inhabitants to state offices and hospitals and to keep a solidarity campaign on social media active.

The placement of this space in the former reception space was fundamental; this space was visible and 'accessible' from the major movement inside the squat, and everyday almost everyone passed in front of the reception space. This decision provided a sense of caring in and about the project and, at the same time, an impression and realization of a well-organized space.

The 'reception desk' was the threshold of organization. The tension embodied if the reception shift would attempt to take control and collect power was neutralized by the visibility of the space, and an accessible desk, rather than a closed office. 'Hierarchical management' as the domain of experts was confronted and contested by a collective decision-making process: paternalistic relations were balanced with empowering practices. The host identity of the reception shift was dissolved when the people of this shift were part of the kitchen or cleaning shift, for example.

Everyday life spaces

Kitchen, dining room, bar and house assembly: Equalizing threshold

City Plaza's first floor was the generator space for the collective identity of the squat. Cooking and dining were core micro-social practices which shaped the inhabitant's relations with the kitchen, bar and dining room spaces providing the loci for interaction that took place between the shifts and among the inhabitants.

Each inhabitant was supposed to be part of a shift at least once per week; and the kitchen, bar and cleaning shifts were the first shifts in the squat that a newcomer would be introduced to. The simplicity of these practices, but the importance they had for the operation of the project, gave them a significant meaning in the everyday life of inhabitants. Friendships and conflicts began during the collaboration in the shifts. In these spaces, everyday life was formed but this alternative everyday life also appropriated and transformed the former hotel spaces. The dining space was also used for the house assembly. Likewise, many different organizational forms were used in order to achieve maximum participation in the shifts (cooking, cleaning, bar, security, etc.). The need for participation as a collective way to keep the project working was always an important issue; however, assuming responsibilities was not the case for everybody, and this led to conflicts. Participation was perceived as a multifactor issue which was dependent on the various identities of each resident including factors such as language, age, family situation and anticipations:

> projected onto the building's walls [. . .] governance processes were widely communicated through signs, notice boards, posters, and notes in different languages throughout the building in a possibly hopeless attempt to engage all residents with day-to-day governance and the coordination of responsibilities. (Katrini, 2020, p. 45)

These contradictions were the concern of the house assembly. The fact that it took place in an intimate space where everyone had spent time enabled potential encounters, and the goal of the assembly was to gather all residents, share information and take decisions. The house assembly was a horizontal structure based on the notion 'one man one vote'. However, there were many instances where exclusions and hierarchies became obvious. Differences created multiple borders, which needed to be traversed, and the dining room created a threshold where the constant reflection on differences, exclusions and borders shaped and equalized potentiality: 'relationships of dependence are, in a sense, transformed in to relationships of interdependence and cooperation within a community' (Lafazani, 2018b, p. 901).

Dormitory, protected sociality spaces: Privacy-empowering thresholds

Above the first floor, there were more private spaces and conditions; these were intermediated by a staircase and corridors where, mostly, children would appropriate them as a playground during the day. The ends of the corridors cultivated a neighbourhood setting where groups of people, mostly women, could gather and have a cup of tea. The appropriation of these out-of-use spaces of the former hotel created an unexpected multiplicity which constituted a threshold between the first floor and the private rooms: a threshold that was demanded by children whose games disturbed adults.

In this unit of the squat, some classrooms and the women's space were placed because of the fact that on the upper floors there were bigger rooms. The decrease in movement on the upper floors, partly due to the lack of elevator, created a more intimate character, which meant that the classrooms and women's rooms that were placed there attained the character of intermediate spaces with protected publicity. The intention was to empower these groups of inhabitants so as to be equal members of the common.

Due to the lack of extra space, private rooms and households would keep their doors open and the required extra space was found in the corridors or in the everyday spaces on the first floor. Especially for families that had children, the open door was a way for children to play in the corridors and then return to their 'home'. To address this quality, curtains were added at the door thresholds that could retain the privacy of the room and, at the same time, allow movement in and out. This minimal spatial intervention could reshape the relation between private and semiprivate spaces in a more flexible way. The former hotel rooms imposed very strong limits between the private rooms of hotel patrons and the corridors; however, the City Plaza community was in need of a porous distinction that could give opportunities of passages due to the density of the living space. This threshold could enable a family to live with dignity in a small 14 square metre room. In the case of individuals, their private space was minimized to their bed, with each room being shared by two to three individuals. A private phone call during night could take place in the corridor.

Thresholds on the upper floors of the squat create small passages between the very private spheres of each person. Different cultures and imaginaries, shaped over many years prior to arrival in the squat, had to be transformed rapidly and find mutual channels of communication. Co-living does not necessitate the erasure of private space; however, in this instance, there was the need to deal with an unstable and constantly changing privacy.

Conclusions

Squats give life to urban networks of political contestation and experimentation in the here and now, where grassroots forms of self management, solidarity and autonomy are constituted [. . .] therefore, these struggles are interpreted here as forms of commoning, as they constitute livable spaces, autonomous socio-political infrastructures and networks of solidarities beyond (and against) the state and humanitarian provision.

(Martinez, Dadusc & Grazioli, 2019, p. 3)

The discourse on commons can be infused with the experience of the refugee squats in Athens. The representations of these practices in social media create illustrations of emancipative spaces. These representations underlined the 'we' that in the case of City Plaza made the slogan 'we live together, we fight together, we celebrate together'. In the case of City Plaza, life in common was captured constantly by residents, journalists and activists from all over the world. The majority of squats had a Facebook page on which uploaded photos became an international solidarity threshold of these shared heterotopias (Iliadi, 2016). Through these forms of envisaging represented through social media posts and articles, a new set of meanings regarding the term 'solidarity' were introduced (Siapera, 2019). The snapshots of everyday life constitute bridging passages between the local community and an international solidarity community which support the projects. Commoning, as a survival strategy and as a political action, became exemplar despite the contradiction that had arisen: 'Imagining spaces of transition, spaces-as-thresholds, may, conversely, contribute to the prefiguring of possible practices of space-commoning' (Stavrides, 2016, p. 241).

Refugee squats, the majority of them not existing any more, can be perceived as potential urban commons produced informally and outside of the legal framework. Refugee housing squats as shared heterotopias still affect a way of living which can be traced in contrast to, and beyond the idea of, homogeneity. Everyday life expressed openness to otherness. The groups of difference came together in each squat and based their everyday life on anti-racism, anti-fascism and anti-sexism, and horizontality created various realized projects in the city centre (Tsavdaroglou, 2018; Papataxiarchis, 2016a). Life in common in the centre of the city, as a communal life based on heterogeneity forms a new way of interpreting urbanity. Squats as buildings, communities and their networks in the city constructed an alternative experience of difference in the contemporary city: 'the Athenian refugees' occupied buildings pushes the boundaries of the symbolic, material and social meanings if the common space' (Tsavdaroglou, 2018, p. 393).

Refugee squats as shared heterotopias produced by the praxis of autonomous solidarity between host/guest relations create transitional forms of organization. The liquidity of the external borders affects the internal dynamics by regrouping the host/guest division. As a result, internal borders are never fixed but always create territories of negotiations. Transitional areas emerge as thresholds that enable interactions and inter-affection by the virus of solidarity. Openness to newcomers is the key to keep these thresholds procedural, dynamic and vivid. Newcomers, the moment they appear as threat, are simultaneously the promise of revitalization. Squats as shared heterotopias open to otherness develop a liminal strategy. Openness is both vulnerability and an opportunity. The host/guest division is the mechanism which can digest difference in a way that does not erase deviance but enables channels of interaction based on the praxis of solidarity.

Guests disrupt host's normality and the tension to feel safe and stable. Hosts canalize guest's power and the external tension to reproduce norms and behaviours incongruent with the programmatic concepts of the squat. Squats as shared heterotopias include a spectrum of inner thresholds radiating 'outside'.

> Threshold spatiality may host and express practices of commoning that are not contained in secluded worlds shared by secluded communities of commoners. Thresholds explicitly symbolize the potentiality of sharing by establishing intermediary areas of crossing, by opening the inside to the outside. (Stavrides 2014, p. 547)

After the eviction of the majority of squats in September 2019, there is a new period for the city. The fact that it was very easy for the government to evict all of these squats can be interpreted in two ways. The first is the power of the state to impose a decision: the general political decision for the management of the 'undesirables' (Agier, 2010) is to hide them in closed camps out of the sight of the 'citizens'. The second is the lack of openness, as described earlier, towards the 'other' as it can be understood in the supportive local and international networks. Antagonistic practices between squats (Raimondi, 2019) and outlaw networks trying to manage these spaces sometimes left limited opportunities for openness, and shared heterotopias could transform into enclaves. Borders could arise and cut the channels of communication with the neighbourhood, the city and the social media international community.

Refugee housing projects as heterotopic moments have the power through collective memory to leave lasting impressions and to continue to travel through representations that demonstrate new possibilities for social movements. A contemporary utopia will not be based on the idea of a homogenous society; moreover, the utopia of hospitality is based not only on the acceptance of the other but also in centralizing the difference as the core of the utopian society. Thus, we

> cannot formulate a utopian proposal that does not include hospitality: neither a jealous, reserved utopia, nor a possible ideal society that is not initially oriented towards the foreigner and his/her reception – Schérer, op.cit., p. 113-. (Kakoliris, 2019, p. 37)

The power of sharing, joy and self and the collective fulfilment – that the encounter with the 'other' offers – are experiences which have affected many people all over the world. Athens city centre, after the three years of experience with the refugee housing squats, maintains the hospital attribute so as to welcome again the 'other' under no conditions: the 'other' who can revitalize the unbearable atmosphere of enforcement and oppression.

Acknowledgements

I would like to thank City Plaza community, Stavros Stavrides and Melissa Harrison for editing this chapter.

References

Agier, M. (2010). Forced migration and asylum: Stateless citizens today. In C. Audebert and M. K. Dorai (ed.), *Migration in a Globalised World: New Research Issues and Prospects* (pp. 183–90). Amsterdam University Press. http://www.jstor.org/stable/j.ctt46mwxq.12.

Agustín, Ó. G., & Jørgensen, M. B. (2019). Autonomous solidarity: Hotel City Plaza. In Ó. G. Agustín and M. B. Jørgensen (ed.), *Solidarity and the 'Refugee Crisis' in Europe* (pp. 49–72). London: Palgrave Macmillan.

Agustín, Ó. G., & Jørgensen, M. B. (2019). Conceptualizing solidarity: An analytical framework. In *Solidarity and the 'Refugee Crisis' in Europe* (pp. 23–47). Cham: Palgrave Pivot. https://doi.org/10.1007/978-3-319-91848-8_2

Auge, M. (1995). *Non-places: An Introduction to Supermodernity* (J. Howe, Trans.). London and New York: Verso.

Bayat, A. (2010). Introduction: The art of presence. In A. Bayat (ed.), *Life as Politics: How Ordinary People Change the Middle East* (pp. 1–26). Amsterdam: Amsterdam University Press.

Benjamin, S. (2007). Occupancy urbanism: Ten theses. In Monica Narula, Shuddhabrata Sengupta, Jeebesh Bagchi, and Ravi Sundaram (eds.), *Sarai Reader 2007: Frontiers* (pp. 538–563). Sarai. https://sarai.net/sarai-reader-07-frontiers/

Bhide, A. (2009). Shifting terrains of communities and community organization: Reflections on organizing for housing rights in Mumbai. *Community Development Journal*. doi: 10.1093/cdj/bsp026

Bollier, D. (2014). *Think Like a Commoner: A Short Introduction to the Life of the Commons*. Gabriola Island, BC, Canada: New Society Publishers.

Borch, C., & Kornberger, M. (2015). *Urban Commons: Rethinking the City*. London: Routledge, https://doi.org/10.4324/9781315780597

Bresnihan, P., & Byrne, M. (2014). Escape into the city: Everyday practices of commoning and the production of urban space in Dublin. *Antipode, 47*(1), 36–54.

Bulley, D. (2015). Ethics, power and space: International hospitality beyond Derrida. *Hospitality & Society, 5*(2), pp. 185–201.

Burte, H. (2017). *Trajectories of Place.* Doctoral dissertation, CEPT University.

Caffentzis, G. (2009). The future of 'the commons': Neoliberalism's 'plan B' or the original disaccumulation of capital? *New Formations, 69: Imperial Ecologies,* 69, pp. 23–41. doi:10.3898/NEWF.69.01.2010

Candea, M., & Col, G. (2012). The return to hospitality. *Journal of the Royal Anthropological Institute,* 18, pp. S1–S19.

Casey, E. S. (2001). Between geography and philosophy: What does it mean to be in the place-world? *Annals of the Association of American Geographers, 91*(4), pp. 683–693.

Chattopadhyay, S. (2012). *Unlearning the City: Infrastructure in a New Optical Field.* Minnesota: University of Minnesota Press.

De Angelis, M. (2011). Η τραγωδία των καπιταλιστικών κοινών [The tragedy of the capitalist commons]. *Commons vs Crisis,* 1, 64–72. http://www.turbulence.org.uk/turbulence-5/capitalist-commons/.

De Angelis, M. (2019). Migrants' inhabiting through commoning and state enclosures. A postface. *Citizenship Studies, 23*(6), pp. 27–636.

Derrida, J., & Dufourmante, A. (2006 [1996]). *Περί Φιλοξενίας (Of Hospitality)* (Μ. Βαγγέλης, Trans.) ΕΚΚΡΕΜΕΣ [ekkremes].

Econ Pollution Control Consultants. (2002). *Community Environmental for Environmental Management Plan (CEMP) at Permanent Resettlement Site at Plot No. CTS No. 190 (pt) Majas Village.* MMRDA, MUTP. Mumbai: MMRDA.

Fuchs, M. (2005). Slum as achievement: Governmentality and the agency of slum dwellers. In E. Hust, & M. Mann (ed.), *Urbanization and Governance in India* (pp. 102–23). New Delhi: Manohar.

Fullilove, M. T. (1996, December). Psychiatric implications of displacement: Contributions from the psychology of place. *American Journal of Psychiatry, 153*(12), pp. 1516–23.

Galgano, A. (2017). Tomorrow's neighbors: Strategies for temporary refugee integration in Athens, Greece. *NYU Abu Dhabi Journal of Social Sciences,* pp. 1–28. https://sites.nyuad.nyu.edu/jss/wp-content/uploads/2017/12/annalisa_final.pdf.

Gidwani, V., & Baviskar, A. (2011). Urban commons. *Economic and Political Weekly, 46*(50), pp. 42–3.

Gutiérrez Sánchez, I. (2017). *Commoning Spaces of Social Reproduction. Citizen-led Welfare Infrastructures in Crisis-Ridden Athens.* UniFi, School of Architecture, Φλωρεντία [Florence].

Haddad, E. (2016, 2 May). Solidarity, squats and self-management assisting migrants in Greece. *Equal Times.* https://www.equaltimes.org/solidarity-squats-and-self?lang=en#.YdwsC_5BzBU.

Iliadi, A. (2016, Οκτώβριος 12). *Re.Framing Activism.* Retrieved from http://reframe.sussex.ac.uk/activistmedia/2016/10/the-radical-potential-of-media-publicity-the-case-of-city-plaza-refugee-squat-in-athens/

Kakoliris, G. (2015). Jacques Derrida on the ethics of hospitality. In: Imafidon E. (eds.), *The Ethics of Subjectivity*. London: Palgrave Macmillan,. https://doi .org/10.1057/9781137472427_9.

Kakoliris, G. (2019). Jacques Derrida and René Schérer on hospitality. *Dianoesis: A Journal of Philosophy*, 6, pp. 23–42. Location: Thessaloniki, http:// dianoesis-journal.blogspot.com.

Kanavaris, N., & Makaronas, S. (2017). *Refugee Accommodation Squat City Plaza: A "Weird" Village*. Athens: Dspace NTUA Library.

Kanavaris, N., Makaronas, S., & Stellatou, D. (2018). *Bridging the Diverse – Social Center Jasmine*. Athens: dspace NTUA Library.

Kapsali, M. (2019). *The Politics of Urban Commons: Participatory Urbanism in Thessaloniki during the 2010 Crisis*. Thessaloniki, National Archive of PHD Thesis: Aristotle University of Thessaloniki (AUTH). doi: 10.12681/ eadd/45891.

Karaliotas, L. (2017). Towards commoning institutions in, against and beyond the 'Greek crisis'. Retrieved from Eurozin: https://www.eurozine.com/ towards-commoning-institutions-in-against-and-beyond-the-greek-crisis/

Karyotis, T. (2016). The eviction of three occupied refugee shelters in Thessaloniki marks another episode in the Greek government's war on grassroots solidarity efforts. *ROAR Magazine*.

Katrini, E. (2020). Spatial manifestations of collective refugee housing – the case of City Plaza. *Radical Housing Journal*, 2(1), pp. 29–53.

King, A., & Manoussaki-Adamopoulou, I. (2019, Αυγούστου 26). Greek police raid Athens squats and arrest migrants. *The Guardian*.

King, A., & Manoussaki-Adamopoulou, I. (2019, August 29). Inside exarcheia: The self-governing community Athens police want rid of. *The Guardian*.

Koptyaeva, A. (2017, June). Collective homemaking in transit. *Forced MIgration Review: Shelter in Displacement*, 55, pp. 37–8.

Kotronaki, L. (2018). Outside the doors: Refugee accommodation squats and heterotopy politics. *The South Atlantic Quarterly*, 117(4), pp. 914–24.

Kotronaki, L., Lafazani, O., & Maniatis, G. (2018). Living resistance: Experiences from the refugee housing squat in Athens. *The South Atlantic Quarterly*, 117(4), pp. 892–5.

Lafazani, O. (2012). The border between theory and activism. *ACME An INternational Journal for Critical Geographies*, 11(2), pp. 189–93.

Lafazani, O. (2016). documenta14.

Lafazani, O. (2017). *1.5 Year City Plaza: A Project on the Antipodes of Bordering and Control Policies*. (Antipode, Editor) Retrieved from Antipode Online: https://antipodeonline.org/2017/11/13/intervention-city-plaza/

Lafazani, O. (2018a, June). Κρίση and Μετανάστευση in Greece: from illegal migrants to refugees. *Sociology*, 52(3), pp. 619–25.

Lafazani, O. (2018b, October). Homeplace plaza: Challenging the border between host and hosted. *The South Atlantic Quartery*, 117(4), pp. 896–904.

Lefebvre, H. (2002). *Critique of Everyday Life* (Vol. II). London; New York: Verso.

Lima Camargo, L. O. (2015). The Interstices of hospitality. *Research in Hospitality Management, 5*, pp. 19–27.

Linebaugh, P. (2010). Some principles of the commons. *Weekend Edition*, January 8–10.

Lombard, M. (2014). Constructing ordinary places: Place-making in urban informal settlements in Mexico. *Progress in Planning, 94*, pp. 1–53. https://doi.org/10.1016/j.progress.2013.05.003.

Lynch, K. (1984). *Good City Form*. Boston: MIT Press.

Maniatis, G. (2018). From a crisis of management to humanitarian crisis management. *The South Atlantic Quarterly, 117*(4), pp. 905–13.

Martinez, M. A., Dadusc, D., & Grazioli, M. (2019). Introduction: Citizenship as inhabitance? Migrant housing squats versus institutional accommodation. *Citizenship Studies, 23*(6), pp. 521–39.

McGuirk, J. (2015, June 15). Urban commons have radical potential – it's not just about community gardens. *The Guardian*, International Edition.

Mezzadra, S. (2018). In the wake of the Greek spring and the summer of migration. *The South Atlantic Quarterly, 117*(4), pp. 925–33.

Montagna, N., & Grazioli, M. (2019). Urban commons and freedom of movement – The housing struggles of recently arrived migrants in Rome. *Citizenship Studies, 23*(9), pp. 577–92.

Nijman, J. (2010). A study of space in Mumbai's slums. *Tijdschrift voor Economische en Sociale Geografie, 101*, pp. 4–17.

Papataxiarchis, E. (2006a). Τα άχθη της ετερότητας, Διαστάσεις της πολιτισμικής διαφοροποίησης στην Ελλάδατου πρώιμου 21ου αιώνα [Burdens of alterity: aspects of cultural differentiation in early 21th-century]. In E. Παπαταξιάρχης (ed.), *Περιπέτειες της ετερότητας: Η παραγωγή της πολιτισμικής διαφοράς στη σημερινή Ελλάδα [Adventures of Alterity: The Production of Cultural Difference in Contemporary Greece]*. Athens: Alexandria, 12–78

Papataxiarchis, E. (2006b). Το καθεστώς της διαφορετικότητας στην Ελληνική κοινωνία, Υποθέσεις εργασίας. In E. Παπαταξιάρχης (ed.), *Περιπέτει ες της ετερότητας: Η παραγωγή της πολιτισμικής διαφοράς στη σημερινή Ελλάδα [Adventures of Alterity: The Production of Cultural Difference in Contemporary Greece]* (pp. 407–69). Alexandria.

Papataxiarchis, E. (2014). Ό αδιανόητος ρατσισμός: Η πολιτικοποίηση της 'φιλο ξενίας' την εποχή της κρίσης' ['The inconceivable racism: the politicization of "hospitality" in the age of crisis']. *Synchrona, 127*, pp. 46–62.

Papataxiarchis, E. (2016a, April). Being 'there' at the front line of the 'European refugee crisis' – part 1. *Antropoly Today, 32*(2), pp. 3–7. doi:10.1111/1467-8322.12237

Papataxiarchis, E. (2016b, June). Being 'there' at the front line of the 'European refugee crisis' – part 2. *Anthropology Today, 32*(3), pp. 3–7. doi:10.1111/1467-8322.12252

Papataxiarchis, E. (2016c, May). Unwrapping solidarity? Society reborn in austerity. *Social Anthropology, 24*, pp. 205–10.

Papataxiarchis, E. (2016d, October). Μία Μεγάλη Ανατροπή: Η Ευρωπαϊκή Προσφυγική Κρίση και ο Νέος Πατριωτισμός της Αλληλεγγύης. *ΣΥΓΧΡΟΝΑ ΘΕΜΑΤΑ, 132-133*, pp. 7-28.

Pred, A. (1984, June). Place as historically contingent process: Structuration and the time- geography of becoming places. *Annals of the Association of American Geographers, 74*(2), pp. 279-97.

Raimondi, V. (2019). For 'common struggles of migrants and locals'. Migrant activism and squatting in Athens. *Citizenship Studies, 23*(6), pp. 559-576.

Rakopoulos, T. (2016, May). Solidarity: The egalitarian tensions of a bridge-concept. *Social Anthropology, 24*, pp. 142-51.

Roy, A. (2011). Slumdog cities: Rethinking subaltern urbanism. *International Journal of Urban and Regional Research, 35*(2), pp. 223-38.

Rozakou, K. (2012). The biopolitics of hospitality in Greece: Humanitarianism and the management of refugees. *American Ethnologist, 39*, pp. 562-77.

Rozakou, K. (2016). Crafting the volunteer: Voluntary associations and the reformation of sociality. *Journal of Modern Greek Studies, 34*, pp. 79-102.

Rozakou, K. (2016, May). Socialities of solidarity: Revisiting the gift taboo in times of crises: Socialities of solidarity. *Social Anthropology, 24*, pp. 185-99.

Schindler, S. (2014). Understanding urban processes in Flint, Michigan: Approaching 'subaltern urbanism' inductively . *International Journal of Urban and Regional Research, 38*(3), pp. 791-804.

Siapera, E. (2019, April). Refugee solidarity in Europe: Shifting the discourse. *European Journal of Cultural Studies, 22*, pp. 245-66.

Simone, A. (2004). People as infrastructure: Intersecting fragments in Johannesburg. *Public Culture, 16*(3), pp. 407-29.

Solidarity2Refugees. (n.d.). Retrieved from http://solidarity2refugees.gr /39-mines-city-plaza-oloklirosi-enos-kyklou-archi-enos-neou/?fbclid =IwAR21QYRNWLJvYwYGXzzF_01RiL3c-YmMYzqKs13zJuXfD -AlWcVCUwqok18.

Squire, V. (2018, July). Mobile solidarities and precariousness at City Plaza: Beyond vulnerable and disposable lives. *Studies in Social Justice, 12*(1), pp. 111-32.

Squire, V., & Darling, J. (2013). The "minor" politics of rightful presence: Justice and relationality in city of sanctuary. *International Political Sociology, 7*, pp. 59-74.

Star, S. L. (1999). The ethnography of infrastructure. *American Behavioral Scientist, 43*(3), pp. 377-91.

Stavrides, S. (2014). Emerging common spaces as a challenge to the city of crisis. *City, 18*, pp. 546-50.

Stavrides, S. (2015). Common space as threshold space: Urban commoning in struggles to reappropriate public space. *Footprint, 16*, pp. 9-19. https://doi .org/10.7480/footprint.9.1.896

Stavrides, S. (2016). *Common Space: The City as Commons.* London: Zed Books Ltd.

Tsavdaroglou, C. (2018). The newcomer's right to the common space: The case of Athens during the refugee crisis. *ACME An International Journal for Critical Geographies, 17*(2), pp. 376-401.

Tsavdaroglou, C. (2019). Reimagining a transnational right to the city: No border actions and commoning practices in Thessaloniki. *Social Inclusion*, 7(2), pp. 219–29.

Tsavdaroglou, C., Giannopoulou, C., Lafazani, O., Pistikos, I., & Petropoulou, C. (2018). De(constructing) the refugees' right to the city: State-run camps versus commoning practices in athens, thessaloniki and mytilene. Vol. Refugees and forced immigration '18 conference proceedings. Istanbul.

Tsavdaroglou, C., Giannopoulou, C., Petropoulou, C., & Pistikos, I. (2019). Acts for refugees' right to the city and commoning practices of care-tizenship in Athens, Mytilene and Thessaloniki. *Social Inclusion*, 7, pp. 119–30.

Tuan, Y.-F. (1977). *Space and Place: The Perspective of Experience*. Minneapolis: University of Minnesota Press.

Turner, J. F. (1976). *Housing by People: Towards Autonomy in Building Environments*. London: Marion Boyars.

Velegrakis, G., & Kosyfologou, A. (2018). The city plaza immigrants' housing project in Athens and the social solidarity medical center of Thessaloniki. In Miriam Lang, Claus-Dieter König and Ada-Charlotte Regelmann (eds.), *Alternatives in a World of Crisis* (pp. 222–55). Brussels: Rosa Luxemburg Stiftung.

10

The Dandara community-occupation

Destitution-constitution movements towards urban commons in Belo Horizonte (Brazil)

Lucia Capanema Alvares, João B. M. Tonucci Filho
and Joviano Maia Mayer

Introduction

Some insight into the Brazilian housing situation can be gained from the fact that among fifty-seven million permanent private households, only thirty million (52.6 per cent) were considered adequate by the 2010 Census.[1] According to IPEA[2] and building on data from the National Household Sample Survey (IBGE), the country's fragile housing policies resulted in a deficit of 5.24 million units in 2012, 73.6 per cent of which consisted of families with an income of up to three minimum wages. These families have very few, if any, alternatives within their reach in metropolitan areas, where they end up living in densely populated and precarious areas where the real estate market is absent: preservation areas defined by federal law, or unhealthy zones like landfills and swamps. In rare cases, plots fit for occupation remain empty due to tax debts, pending inheritances and other legal problems. Such was the case with the land targeted for occupation by the Popular Brigades[3] in 2008, initiating Dandara's history and an occupation movement that now numbers more than fifty occupations and somewhere between 15,000 and 20,000 families in the Belo Horizonte Metropolitan Region (RMBH) – the third largest in Brazil, with more than five million

[1] IBGE – Instituto Brasileiro de Geografia e Estatística. 2010 Census.
[2] IPEA – Instituto de Pesquisas Econômicas Aplicadas. Available at http://www.ipea.gov .br/portal/index.php?option=com_content&view=article&id=20656. Accessed October 2014.
[3] The Popular Brigades is a socialist political organization which aims to establish a sovereign and popular political regime in Brazil.

people. The new occupations are organized through diverse networks of new social movements, homeless families and supporters.

Its resistance has led Dandara to gain a prominent position in Brazil's alternative housing sector. While it obtained several victories during its destitution-constitution movements, including recognition of the families' rights to tenure, the institution of a common culture and the formation of grassroots leaders, it has recently also shown movements, like giving up the ideal of common landownership, the loss of control to outsiders and internal power struggles. Whether the community is going to fall prey to Olson's predicament by losing its commonality and sense of community remains to be seen.

In order to tell Dandara's history in these terms, we build on the critical literature on the common and on our own participation in events, including Joviano Maia Mayer's work as a voluntary lawyer with the Popular Brigades, witnessing the most important events, and hosting a number of focal group discussions. The authors deepened this experience further by interviewing local leaders and staff from the Belo Horizonte Housing Authority, as well as visiting the community several times. The chapter begins with a brief discussion of critical approaches to the common, and then presents Dandara's destitution and constitution movements, before finally offering an appraisal of the overall process.

The concept of the commons, private property and urban commoning as practice: A brief review

The commons is a tensioned and disputed field of power relations: it is inherently political. The current debate about the commons spans a wide universe of authors and approaches, from studies on the history of communal lands, enclosures and the formation of capitalist private property, to the commons as a foundation of social reproduction and as a political project for fostering communism beyond capitalism and socialism. Seen from this perspective, the common is a social relationship and a political concept, rather than some type of economic good, and thus a conflictual field defined by social relations (of production, labour, property, etc.) and historically determined productive forces.

According to Dardot and Laval (2015a), the common as a political principle includes the political co-obligation that comes entirely from acting in common and jointly elaborating the rules of an activity. The definition of what is the 'common good' is the principle; it is precisely what needs to be decided politically in common. The activity is what communizes, inscribing things in an institutional space through the production of specific rules, and becoming the subject of institution and government: it is the instituting praxis, not in any way similar to 'management' (the consensual organization of things), but closer to 'government', insofar as it assumes social interests and seeks to overcome conflicts through decisions concerning the rules. Furthermore, the common is not spontaneously born either from social life (as in Proudhon) or from its historical production by capital (as in Marx); it emerges out of collective struggles not only as resistance and protest but also as sources of institution and law (Dardot and Laval, 2015b).

Negri, however, criticizes such formulations for abolishing historical materialism and dematerializing the class struggle for the sake of a 'metaphysics of the common', of the common as a principle (2014, p. 282): we can no longer understand how the common is claimed, where the subjects that constitute it are, or which are the figures of capital development that fill its background. For De Angelis (2007), the increasing hegemony of capital finds resistance in alternative ways of life and value practices, generating an 'outside' – constituted as antagonistic and contradictory to capital – which is the scope of the common production. What the author argues for is a political discourse that overcomes capital, not oriented towards the creation of a utopically idealized 'system', but towards the production of conditions that favour the blossoming of alternative practices of value.

The urban commons

With rare exceptions, theorists of the common have not intend to discuss in depth how to explore contemporary urbanization from a common perspective, either to think about the ways in which resources and common spaces in the metropolis are produced and appropriated or to think the metropolis itself as a common. By failing to articulate the dimension of common resources that exist in the city – community gardens, housing occupations, self-managed cultural spaces and so on – with the idea of the city itself as a common, they have effectively denied its potential for generating resources, spaces and common practices, and its capacity to function as a space for life in common.

If the city is a diverse space of numerous urban commons (goods, resources and common spaces), it is also a common as a whole, its relationships and opportunities associated with the complexity and richness of urban life. In Henri Lefebvre's work, the urban common appears as a mutually illuminating reality and concept, asserting itself in the insurgent and counter-hegemonic socio-spatial practices that populate the folds and interstices of abstract space, in emerging processes of appropriation and spatial experimentation that cultivate the meaning of use, of the work of art and of difference. The common is based around the experiences of producing space in everyday life, in usage, in collective appropriations, and in the self-management of the city as a collective work, which may converge towards the realization of the right to the city (Tonucci Filho, 2017).

The struggles for the common in the metropolis intersect and add to the struggles for the right to the city in the resistance to the enclosures, privatizations and dispossessions associated with neoliberal urbanism, as well as in the alternative experiences of building new common spaces, through art and politics, activism and parties, intentionally or intuitively approximating everyday life, production and reproduction. According to Tonucci Filho (2017), practices and spaces considered as pre-modern, archaic and informal, found in the favelas, peripheries and other metropolitan popular territories, are potential cultivators of commonality, sharing and cooperation.

The common against private property

At the centre of the philosophical and political debate about the common in Critical Theory (in dialogue with Marx) is its opposition to private property, pointing towards a field of more autonomous and collective practices of production and social reproduction (Tonucci Filho, 2017). For Dardot and Laval, the political principle of the common is antagonistic to private capitalist property and to public state property, both based on the logic of exclusivist appropriation; private property is opposed to collective use and appropriation aimed at social purposes.

> The principle of the common that emerges today within all social movements must make this articulation possible: it is not at all opposed to the public, but it is no longer defined in terms of 'property'. More precisely, in the public realm it retains the emphasis on the social purpose of ownership and not just its legal form. [. . .] It is not a question, then, of opposing 'good' appropriation to 'bad' appropriation [. . .] but of opposing any appropriation to the preservation of a 'common' subtracted from any appropriative logic. (Dardot and Laval, 2015b, p. 270)[4]

---

[4]   Authors' free translation from the original in Portuguese.

Hardt and Negri (2014) emphasize the underlying difficulty in the transition process from public and private property to common property: 'To speak of common goods, then, means constructing a constitutional process regarding a set of goods [efficiently] managed through the direct participation of citizens' (p. 99):

> The commoner is thus an ordinary person who accomplishes an extraordinary task: opening private property to the access and enjoyment of all; transforming public property controlled by state authority into the common; and in each case discovering mechanisms to manage, develop, and sustain common wealth through democratic participation. (Hardt and Negri, 2014, p. 140)

But this transition from the public to the common can only occur through struggles against privatization, 'questioning practically and theoretically the fundamentals and effects of property rights, opposing them to the social imperative of common use' (Dardot and Laval, 2015b, p. 261).[5] Moreover, from the institution of the common arises a political obligation linked to the exercise of participation in a collective activity: co-activity is the foundation of political co-obligation.

There is no common without commoning and community

An important question posed by the urban common concerns one of its constitutive dimensions: the community. The historical and theoretical meaning that Linebaugh (2014) and other authors confer today to the commoner does not correspond to his/her housing status, but to participation in commoning practices that situate the person in relationships based on sharing and reciprocity. Harvey (2012) sees resources, community and commoning as integrated elements that form an interdependent whole. In other words, the common must be treated inseparably as a practical reality, a theoretical concept and a political discourse.

Although working from an economic-functionalist perspective, Ostrom (1990) demonstrated how common resources can count on sustainable collective management practices and on use and access rules defined by communities, departing from some principles such as the institution of

---

[5] Ibid.

barriers, rules and sanctions, and their interscale recognition. In De Angelis and Stavrides (2016), the common, as a social dimension of sharing, points to a path based on community self-management and self-government. The common should not be seen as a matter of individual interest versus the common interest, therefore, but of how certain individual interests can be articulated in order to constitute common interests. Hardt and Negri (2014) also stress the political importance of instituting democratic forms of producing and managing our common wealth, which aligns them both with Ostrom, and Dardot and Laval, and with the argument that the common is a sharing practice that presupposes co-obligations and reciprocities.

The common is not produced only in acts of contestation and resistance, because its survival, against all opposing pressures, requires perpetuity, continuity, rooting and expansion. It is also through everyday life that the bonds of reciprocal obligations and political co-responsibilities that constitute the community are interwoven (Dardot and Laval, 2015a; Esposito, 2010). In this sense, the production of the common requires the transformation of daily life, recombining what was separated by the social, gendered and spatial division of labour under capitalism, redefining reproduction in a more cooperative way, bringing the personal closer to the political and recreating ties and relationships based on sharing and reciprocity (Federici, 2010). As Dellenbaugh et al. write (2015, p. 18), 'urban commoners thus constantly need to negotiate and rearticulate the "we"'.

In political and organizational terms, Lefebvre (2009) considers that appropriation is only concretely achieved through self-management. He argues that the principle of self-management revives the contradiction between use value and exchange value, restoring primacy to use against the commodity world, without denying that this world has its own laws and that these need to be tamed, not neglected. The limits to commodity logic must be put in place by self-managed democratic planning projects, in which the social needs formulated and controlled by those who have some real participation are prioritized over purely economic concerns.

Destitution-constitution movements and the counter-power construction

Hardt and Negri highlight three elements that make up the concept of counter-power construction: resistance, insurgency and constituent power. While resistance and insurgency are premises for the very installation of movements and networks in metropolitan spaces, constituent power, undertaken by the multitude in the defence and construction of the urban commons, has the potential power to create another society that can organize and govern itself, independently of the logic of representative democracy, forming new affection networks and new democratic forms of deliberation through creative processes of cooperation and communication, and new ways of life based on the production and defence of common goods and developed through constituent processes of commoning. The production of subjectivity operated and determined by the instituted power always leaves room for resistance through 'irresistible devices' (Negri, 2016). It is, therefore, in the context of urban struggles and resistances that the production of new subjectivities in the course of political action can potentiate the formation of counter-powers, networks and subversive connections, under the perspective of the production of the common and based on communication, cooperation and creativity, filled with destitution and constituent contents at the same time (Hardt and Negri, 2014).

> How can people associate closely together in the common and participate directly in democratic decision making? How can the multitude become prince of the institutions of the common in a way that reinvents and realizes democracy? This is the task of a constituent process. (Hardt and Negri, 2014, p. 65)

> [It] is a decision that emerges out of the ontological and social process of productive labor; it is an institutional form that develops a common content; it is a deployment of force that defends the historical progression of emancipation and liberation; it is, in short, an act of love. (Hardt and Negri, 2004, p. 351).

If the whole space has become the place of reproduction of productive relations, it has also become the primary locus open to the construction of new relations of production and new forms of existence in the world, the outcome of the constituent dimension that biopolitically empowers the metropolitan multitude in the development of a future common. But the common is confirmed on the horizon of the biopolitical metropolis precisely because the present already brings with it a production that is common; in other words, it is not a question of utopia because the bet in the common comes from the field of immanence, from the constituent dimension of biopolitical production that has the common 'more as a premise than as a promise' (Pelbart, 2016, p. 30).

Dandara's history

In August 2008, the Popular Brigades, together with the Landless Workers Movement (MST) and the Catholic Land Pastoral (CPT), started to plan the occupation of a 315,000 metre[6] tax-indebted plot of land in Belo Horizonte's periphery. It was meant to be a planned and innovative initiative, based on common ownership, on preservation of commons such as green areas and orchards and on an open conflict with local authorities and facilities companies in order to force them to provide public services. After planning the occupation for nine months, during which they contacted a number of activist groups and homeless families willing to take part in the endeavour, 150 families invaded the plot in April 2009. In the evening, breaking the law and without any order to reinstate possession, the military police tried to expel the occupants. Other families rushed to join this unique endeavour. By 2010, the site contained 981 registered and numbered tents, with an estimated population of 4,000 people and a waiting list of 300 families. Tents gradually became more substantial, sheltering 'mattresses, stoves, children and dreams' (Ocupação Dandara, 2011). In their own words:

> We exist, we are many and we will fight to continue to exist. . . . Those who try to massacre us not only want to expel 1,159 homeless families, they also want to expel dignity, expel those who do not comply with poverty and wealth, they want to expel an 'internal enemy', a non-conforming voice. [. . .] We occupy abandoned land [. . .] cluttered with unpaid taxes, full of nothing. When we build our homes, we build a community, [. . .] we build our dignity, we are building ourselves. (Ocupação Dandara, 2011)

Enduring police attacks for months, they held regular assemblies with up to 2,000 participants while occupying the area in orderly fashion and, with the help of a local lawyers' collective, suing water, electricity, healthcare and postal providers for failing to provide services to the community. Architects from the Catholic University designed a prize-winning urban plan as they went to court claiming collective ownership of the plot (Figure 10.1). From 2009 to 2014, they led at least five marches to downtown and seven occupations of the City Council, including one-week occupations of City Hall and of the city's main square, which gave Dandara visibility and generated a huge support network; their representatives obtained meetings with the National Secretaries of Cities, the Presidency, Women Policies and Human Rights, and

---

6   Fictitious name.

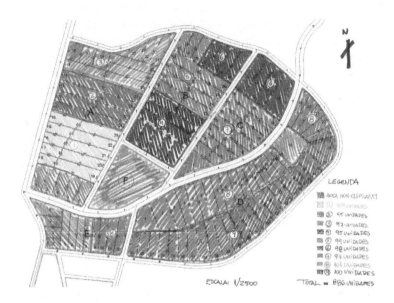

Figure 10.1 Community centre and healthcare facility. (Photograph by authors.)

with the National Congress, the Lawyers Federal Council and the National Conference of Bishops in Brazil.

In 2014, during the Fourth Belo Horizonte Urban Policy Conference, Dandara was recognized as AEIS-2 (Special Area of Social Interest 2), giving it legal recognition and the possibility of applying for Participatory Budget (PB) funds. Since then, the Dandara Community Residents Association (AMCD) has been carrying out social work and campaigning for the installation of water and electricity in the area, as well as making referrals to health and education public services. In 2015, Dandara saw a groundbreaking mobilization regarding the PB. Angela, a veteran leader, learnt about a local PB meeting just three days in advance and appealed to community bonds:

> Each one was at a corner; four people calling the residents, the residents calling us. This was our alternative to participating in the participatory budget, although we had not been invited. It was by chance that I found out about it [. . .]. Arriving and seeing what it was, I thought, 'this is our chance to get into that budget, no matter what.' We had no official right because [Dandara] was not legal. We gathered around 900 people and went down to where the participatory budget meeting was due to he held. When we got there we had no rights, but they had to let us in. As

we were not legalized, they wrote us down as *'Dandara Trevo,'* which is another community down the road. So, we showed up well organized! Belo Horizonte had never seen such a case in its participatory budget. We had 66 representatives, including delegates and substitutes. So, the victory came about because of the fight. We put up a fight and we won.

The endowment was directed towards a comprehensive urbanization and land regularization plan, which started in 2017. By 2018, URBEL (Belo Horizonte Housing Authority) began the land regulation process and the urbanization of the plot. The sewage and water company, together with the power company, also started to work on the infrastructure, while City Hall installed garbage collection and a public healthcare facility. During 2019–20, URBEL was still urbanizing the area and the mayor had recognized the lawful possession of individual plots by Dandara inhabitants. Due to the strength of its resistance, the consolidation of occupation and its national and international visibility, Dandara has played a decisive role in the new cycle of struggles for housing.

In the course of the occupation, the large plots destined for agricultural activities had to be reduced, given the immense pressure for housing. This led to the abandonment of the project based on common areas in favour of a denser occupation model. Both Dandara and the Popular Brigades movement lost power and control over the real estate market to informal agents, including drug traffickers. In addition to the clash between these two forms of para-state power, and the multiple interests of residents themselves, conflicts also exist between the de facto modus operandi of social movements and the ideal horizons of constitution of the common – principles and demands for direct democracy, horizontality, self-management and local government. As URBEL staff member Gui[7] has put it, in the course of the Regulation Plan, 'they have already decided to break apart and go for individual lots. Then you see the conflict between community, an idea of commoning, and the individuality of people. [. . .] When the movement swelled in size and a lot of people came from outside, individual interests ended up undermining these ideas.'

Families have been establishing small businesses (mainly tire shops, stationary/LAN houses, construction material stores, bars and bakeries/grocery stores) in their residential plots, indicating that they feel secure enough about their land possession status to invest in residential expansions and the development of economic activities. This demonstrates that duly registered private property rights are not essential to transform the 'dead

---

[7]   Fictitious name

capital' of informal settlements into productive capital. On the other hand, and despite the economic gains made by some families, the capitalist business model means there is no prospect of sharing the means of production or the profits.

Dandara as common

Located at the beginning of the avenue that bears the same name as the community, a broad open area used for parties and local events ushers incomers to the Professor Fábio Alves Community Centre, the venue for the occupation meetings and gatherings and the location of the Popular Brigades local base. The centre also functions as an important cultural space where instruments are stored for the music and dance rehearsals and performances. It is used as a common: built, administered and maintained by residents.

The few squares and open spaces are also common, publicly used and not owned by the state, but the Dandara community orchard no longer exists. It was located in one of the green areas originally preserved (which, under federal legislation, cannot house people) that ended up being transformed into individual lots by the real estate informal market, dominated by drug dealers. According to Gui, 'there is an internal conflict between the people who are in the preservation areas [on the fringes of] Dandara and those who are inside. The conflict is with the people who occupied this green area and the group who divided it up.' Angela seems to agree with Hardin (1968) on the issue of the collective orchard: 'the project here was for everyone to plant and harvest at the same time, but that doesn't work. I think it is unfair for some to plant and others to reap.' Despite this loss and with it the meaning of the original rur-urban character of the occupation, many families still grow orchards in their backyards. Some sell the surplus, but they mostly engage in sharing among their peers. Some houses have well-kept gardens and flower beds that advance over the 'public' space of non-existent sidewalks, contributing to the environmental and urban quality of the occupation. Maintaining the streets safe and clean is also an everyday chore: 'If a new resident arrives here, there is already someone who goes and explains how things are done here in the Community. And, like it or not, the person adapts,' says Angela. Along Dandara Avenue, one can see gardens in the green and well-maintained central beds, in spite of the previous conflicts with new incoming residents, who wanted to use the middle of the widest roads for housing purposes.

Another commoning activity was the infrastructure laid down before City Hall started to implement its urbanization plan. This involved use of a bulldozer, hired on a pro-rata basis. Luciana, a young leader who grew up in the occupation, reminds us of other commons: 'The "Struggle time" is a two-year-old space initially conceived and built to help women who have experienced some type of violence, with a focus on sexual violence, [. . .] but it is really about empowering women, giving them visibility.' In order to support and complement this space, community women also founded 'the sewing cooperative, which is a way of mobilizing women to work on income generation, but also to have time among themselves to discuss daily abuses and think about proposals and strategies to fight and, in some way, overcome their current pains and try to prevent others'. A school directed towards preparing Dandara's youngsters for university entrance exams 'also assists neighbouring communities in order to counter the prejudice against the occupation' and constantly discusses 'political issues that place occupations in context'. According to her, these are 'ways to show the State how organized the community is'. Though sparse, commoning activities that build a sense of community are part of Dandara's history: when 'Tiq'[7] moved to a plot 'she was in no condition to build a house, so we got together and built the first room for her. Afterwards I named her house "little-bit house" – a little bit of each one of us was there,' recalls Angela, one of the first leaders of the occupation.

According to Angela, Dandara has 'won all the fights; everything we won here was through joint efforts'. She proudly states that AMCD is alive and well. 'It does not aggregate everybody, just those who want to participate. But when there is something that interests the community, everyone comes together no matter what they think.'

A critical look at Dandara's destitution-constitution moves

At the same time, the Dandara occupation-community provides an example of Simmel's dialectical construction of antagonism unity through its opposition to and relation with the state, forcing it to increasingly supply goods and services and to recognize its existence outside the existing property laws (as Kip 2015 calls for). It builds Durkheimian social cohesion and works to dilute the fear caused by exposure to difference (Bauman 2007) in its neighbourhood. In addition to a convergence of interests, the mobilization and unification of the inhabitants attain an ideological and value goal, where all residents see themselves as members of a group that represents an ideal and an objective more important than individual wishes. According to Simmel (1903), personal aggravation is reduced and social struggle intensified. The overarching supra-personal cause also reduces the possibility of dissolution and desertion from the group, as Luciana put it: 'now that housing is secured, we need to fight for other things, not only for Dandara, but for the city, for the country.' The newcomers, on the contrary, 'do not carry the marks of the struggle for the community: the manifestations that we led, the marches downtown, the political meetings, the meetings with the Police and with the State. . . . They don't carry those marks [. . .]. That demobilizes the community now.'

Once housing was secured, a number of inhabitants – and not only newcomers – ceased participating in community meetings. For Gui, 'from that moment on, other interests, interests that came from outside, took over. It seems like when the group opens up, outsiders become very powerful.' 'The bond [of participation], in a way, existed through fear: [some people say] "now that housing is already guaranteed, I don't need to participate so much in the collective struggle"', Luciana reports. Angela reminds us that people are somewhat tired of struggling and want to prioritize their personal sphere: 'Saturdays and Sundays, people you will never stop doing your house to work in the community garden. . . . You know, right? Each one has its own projects.' Overcoming Olson's (1971) description of the predicament surrounding the end of the movement once the main objectives are achieved, and instead working continually to constitute the common against the private and found new ways of life outside capitalist subjectivity, is indeed very difficult. The initial resistance against private property and the following insurgency – the occupation itself – mobilized the dimension of conflict as they opposed their eviction. Once the threat of eviction was overcome, the constituent dimension must be elevated to the forefront of political action without being deprived of the indispensable antagonism towards capital and its forms of expression, as Hardt and Negri emphasize.

According to Gui, 'from what has been happening in the favelas, we recognize a loss of commoning practices in the housing movement: "It's really cool, but not in my backyard." I think the goal of the Brigades, as a movement, was to occupy in and of itself, as a way of guaranteeing the plot for those families, and that really was achieved.' The origin of most families, who previously lived under rent or favour in overcrowded spaces, as Luciana stated, may have also played a crucial role in the prejudice expressed against more collective forms of housing and property arrangements. This feeling, combined with the pressing need to settle participant families, undermined the ideal of Dandara as a common (Lourenço, 2014). Collective land tenure was left behind as soon as the state entered the process with its regularization plan, producing the abstract space in the occupation and bringing it into the commodity world. Although the challenge to overcome the narrow limits of private property was not met, their collective economic, political and cultural practices deepen the production of new subjectivities and advance the constituent dimension of resistance (Mayer, 2015).

There are a number of important contradictions regarding urban occupations. On the one hand, they are spaces in the making that seem very powerful zones for the flourishing of practices based on sharing and solidarity, in part because they are peripheral spaces where the presence of the state and capital is smaller. On the other hand, most of this autonomy derives from the fact that they exist as a product of a very heteronomous and unequal capitalist society. Occupations thus experience these contradictions and ambivalences, living between the potentialities of autonomy and collective construction of commons, and the harsh realities of an extreme condition of exclusion, deprivation, segregation and violence (Tonucci Filho, 2017).

Among the commoning rules articulated by Bollier (2014), however, defending the collective against foreign interests and easy riders has proven to be almost impossible in Dandara's reality. In spite of collective efforts and investments, the experiments with community gardens in the occupation proved to be quite fragile and discontinuous, exposing important limits to the production of the common. Created at the beginning of the occupation, Dandara's community garden, for example, no longer exists. Moreover, according to Angela, when the movement's coordination team was turned into a neighbourhood association in compliance with PB rules, the group opened participation to newcomers and inadvertently yielded control. Luciana also identifies another troubling movement that came into play in the association: 'today [they put] that energy into fighting each other to remain in that small position of power, in so-called leadership.' What might be the most problematic influence over the community, however, is drug trafficking, since it subverts constituent movements by seizing common and vacant plots of land and transforming them into privately owned public spaces ('POPS') through its coercive power. With the advance of the private over the public, the potential of public space to be open to encounter, spontaneity and alterity is drastically curbed, together with the possibilities for the appropriation and collective use of open areas.

The challenges surrounding the production of the common became more instigating when the community won its direct conflict with the state and capital over the territory's possession. Other devices for activation of mobilization, in addition to the struggling dimension of conflict – endless horizon of constituent positivity – are needed in order to enhance the exercise of democracy and the production of new ways of life.

Focusing on the struggle through the common, not for the common (De Angelis, 2007), the process has been highly successful. The abstract space of property and taxes left its folds and interstices (Lefebvre, 1991) or the 'out' opportunity suggested by De Angelis (2007), giving Dandara the chance to occupy and legally possess a tax-indebted plot. Its leadership position in the local occupation movement, maintained throughout its existence, has turned Dandara into one of the main nodes of the housing movement, articulating a consistent net of communities. Angela recalls their role as commoners: 'Many times children grow up thinking that those who live in communities are slum dwellers, thieves. . . . You know how it is, right? So, we go to schools to show that we are all the same, there is no difference. The difference is only money.'

References

Bauman, Z. (2007), *Vida Líquida*. Rio de Janeiro: Jorge Zahar.

Bollier, D. (2014), *Think Like a Commoner: A Short Introduction to the Life of the Commons*. Gabriola Island, CA: New Society Publishers.

Dardot, P. and Laval, C. (2015a), *Común: ensayo sobre la revolución en el siglo XXI*. Primera edición. Barcelona: Editorial Gedisa.

Dardot, P. and Laval, C. (2015b), Propriedade, apropriação social e instituição do comum. *Tempo social, São Paulo*, 27(1): 261–73.

De Angelis, M. (2007), *The Beginning of History: Value Struggles and Global Capital*. London; Ann Arbor, MI: Pluto.

De Angelis, M. and Stavrides, S. (2016), On the Commons: A Public Interview. *e-flux*, [New York], journal #17. An Architektur. Available at: http://www.eflux.com/journal/on-the-commons-a-public-interview-with-massimo-de-angelis-and-stavrosstavrides/ (Accessed on 04 Aug 2016).

Dellenbaugh, M., Kip, M., Bieniok, M., Muller A.K. and Schwegmann, M. (eds) (2015), *Urban Commons: Moving Beyond State and Market*. Basel: Birkhäuser Verlag GmbH. [Seizing the (every)day: Welcome to the urban commons!].

Esposito, R. (2010), *Communitas: The Origin and Destiny of Community*. Stanford, CA: Stanford University Press.

Federici, S. (2010), Feminism and the Politics of the Commons. In *The Commoner: Other Articles in Commons www.thecommoner.org*. Available at: https://selforganizedseminar.files.wordpress.com/2012/05/federici-feminism-and-the-politics-of-commons.pdf (Accessed on January 7, 2022).

Hardin, G. (2009/1968), The Tragedy of the Commons. *Journal of Natural Resources Policy Research*, 1: 3.

Hardt, M. and Negri, A. (2004), *Multitude: War and Democracy in the Age of Empire*. London: Penguin Books.

Hardt, M. and Negri, A. (2014), *Declaração – isto não é um manifesto*. São Paulo: n-1 edições.

Harvey, D. (2012), The Creation of the Urban Commons. In: Harvey, D. (ed.) *Rebel Cities: From the Right to the City to the Urban Revolution*. London; New York: Verso, 267–88.

Kip, M. (2015), Moving Beyond the City: Conceptualizing Urban Commons from a Critical Urban Studies Perspective. In: Dellenbaugh, M., Kip, M., Bieniok, M., Muller A.K. and Schwegmann, M. (eds) *Urban Commons: Moving Beyond State and Market*. Basel: Birkhäuser Verlag GmbH. [Seizing the (every)day: Welcome to the urban commons!].

Lefebvre, H. (1991), *A vida cotidiana no mundo moderno*. Trad. de Alcides João de Barros. São Paulo: Ática.

Lefebvre, H. (1999/1970), *A revolução urbana*. Belo Horizonte: Editora UFMG.

Lefebvre, H. (2009), *State, Space, World: Selected Essays*. Brenner, N. and Elden, S. (ed.). Minneapolis; London: University of Minnesota Press.

Linebaugh, P. (2014), *Stop, Thief! The Commons, Enclosures and Resistance*. Oakland, CA: PM Press.

Lourenço, T.C.B. (2014), *Cidade ocupada*. Belo Horizonte: UFMG, Dissertação de Mestrado em Arquitetura e Urbanismo.

Mayer, J.G.M. (2015), *O comum no horizonte da metrópole biopolítica*. Belo Horizonte: UFMG, Dissertação de Mestrado em Arquitetura e Urbanismo.

Negri, A. (2016), *Comum, entre Marx e Proudhon*. Originally published in: Il Manifesto, 06/05/2014. Translation UniNômade. (pp. 282–6). Available at: http://uninomade.net/tenda/comum-entre-marx-e-proudhon/ (Accessed on July 20, 2016).

Ocupaçao Dandara (2011), *Ocupação Dandara*. Available at http://ocupacaodandara.blogspot.com/(Accessed on January 3, 2011).

Olson, M. (1971), *The Logic of Collective Action: Public Goods and the Theory of Groups*. Cambridge, MA: Harvard University Press.

Ostrom, E. (1990), *Governing the Commons: The Evolution of Institutions for Collective Action*. New York: Cambridge University Press, 1990.

Pelbart, P. P. (2016), *Cartography of Exhaustion: Nihilism Inside Out*. Minneapolis: University of Minnesota Press.

Simmel, G. (1903), The Sociology of Conflict. *American Journal of Sociology* 9: 490–525.

Tonucci Filho, J.B.M. (2017), *Comum urbano: a cidade além do público e do privado*. Belo Horizonte: Tese de Doutorado em Geografia.

Part III

In defence of the collective right to housing

11

Materializing the self-management

Tracking the *commons* in Yugoslav housing economy

Jelica Jovanović

Introduction

The housing economy of socialist Yugoslavia and the housing stock it produced have been a result of top-down housing policies, administered and implemented by the federal socialist government, which drew its legitimacy from the grassroots People's Liberation Struggle and the Revolution during the Second World War. Deeply intertwined with the self-management practices, and influenced by the society's economic and political circumstances, Yugoslav housing economy mirrored the processes unravelling in the country. Because of the severity of the housing crisis in post-war Yugoslavia, the system was rigid on material side, planning and controlling the land allocation, production and distribution of the construction material and expertise. However, due to the unfavourable conditions from which it emerged, the system was quite flexible on the organizational side, allowing many forms, scales and modalities for investment, development and ownership. Furthermore, dwelling – especially in collective (multifamily) housing – was entangled with the communal policies of urban and rural development: housing communities as the lowest organizational unit of the municipalities acted as legal entities representing all 'housing councils' of the corresponding territory. Practices of self-management, self-organizing, self-financing and embedded solidarity model of the housing distribution were integral part of the housing economy. The society relied mostly on its own resources to (re)build and develop, using whenever possible the youth and workers brigades, which were employed throughout the existence of socialist Yugoslavia, mostly engaged in building infrastructure like highways and railroads. Finally, the societal companies and enterprises, which were planning, designing and developing housing, were based on the principles of self-management and practically implementing the 'agreement-based economy', materializing the needs and aspirations of all the members of the society. There were many problems and mistakes that happened along the way, fuelling severe and unforgiving critique, but for decades this system worked and was delivering results. It constantly evolved, branching out and reshaping, thus further complicating its (present-day) research and understanding. Today, in retrospective, its results are resonating even stronger as the problems of our society multiply – the need to reassess and potentially reintroduce and reuse some of the elements of the Yugoslav housing economy, at least in reconstruction of the existing stocks, is growing stronger and louder. We could argue that many aspects of this housing economy could be interpreted as a form of *commons*, as it produced the knowledge and the material conditions for housing the largest number of people, creating frameworks and infrastructures to achieve this goal.

The emergence: Self-management bestowed from the above

On 15 August 1945, the Presidency of the National Assembly of Serbia adopted the *Law on the Use of Apartments and Commercial Premises*, which was published in the *Official Gazette of Serbia no. 25* three days later, thus entering into force. Under the auspices of local peoples' councils and the Ministry of Social Affairs, the law introduced new policies, effectively de-commodifying housing, which aligned with the ideological character of the new revolutionary and socialist authorities. An institution of the *housing authority* was introduced, to manage and (re)distribute the residential and commercial premises in the country. The law governed the redistribution and basic organizational aspects of the housing and commerce, since the significant part of the built stock and infrastructure was either damaged or destroyed during the war. According to this law, no one could own more than one flat/commercial premise, except for premises adjacent to agricultural and economic capacities. It also set the rules of priority in distribution for families with children, hors de combat and war veterans, the procedures for repairs and the use of the empty and abandoned flats/premises, to name a few instrumental paragraphs. Already in January 1946 the constitution was adopted, confirming the paragraphs of the law and proclaiming that the state will take care of 'the housing situation' of its citizens, alongside acting as a guarantee of the new way of life: the rights to assembly, limiting working days, securing entitlement to paid annual leave, control of working conditions and care for social security. Housing becomes an integral part of this new social contract.

In April 1947, the first *Five Year-Plan of Yugoslavia's economy* was adopted by the federal assembly, setting in motion the planned economy of Yugoslavia based on experiences of Soviet Union, remodelled to fit the local conditions. The plan would address the issues of the country via two major strands: development of production capacities and planning of the 'material and cultural elevation of the people' in all the Yugoslav republics. These legal documents were, essentially, enacting nationalization of the land and real estate, a prerequisite for the forthcoming socialist modernization of the country. However, individual and private property was never abolished, which was one of the causes for the dispute with Stalin and expulsion of Yugoslavia from Cominform in 1948, though the limitation in size and numbers of units was stipulated through the legal framework of the country.[1] The state also started sequestering and (re)assigning other resources: scattered and pauperized industrial capacities, workforce and intelligentsia, even by tapping into the pool of 'class enemy' for latter (Lekić and Zečević, 1995: v.1, 94). Slowly, the state would gain the basic resources to start building socialism on a large scale, *commoning* and transferring back to the society what deemed needed for this endeavour. Within ten years, the society had modest but well-organized capacities for mass production of housing. The upgrade to industrialization was the next step (Figures 11.1a and 11.1b).

In relation to the overall issue of housing, the plan addressed the problem of reorganization and the output of the construction industry. Focusing on the particular regional conditions for production of construction material – bricks, concrete, stone – the general guidelines stipulated the path of maximized industrialization, setting up the capacities for production of the prefabricates and semi-prefabricates, as well as fully prefabricated family houses. The plan also dealt with 'housing and communal economy', crunching the numbers and prescribing the norms per republic. The plan defined the priorities: urgent number of kilometres of roads, sewage, water supply systems, the regulation plans for major cities, the programmatic briefs for public facilities, the number of square metres or pieces of housing units, etc. However, the above-mentioned legal documents were passed during the two-year period of the country's *Renewal*[2] and prior to the Cominform-

---

[1] Depending on the region, the size of individually owned land was limited to 16–25 hectares per household.

[2] A two-year period, 1945–7, in the development of the Yugoslav post-war economy, aiming to restore the capacities and achieve the pre-war production outputs of the economy.

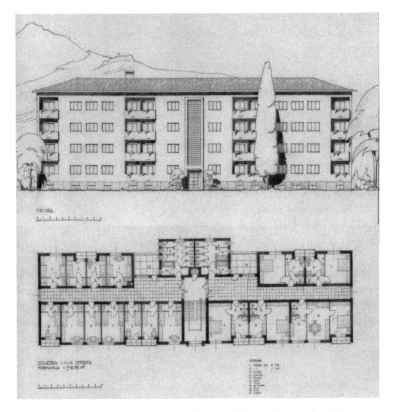

Figure 11.1a and 11.1b Designs for typified residential buildings, call for proposals by the Ministry of Construction FPRY in 1949, competition entry, arch. Branislav Marinković. (Source: Personal archive of Branislav Marinković with copyright permission.

Resolution crisis of 1948. In this period, the economy was organized around two major principles: first, the experience of the People's Liberation Struggle, from which most of the administrative and organizational network of the country stems,[3] and second, the experiences of the Soviet Union, often referred to as the 'first socialist country of the world'. Within this set-up, housing was a part of the *communal economy*, which was governed top-down, by the state, which also acted as investor, distributor and governing entity via its competent bodies. This period is often called the *administrative*

---

[3] Researchers consider committees to be the stem of the country's municipal network, directly addressing the needs of the local community.

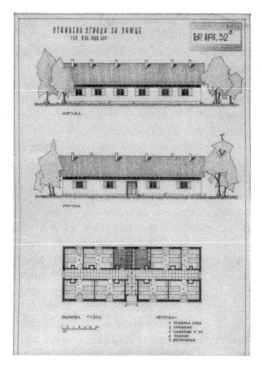

Figure 11.1a and 11.1b (Continued)

budgeting period (1945–55), meaning housing was basically financed by the state budget, while municipal organs were managing, maintaining and distributing the flats and deciding on the monthly rent (Antić, 1978: 82–3). During this period, the state also started giving loans for the individual housing construction, and in total, 310,000 flats were built in Yugoslavia.

Although for a while considered the best and most loyal ally of the USSR, Yugoslavia took on a different path of socialism. Already during the Second World War, the basic foundations were laid for the society embedded in local experiences, which was per se divergent from USSR model.[4] Yugoslav

---

[4] Except for Scandinavian countries, the post-1948 pressure on Yugoslavia was unanimous from East and West. The expulsion from Cominform (28 June 1948) triggered the expulsion from the international socialist movement, economic sanctions and clashes at the borders to the East. Meanwhile, the West conditioned any relief or loans with favourable resolution of the nationalization of the foreign companies' property in Yugoslavia, end of support to Greek communists, resolution of *Trieste question,* etc. Yugoslavia strayed away from the model of administratively planned economy, striving to create its own path to socialism. The government went back to classics in search for

leadership was considering the (Yugoslav) socialism as a transitional stage towards communism, hence utilizing as much as possible the potentials of the already-existing natural economy as a part of this transition, while striving to avoid capitalist relations with other countries, especially those recently decolonized (Lekić and Zečević, 1995: v.2, 118–20). Owing to the decades-long illegal work of the Communist Party before the war, the resistance in Yugoslavia was organized via network of locally based peoples' liberation committees, whose work relied extensively on well-organized networks of solidarity. People's Committees continued to exist well into the 1950s, when administration reorganized. The long tradition of self-organization, self-sufficiency and self-help of the rural and peri-urban communities, especially in the post-Ottoman areas, proved to be very useful both during the war and during the Cominform crisis. Self-financing and self-building the communal infrastructures, such as schools, churches, roads, water cisterns and housing, were a rule, not exception – both in the monarchy and in the socialist republic. Building upon this kind of social base, the housing production of the first post-war years relied heavily on the existing commonalities, vernacular practices, typologies and craftsmanship, utilizing traditional construction materials and techniques (Jovanović, 2020: 35–8). *Moba*, a form of centuries-old collective assistance rooted in customary law, was especially important during this period, as the communities were accustomed to it in their daily practices. The construction of a house, including the preparation of the building material, was a costly and complex process, an expense that a regular household would struggle paying from its own budget. *Moba*, therefore, was considered as a long-term collective loan, repaid exclusively through community members' reciprocal labour: when building a house, members of the community either return the assistance they had previously acquired, or 'credit' the future construction of their own houses. In case of housing, this form of assistance was exclusively connected to the housing construction: *moba* vanished in the areas where construction could be swapped for fieldwork (Vukosavljević 2012: 40–3).

The post-war socialist government utilized these existing practices. The first stage of the construction industry's development (re)organized around the regional and local (field) brickyards (Mihailović 1953: 433–5), and the customs were absorbed into the housing economy, while arguably appropriating and expanding them through nationwide coordination of the

inspiration: 'the restoration of original Marxist ideas about the transitional state period (after proletarian conquest of power), in transitory experiences of the Paris Commune, the Soviets in two Russian revolutions, the works councils in Bavaria, Austria and Hungary after the First World War, as well as the experiences of the Yugoslav Revolution, especially the National Liberation Committees' (Petranović, 1988: 288).

voluntary labour brigades (Adžić 1970: 15, 29, Izgradnja 1948/2-5: 45–53, 1954/8-9: 56–68, 1954/10:39-49; AS-134-f-204-2-49, AS-134-f-213-14). Furthermore, throughout entire socialist period the practices of self-building and/or self-financing were quite common, especially in the construction of the communal infrastructure, occasionally raised to a higher level through self-financing bonds for large-scale projects: Sava Center in Belgrade, post-earthquake reliefs of Skopje and Montenegro coast, etc. Various forms of self-organization and solidary work, which were already instilled in the society, were encouraged, elevated and legitimized by the post-war policy, but with different core group – shifting the focus towards (industrial) workers and proletariat.[5] During the administrative budgeting period, the housing stock of the public administration and core industries had significantly improved, which remained in the public/societal ownership until its privatization in the 1990s. The goal was for this stock to be used within the framework of the societal property, distributed and redistributed according to the needs of the society's members, for many generations to come. Besides the construction of the physical commonalities, such as roads, railways and cooperative's houses, the logistics of the housing production was established through the consolidation of the professional realm, communal sphere, and industrial production and procedures. The crafts, predominantly vernacular in education and practice, were gradually reorganized and professionalized, because they were essential for further development of the construction capacities. The *commons* of this period could be tracked through organized, large-scale collective efforts for building various capacities to impede the (housing) construction.

The complexities and the paradoxes: Absorbing and navigating practices from below

Although self-management was official state policy since 1950 and therefore a part of its administrative bodies' practice,[6] the administrative budgeting and state investments in housing continued at least until 1955. Nevertheless,

---

[5] Due to the nature of the Yugoslav industry and economy, the working class was small in total numbers, and consequentially the urban population. Yugoslavia was a predominantly agrarian society well into 1970s (Petranović, 1988: 30).

[6] On 26 June 1950, the *Basic Law on the Management of State Business Enterprises and Higher Economic Associations by Labor Collectives* (colloquially named the *Law on Workers' Councils*) was adopted. However, from summer 1949, when the first experimental workers' councils were founded, until the next year's law, there were already 520 workers' councils in enterprises all over the country.

all the aspects of life in the communities were covered by self-management: work, education, culture, healthcare and housing, both in countryside and in cities. The idea was that through their delegates in key positions, the workers' councils would eventually take over the decision making in the municipality, since it was them who brought the income to the municipalities by working in the local production capacities. By choosing the investments allocation, these councils would work in self-interest, benefiting the municipality and preventing the outflow of funds. This worked well in towns with longer industrial tradition with more homogenous working class, usually employed by a single sprawling enterprise, such as mono-industrial towns of Bor[7] or Borovo,[8] but challenging in the municipalities where multiple enterprises had to come together and discuss the communal development. The municipal organs were facilitating and coordinating these processes, as the various planning documents were developed by them. Housing was considered a basic necessity for social reproduction, but it also had productional and communal value – hence being of tripled value to the society, especially in the municipalities where construction companies were located.

However, in the post-war years, especially from 1948 until 1952, the circumstances were especially dire. While politically one of the most trying periods of the country's history was unravelling, all the orders of equipment were on hold indefinitely, technical assistance were withdrawn and bank loans were cancelled – housing shortages still had to be addressed. The features of the industrialization of the country were rather typical, causing typical problems: the workforce from the countryside was flocking the cities, which were just being urbanized and their communal infrastructure (re)built and expanded. The lack of housing in the cities was chronic for many years, and could not have been resolved by the surplus in the countryside. Nevertheless, the villages were the first to build infrastructures such as schools, ambulances and community centres. Some factories would rather invest in workers' transportation than relocation to the cities, if they had their housing needs met in nearby villages. Many employees took loans for improvement of their housing conditions, later in 1960s even going abroad to earn extra money. However, the housing typologies prevalent in the countryside were something that socialist countries strived to eliminate: traditional structures built in adobe, rammed earth and timber. The professional organizations even experimented with earth and clay, since it was the only abundant construction

---

[7]   Bor is a mining town in Eastern Serbia, developed around the copper mine during the twentieth century.
[8]   Borovo is one of the *Bat'a towns*, developed in 1931 around the shoe and rubber factory in Borovo in Eastern Croatia, today a part of Vukovar. For further reading, see *Kome treba poduzeće? Borovo 1988–1991. Samoupravljanje.*

material, providing numerical data, examples of experimental buildings and typified designs (Izgradnja 1950/5-6: 27–9). Ironically, the modest capacities for industrial production of the construction material and lack of trained builders, especially in rural areas, caused traditional techniques and materials to remain in use until 1963, when they were legally banned after the earthquake in Skopje. For the individual construction, from the onset the system absorbed the customary law of *moba*, in which an entire community would gather to help build individual house, especially when building with traditional techniques, as they were labour intensive. However, this practice also remained an indispensable part of informal/rogue construction in 1960s and 1970s, as the rogue builders – most of which employees of the large construction companies, the very builders of housing – struggled to settle in the outskirts of Belgrade and other industrial centres (Le Normand 2014: 148; Kulić and Mrduljaš, 2012: 276–92). A significant portion of the housing in this period was just sheltering, often with very basic amenities, such as barracks. Many workers' colonies were built during this period, especially in the cities where the key industries were situated. In the cities, the 'infills' would appear in place of demolished buildings, while estates were built very cautiously, where absolutely needed: near essential industries such as metals production in Železnik, Svetozarevo (Jagodina), Trstenik, Nikšić and Zenica.

The period from 1956 to 1965, when self-management became a ubiquitous practice, can be divided into two subperiods (Antić, 1978: 82–3). From 1956 to 1959, the financing was still coming from the budget. However, the institutes of the *(self)contribution* for housing construction and specialized *social funds for crediting the housing construction* were established in this period. Moreover, one of the crucial laws was adopted in 1958, the *Law on Nationalization of Residential Buildings*. Subperiod from 1960 to 1965 is called 'the first housing reform', framing the period when several legal acts were adopted, effectively moving the housing into the category of consumption goods. Housing shifted more towards market-driven relations and pricing, crediting system improved and expanded, and the institute of *tenancy subscription* was introduced to alleviate the clutter and provide some guarantees to the future tenants. The cooperative housing was particularly thriving during this period, and together with the private initiative accounted for roughly 59 per cent of housing production. A total of 838,160 housing units were built in Yugoslavia within these ten years. During this period, the housing production shifted more towards industrialized processes as the enterprises continued to invest into the societal stock, while the maintenance of the societal housing became more centralized and bureaucratized in the municipal housing companies. The coordinated activities of the government in financing and legislature of housing economy further advanced the housing production, while diversifying and decentralizing its organizational and proprietary modalities. However, despite the efforts to better connect and organize the actors in the process, housing and communal economy remained too fragmented to meet the mounting demand for housing units.

Third period spans from 1966 to 1975 and is named 'the second housing reform'. Its beginning coincided with the (in)famous economic reform of 1965. During this period, the *housing maintenance companies* for societal housing were established with the single purpose of maintenance of the society-owned housing, and the self-managed enterprises were legally obliged to hand over their stock to these companies as a so-called *input*, and basically give over some of their rights as investors, while maintaining the right to use and distribute this input to their employees (Društveni: 48). These steps were taken with the goal of equalizing and improving the level of maintenance through centralizing the rent collection. The municipal and republic funds for housing construction were cancelled, while their monies were transferred to the commercial banks as credit potential. On the other side, the monies of the enterprises remain within, for the workers' councils to utilize them. Later during this period, the construction companies take over the development of the housing for the market, which at first improved production of housing and pushed the rise of rent, which was insufficient to cover even the basic maintenance of the stock. This step further advanced professionalization of the housing construction, hence further removing the agency and funding from the hands of the end user and placing the resources in the hands of various institutionalized keepers, depending on the phase of the housing development: banks, planning offices, construction companies, workplaces and maintenance companies. The unresolved issues with the land policy, which was never integrated within the housing economy, paired with market-driven production, started pushing the prices up. Nevertheless, during this period there were 1,319,515 flats built in Yugoslavia. The distribution was regulated within the self-managed organizations/enterprises with ranking lists: those with most dire housing situation would be prioritized, points would be awarded if the said person had children, spouse, elderly parents or higher qualifications. The scoring system resulted in many of the employees becoming more involved with the processes of decision making. Similarly, many have given up navigating the self-managed landscape and monitoring the long waiting lists, and started building on the outskirts of the cities, either with or without permits and plans. The housing economy started becoming increasingly hybridized, which resulted in not only the rise of the number of built housing units but also being more entropic, thus resulting in the mounting of new challenges. Besides financing, the pace of industrialization, lack of communal construction land and discrepancy or non-existence of the plans were causing a lot of halts and delays. By liberalizing the society and opening to the market-driven economy, paradoxically, the government itself introduced the processes and relations which gradually led towards the fatigue and braking of the housing economy in 1980s.

The knowledge: Learning by doing

Yugoslavia did not have a tradition in organized housing production, like Czechoslovakia, USSR or Austria did. The exceptions were the post-Habsburg areas, where the regulated settlements existed since the eighteenth century. In Belgrade, the country's capital, there were only few examples of multifamily housing estates, developed by the municipal administration: workers' housing in Dorćol by Jelisaveta Načić in 1911, Topčider Hill by Branko Maksimović in 1929, or the largest estate in Northern Boulevard by Mihailo Mijatović, with 118 flats designed and 102 built by 1941. Other options for housing construction would involve bank loans for individual buildings, or cooperative construction. There were even cases of neighbourhoods urbanized and built by the organized associations of future house owners, such as Professors' Colony, since these schemes were less expensive and precarious than renting out. Meanwhile, the urban poor lived in unhygienic provisory settlements, scattered all over the city, even paying rent for the horrible housing they lived in.[9] The situation was not better in other regions of the country either. The architects, especially the ones involved with the professional associations, started advocating for organized housing construction, citing examples from Czechoslovakia and Red Vienna (Kulić and Mrduljaš, 2012: 397-404). While modernists in other countries experimented with new materials, layouts and urban planning, in interwar Yugoslavia the modernization would finish at the facade: it was a style, not the overarching process, as it depended on the taste of the bourgeoise investors. However, in first post–Second World War years, some of these modernists were the most active in reconstruction efforts and reorganization of the profession.

---

[9] Researcher Zlata Vuksanović Macura writes extensively about settlements such as Jatagan Mala and Pištolj Mala, and has documented the housing conditions of the urban poor in interwar Belgrade. Some of these typologies remained in the post-war period: dugouts' (zemunice) settlements on the territory of New Belgrade (resettled to Ledine), shanties near highway, wagon-housing (partaja), etc. Furthermore, in 1985, during the peak of the distribution crisis, Miloš Bobić, architect, and Sreten Vujović, sociologist, edited an anthology titled 'Roof Over Your Head: Essays on Housing Destitution and Poverty', mapping and analysing slum-like conditions in Yugoslav cities and their position within the country's housing economy.

Prominent architects continued their work at the universities, institutes or construction companies after the war, on a new socialist platform. Nikola Dobrović, who started working while on liberated territories in 1943, was indispensable for establishment of the urban planning institute of Peoples' Republic of Serbia, Milan Zloković elaborated the modular coordination essential for industrial prefabricated housing, Branislav Marinković worked in Srbijaprojekt's housing department, and Vera Ćirković designed housing, schools, etc. During this period, the crucial systems for space production were established: planning, designing, survey of the territory and detailed mapping, land acclamation and amelioration of the largest rivers, and basic infrastructural networks. The housing typologies built during this period relied heavily upon the designs of the pre-war architects, some of which were modified and repeated as those were the only ready-made solutions available. To tackle the issue of sluggish housing economy, the state administration assigned the Economic Institute of Serbia the project of collecting proposals and publishing them in catalogues of typified housing units from 1952 onwards, as there were too few architects to meet the demand. This practice remained until the end of 1980s; later, it was mostly reserved for individual housing, as the cheapest and fastest way to get the construction permits. Meanwhile, the professional associations were organizing counselling and competitions, and the competent publishers commissioned and published the much-needed manuals for scarce and predominantly unqualified workforce.

The post-war government was constantly pushing for the industrialization of housing production. Based on other countries' experiences, this was the only way to provide enough units. However, modest expertise existed in Yugoslavia, with no practical experience in this field. It had to be created from scratch, after a thorough preparation and sending both scholars and workers abroad for apprenticeships. For a while, the construction was done in traditional techniques, pushing the existing industrial resources to the limits. All the efforts prior to 1955 were not enough: although the industrial capacities were put in motion, the outputs were not standardized, so their use or installation were more difficult, and demanded a lot of extra craftsmanship involved. Many 'provisory' and temporary standards were enacted, just to have some minimal level of compatibility, but as the construction sites grew in number and scale, so did errors in the process. After numerous pleas from professional associations, the state allocated resources for various uses, purposefully for the field of housing. In 1956 the call for typified multistorey housing took place, and in 1957 the call for innovation in field of structural systems for housing. The federal assembly enacted the Resolution on the Perspective Development of the Building Sector in 1957 and pushed for measures to enhance investments and activate scientific research. By pouring funds into societally owned housing production, the state managed to elevate the quality of housing production in general, as the standards rose, and the achievements were utilized by the citizens: spatial and industrial standards, products and scholarship. By 1970 there were seventeen independent research institutions in the country, coordinating their programmes with Federal and Republic Funds for Research, and Construction Council of the Federal Economic Chamber, Yugoslav Construction Centre and the Association of Laboratories. The organizations[10] – construction companies, design offices and producers of construction material – active in field of housing, were also encouraged to allocate funding and resources for research, which they did because of better competitiveness. Architects were skillfully navigating this complex landscape, negotiating between authorities, investors, construction companies and residents (Kulić and Mrduljaš, 2012: 41–54). This is how Belgrade-based Housing Centre (Centar za stanovanje) emerged within the Institute for Materials Testing of Serbia, or Ljubljana-based Construction Centre (Gradbeni centre). In time, these units became Yugoslavia's leading research organizations in field of *habitology*, the accomplishments of which are still used today. Within this field, a particular phenomenon emerged, known as *Belgrade School of Housing*, naming somewhat elusive synergy of architectural practices, urban planning laboratories such as New Belgrade or New Zagreb, institutionalized competitions of various scales, large-scale investments into entire neighbourhoods and estates and construction companies experimenting with prefabrication technologies. The large, organized investors, such as Yugoslav People's Army and cities' housing communities were systematically investing into research, development and publishing of own standards for housing construction, since they operated with public funds and needed to have equable standards of housing on entire territory they covered. Some of these standards were, paradoxically, classified, but since the same protagonists operated in 'civil' sector, soon enough these became the operational standards in entire country. All this scholarship has been used since then effectively as *commons* and the 'golden standard' for quality design in housing architecture.

The vivid variety of shapes and forms came from the locally developed structural systems. Many prefabricated systems – Jugomont panel systems and IMS Žeželj prestressed skeleton system being most known – were developed and patented during this period. Some companies proceeded to buy the patents of the already-existing systems abroad. By late 1970s, there

---

[10] Within context of self-management, 'organization' would be the most inclusive term, since all the companies, enterprises, industries, businesses, etc. were organized via organizations of associated labour (acronym OUR – *organizacija udruženog rada*), either basic (*osnovna*, OOUR) or complex (*složena*, SOUR).

were total of fifty-seven systems promoted by the local construction sector. The precise number of applied systems is impossible to know and untangle from the splice of trade secrets and motifs of various actors, as in 1970s a wave of direct imports of foreign prefabrication technologies had occurred. Fading giants from abroad, such as French Camus, were seeking for new markets and shortcuts to post-colonial and non-aligned countries via Yugoslavia (Cagić, Otović and Lojanica, 1978: 8–9). However, although the initial goal of industrialized housing construction was set along principles of Fordism – as a continuous production line for the unknown user, with nuclear families in focus as core 'consumer' – the goal of the so-called full industrialization was never achieved. Many continued to use improved traditional techniques and craftsmanship, especially in the smaller cities and towns, since prefabrication was too expensive if the output series were low in numbers. Yugoslav industrial production in general, arguably by design, maintained high dependency upon craftsmanship and was never fully industrialized. The path taken by the Yugoslav housing economy and construction industry was open-system production and small-piece prefabrication. Often, a prefabricated system would have numerous modifications as the time passes and new sites open, potentially making every single building a prototype of a certain technology, which gives an insight into the atmosphere of the era and the drive for experimentation. The envelopes were custom-made prefabricated pieces, or brick-laid facades, and the layouts were obtained through public competitions, designed independently around a certain structural system. The serial production was accomplished by large-scale production of typified load-bearing structural elements: pillars, beams, slabs and panel walls (Kulić and Mrduljaš, 2012: 404–20). This was not the usual path of other countries, especially those with grave housing crisis. Usually, a few prefabricated systems would be selected and high-output capacities built around them. Yugoslavia, due to its difficult beginnings, could never make such a commitment: with limited resources, the country had to create a genuinely self-managed and self-reliant housing economy. Open prefabrication was best suited for such circumstances: highly flexible, scalable, transformable and transportable. It was adaptable both for on-site, manual prefabrication and for industrialized environment, that is, in a plant. Many breakthroughs were accomplished in this framework – new structural systems, new machines, new schools of housing architecture, etc. The country also started exporting, both the technology and the experience of the Yugoslav housing economy to the NAM countries, because it was relevant for their situation as well. Finally, the housing landscape this economy created through societally owned housing was very diverse and varied. Although it did not fully resolve the housing crisis, it managed to

Figure 11.2 Cerak Vineyards housing estate, 1978–86 (arch. Milenija Marušić, Darko Marušić, Nedeljko Borovnica). (Source: Personal archive of Milenija and Darko Marušić with copyright permission.

successfully escape the trap of uniformity and not create belts of 'sameness' with the estates around major cities[11] (Figure 11.2).

The tragedy:[12] Inertia and distrust

With the introduction of the *Socially Directed Housing Construction (SDHC)*[13] alongside the *Associated Labour Law (ALL)* in 1976, after the constitution

---

[11] This variety can be best seen in new database of Docomomo Serbia, Housing Atlas http://www.docomomo-serbia.org/atlas/
[12] As defined by William Forster Lloyd.
[13] DUSI – društveno usmerena stambena izgradnja.

changes in 1974, the last, fourth period of Yugoslav housing economy begins. It is a far more radical shift towards market-driven economy and less welfare, which gained traction especially post-1980 with the neoliberal turn of the world economy and the consequent destruction of socialism. The purpose of the SDHC was to connect and organize *Self-management Interest Associations*[14] established by the ALL, especially since there was a legally stipulated percentage of the wages of every single worker, who was also a self-manager, allocated to the self-managed enterprises' common fund for housing. There was the notion of common good and common interest, as well as legally defined solidarity housing which could have been distributed independent from the workplaces. However, the concept wasn't more successful compared to the previous models. This was in part due to not only the embedded problems, such as the organizations involved in the development procedures increasingly monopolizing various aspects of the process instead of facilitating it, but also the external issues, such as the foreign debt crisis Yugoslavia struggled with during the 1980s. Still, more than a million of housing units were built during this period.[15] The *Interest Communities in Housing – ICH*,[16] established with the goal of managing and coordinating the construction and distribution of housing, but often contributed to more clutter, especially in large cities, eventually caused the numbers of built units to stagnate and drop. The problem was severe, since ICHs had direct access to funding provided by the Common Consumption Funds of the organizations, allocated per annual financial statements. In other words, all the employed citizens allocated a mandatory part of their income to these funds, but only some got their housing from it, while the others were never compensated as the funds went bankrupt in 1990s. Although there were other means to alleviate this injustice, such as tax-free purchase of the construction material via cooperatives, the discrepancies in housing distribution between blue-collar and white-collar workers caused cumulative distrust in the system, and pervasive corruption and anomie in later stages prior to the federation collapse. All the periods of Yugoslav housing economy, from 1956 onwards, are characterized by the emergence of the (proto)capitalist tendencies.[17] The privatization of the public housing stock or the stock of the federal administration starts appearing in archival

[14] Often the acronym SIZ was used, which stands for *samoupravne interesne zajednice.*
[15] From 1976 to 1983, 1,140,029 flats were built in Yugoslavia, and although the production declined towards 1990, we can assume that around 100,000 flats were built annually.
[16] *SIZ stanovanja.*
[17] Kirn, 2019, location 439, states this about the period of post-reform of 1965; however, I would argue that in housing, indicated through the ownership, these tendencies are visible much earlier, or never disappeared.

documentation in early 1950s.[18] The *construction for the market* as a defined legal format appears in 1966: construction companies then started building and selling the flats via closed market, to various organizations purchasing them for their employees. This stock could either remain in ownership of said organization to be rented to the employees or sold to them as a form of loan given by the organization.

However, the distribution remained an issue: paradoxically, white-collar workers would always get housing first, resulting in freeing up significant part of salaries for consumption: travel, (luxury) goods or even secondary housing (weekend houses), thus climbing further on the social ladder while narrowing down the possibilities for social upward mobility for the others. Meanwhile, blue-collar workers remain shorthanded – the less qualified, the worse situation – resulting for them to turn to individual construction. Most often, they would join housing cooperatives, either for housing or for purchase of the tax-free construction material, and build themselves, which was more expensive, time consuming and labour intensive. This type of housing construction was often paralegal or illegal, since the construction land in urbanized areas was scarce, expensive and already allocated to large investors, while agricultural land on the periphery was not conversed into construction land and hence not covered by urban plans – therefore, legally unavailable for construction. The Yugoslav People's Army has been a major concern for city authorities in Zagreb, Split and Belgrade, since most of the retired officers tended to demand housing in these cities. Hence, the army invested into estates and appeared as major and most powerful investor, swarming the market and pushing out the other organizations, with less cash at disposal for their employees.

Another prevailing problem was the accumulation capacity of the associated labour organizations. Best example is the case of two housing cooperatives from Croatia: 'Uljanik' from Pula and 'Medicinar' (medic) from Zadar (Antić, 1978: 103–5). 'Uljanik' cooperative was established in 1983 by the employees and unions of the 'Uljanik Shipyard' in Pula, who were dissatisfied with the constant delays of the resolution of their housing problem – some members were waiting for seventeen to eighteen years. 'Uljanik' managed to get the low-interest rate loan because the enterprise could guarantee its return. On the opposite side, the fifty-four members of 'Medicinar', founded in 1985, were coming from public sector; their employer

---

[18] AJ-F130-SIV-f750: a letter to republican assemblies, noting the need to scrutinize the faulty procedures during sales of housing stock of federal administration, 18 November 1955. In many local newspapers, there are ads announcing public biddings for sales of 'residential buildings from people's property', that is, *Krajina – newspaper of regional and city committee*, Negotin, 1 July 1953, p.6.

had no accumulation at all, hence not being a lucrative customer of the bank, which resulted in less favourable loans and the rise of construction costs. However, both co-ops had the same problem while getting the construction land – the cities did not have the land at disposal, causing more delays and loss of value of the monies. Furthermore, there was no model which would have accounted for own labour in the construction, to reduce the size of the loan, or halfway solutions such as sales of incomplete units, without finishing, which might have alleviated the housing issues. The state often overlooked these fragmented and hybridized practices in favour of construction companies, since they were numerous, had many employees and brought significant revenue – but were facing crisis in the 1980s with the onset of the collapse of their key markets in Asia and Africa. The maintenance was often put aside, although it should have also been self-managed and self-financed by the residents.[19] It was often postponed and underfunded, causing disrepair which spurred further alienation of the residents.

Other problems were result of self-management in market economy: there was solidarity among colleagues within the same organization, but vicious competition between organizations, resulting in lesser cooperation to pressure the municipal governments to provide construction land and planning documents within their jurisdiction. In case of essential, lucrative industries such as ore extraction and processing, or large construction exports abroad, either self-management was suspended or the role of workers' councils was subdued to advisory. Then, there were the maladies of the system itself: from early stages, the reports of the time speak of the self-management *on paper*, individuals or oligarchies usurping the councils and union bodies, resulting in alienation of the workers and discreditation of the system. 'Economic units do not function in enterprises. . . . The above examples clearly speak of the distrust and reservations of certain communists in the ability of economic units to perform self-governing functions, as well as the fear that they would lead to breaking the unity of the collective' (HAB-F893-f369). Branko Horvat, the prominent economist, theorist and chronicler of the Yugoslav socialism and self-management, ascribed many of the above-mentioned problems to the etatism disguised as socialism in Yugoslavia – as well as in other socialist countries for that matter. In his opinion, the societal ownership is the prerequisite for self-management and consequentially socialism, but Yugoslav society was supposed to function on two conflicting organizational principles: economic system based on collaboration and

---

[19]   In 1960s various housing maintenance companies were established; many of them are still operating today, but are notorious for their lack of transparency and inadequate reaction.

solidarity and political system based on subordination and issuing orders. In Horvat's opinion, the 'political vulgarization' of the self-management was epitomized in the 1976 ALL, which eroded the self-management (Horvat 1989: 25, 33-7). The workers' councils were exposed to pressure from the political bodies, executives gained power while workers were leaving unions and felt alienated from the work of the councils (Arzenšek, 1981: 3-12). This is how the self-management was gradually discredited: the atomization of the enterprises into operationally and financially independent units, stipulated by the ALL, demanded more energy invested into negotiation, arbitrating, thus enabling the infiltration of the political monopoly and cartelization. Paired with the (consequential) drop of the production and growth of the administrative staff, led further down the path of more etatization (Horvat 1989: 5-12). Furthermore, Yugoslav societal property was founded by the state funds, given as seed money to the enterprises, and tangible property, which was basically leased to self-managed enterprises in 1950s. The problems of housing economy were obviously inseparable from the rest of the economy, which suffered from the rise of bureaucratism and technocratism from lack of true democracy, which discouraged individual initiatives, and which was believed would be amended by privatization and financing of individually (self-)built housing (Pjanić, 1972: 249-90; Horvat and Štiks 2015: 45-75).

The legacy: Forgotten, fragmented, forbidden history

Every now and again, the spectre of self-management peaks out of the blissful oblivion it was sent to some thirty years ago. It is neither the exhausted workers that speak of it nor the teachers at schools and universities. The politicians in power, the post-socialist and post-Yugoslav elites, are the ones who still see the apparitions of self-management, even though it is long gone – or never existed as many would argue (Zorkine, 2020: web). They proclaim that self-management will not come back, while explaining why the employees should put up with the preposterous working conditions in today's private factories in Serbia (Ivanović and Marinković, 2020: web). Even the faintest idea of diverging from the usual capitalist practices and etiquette is declared self-managerial tendency, which needs to be ousted. The successful stories of former self-managers – some of whom eventually turned into shareholders salvaging their companies – are pushed aside, while most problematic examples are amplified and used as the proverbial boogeyman in smear campaigns, placed in public media outlets. This comes as no surprise since the fiercest opposition to bad privatizations came from companies such as 'KMG Trudbenik' or 'Jugoremedija'.[20] The 'curse word' *self-management* is trending nowadays, which is unusual for a policy that is widely considered deadbeat, failed, forgotten and defeated. With the current crisis of capitalism, people are looking for possible alternatives to it. Despite all its problems and deficiencies, Yugoslav self-management is capturing attention of scholars and activists worldwide, with the goal of at least understanding its failure. Since it is recent history, the memory and the documentation still exist, and interlocutors are willing to partake in an organic effort to resurface and systematize the knowledge. The testimonies of the workers speak of the decision-making processes as much more transparent and democratic, especially compared to the present day (Markuš, 2016: web). These organizations also played a role in communal development and equipment, today effectively a wasteland of impoverished communities living off the remnants of these structures. For example, Borovo Combine had a long history of a socially responsible self-managed enterprise, whose workers' councils decided to keep their own wages low; and instead of splitting the profits, they invested generously into the city's infrastructure: housing, heating, healthcare and workers' education. The Combine employed more workers than needed, to help the unemployed and prevent them from idling and indulging in vices such as alcohol or gambling. Today, after the war, after transformation of societal to state-owned property in 1990s, and bankruptcy and privatization in 2000s, these workers have lower pensions and limited-to-none access to the benefits of their investments.

The Borovo example shows how the housing policy of Yugoslavia was deeply intertwined with country's social policy, while both embedded in the self-management system and rooted in the societal property. The societal property was the product of the joint labour based on the joint rights and joint responsibilities in directing and distributing the earnings. These earnings, although belonging to the collectives, were simultaneously raised to the status of a societal property (društveno dobro), which were invested into the housing construction from the resources allocated through the legal institute of the *common expense*. Through commoning of the housing production and housing policy, there was also a common interest of the working people to enlarge this societal property. Social policy was an integral part of the developmental policies, and was optimizing economic development to fulfil the necessities of the citizens. The government's role in

---

[20] Most insightful publication on the issue of privatization of societally owned companies was written by historian Marija Obradović: *Hronika tranzicionog groblja: Privatizacija društvenog kapitala u Srbiji 1989-2012. Ekonomsko-istorijska analiza.* Beograd: NSPM, INIS, 2017.

this case was to ensure the enforcement of the laws and guarantee the future use of the societal property – in other words, to ensure the *governmentality* of the common good for the present and future use. Although faced with many difficulties, Yugoslav society did function as a polycentric system, and societally owned and financed housing was one of the basic commonalities that was ensuring the reproduction of this society. Marx's 'federation of self-governing communes' was applicable in Yugoslav case in Horvat's iteration of the *association of associations*, since the communal/municipal system of the country was established in 1950s along the lines of Marx's concept, and the self-government of the enterprises/companies was intertwined with the communal government (Dolenec and Žitko, 2016: 8–10).

Many researchers agree that the mistake of self-managers was trying to compete in the international market with capitalist countries, while trying to eliminate disparities and injustices within the country by utilizing modernization via industrialization and development-driven economy. The country was encircled by the Cold War powers the entire time of its existence, and occasionally had to spend up to 20 per cent of its budget on defence. The government believed in strength of Yugoslav society's ability to see through manipulations and utilize the mechanisms to call out and stop those who are misusing common resources. Eventually, these mechanisms were not enough, since in time of political turmoil and public debt crisis in 1980s, the market mechanisms prevailed, propped up by the bureaucrats and technocrats greedy to grab the profit of these enterprises for themselves. Subsequent wars and all-pervading privatization – housing stock included – further exposed these processes. However, many practices, stemming from self-management period, are still present in the post-Yugoslav societies, only under different names and in different contexts: tenants councils, informality and paralegality, self-building and self-maintaining, and DIY construction and maintenance. In times of crisis, these are the practices that take the lead, not the other way around: we have seen citizens all over the post-Yugoslav region self-organizing promptly and efficiently during floods, wildfires, even COVID-19 pandemic, while the state would chime in with days of tardiness. With the variety as a main result of self-managed housing economy of Yugoslavia – of shapes, forms, hybrids, technologies, sizes, densities, ownerships, knowledges and practices – as well as the volume of around 3,000,000 newly built and around 800,000 reconstructed housing units in socialist Yugoslavia, the usual narrative surrounding Yugoslav housing production must change. The diversity, decentralization and vernacularity of Yugoslav housing economy were a manifestation both of the hardship and of the resilience of country's self-management system and were a good and optimal strategy in country's complex geopolitical and economic circumstances.

References

Adžić, Mara (ed.) (1970). *25 godina građevinarstva socijalističke Jugoslavije.* Beograd: Tehnika.

Antić, L. (1978). *Programirano zadovoljavanje stambenih potreba.* Beograd: Ekonomika.

Antipolitika (2020). 'Yugoslav workers' self-management: emancipation of workers or capitalist division of labor?. *Antipolitika: Anarchist Journal from the Balkans.* https://antipolitika.noblogs.org/post/2020/07/17/self-management/, accessed 10.11.2020.

Archer, R. (2013). 'Imaš kuću – vrati stan': housing inequalities, socialist morality and discontent 1980s Yugoslavia. *Beograd: Godišnjak za društvenu istoriju,* 20(3), 119–39.

Arzenšek, V. (1981). Samoupravljanje i struktura moći: stabilnost sistema dominacije. *Revija za sociologiju,* XI(1–2), 3–12.

Cagić, P., Otović, S. and Lojanica, M. (1978). *Prethodna studija za izbor optimalnog sistema za industrijsku proizvodnju stambenih, javnih i industrijskih objekata.* Beograd: Institut Kirilo Savić, IAUS, Arhitektonski fakultet Univerziteta u Beogradu.

Dolenec, D. and Žitko, M. (2016). Exploring commons theory for principles of a socialist governmentality. *Review of Radical Political Economics,* 48(1), 66–80. doi:10.1177/0486613415586986, accessed 18.02.2021.

Đuričić, M. (1987). *Ostvarivanje prava radnika (obrasci i sudska praksa).* Beograd: Službeni list.

Filipović, S. Izgradnja 1948, v. 2, n. 2-5, pp. 45–53.

FNRJ (1961). *Društveni plan privrednog razvoja Jugoslavije od 1961. do 1965. godine.* Beograd: Službeni list FNRJ.

Horvat, B. (1989). *ABC jugoslovenskog socijalizma.* Zagreb: Globus.

Horvat, S. and Štiks, I. (2015). *Dobro došli u pustinju postsocijalizma.* Zagreb: Fraktura.

Ivanović, Marinković (2020). Vučić o 'Juri': Socijalizam neće da se vrati. *JuGmedia.* https://jugmedia.rs/vucic-o-juri-socijalizam-nece-da-se-vrati/, accessed 3.6.2020.

Jovanović, J. (2020). Lessons of Yugoslav housing economy of the First Five Years Plan: permeable boundaries between tradition and modernity. *Život umjetnosti,* 107, 32–59.

Kardelj, E. (1979). *Samoupravljanje i društvena svojina.* Beograd: BIGZ.

Kirn, G. (2019). *Partisan Ruptures. Self-Management, Market Reform and the Spectre of Socialist Yugoslavia.* London: Pluto Press.

Kostadinović, S. (1989). *Zadovoljavanje stambenih potreba i razvoj socijalne strukture Jugoslavije.* Beograd: Zavod za novinsko-izdavačku i porpagandnu delatnost JŽ.

Kulić, V. and Mrduljaš, M. (eds.) (2012). *Unfinished modernisations: Between utopia and pragmatism.* Zagreb: Association of Croatian Architects.

Le Normand, Brigitte. (2014). *Designing Tito's Capital: Urban Planning, Modernism, and Socialism.* Pittsburgh: University of Pittsburgh Press.

Lekić, B. and Zečević, M. (eds.) (1995). Privredna politika Vlade. *FNRJ: zapisnici Privrednog saveta Vlade FNRJ: 1944–1953,* 1–4, Beograd: Arhiv Jugoslavije.

Markuš, B. (2016). Radničko samoupravljanje, moje iskustvo. Zaboravljena vrednost ili strah da se ne setimo tih vrednosti. *SRP.* http://www.srp.hr/radnicko-samoupravljanje-moje-iskustvo-zaboravljena-vrednost-ili-strah-da-se-ne-setimo-tih-vrednosti/, accessed 14.04.2020.

Miler, J. and Bečejac, S. (eds.) (1974). *Savetovanje o društvenom organizovanju usmerene stambene izgradnje.* Beograd: SITM, SITJ.

Mihailović, K. (ed.) (1953). *Proizvodne snage NR Srbije.* Beograd: Ekonomski institut NR Srbije.

Mitrović, M. (2016). Samoupravljanje: budućnosti jedne utopije. *Peščanik.* https://pescanik.net/samoupravljanje-buducnosti-jedne-utopije/, accessed 14.04.2020.

Narodna armija (1978). *Zajednica stanovanja JNA: zbirka propisa o upravljanju stambenim fondom JNA.* Beograd: Narodna armija.

Obradović, M. Izgradnja, 1950, v. 4, n.5-6, pp. 27-29.

Pantelić, Č. K., 1954, v. 8, n. 8-9, pp. 56–68.

Pantelić, Č. K., 1954, v. 8, n. 10, pp. 39–49.

Petranović, B. (1988). *Istorija Jugoslavije III – Socijalistička Jugoslavija 1955–1988.* http://znaci.net/00001/95.htm, accessed 14.04.2020.

Pjanić, Lj. (1972). *Prostorna ekonomija.* Beograd: Službeni list SFRJ.

Putnik Prica, V. (2019). About the development of small apartment typology in Belgrade interwar architecture. *Matica Srpska: Journal for Fine Arts,* 47, 225–234. Novi Sad: Matica srpska.

Račić, J., Cvek, S. and Ivčić, S. (2015). Neko se za to znojio. *Masina.* http://www.masina.rs/?p=1266, accessed 14.04.2020.

Samoupravljanje na izmaku. Šalabahter. http://borovo1988.radnickaprava.org/pdf/rjecnik-samoupravljanja.pdf, accessed 14.04.2020.

Savezna planska komisija (1947). *Petogodišnji plan razvitka narodne privrede FNRJ 1947-1951'.* Beograd: Savezna planska komisija.

SFRJ (1981). *Zakon o stambenim odnosima (prečišćen tekst). Zakon o finansiranju stambene izgradnje (prečišćeni tekst).* Beograd: Službeni list SFRJ.

SFRJ (1982). *Zakon o osnovnim pravima iz penzijskog i invalidskog osiguranja.* Beograd: Službeni list SFRJ.

SFRJ (1986). *Zakon o udruženom radu.* Beograd: Službeni list SFRJ.

SFRJ (1991). *Zakon o preduzećima sa ugrađenim izmenama.* Beograd: Službeni list SFRJ.

Stierli, M. and Kulić, V. (eds.) (2012). *Toward a concrete utopia. Architecture in Yugoslavia 1948-1980.* New York: Museum of Modern Art.

Stojković, M. and Grujičić, R. (1978). *Prostorno planiranje.* Beograd: IC Ekonomika.

Stručna štampa (1974). *Statut grada Beograda.* Beograd: Stručna štampa.

Ustav FNRJ (2020). http://www.arhivyu.gov.rs/index.php?download_command =attachment&file_command=download&file_id=42688&file_type=oFile &modul=Core%3A%3AFileManagement%3A%3AcFileModul, accessed 14.04.2020.

Vukosavljević, S. (1960). *Savetovanje o industrijalizaciji stambene izgradnje*, ed. Mole, Milan. Beograd: Savezna građevinska komora.

Vukosavljević, S. (1971). *Društveni stambeni fond*. Beograd: Poslovno udruženje stambenih preduzeća Beograd.

Vukosavljević, S. (2012). *Istorija seljačkog društva II – sociologija stanovanja*. Beograd: Službeni glasnik.

Zorkine, P. (2020). The myth of workers councils under Tito. *Antipolitika: The Anarchist Journal from the Balkans*. https://antipolitika.noblogs.org/post /2020/07/27/tito/, accessed 10.11.2020.

12

A Greek activist's reflections on the housing struggles and the movement against foreclosures in Athens

Tonia Katerini

Introduction

This text is not merely a theoretical contribution to the interpretation of the current housing situation in Greece (a particularly difficult one for the social struggles for the emancipation of the oppressed classes). It stems from the urge to discuss some important questions that have arisen over the last six years of our continuous involvement with the movement for housing rights and against foreclosures in Athens, Greece. This struggle has brought together a significant number of individuals and local collectives and has managed to prevent all home foreclosures in the past four years. The Greek government has responded to this struggle with new, and more authoritarian, legislation. In this most unfavourable present context, the movement struggles for the protection of 'the right to a primary home' (aiming to prevent the foreclosure of houses that are the primary residence for those who live in them). This struggle has been criticized by both the government and the media and, also, by parts of the left. The criticism from the left stems from the identification of our struggle as a struggle to protect (private) property. This criticism underpins the reluctance of parts of the left to engage in this struggle.

To organize our struggle more effectively, it is necessary to understand the mechanisms and instruments deployed by the ruling classes in their current attack on housing rights. In the current situation, it is imperative that movements and collectives around the world take action while also producing significant knowledge. In particular, the European Action Coalition for the Right to Housing and the City has published two research brochures based on the knowledge collated by the social movements participating in the coalition. This research has contributed greatly to the interpretation of the policies and strategies pursued by capital.

Whether in Greece, where the commercialization of housing is not only a universal practice for addressing the housing need but also a dominant tool of (a distorted) economic development, or in Northern and Central Europe, where a long tradition of social housing has been eroded in various ways that, in recent years, the weaker social classes are now confronted with an onslaught on their right to housing and the spatial identity this right entails. Numerous people are being stripped of all ties of empowerment, retaining only those elemental ties that ensure their own reproduction (for which, most of the time, they bear the sole responsibility). The 'welfare state' becomes exempt from the obligation to provide even a modicum of welfare, which, at best, maintains the minimal degree of social cohesion needed for the operation of the established system of exploitation. In these conditions, the erosion of the right to housing (in a secure home) is universal.

The exploitation of small private property, communal land and housing, and public land and property by capital forms the three prongs of this attack. The tactics of lending and overindebtedness, taxation, the marketization of the housing stock and the deregulation of the tenant protection framework are some of its weapons.

Today, we are witnessing a shift in the attitude of the dominant classes towards housing (and, more generally, towards the reproductive means of the workers). The financial crisis of the recent years has led to a new cycle of tougher policies. The redistributive policies of the past fifty years have been abolished, and the welfare state is shrinking to a mere manager of extreme poverty (Kourachanis 2017). It is at this very moment that the state facilitates an attack on secure housing and small property for the benefit of capital. The policies of the previous decades enabled the working class to obtain private housing through market processes (compensation, low taxation, cheap loans) in Greece, or through the production of social housing purchased with low-interest instalments, or rented at low rates, in other countries. These policies, and the legislation that protected tenants, have been withdrawn. The contract of the ruling class with the middle class, based on the transformation of the latter into small-scale landlords, has been ruptured. At the same time, the ruling class' interest in the workers having a secure residence where they can maintain and develop their productive potential in stable and tolerable conditions of daily life has also disappeared. The new, threefold strategy of variability, mobility and precariousness ensures the greatest possible disciplining of employees to the requirements of capital. This situation significantly changes the context in which we now have to understand the conflict between labour and capital.

As David Harvey (2013) aptly points out, workers can struggle for higher wages and better working conditions, and potentially succeed. But when they finish work, they come back home from the workplace to find out that they have to give much of their earnings back to the bourgeoisie, to pay for the increased rent, credit card, phone bill and so much more. From the workers' perspective, therefore, the concern is not only about what happens at the point of production but also about the cost of housing, services, goods, commodities, hidden mortgages, loans, etc. To codify the fronts that this new phase opens, we need to understand the following:

- The consequences of the withdrawal of home and small property for the process of reproduction of the working classes;
- The destruction of the middle social layers;
- The concentration of land and real estate ownership, and the return of capital to profiting from land rent;
- The financialization of the housing stockpile, and its role in converting non-productive money into efficient investment, that is, into capital.

The regression of the care for housing, and the security of housing as a social asset, in developed countries is a direct consequence of the emancipatory struggles of the working classes in previous decades: these struggles reduced the ability of capital to derive profit from the workers. Social security rendered workers less obedient to employers' demands; at the same time, it enabled them to formulate individual plans for 'advancement' to the status of the petty bourgeois. Characteristically, the ratio of wage earners to the working population is inversely proportional to the ratio of owners to tenants.

The exploitation of small private property (e.g. whether this is a second home for financial reserve, small plots of productive or construction land, etc.) by capital has many and far-reaching impacts. The strategy of overindebtedness and multiple forms of taxation (that now also include the social security system) result in the destruction of the weakest segments of the middle class. This process often leads to an oversupply of highly skilled labour. The vulnerability generated by homelessness is further reinforced by the rupture of spatial and social identity resulting from the mandatory relocation in search of affordable housing.

At the same time, capital pursues an aggressive policy of acquisition and concentration of large parts of the housing and land stock devalued through the process of overindebtedness (public and private), as this stock has been set as collateral for borrowing. Banks, real estate and other companies are currently planning a new profitability cycle for capital, and a new framework for social and economic control. The features of this new cycle are not yet clear; nevertheless, it is interesting to observe these new dynamics in relation to emerging areas of labour–capital conflict.

Do these phenomena constitute a new phase of social competition? Could they be described as a new cycle of primitive accumulation? And what does this entail for the labour–capital relationship? We need to look at these issues in some more detail.

Primitive accumulation and housing struggles

To approach these questions, we begin by looking at the concept of primitive accumulation as formulated by Karl Marx and interpreted by his successors. In particular, we should clarify whether primitive accumulation should be understood as a process that occurs at a specific, historically defined moment in the development of capitalism, or, as we argue, as a process that recurs within capitalism, even if, at first sight, its recurrences appear to be something else.

Looking at Rosa Luxemburg's (1951/2003) approach to primitive accumulation, we find what she termed 'inherent or continuous primordial accumulation'. She argued that this is a characteristic of the separation of people from the means of production, and thus a permanent and inherent process of capitalist production (Kalabokas 2013). Sylvia Federici (2018) explains that primitive accumulation is a strategy, used especially in times of crisis, to redefine class relations and reshape subjectivity. In a complementary approach, primitive accumulation is, according to Braudel, consistent with the understanding of the capitalist economy as a global economy in which accumulation at one place may correspond to primitive accumulation at another place.

Massimo de Angelis (2001) supports and further develops this approach in his interesting article on the concept of primitive accumulation in Marx. In this, he identifies three conditions for the permanent recurrence of the process of primitive accumulation: The first condition concerns the alienation of the working classes, not only from the means of production but also from the means of reproduction. The second concerns the existence of guaranteed rights to health, education, etc. (as shaped by social struggles in the post-war welfare state), which function as common goods and, as such, are subject to an onslaught of new enclosures. The third condition concerns social conflict, through which producers question the reproduction of their separation from the means of production, as well as the current processes of accumulation of capital.

If we are interested in understanding these social processes today, it is because we do not want to underestimate the significance of the current conflict around housing, and also the urban landscape, as a part of the capital's ongoing quest for profitability. Ignoring the circumstances of the current conjuncture, and the consequences of these circumstances for the constitution of the workers' emancipatory project, could lead to such an underestimate.

Today, the defence of home and small property does not, therefore, reflect the demands of a social class in crisis – a social class that, in the dominant capital–labour opposition, appears to be the residue of an incomplete system of relations. In fact, what we defend are the rights that allowed workers a modicum of emancipation. Historically, workers' complete deprivation of the means of production and reproduction has never contributed to the emancipation of the working class.

The defence of home and small property today enters into the conflict between the logic of boundless accumulation of capital and the struggle of people for freedom and dignity, and helps us to understand the recurring character of primitive accumulation. By doing so, it also helps to position alternatives to capitalism – the direct access to the means of existence – to the centre of political discourse.

A great debate about the nature of our struggle continues to take place within the housing rights movement: Is this a struggle about the protection of private homes (e.g. from foreclosure and repossession), or about claiming adequate quality public housing for everyone? Beyond the obvious priorities imposed by the current condition, the answer to these questions is synthetic and multifaceted. We also recognize a further, strong reason to overcome such dilemmas synthetically. The present surge of primary accumulation, if not orchestrated, is certainly facilitated by a combination of capital strategy and the institutional violence stemming from an increasingly authoritarian state that promotes the proletarianization of many social strata and the exploitation of common goods. In particular, countries where the state is administered by governments self-defined as progressive (such as Greece and Portugal) confirm Marx's identification of the role of the state in primitive accumulation: to promote the separation of the producers from the means of their subsistence. This is why, for Marx, an emancipated society will take the form of 'an association of free men, working with the means of production held in common, and expending their many different forms of labour-power in full self-awareness as one single social labour force' (Marx 1976: 171).

House grabbing, however, is not part of the construction for a more equitable society, as it is not accompanied by any kind of transition to public or community management of the existing housing stock. Quite the opposite: house grabbing promotes further separation of the producers from the means necessary to ensure a life worth living.

The housing crisis in Greece

European housing movements have initiated the debate about the present and future of housing as a human right and a common good. This debate has to do with the many practices and concepts through which housing is defined as a good that should become accessible to all: public, social, affordable or cooperative housing; alternative forms of housing; self-housing; common housing. Each of these concepts corresponds to particular practices that need to be valued in order to empower social struggles attuned with the specific conditions in each country, city or region. In the European context, especially, all of these models coexist to a different degree, with each model underpinning different priorities. The coordination of housing movements facilitates the exchange of experiences and strengthens the movements' ability to understand the trends and tactics of capital and formulate an effective resistance.

Greece has a strong tradition of home ownership. In recent years, as Greece's banking system was deleveraged, and a different model of development was pursued (The Economist 2020), home ownership – especially that of the weakest section of the middle class – was hit hard. Greek housing movements – and especially the movement against foreclosures – are confronted with this new reality. The action of the housing movements should thus develop simultaneously in two directions: defending the housing rights of overindebted households (faced with the prospect of homelessness as their financial situation deteriorated dramatically due to the crisis) on the one hand and seeking new housing patterns in the face of the severe decline of home ownership (the dominant ownership model in post–Second World War Greece) on the other.

The institutional framework for the protection of primary residence has been gradually eroded since 2014. On 30 April 2020, the last legislative tool for the protection of primary residence, applicable only under very strict stipulations, was withdrawn. In October 2020, the parliament approved a new bankruptcy law that permits the foreclosure of all the property of indebted persons, including the house they live in. As far as the right to housing is concerned, this law marks the beginning of a new era in Greece.

The new bankruptcy law puts more than 150,000 households at risk of homelessness. This number only includes debtors to banking institutions; the addition of debtors to the state and those who own tax or insurance contributions would make this number much higher. The state's response to the imminent housing crisis is a plan to subsidize part of the rent for those who lose their homes as long as they can demonstrate that they lack other resources and are declared bankrupt.

At the time of writing, more than 10,000 foreclosures have been announced. Contrary to the claims of the current and previous governments, many of these foreclosures affect low-income borrowers rather than strategic defaulters. A large number of the houses to be auctioned are in low-income neighbourhoods. These foreclosures will enable banks, funds connected with them and real estate funds to buy numerous houses, control the future housing market and develop gentrification plans for certain areas.

To date, there has been no large wave of evictions. Some evictions have been publicized; we know that many more have not come to light because of the fear and the shame of those affected.

At the same time, and as the demand for rented accommodation increases, the arrival of Airbnb-type short-term rental in Greece has resulted in a dramatic increase in rents, especially in the cities that attract tourists. With the exception of a special taxation policy for short-term lease, no measures are in place in Greece to control the spread of Airbnb, and the legal framework for the protection of tenants is very weak. Precisely because of the previous condition of widespread home ownership, the tenants' movement is in its infancy.

A special but very important issue concerning housing in Greece is the housing for immigrants and refugees. Deficient policies and miserable conditions are its key features. According to the agreements between the EU and the Greek government, most immigrants and refugees arriving to Greece have to stay in the country and are not permitted to travel further. These agreements treat a large and long-term problem as temporary. Thousands of migrants have been evicted from their (temporary) accommodation. Many of these people now live in the streets or in overcrowded refugee camps and detention centres.

In these conditions, the movement for the right to housing takes various initiatives. Yet, it remains a minority movement, mainly involving politicized and radicalized persons rather than those directly affected by the housing crisis. The actions of this movement focus on four main objectives: the defence of overindebted people from the looting of their home, resistance to Airbnb, the protection of tenants against rent speculation by landlords, and decent housing for refugees-immigrants and, also for the homeless, whose numbers are on the rise.

The right-to-housing movement in Greece proposes a framework of three baseline conditions for the protection of primary residence: homes of a quality sufficient to provide dignified living conditions, secure from eviction, and at a total cost (including rent or loan, tax and energy costs) not exceeding 20 per cent of a household income and, in any event, not affecting the minimum 'dignified living' income (which would need to be updated).

To this perspective it is necessary to add a qualitative dimension related to the territoriality of residence, the personal integration and identity implemented in space, the social reference networks and the risks from their disruption, and the association of residence with all activities, starting with work. The latter relationship is of particular importance as the recent Yellow Vest demonstrations in France have demonstrated.

The current attack on Greece's historic model of home ownership can be resisted by defending the home. Thinking about the home in a different way is also important. The key direction should be towards removing housing from the mechanisms of the market. This can be a point of departure for the emergence of a number of new types of housing within a system of sharing and exchange that serves the real needs of the home occupants, as these are reshaped and transformed in the course of the occupants' lives. A new ethos of commoning may thus emerge through demands and actions that reframe the housing question to this direction.

As a movement, today, we are faced with a major challenge. We must act on three goals at the same time. We need to (a) make apparent the dimensions of the housing problem and strive to make it better understood by the wider society; (b) approach those affected, and empower them to claim their rights; (c) stop any attempt of home foreclosures and evictions.

These three goals are closely interlinked. In the last seven years, numerous articles, posters, videos and radio and social media presentations have helped to deconstruct the government and banks' narrative that reduces the housing problem to a matter of individual responsibility and self-management. At the same time, by our presence in the courts every Wednesday afternoon, we have managed to prevent many foreclosures. This was the reason why, in 2017, the EU institutions and the Greek government decided to move the foreclosure procedures to an e-platform that does not permit us to block an auction while it is running. The movement had thus to resort to new forms of action: by demonstrating at the banks and notary offices responsible for the repossessions, we forced them to postpone the auctions and negotiate a settlement with the debtors. In many cases, we succeeded. This has strengthened the confidence of many of those affected that fighting for their right is worthwhile. In anticipation of a forthcoming wave of evictions, the words of a woman whose house was saved from foreclosure fill us with optimism:

> I am sixty-five years old and have lived my life working and taking care of my family. It is the first time that I felt that people fighting together can succeed a lot. And I am thankful for this!

Acknowledgements

This chapter has been edited by the authors and proofread by Dr Nikos Kourampas, University of Edinburgh.

References

De Angelis, M. (2001). Marx and primary accumulation: the permanent character of the capital enclosures. *The Commoner*, 2 September 2001 [online]. http://www.thecommoner.org

Federici, S. (2018). *Witches, Witch-hunting, and Women*. Oakland: PM Press.

Harvey, D. (2013). *Rebel Cities: Rebel Cities: From the Right to the City to the Urban Revolution*. London: Verso.

Kalabokas, G. (2013). *Violence, History, Encounter: Marx's Theory of Prime Accumulation*. Masters Thesis. Athens: Panteion University (in Greek).

Kourachanis, N. (2017). *Social Housing Policies – The Greek Residual Approach*. Athens: Papazisi Publications (in Greek).

Luxembourg, R. (1951/2003). *The Accumulation of Capital*. London: Routledge.

Marx, K. (1976). *Capital: Volume 1*, translated by B. Fowkes. Harmondsworth: Penguin.

The Economist (2020). The horrible housing blunder: home ownership is the West's biggest economic-policy mistake. *The Economist*, 18 January 2020 [online]. https://www.economist.com/leaders/2020/01/16/home-ownership-is-the-wests-biggest-economic-policy-mistake

13

The power of public participation

Socio-economic impacts of urban development on the local commons in Egypt

Mohamed Magdi Hagras

The gap

I did not realize this gap between how the government is handling the informal housing crisis and the residents' motives for still living in it until I witnessed an official governmental visit to Manshiet Nasser – one of the largest slums in Cairo and the Middle East with a population of one and a half million – and I observed the scene with great concern. I watched the motorcade as it stood on the outskirts of the area next to the main road without penetrating into the depths of the urbanism. Government officials, in their black suits and white collars, rolled out of their cars amid their guards, waving their hands on the dilapidated houses and narrow streets, discussing the demolition of those homes and the transfer process of its people, to house them in the previously built units in the desert outside Cairo, without taking their opinion or discussing the process with the people! Those people on the other side, suspicious yet do not come close, and warn their children not to approach the procession. A scene that indicates separation from reality and the loss of dialogue between the two parties. The visit ended with many decisions, most of which ensued demolitions and removals. This portrayed that they feel as if this community and their homes are just a burden on the state.

Years later, while I was working in ADAPT – an architecture and urban planning firm – I was on a site visit to follow up on the project of developing the same area – Manshiet Nasser – and we went to the same place, but this time it was not to make decisions, it was to discuss solutions with the people as we used to share our visions and work with public participation. In a different way, I began to think about the huge efforts that these people made to obtain the most basic rights, like housing, and the amount of creativity they cultivated in reusing materials and merging them together to build adjacent rooms that will eventually form a shelter for a family. I observed the children as they extracted from the trash an old stick and installed a round metal cover at its end to make a wheel and play with it; yes, they are making their own toys because they do not have the luxury of buying them. It is the same scene, and the only difference is our perspective, which assured me that this community is not a burden but rather an example of struggle and an evidence of our shortcomings as urban planners.

Between the first and second scenes, my perspective changed due to my years of work with the Egyptian architect Hany El-Miniawy, founder of ADAPT – Appropriate Development Architecture and Planning Technologies – and one of the most important architects and urban planners in Egypt. He earned his bachelor's degree in 1975 from the Faculty of Fine Arts in Cairo, and then travelled to Germany for postgraduate studies. As part of his studies in Germany, he went to Algeria for a four-month practical training, but spent fourteen years there! He always says: 'When I went to the Algerian desert, I saw that there was a need for my work' (Ashoka, 2004).

Miniawy started his work in the southern Algerian desert by perceiving the housing system and the local houses built over 600 years ago yet still standing. He began to analyse the materials which the houses were built from; he then developed and used them in building modern units instead of importing building materials from outside the place. He was confident that those local materials established the identity of the desert communities and resisted its harsh climatic factors.

During his fourteen years in Algeria, Miniawy utilized the method of building with local materials and local labour to establish housing projects. This started with a project of building 400 housing units that ended with 8,000 housing units instead, and educational projects that started with a 6-classroom school but ended with 15 schools (Bellal, 2010). However, his greatest success is that although he left the desert and returned to Egypt in 1989, the Algerian people continued the work with the same approach, until the number of housing units built with his technique reached 20,000 housing units today.

Urban fabric versus social fabric

Miniawy returned to Egypt in the late 1980s, determined that his main goal is to develop informal areas, on the levels of urban, social, cultural and economic development levels (Ashoka, 2004). Armed with his personal conviction that whoever wants to succeed in any traditional work must start outside the centre of the capital, he started work on the project of the High Dam workers city, known as 'Nasiriyah'. He began to analyse and develop local building materials and obtain the necessary permits for their use in the development of the city. From the far south, after the success of the project, he returned to the capital, Cairo, to work in Imbāba, Manshiet Nasir, Bulaq al-Dakrur and various areas of Giza; this is when I began to work with him.

In our work, we believe that the most important solutions to the housing problems in the informal settlements are, first, to recognize the power of the targeted community and to believe in the capabilities of the local people of these areas and, second, to exploit their knowledge and experiences in using local materials in construction, and to expand public participation. Then, to bring together old generations of craftsmen with young people to transfer the knowledge of these crafts to new generations.

With the same public participation approach, his project started in Manshiet Nasser while he was teaching a course for students of the architecture department, Al-Azhar University. After their first lecture, he took the students to Manshiet Nasser youth centre, and they started to get to know the youth and people of the area. The targeted community in this case was the residents of Manshiet Nasser, one of the largest informal areas in Egypt, and is the most densely populated area not only in Egypt but in all of Africa. Although there is a perception among some groups in Egyptian society that these informal areas are associated with criminal activity and danger, the university students felt safe during the site visit, which encouraged them to bond with the residents and develop ideas for developing the area.

Together, they started cleaning the streets and planting trees. Then the design process started with public participation. On the way to implementing the buildings, the students realized the local youth's energies, and the need of providing them with a place to release these energies. So, the result was the construction of an open theatre in the heart of the mountain, on which the people of the region presented theatrical and musical performances of their production, dazzling the world and changing the negative connotation of the informal areas.

The student experiment was repeated with Cairo University students at the Faculty of Urban Planning in other informal areas such as Imbāba and Bulaq Dakrur, Cairo, and the result was the transformation of 'garbage dumps' into cultural centres that the General Authority of Culture Palaces later placed their banners on and completed its development. 'Every university should have a tangible role in urban development of its geographical scope,' Miniawy says (Ashoka, 2004).

In most public participation housing projects carried out by Miniawy, the first step was always the participation of the residents in the DPs, then workshops, questionnaires and community dialogue with the people, before reaching the final plan. He believes that studying the social fabric is just as important as studying the urban fabric, so before going through the planning and design details, Miniawy and his team used to study the social relations between the residents, their daily life, their main economic activities and resources. Then he would engage the residents, focusing on their potentials to plan the development project phases.

Later on, before implementation, El-Miniawy would head to the project area in search of old generations of construction workers, so that he could learn about local building materials from them, in order to develop and use them in construction. He also requested that the older generation craftsmen teach and train some of the region's youth on the use local building methods, allowing for a new generation of local workers to emerge (Ashoka, 2004).

Miniawy introduced, in Egypt and Algeria, a new method to solve the problem of housing and architectural and urban treatments, represented in the concept of public participation and building with local materials and by local labour. Other successful applications of this system in medium-sized projects include the 'Howard Carter House', discoverer of the 'Tutankhamun' cemetery in Luxor, the Danshway Museum and the rest of St Catherine's visitors in Jabal Moussa in Sinai, and housing projects such as the New Duwaiqa and the development of Manshiet Nasser.

Armed with these experiences, Miniawy gives lectures in Egyptian and international universities, to bestow upon the students the knowledge gained through years of working with the community. And although his record is filled with dozens of honours and awards, his most precious prize remains the appreciation of people for his work, and how they follow his approach with passion. Evidently, it is the most valuable lesson for architects and urban planners.

At the end, Miniawy was not the first to provide different and sustainable solutions for informal housing, as there are many valuable experiences worth mentioning that preceded El-Miniawy. Some of which were to tackle the slums that appeared in major centres, especially Cairo, and some provided solutions to the root causes of the problem, such as the migration from rural to urban areas. So what if the nature of housing in the countryside was developed to be more connected to the people, their job opportunities, their future and their families? Would they still opt for immigration, or would they stay in the countryside?

Creative commons (art as commons)

So many people aspire for a better future, for a chance to realize their dreams of change. People may differ in their characters, habits and backgrounds, but they all share the ability to dream. The dream of change, of innovation, of creativity can lead someone to risk everything they have for a chance to turn their dreams into reality. One of those people was the Egyptian architect Ramses Wissa Wasef, who had a different vision regarding the issue of housing and rural abandonment, which will be presented in the following text.

So, at a time when it was common for the inhabitants of rural areas to pursue job opportunities and better quality of life in the capital city of Cairo, another school of thought emerged to advocate the role of the countryside and the characteristic inherent ability of its people to create change while preserving their unique identity. This view was adopted and advocated by the Egyptian architect Ramses Wissa Wassef as he believed that children who were brought up surrounded by nature had an immense reserve of talent and creativity. He also noticed that women in these areas were often selflessly giving as they held a great sense of responsibility towards the community.

Consequently, Wassef saw that the key solution to the rural–urban migration issue lies in creating job opportunities that strengthen the people's bond/attachment to their natural habitat along with obtaining a healthy wholesome standard of living for the entire family (Berger, 2013), a concept he called the integration of humans and nature.

Egyptian architect Wassef, born in Cairo in 1911, travelled to France to continue his study in architecture; he received his diploma degree in 1936, and then returned to Egypt to work as a professor of art and architecture history in the Faculty of Fine Arts (AbdelTawab, 2013). And maybe it was due to the time he spent abroad he was able to see Egypt in a different way. He appreciated the value of the Egyptian cultural heritage as compared to the other places he had been to, and he came back with the full realization that his country had a magnificent history that was not fully appreciated as the people had got used to its presence.

Wassef worked in architecture when he returned as he was hired in an art technical school in 1936. At the time, the construction industry was trying to rise by integrating local elements. Wassef was a pioneer during this renaissance as he had a unique architectural style that utilized the help of craftsmen such as gypsum crafters and stained-glass crafters, as he believed that the work needed to be fully integrated.

'What I fail to understand is why our artistic cultural heritage would create such monstrosity in place of authentic artistic architecture, even in archaic neighbourhood an outbreak of new hideous buildings has emerged, it's an offense to the human artistic sense' (AbdelTawab, 2013). Wassef clarified his point of view of modern architecture and tried to present the principles of modern architecture while maintaining the heritage within the architectural elements of the Egyptian identity; he was also more practical and functional as he wanted an average-sized home with the kitchen and bathroom in close proximity to the other rooms, as opposed to the classical style where these rooms were spaced out to eliminate mingling of the house owners with the hired help. His style was more relevant and up-to-date, which allowed many architects to draw inspiration from him.

Then, in the village of Al-Harrania, Giza Governorate, Wassef's creative story made its way towards community development. Wassef started with the children in the village as they are the future of this community, so he established the Harrania Art Centre, where he divided work groups of children between the ages of eight and twelve years and attached them to this Art Centre to learn how to produce handmade carpets.

The centre was based on experimental methodology in art. There were no prior drawings or plans for the form of artistic work that these young boys and did, as their work was all due to the creative sense that they were born with. The children were very quick learners. After several years of work, Harrania Art Centre achieved unprecedented achievements. The children excelled in producing unique shapes and artistic styles of handmade carpets, and the sales achieved great profits for the people of the village.

As a result, their creative products went out of the village to reach the capital, Cairo, and then to the world. The handmade carpets of the Harrania participated in art exhibitions in Paris and many cities around the world.

At that time, people of Harrania realized that their creative commons became a means of living, which improved the quality of life in the village. On the other side, Wassef, with his creative project, achieved real development on the social, technical and economic levels for the people of the village (AbdelTawab, 2013).

Wassef died in 1994, at the age of sixty-three, and all the villagers mourned him. They still love and respect him, and they are still working in the jobs he created for them and live in the homes that they designed together. Lastly, he still lives in their memories and will remain so forever.

The impact of 'one million housing units'

'Places as the products of common cultural and symbolic elements and processes': this is how Edward Relph defines places. He adds that the basic elements required to form a place are a static physical setting, activities within that setting and meanings which come out with the activities there (Relph, 1976). Consequently, place formation is largely a social process. Therefore, the impacts of development on social relationships and activities should be considered in any process of planning for urban development, and such impacts need to be assessed like the social, economic or environmental impact of the urban development.

The aforementioned statement leads us to the main problem of this part, which is how to consider the social dimension while planning for informal urbanism solutions, in order to achieve socio-economic sustainable development. After reviewing the previous housing projects, which proved the success of the public participation approach, and the recognition of people and their needs in solving the housing crisis, with evidence that people loved the projects, interacted with them and lived in them (Dempsey, 2006), this part of the chapter attempts to analyse a larger experience with a very different approach, that is, the 'Social Housing Project' in Egypt.

What is the Social Housing Project (SHP)? It is a national project that is implemented by the model of supply, not demand, first construction, and then offering to applicants (UN Habitat and UNDP, 2012), an approach that is completely different from the projects presented earlier in this chapter that depended on building the project according to the needs of a specific group of society.

In 2011, the SHP was launched in Egypt, known to the public as the 'One Million Units' project. It is a subsidized housing project that aimed to build one million housing units for low-income families over five years; however, it remains active until 2020, with total investments exceeding US$9.50 billion (Tadamun, 2015).

The SHP is a continuation of the National Housing Project (NHP), a project which started in October 2005, in fulfilment of an electoral promise that Ḥusni Mubarak had made during his presidential campaign during Egypt's first multicandidate presidential election held in September 2005. The NHP aimed to provide 500,000 housing units within six years through implementing seven different programmes (UN Habitat and UNDP, 2012).

Back to the SHP, the project provides a solution to the housing crisis through ready-made housing units in multistorey buildings, located in remote locations, outside the cities in most cases. Except for a few rental units, most units are sold to beneficiaries, through mortgage-backed loans from the state with an interest rate lower than the market price.

Despite the magnitude of the project, many problems have arisen among the residents since its inception. This led to residents leaving their housing units and homes in many places of the SHP, due to their dissatisfaction with the project, or due to some difficulties in paying the units. This gave the project a bad reputation despite the efforts and costs spent on it (Abdul Karim and Hashim, 2012).

Figure 13.1 Masaken Uthman, the National Housing Project. (Source: Mohamed Hagras 2018.

Subsequently, this part of the chapter presents a socio-economic impact assessment of SHP, which will explain the reaction of the people towards the project. This part also provides several reasons and argues that by using the socio-economic impact assessment (SEIA), we will be able to investigate whether the project took into account the community's social aspects or not, concluding with the results and recommendations that shall be considered during the SHPs (Figure 13.1).

The impact assessment

The SEIA of SHP in Egypt: this study is divided into three sections and depends on the three dimensions of the impact assessment process, that is, the economic dimension, the social dimension and the environmental dimension (Gammaz and Hagras, 2020). They will be discussed in the following text.

The economic dimension

The economic dimension came at the head of the influencing dimensions in society. After the relocation, the people of the informal areas suffered from economic problems, which became more dangerous to them than their old houses (Becker and Vanclay, 2006), and which the government had previously labelled as 'dangerous areas'. The following are the most important issues of the economic dimension and its variables:

A. *Job, work and the workplace*: Employment opportunities are considered one of the most affected variables after the transition to the SHP, mostly because residents see that no jobs are available in new housing projects. With the aim of earning a living, some of them resort to opening kiosks and small commercial projects in the region, while others search for work in the neighbouring areas such as factory workers, cleaners, security personnel in malls and other professions that do not require specific skills (ISDF, 2011).

B. *Shops*: Because the more general profession is manual labour of all kinds, the people of the SHP have found it very difficult to keep their old shops and workshops in the previous residence, either because of their removal or because of the distance of the new residence, and at the same time they did not find in the SHP the market best suited for completing craft or commercial work.

B. *Transportation*: One of the main problems in SHPs is the absence of public transportation. Those people with a limited income cannot afford high transportation costs to carry out the simplest tasks, such as purchasing affordable food, going to work or schools and getting medical care.

C. *Public utility*: The remoteness of the SHP and their secluded location is not only a nuisance to the inhabitants, but it represents a great difficulty for them as well, especially as these areas lack basic facilities, effective services and job opportunities. Although the residential area was originally designed to create a sense of order and harmony, now it is showing increasing resemblance to the manifestations of slums – those same areas that the state aims to limit their growth.

D. *Housing*: Perhaps the issue of people abandoning their assigned units and then leasing them to a new population is one of the most important housing issues in the SHP. The phenomenon of subletting spread very quickly due to the return of the residents (who were originally assigned units) to their previous place of residence in the informal areas in search of the nature of their work and their previous lives, and this was helped by the appetence of other groups like immigrants or illegal residents to reside in those projects (Tadamun, 2015).

The social dimension

After the economic dimension is the social dimension, at the population level, where the movement of population and static groups in SHP is a rapid movement that must be considered in the development processes (Mathur, 2016):

A. *Population, demographic movement and society*: As some of the residents were unsatisfied with their homes in the SHP, they abandoned them and started searching for tenants at the lowest prices; as a result, another group of untargeted population emerged.

B. *Culture and lifestyle*: After the transfer, the largest percentage of residents did not see any effect on the culture they acquired from the previous residents. Most of the residents of the SHP were residents of informal areas previously; this allowed the merging process of cultural backgrounds, customs and traditions, and other social frameworks.

C. *Social interference and population groups*: There is an undeniable need to strengthen the social fabric in SHP. The social fabric is fragmented and volatile.

D. *Right to equality and empowerment*: The resettlement process itself caused more harm to the population as it was conducted most of the time in haste and without regard to the circumstances, as the residents disclosed in some of their interviews. As for services, they have not improved over time from the viewpoint of long-term residents. Most of the planned services have not been implemented despite the passage of several years since their resettlement.

E. *Community organization and local organization*: Policymakers must develop a true understanding of the region and take into account the developments that the authorities have long ignored or were not aware of (World Bank, 2003). To achieve this, they should always strive to welcome the active participation and cooperation of the community representatives on the ground who have a lot of activity in the region.

F. *Local government*: The people are fully prepared to cooperate with the government if it provides a joint work mechanism. For example, in some places, free mass transit buses were allocated to connect residents with their previous workplaces and to provide services. This had a positive impact on people on gaining trust in the government.

The environmental dimension

Finally, unlike the economic and social dimensions, the environmental dimension is one of the positive dimensions compared to the environment in which they were living in their previous place of residence (ISDF, 2011):

A. *Natural resources and infrastructure*: Of course, the SHP have a better infrastructure than the informal areas that the residents used to inhabit before. However, the repeated cut of water and electricity services in most of the SHP is one of the most important problems for the population.

B. *The environment*: When compared to the previous living quarters, the population unanimously agreed that there is a better environment in the SHP as compared to those they used to live in, especially in natural resources, which makes the environment a positive point in the development process.

C. *Threats and risks*: Residents of SHP generally feel insecure as a result of a number of pressures. The most important of these are the lack of confidence of people in one another, the lack of social ties between them, and the complete lack of confidence in the governmental housing system.

Findings

From the previous presentation and analysis, we come to a set of general findings and recommendations that can be implemented in similar and general urban development projects:

The most important thing that a human being seeks is to meet his vital physiological and psychological requirements that vary according to the surrounding environment and culture, here we find that architecture and urbanism affect the fulfilment of these requirements and are affected by them as well (Dempsey,2006).

SEIA includes positive and negative analysis, monitoring and management of intended and unintended social impacts, from planned interventions (policies, programmes, plans, projects, as well as any processes of social change that include these interventions). Its main purpose is to achieve a sustainable and equitable development of the human environment as a methodology. It is concerned with monitoring planned interventions or events and setting monitoring and management strategies (Colantonio and Dixon, 2009).

There should be a general, controlling and motivating basis for the development process within the city to act as support for its goals, and it should be part of a strategy that encourages global and local sustainability. It must also be analysed and developed based on three guiding principles: social sustainability, environmental sustainability and economic sustainability (Becker and Vanclay, 2006).

To achieve the goals of social sustainability, which include creating sustainable successful places that promote well-being, by understanding what people need from the places they live and work, the SEIA can be used as a tool to ensure the integration of the social dimension in urban planning and development projects for formal or informal areas. This evaluation will be able to investigate social aspects and then highlight the factors that must be considered in the project. It works to bridge the gap between urban planning mechanisms and society leading all the parties to a socially sustainable development (Cocklin, 2006).

SEIA study identifies the social, cultural and economic impacts associated with the proposed planning or development in the region, in addition to factors related to the public interest. This results in a set of recommendations that identify the strengths, weaknesses and determinants resulting from that project and then offer alternatives to the proposed planning or development. It is also clear that it is important to consider all these impacts – negative or positive – at all stages and processes related to the project (Barton and Grant, 2012).

By studying the economic, demographic and environmental impacts, and merging them with the concepts of social sustainability and sustainable urban development, issues affecting each of the following dimensions were reached: *the socio-economic dimension, the population social dimension* and *the socio-environmental dimension.* Thus, it is possible to deduce the evaluation variables in each case, in order to form an integrated evaluation model (World Bank, 2003).

Conclusion

At a time when the world is striving to develop tools and mechanisms to predict the social, economic and environmental impacts of urban development projects on communities, this chapter addresses the importance of the community engagement within the development process and presents the SEIA for the urban development projects as a tool which indicates the community needs and potentials.

To apply this tool, each site has its own criteria for the surrounding environment and factors affecting society, and therefore social issues, influences and measurement indicators will differ from one project to another. Therefore, the social and economic impacts assessment process is an independent process in which tools, variables and measurement indicators are formed according to the nature of the project (Brown, 2002).

In projects relying on population transfer, a SEIA procedure allows us to access a list of social issues, classified according to their importance (as determined by the population) and then address the social impact of their transfer to their new housing units in the new or redeveloped urban project. This procedure will help to recommend a set of factors to be considered during urban planning and development processes. This allows us to redress the social impacts of the population to be relocated or the population that needs to be attracted to the project, and to compensate the population that has already been socially relocated.

SEIAs are flexible processes that can be applied in urban planning at different levels, starting with local community development projects, planning new urban communities, that is, urban development for an existing formal or informal area, and reaching strategic and regional development projects (Brown, 2002). Urban development stresses the importance of conducting a SEIA in the early stages of project planning (Colantonio and Dixon, 2009), to highlight the social issues that affect or are affected by the project.

As for the urban context in Egypt, the housing projects and new urban communities proposed to solve the problems of residents of informal areas, or those who in need of the right to housing, usually carry many development visions and intentions but they lack support for social sustainability within the feasibility studies of those projects (ISDF, 2011). These are important as they study the social urban fabric of the areas the population previously inhabited before their transfer, thus providing social services appropriate to the people's needs of housing, work and daily-life activities in a safe and sustainable manner (IAIA, 2003).

The case studies presented in the previous chapter clarified the importance of public participation in the planning and following-up phases in the urban development. It has also been shown how useful to use SEIA as a tool for measuring community satisfaction with the project, its adaptation, and the changes occurring, negative or positive, even if they were not engaged from the beginning.

As mentioned in the two successful examples: First, the work of Hany El-Miniawy was based on public participation depending on the community needs in the neglected areas like the desert in Algeria and the informal settlements in Cairo. This made the community lead the DP and control its priorities on the social and economic levels, which resulted in community development and satisfaction. Second, Rameses Wassef project in Harrania, which was completely based on raising the standard of living by teaching the people of the village new handicraft and then achieving economic growth for the entire village, which led to social and economic sustainable development.

On the other side, the analysis of the third example, 'The One Million Units Project', presented how it could be useful and informative to re-evaluate a project – which did not include any community engagement – using tools like the SEIA, to follow up with the DPs (Tadamun, 2015).

All of this contributed to reaching several recommendations that will be put forward later to benefit from the SEIA model.

When and why to use SEIA

SEIA is just a tool which could greatly help decision-makers to build framework and identify the variables and indicators of similar urban development projects that affect the social and economic life of the targeted communities (Mathur, 2016). So, after reaching the previously listed findings, a set of recommendations was reached for using SEIA in each stage of the project:

The stage of general planning and policy development

Incorporating the SEIA tool into the primary mechanisms for setting urban DPs, as well as making SEIA one of the decision-making tools in the various stages of the project, from planning to implementing and then following-up, all contribute to achieving socially sustainable urban development.

To make a SEIA for a new project, evaluation processes can start during the general plan stage. For example, if it is a housing project, the evaluation will be done once the urban design proposal is submitted. If the results indicate that the proposal achieves the desired level of social sustainability, the project will move to the next stage. If this limit is not achieved, the project plans will be modified according to the positive or negative effects reported by the evaluation result (IAIA, 2003). There is an urgent need to start preparing detailed statistical and graphic reports on social issues in informal areas. This will contribute to shaping urban DPs and future visions, either by developing an existing urbanism or by planning for a new one (World Bank, 2003).

It is recommended that the general plan consider formally reinforcing the role of NGOs in society as a local representative in any DPs from the government. These NGOs are the spine of the informal communities and provide means of communication between them and decision-makers in the government. Also, NGOs will be the best way to achieve public participation with the targeted communities, as most of the people working in these NGOs are locals who know and understand the needs and capacities of the community (the Interorganizational Committee on Principles and Guidelines for Social Impact Assessment, 2003).

The detailed planning stage

The outline should establish a general participation plan for managing decision-making consultation processes, ensuring the population equal opportunities to participate, and identifying positive influences that must be strengthened, and negative influences that must be mitigated as part of a general effort required to make sustainable development (Clarck and Stankey, 1994).

Residents must know their transfer plan; when and where they may be transferred and the impact on their lives and their sources of income, so as to be able to plan for their future lives and participate in planning their new community, whether that participation is in groups or through community representatives.

The population is greatly affected by the availability of transportation and public transport in terms of cost and infrastructure, so detailed plans for urban development and design projects must include sustainable plans for transportation to and from the project. Newly developed areas must be planned to include major pedestrian and bike lanes. By facilitating these alternatives, the demand for vehicle movement decreases, pollution and spending decreases and a healthier lifestyle is promoted.

Construction and implementation phase

The construction and implementation processes must undergo periodic follow up from the competent supervisory authorities, which monitor the implementation stages and ensure that they are moving properly towards achieving sustainable development in the general and detailed plans. Final approvals are not granted unless the aforementioned details are considered (IAIA, 2003).

A framework can be organized that contains the target groups for inhabiting or using this project. Work must be done in a participatory manner, whether in theory by making visits and questionnaires during the implementation stages or in practice by integrating those groups into the implementation and construction work.

Operation and maintenance stage

To measure the levels of sustainability that were reached in the projects actually implemented and already inhabited, it is recommended to conduct a SEIA to measure the variance and the extent of the difference or resemblance of what has been implemented from what was planned. This process of monitoring and evaluation will contribute positively before making any decisions in developing, improving and maintaining the built environment, facilities and services (Mathur, 2016).

In the event that the initial planning of these projects lacks consideration for social sustainability from the beginning, it is still recommended to assess the social impact, as it is the most appropriate tool to remedy the negative effects reached and to reach mechanisms for developing and recreating the built and social environment (the Interorganizational Committee on Principles and Guidelines for Social Impact Assessment, 2003).

Epilogue: Back to the people

Finally, after the SEIA studies of projects like SHP in Egypt, is there reason for hope? Yes, of course; addressing the main problems, supporting services and providing them will make these projects more suitable for housing and accommodating larger numbers of people (Clarck and Stankey, 1994).

Sharing the dream and vision with people, ensuring the provision of basic services such as health, education and public transportation, and activating their work is at least a step that puts these projects on the path of sustainability. However, if by socio-economic sustainable development we mean development which meets the needs of the present without compromising the ability of future generations to meet their own needs, we must, first and foremost, resort to a different approach in containing problems, an approach that depends on the social and economic aspect of people, their needs, their capabilities and then work for their future.

References

AbdelTawab, A. G. (2013). Evaluating the authenticity of earthen heritage: The case of Ramses Wissa Wassef Art Centre in Egypt. *Alexandria Engineering Journal*, 52(3), 489–98.

Abdul Karim, H., & Hashim, A. H. (2012). The effect of a resettlement scheme on the social-cultural changes of the Temuan Community. *Procedia – Social and Behavioral Sciences*, 42, 362–73.

Ashoka (2004). Hany El-Miniawy. ADAPT, Everyone a Changemaker. [online] Available at: https://www.ashoka.org/en-eg/story/hany-el-miniawy-adapt [Accessed 8 April 2021].

Barton, H. and Grant, M. (2012). Urban planning for healthy cities. *Journal of Urban Health*, 90(S1), 129–41.

Becker, H. and Vanclay, F. (2006). The international handbook of social impact assessment. In: H. Becker and F. Vanclay (ed.), *Concept and Methodological Advances*. Cheltenham, UK: Edward Alger. pp. 74–91.

Bellal, T. (2010). Housing as an expression of self-identity in contemporary Algeria: The work of El-Miniawy Brothers. *Journal of Islamic Architecture*, 1, 87:93.

Berger (2013). *Health and Urbanism Report*. Cambridge, MA: MIT Press.

Brown, J. (2002). Social infrastructure and sustainable urban communities. *Proceedings of the Institution of Civil Engineers. Engineering Sustainability*, 165(ES1), 106–07.

Clarck, R. N. and Stankey, G. H. (1994). FEMAT's social assessment: Framework, key concepts, and lessons learned. *Journal of Forestry*, 92(4), 32–5.

Cocklin, C. (2006). *Strategic Environmental Assessment and Land Use Planning: An International Evaluation*. Edited by C. Jones, M. Baker, J. Carter, S. Jay, M. Short and C. Wood. *Geographical Research*, 44, 224–5.

Colantonio, A. and Dixon T. (2009). *Measuring Socially Sustainable Urban Regeneration in Europe*. Oxford: Oxford Institute for Sustainable Development (OISD), School of the Built Environment, Oxford Brookes University.

Dempsey, N. (2006). *The Influence of the Quality of the Built Environment on Social Cohesion in English Neighbourhoods*. Oxford: Oxford Brookes University.

Gammaz, S. and Hagras, M. (2020). Social impact assessment as a tool for achieving social sustainability in urban development processes. *Journal of Engineering and Applied Science*, 67(7), 1669–87.

IAIA (2003) *Social Impact Assessment, International Principles*. International Association for Impact Assessment IAIA, Special Publication Series Number 2.

Impact Assessment and Project Appraisal (2003). *Principles and Guidelines for Social Impact Assessment in the USA*. The Interorganizational Committee on Principles and Guidelines for Social Impact Assessment. 21(3), 231–50.

ISDF (2011). *The Committee's Report on the Service Needs of Residents Resettled from Unsafe Areas to 6th of October City in Egypt*. ISDF – Informal Settlements Development Fund, Egypt.

Mathur, H. (2016). *Assessing the Social Impact of Development Projects*. Springer International Publishing.

Relph, E. (1976), 'On the Identity of Places', in Relph, E., Place and Placelessness, Pion, London, 44–62.

Tadamun (2015). *Masakin Uthman*. Published online on 30 April 2015 [online] Available at: www.tadamun.co/masakin-uthman [Accessed 8 April 2021].

UN-HABITAT, UNDP, GOPP (2012). *Urban Development Strategy for Greater Cairo*. Part 1: Future Vision and Strategic Directions.

World Bank (2003). *Good Practice – Addressing the Social Dimensions of Private Sector Projects*. Environment and Social Development Department, International Finance Corporation, World Bank Group, Number 3.

14

From social urbanism to strategies of collective action in Medellin

Catalina Ortiz and Harry Smith

Penny Travlou (PT): In recent years, Colombia's economic growth has placed the country among the world's 'emerging economies', while Medellin has been branded as 'a city of urban innovation'. However, over 30 per cent of Medellin's population still live in poor housing conditions and/or inadequate homes. Could you please give us an overview of the housing situation in Medellin in the last twenty years?

Catalina Ortiz (CO): This is a very broad question, but let me point out to two scales. Housing policy in Colombia has largely focused on the construction of new housing or the resettlement of informal dwellers in new housing. [In Colombia], much of the effort and public budget are just following, in a way, the general model that the Chilean government championed in the region, the policy of subsidies to the demand of housing. Under neoliberal regimes, this is the strategy that has become predominant all across Latin America: subsidies for building in the outskirts of the city, in areas that do not necessarily have the best conditions to be urbanized – with all the problems associated with this. These problems are very well known to urban scholars. So, I think that there is a mismatch of priorities at the national *versus* the local level.

At city level, one singularity stands out – the generation and investment of public revenue is very high in comparison to the whole region. Nonetheless, there are persistent inequalities, and the qualitative deficit in housing is still large. When we approach the case of Medellin, we always have to ask, how come one of the most 'innovative' cities remains so unequal despite all the public investment? The city still has a lot of work to do towards more redistributive measures: redistribution not only in terms of access and public facilities but also in terms of income and real opportunities for social mobility, and with that, of course, political recognition. In a research we did several years ago, in which we tried to map the trajectory of urban change [in Medellin], we discovered that most of Medellin's urban footprint (almost 40 per cent) has informal origins. The 1950s, the time of the great rural–urban migration, was the time when many of Medellin's popular neighbourhoods had begun to be built. That type of construction and self-building processes that happened during the 1950s and all the way to the 1970s produced a large part of the housing that we see now. Another very important peak in migration and new inhabitants arriving to the city occurred mainly in the 1990s, and was aligned with the exacerbation of armed conflict and the resulting forced displacement.

The configuration of a substantial number of self-built neighbourhoods are a by-product of the massive migration from rural areas or other cities. A different pattern of neighbourhoods was built in the city according to the time and trajectory of the inhabitants and the urbanization process. While in the 1970s there was construction of what is called *barrios piratas* ['*pirate neighbourhoods*'], this was still in the lowlands, or in the areas where the slope was not so steep, here the urban layout had provisions for mobility infrastructure and some public facilities making easier the provision of public utilities. In contrast, the neighbourhoods that were built during the 1990s are in areas that are more fragile from an ecological perspective. The population that came to the city during the 1990s are, to a great extent, victims of the conflict and built several neighbourhoods called *invasions* [invasions]. Therefore, the conditions [in these areas] have been very poor in terms of urban standards. These are the more challenging areas for intervention. So, even now, in this very year [2020], an updated *Strategic Plan for Housing and Habitat* was approved, which recognizes the ongoing precarity of the housing conditions in some neighbourhoods. Since the 1990s, of course, there has been a lot of further migration and, also, internal population growth. This has been ongoing.

With the rise of social urbanism since 2004, there has been a new focus on areas of informal settlement, and the strategy of connecting these areas to the general transport system in order to achieve a symbolic inclusion of the more problematic and precarious areas into the fabric of the city. This strategy of social urbanism has been very popular, mostly because it focuses on the generation of public spaces, public facilities of education and culture, and the innovative use of cable cars as part of our massive integrated transport system. These have been the main strategies for improving the conditions of life in these informal settlements. So, in the last fifteen years, there have been three approaches to housing: business as usual real estate speculation; generating new housing, such as vertical social housing; and a focus on reducing the qualitative deficit through this strategy of social urbanism targeting informal settlements. The whole upfront speculation focuses on how the high-income areas have experienced a complete transformation of the landscape with the verticalization of the city, the [expansion of] the very high-end property market, and, also, the consolidation of new frontiers of urban expansion under what we would call 'informality from the top'. Unlike informality from the bottom, this is not criminalized. This very interesting phenomenon is, of course, present in any places, but it is especially blunt in the case of Medellin.

This would be, roughly speaking, a general perspective on the housing conditions [in Medellin]. Of course, there are several further elements to discuss: the number of housing units in downtown tenements (this is estimated to be more than 25,000 units, or more than 8,000 households), and the risks and challenges, such as the spiking homelessness and the new wave of migrants, mainly from Venezuela, who are adding further pressures on the informal settlements and changing the landscape [of the areas] where new housing is intended to be generated.

Harry Smith (HS): My engagement with housing in Medellin was initially through the *Medellin Urban Innovation*[1] (MUI) project, from 2015 to 2017. Together with Professor Françoise Coupé (from the Colombian side), I was responsible for the housing team within that project. There was an exchange of knowledge and experience in housing research among academics [in Medellin] and the team from Edinburgh, and I learnt a lot. Comparing the situation in Medellin with my experience from elsewhere, [Medellin was representative of] what you could see throughout the Global South, and South America in particular. There has been a long experience of state intervention and housing provision [in Medellin], going back to the 1950s and 1960s. This provision focuses very much on owner occupation rather than renting. This remains the trend in

[1]　Medellín: A model for future cities? Harnessing innovation in city development for social equity and well-being #MUI was a research collaboration between academic and non-academic institutions in the UK and Colombia. It was a two-year project (2015 – 17) that received a Newton Institutional Links Grant from the British Council. MUI was about researching to what extent urban innovation in Medellín (Colombia) has helped increase social equity and well-being in the city. This project was led by Dr Soledad Garcia Ferrari (University of Edinburgh) in collaboration with Dr Harry Smith (Heriot-Watt University). http://www.medellin-urban-innovation.eca.ed.ac.uk/ This led to two projects on landslide risk management in Medellin (2016-19) working with communities in *Comuna 8*. https://www.globalurbancollaborative.org/completed -projects

Colombia in general, and Medellin in particular. The other thing to bear in mind is that, in the 1980s, internationally there was a shift from the state providing housing to the state enabling housing, in line with the United Nations' discourse on this. So, how has this played out in Medellin? From what I could see, Medellin still enables developers to provide what we call 'minimum-standard dwellings'. Medellin has some examples [of this], such as *Nuevo Occidente*, which was actually built to temporarily house athletes participating in the games hosted there before being allocated to low-income households, and which, in a way, replicates the model from the 1950s and 1960s. Some of these housing projects, which are very much based on a modernist approach, do reach people of very low income to some extent, because they have to. As we were starting to work on the Medellin Urban Innovation Project, there was a programme just starting, of about 100,000 housing units specifically addressing lower-income residents. Historically, these modernist projects actually reached middle-income and, at a stretch, low-middle-income residents, rather than lower-income ones, although there have been attempts to reach the latter as well. At the other end, you see the so-called informal settlements continuing to spread very rapidly up the hillsides. This is housing that people provide for themselves, because there is still a large influx of internally displaced people. In the follow-up projects that I worked on, we worked in three neighbourhoods, looking at risk and how we can manage it. In two of [these neighbourhoods], the percentage of internally displaced people was about 80 per cent. This shows you how many people were actually still coming to the city. [These people] tend to provide themselves with housing on the perimeter [of the city], in increasingly high-risk areas further and further away from the city centre. That was the other extreme. So, there is both official and unofficial housing provision. You asked about the last two decades. Something that has happened in the last two decades is Medellin coming on the world map as 'the most innovative city in the world', as it was acclaimed in 2013, and promoting its social urbanism model internationally.

Going back to the question about housing, essentially, we do not see [the situation in Medellin] as dissimilar to what occurs in many other rapidly growing cities of the Global South. Now, what struck me in my repeated visits to Medellin was the surprising speed at which some of these so-called informal settlements were appearing and growing. I remember being on a visit in Santo Domingo with some Colombian collaborators who looked across the valley to the western side and said, 'that settlement over there wasn't there the last time I was up here'. Even the local officials were surprised by the speed at which some of these things were happening, so I think that this is generally the case. Another thing to highlight is the increasing polarization and segregation in socio-economic terms. As far as I can see, this is continuing. You get very high-income areas such as *El Poblado*, contrasting with very low-income areas, for example the Northeast, and, also, the Northwest periphery of the city. You can see this very clearly. If you overlap a map of socio-economic stratification in Medellin on the map of the city's topography, you can see that the higher-income people tend to be in the valley and also in the Southeast (there are some exceptions to this, because of high-income areas expanding up the hillsides in some places), but, in the rest of the city, the lower-income residents are concentrated on the periphery and the hillsides. Finally, another thing to highlight is that Medellin very clearly exemplifies two forms of the so-called 'informal housing' provision. One [form] is the 'land invasions' that we typically recognize from other Latin American cities: largely self-built housing without regular layouts, without services. . . . Well, [some] services, such as water and electricity, are present to some extent, but other services are not. [Besides these], there are other settlements, which are not legal or formally approved historically. These [settlements], called *urbanizaciones piratas* ['pirate settlements'], are quite regular. You also find [them] in Bogota, so this phenomenon is not unique to Medellin, but it is very striking there. *Urbanizaciones piratas* have produced a lot of the urban tissue in Medellin, and much of them predates the last two decades. This type of settlement has been present since the 1960s. What I think has happened in the last two decades is that these places may have been consolidating. But, there has been more land invasion and unorganized, informal settlement in the last two decades, rather than *barrios piratas*.

PT: How really inclusive is the '*Medellin miracle*' project in reference
    to housing? Can we speak of a successful policy when we refer, for
    example, to social urbanism? Could you please elaborate on this with
    describing, firstly, what social urbanism is, and, secondly, how social
    urbanism has shaped housing conditions in the city?
CO: We have the official discourse about social urbanism *versus* the
    more critical approach. A lot of my work has been following a more
    critical approach on what [social urbanism] is. I have defined social
    urbanism as [a set] of spatial strategies for monumentalizing the
    peripheries by intertwining partial slum upgrading with a pacification

process. I think that this is very important, because we cannot overlook the role that the militarization of space plays in the 'success' of social urbanism. Also, when I say that slum upgrading is partial, I refer to the fact that the emphasis of the social urbanist project has been mainly on the construction of public infrastructure (public systems), whereas tricky issues such as housing, tenure, risk mitigation, climate adaptation and income generation are less at the centre of this strategy. So, I think that [social urbanism] has been very successful in boosting people's civic pride; also, in terms of mobility and public facilities, it has certainly made a very important achievement. Nonetheless, when you ask who can pay, who can afford to even access the transport system, some assessments have shown that, even if you build the infrastructure, this does not mean that everyone is able to afford the fare and access the system, right? There could be a mismatch in affordability. This is why older transit systems for getting to the downtown are in some cases still active. So, there is a partial 'success'.

I also think that the very idea of 'success' is very problematic. We need to answer the question: Success for whom? [Social urbanism] has been extremely successful for the marketing of the city. In this regard, [it has been] part of removing the stigmatization [of Medellin] in the international arena. This is a very good achievement. On the other hand, this very 'boosterism' and the marketing of the city have also been used against any contestation and dissent within different social movements in Medellin. Slogans such as *'the most innovative city'*, and the legitimacy that international actors give to this success, have also resulted in many setbacks in terms of what a culture of community planning can do. There is still a technocratic approach to planning, and this is interesting and important, but not if it happens at the expense of different voices, different ways of practising planning and of providing spaces (also) for dissent.

HS: I think that, sometimes, there is some confusion about what the 'Medellin miracle' is. There are two stages in this ['miracle']. There is what is known externally as the 'Medellin miracle': social urbanism, which came along with Fajardo [the former mayor of Medellin], from 2004 onwards. People external to Medellin contrast this with what was previously known as 'the murder capital of the world' and tend to conflate these two things. However, there was a prior stage, in the early 1990s: because the situation in Medellin was so bad, a presidential commission was set up to address it, and they started turning around violence back then. One of the elements of that earlier programme was what we call 'slum upgrading' in English, which, I think, is a very often inappropriate term for what, in Spanish, is called 'neighbourhood improvement'. This integrated neighbourhood improvement programme back then [in the 1990s] transformed housing conditions in some parts of Medellin. I think it was the same period when one of the concepts used the National University in Medellin was coined 'habitat', rather than 'housing'. 'Habitat' is a more holistic concept, so it brought about improvements in habitat [when it] came along. So, this is when the 'miracle' started, if you want to put it this way.

Then social urbanism came along, and this is what has been marketed externally. The discourse around social urbanism was about the city owing a historic debt to the poorer areas which were also part of it, and which have to be given more resources, and better access to the kind of resources the rest of the city has. When I say 'access', this did translate into, for example, transport infrastructure, such as the *Metrocable*, and public infrastructure, such as the park libraries. Social urbanism was about both. It tried to combine access to information and culture, and also to open spaces, green areas. It thus produced these park libraries, which are very iconic and produce a new image of the city. These [park libraries] had an impact on both the local consciousness and also the external image of the city. For social urbanism, housing was a much lower priority than it was for the previous interventions of the early 1990s. [In social urbanism, housing interventions were undertaken as] a kind of model project. The advantage in the Juan Bobo project, for example, was that it provided better housing conditions for people who were living in informal settlements around a ravine. In some cases, [these people] were provided with upgraded houses; in other cases, people who were living right down in the ravine at high risk were rehoused in modernist buildings. There was no removal elsewhere [in Medellin] as far as I know. That project won international awards, but it was very costly; so it was not replicated. It was in line with other interventions, such as the major transport infrastructure, *Metrocable*, which is highly visible and, again, a symbol. There was a publication, produced by DPU,[2] which talks about the symbolic importance of social urbanism. To a large extent, a lot of what was done was symbolic rather than actual, substantial change. Even the capacity of the *Metrocable* is not that great: it is not a mass transportation system, since the number of people it can transport [is small], but it does work, it does integrate, and,

[2] The Bartlett – Development Planning Unit

for many people who use it, it has transformed their connection with the city. But there is a lot of symbolism there. So, in terms of housing, what was done tended to be rather symbolic as well, instead of achieving widespread improvement of housing throughout the city. [The latter] is not something that social urbanism achieved.

PT: Following from my previous question, social urbanism has been considered as a means to build an image of the city that is more distinguishable from that of other cities in Colombia. From your own research, what can we draw as best practice when we discuss social urbanism? Obviously, you refer to infrastructures. I was looking back at research on social urbanism, and most studies focus on the public libraries, public space, the transport system connecting the different neighbourhoods, etc. But, then, what about housing within the social urbanism agenda?

HS: To build on what I said previously, the impact of social urbanism on housing was much, much less. Housing was not, as far as I know, a key focus of social urbanism; [social urbanism] was much more focused on infrastructures. [There are also] other things that have not been talked about very widely, but [which] you hear when you talk to the communities, when you dig a little bit more. In some cases, it appears that housing was actually removed to make way for some of [the social urbanist] projects, and that created quite a bit of disparity and distress in some communities. We encountered this when we started our project on landslide risk management in 2016. When we talked to people in the communities where the housing conditions are much poorer, one of the things we found was that there were two discourses. On the periphery of Medellín, one of their key demands is for *vivienda digna* [decent housing]. Even the way they organize themselves reflects this. One of the key players we worked with was the *Mesa de Vivienda*, that is, the Housing Board, which is district-wide. I am talking about *Comuna 8*: There, in particular, housing is such a key issue for them that they are well organized to lobby about this. This is because [housing] has not been addressed properly by the local government from the community's perspective. Judging from recent interventions, when the local government does intervene, it does so in relation, for example, to what they call *macro proyectos* (macro-projects) [that aim] to develop the city by areas, and, also, to address risk. What the community sees when this happens is local government mapping the risk areas and then saying, 'we are

going to have to rehouse you'. This sends mixed messages to the
community because, on the one hand, some households think,
'well, if we get proper housing out of this it might be good', but
many say, 'no, we want to stay here, this is our home'. You get into
this conflicting situation where local communities are saying,
'wait a minute, you are talking about us being in high-risk areas,
but what this really is about is high cost'; 'how come people in El
Poblado [a high-income area] are living in high-rise flats, on exactly
the same kind of steep hillsides as us, and they are not being told
that they need to move out, while we are?' So, housing actually
becomes a bit of a catalyst, or a lens through which you can see the
socio-economic segregation. In that sense, it has not really been
addressed by social urbanism – at least not successfully.

PT: From your past and most recent research in Medellin, what do you
think are the ignored (alternative) voices, memories and learning
spaces that have disrupted upgrading urban practices such as the
ones discussed earlier?

CO: I think that the most incredible and rich set of experiences have
been propelled and championed by grassroots organizations and
long-term NGOs that are very committed to different territories.
Even though I could not point out a specific project that deals
directly with housing, I think that there is a lot of work around
social mobilization. Many collectives – such as the *Movimiento
de Laderas* – are working in what is now called *escuela popular de
autonomias*, or popular school of autonomies. I think that these
practices bring a very interesting new perspective into the old,
traditional popular education movement that is so well established in
Latin America. Initiatives such as the *escuela popular de autonomia*,
or those led by the victims of the Conflict who try to [find ways] to
support the livelihoods of people who have been forcibly displaced,
are very inspiring. Speaking specifically about the *escuela popular
de autonomias*, they started in *Comuna 8* because this has been the
hub of many very interesting and progressive initiatives. The *escuela
popular de autonomias* have also been linked with *Comunas* 3 and 1.
This year, the *comunas* have been consolidating this idea of *escuela
popular de autonomias*, talking about food and energy sovereignty,
and also thinking in terms of harnessing issues of the right to stay
put, community-based risk mitigation, or culture and education
from the bottom. This is a very interesting approach that builds on
popular education and critical pedagogies. They have been meeting
even during the pandemic!

As I mentioned, key to this transformation is how the pacification process enables the state to build new strategies of territorial control and surveillance, which we usually fail to see or speak much about because of the very complicated and opaque nature of these processes. [What is] largely ignored is precisely how the construction of territorial peace – one of the main mantras after the signing of the peace accord with FARC – takes place in the cities. I think that this process (how you build territorial peace) has already been happening within cultural collectives: they have done a lot of incredible work on this. For instance, consider the case of *Agroarte*, a collective that links sowing and hip-hop with performances to honour resistance and memory in the context of *Comuna* 13 legacy of armed conflict and 'military operations'. The more intangible, kinaesthetic expression of reconciliation has featured as part of this transformation. The [discussion on transformation] has not been explicit enough about how [such processes] actually play a role in reconciliation and the building of peace. [Pacification] has been addressed mainly through the lens of militarization and not of the processes through which reconciliation and recognition for the victims are achieved.

Regarding housing, my work approaches it as an infrastructure of care. According to this approach, food and energy are the basis of survival and the protection of life. If we extend this notion of infrastructure of care, then we could think that the *escuela popular de autonomia* could be connected to housing. We understand them at a broader level: of course, they do their advocacy around 'slum upgrading' and the recognition of tenure, the security of tenure, and this, of course, is directly related to housing and the informal settlements.

HS: One of the things that is striking about this is how communities have a really strong voice in parts of the city. I have worked a lot with community representatives, from *Comuna* 8 in particular. My knowledge might be biased towards the people I have been engaging with, because I do get the impression that they are particularly strong. I do not know how strong community voices are in other parts of the city, but they are highly articulate, and housing is one of their key demands: *vivienda digna*. They are very well organized as well. As part of our first landslide project, we piloted community-based approaches to monitoring and mitigating landslide risk with residents in a particular small community. In the second year of the project, this developed into the community organizing a *cabildo abierto* [townhall meeting] – a type of meeting that is recognized in the Colombian constitution. If the local community requests [such a meeting], the municipality has to respond. It has to attend and listen. This does not mean that [the municipal authority] has to act, but at least it has to provide a response to what the community is demanding. Since we were doing action research, we were flexible. We went along with the flow, and I was really impressed by the strong and organized voice the community expressed through that platform. The project itself was instrumental in actually making that [meeting] happen, because you needed two things to happen: you needed those who had the authority to legally convene that [meeting], that is, the *Junta Administradora Local* [Local Administration Board] – the lowest level of local government – the ones who could involve the municipality; you also needed a different type of *junta* [board], the *Junta de Acción Local* [Local Action Board] or *the Junta Communal* [Community Board], who had the power to actually bring people from the community. So, these bodies are the top (recognized) level of the community, and the bottom level of the local administration: one could convene the Municipality; [the other] could convene the community. Françoise Coupé was able to work out an agreement between these two levels to bring about this *cabildo*. The result was that, in the first *cabildo*, in August 2017, up in Sol de Oriente, we had over 600 people from the community, from across the entire *Comuna* 8. The whole thirty-three neighbourhoods of *Comuna* 8 were represented, [including] the ones from the lower-income area.

The other thing that you saw there as well was the important role of supportive NGOs in facilitating communication. There was an NGO there that had been working with the community for a long, long time. They facilitated the whole event, and they organized it so that every community – each one of the community representatives – had three minutes to talk, to present their petition to the municipality. [There were many] communities, and they got three minutes each. I thought that we could learn a lot from how they organize things, because every time one community came up to present their petition, the NGO called out the next one to be ready. It was a constant stream, it was so efficient, it was amazing! And then we had the different departments of the Municipality represented there. The debate got pretty heated. At one point, the [representatives of the municipal] departments stood up and said '*we're leaving*', even though, at the beginning of the session (initiated by Françoise and me), I had explained the project, and Françoise had explained the terms of *concertación*, and how people need to engage under these terms: the thing you should never do is close the door, you should keep the door open to dialogue. And when they all got up to leave, I said to Françoise who was sitting next to me, *'they're closing the door!'*, but they [came back and] sat down again. Then, the following year, there was another *cabildo* around the same issues – risk management and *vivienda digna* – and the tone had changed quite a lot. So, the community has a strong voice, and we have managed to find ways to engage with the municipality, although it has been confrontational at times.

I mentioned NGOs. . . . From the first project, we had learnt that the community we worked with had strong leaders, but focused on just one leader. For a community organization, this is a weakness. But, you cannot expect that community organizations will [be able to resort to their own] resources all the time. They need some other external support sometimes and, also, other types of knowledge. These can come from NGOs, which [can] work really well with the community on the ground. So, in the second landslide project we worked on, we had quite an intense negotiation with two NGOs that were working with the two neighbourhoods we wanted to work with. We discussed all sorts of things: who owns the knowledge that is generated, what is the purpose of what we are doing, etc. They had a very strong voice as well, and very strong experience. This is one of the things that these NGOs can ensure: some continuity of experience and, also, the ability to tap into other types of knowledge that a community may not have access to, or the capacity to deal with. So, these were the strong voices that I came across. As I said, I do not think that [well-organized and vocal communities] are evenly distributed geographically across Medellin (although this [view] may be biased from my own experience), but I get the impression that there are certain parts of Medellin which have very well-organized communities that make their voice heard, with the support of strong NGOs.

PT: Within these alternative voices and urban practices, are there any good examples of grassroots/community-led housing initiatives that we can look at in relation to this book's theme, *'housing as commons'*?

HS: In terms of innovative grassroots experiences around housing, again, I would say that I have not found examples of commons around housing [in the narrow sense of the term]. But if you take the concept of 'habitat' (a concept used extensively by the National University of Colombia in Medellin in their research, teaching and writing), then yes! [The concept of] habitat is another way of seeing how you inhabit the territory, and, yes, I have seen this kind of 'coming together' within the community. This goes back to the history of how many of these informal settlements were created. In the two consecutive projects on landslide risk that followed from

the MUI project, the first element was semi-structured interviews
with residents in three neighbourhoods in Medellin. We asked
people about their history: How had they come here? How did they
provide themselves with their homes? What was their perception
of risk? How much did they feel threatened by landslides and other
risks? What experiences had they had before they came to the
neighbourhood? Many of them had actually experienced all sorts
of threats elsewhere before coming here. Through that storytelling,
we found out a lot about how these neighbourhoods have come
about. There was a lot of mutual help in the early stages of formation
of all three neighbourhoods. The communities had experience in
producing their habitat, their own environment, together – not
necessarily their own house, perhaps, but the neighbourhood:
for example, clearing land, setting out the pathways, etc. This
is a way of coming together which they call *el convite*, which
means something like an invitation to get together, work together
for a day, and then have a meal at the end of that day. There is a kind
of communion around eating and working together, and then
sharing food. This is quite a traditional way of doing things, which
persists to some extent. We found that this practice had actually
waned in recent years, but we revived it as part of the two landside
projects – particularly of the first one. We had some money to
experiment with some low-cost mitigation work and the community
suggested, 'let's do convites'. So, what we did was to identify the areas
of priority. (Figure 14.1)

Originally, the money was for intervening in three volunteer houses to see
what could be done, at low cost, to mitigate landslide risk. After debate,
both the academic team and the community we were working with came
to the conclusion that following the original plan could lead to all sorts of
perceptions of unfairness: some people would benefit and others would not.
This is one of the tricky things about housing: when you see housing in a
narrow sense as only your own home. We decided that the money should be
used for areas that were perceived as part of the wider habitat that [everybody]
shared, so we made a four-tier classification of the types of space linked to
social networks. Generally, we did not intervene in individual homes except
when, for example, installing a gutter in one home would stop water spilling
over onto a home further down the hillside. (We felt that such an effect
between the two homes was a shared issue.) The second level – the next level
up – was shared spaces, which were not streets or lanes but a kind of mutual
space for two or three households. We put a lot of work into that, and also

Figure 14.1 *Convite* in Comuna 8, Medellin. (Photograph by/Copyright: Wilmar Castro)

into the narrow lanes where the municipality does not really intervene. The *convites* focused on these, and people really engaged with [the project]. There was always an element of self-interest, so people were always asking, 'oh, is this work going to be done outside my home as well?' People would engage if they felt that their own home was going to benefit, so there is a kind of balance there between community and your own household's interest. But that worked really well!

You see this kind of community coming together in different types of experiences, even in those that the municipality has tried to foster: for example, allotments, as part of the upgrading of some settlements on the periphery. Some will say that the motivations for that were slightly questionable and, maybe, that the allotment project was not fully successful. For example, some of the allotments [in] some of the communities on the edge were promoted by the municipality as a way of preventing any further land invasions. The community [had a sense of] ownership of some [of these] lands, and they would stop any others trying to build there, so there was a funny mixture of motivations and reactions.

This is the extent to which I have seen communities coming together to intervene as a community in their habitat. This is the experience I have, and this is the kind of thing that we are trying to promote further. At the moment, we are working with the Municipality's Department for Disaster Risk Management. They approached us, but this was because they are in constant communication with *Comuna 8*. So, this voice continues to be heard. They want to develop and integrate a disaster risk management plan for the Northeast of Medellin, so we have been in conversation with them for the last few months about how to do that. Obviously, the community, being a driving force there, is one of the key elements of that. But, as I say, it does not focus on individual houses as such, on housing in the narrow sense, but on improving the habitat.

PT: Catalina, your project, 'COiNVITE',[3] stems from the notions of gathering and working together. As stated on the project's website, *COiNVITE* is 'a celebration of collective actions that result from solidarity and empathy networks among urban dwellers'. Could you tell us a bit more about your project and elaborate on participatory practices for slam improvement?

CO: We recognize that, in many places, collective work for indigenous communities is called *minga*. The idea of *convite* is a similar kind of collective work in the context of the *barrios populares* in Medellin. *Convite* is a practice [whereby a] social organization self-builds neighbourhoods. It is self-management: a strategy of collective action in the informal settlements. So, in a way, this *convite* operates on many fronts: it is used to transform the material conditions of a place – to pave a road, work on risk mitigation, put a ceiling over a collective facility. In a *convite*, you do these; you also come together to celebrate and support these networks of solidarity through public cooking. So, in a *convite*, you also have the pot – a big pot – to feed everyone who is participating in this knowledge exchange while also contributing to the improvement of the living

---

[3] COiNVITE: 'Activating Urban Learning for Slum Upgrading' funded by the Bartlett ECR-GCRF and led by Dr Catalina Ortiz and Gynna Millan (PDRA) at the Bartlett Development Planning Unit (DPU), is a research collaboration between the Bartlett DPU staff, UN-Habitat, United Cities and Local Governments (UCLG), Habitat International Coalition (HIC), Cities Alliance, the Municipality of Medellin and six grassroots organizations part of 'Movimiento de Pobladores' and Sandelion – a local transmedia production organization – to codesign a digital platform that helps to learn about slum upgrading strategies. https://medium.com/@storytelling4urbanlearning

conditions of a particular community. The *convite* also helps to organize and mobilize people, so it is also an act of resistance. It could host acts of resistance. It has a cultural connotation as well. You do a *convite*, a gathering with food, to also bring different cultural representations, such as public theatre or a bazaar. These also produce some funding for doing something else for the community. I think that this collective gathering to transform something, either materially, or symbolically, or organizationally, is a very powerful strategy for organizing. This has been at the core of the founding of informal settlements, particularly in Medellin.

I think that this recognition has been largely absent when the 'Medellin miracle' is talked about. The story of the 'Medellin miracle' is only told from the perspective of the state, while not recognizing how, for several decades, transformation has been [achieved through] the ingenuity of the inhabitants themselves. I think that this was the reason why a project that begun with a focus on translocal learning ended up shifting its focus to the idea of *convite*, to understand and use *convite* as a learning space for critical pedagogies. In a way, *convite* provides methodological tools inspired by this practice, ideas for more horizontal knowledge exchange and co-creation. The COiNVITE project has three aspects: Firstly, it aims to bring [together], or foster, a network of urban storytellers. We place at the centre this idea of storytelling as a strategy to build empathy and exchange knowledge. Secondly, it generates a digital platform as a repository that [enables us] to see and understand the transformation of the city, particularly around 'slum-upgrading', and to bring up perspectives that are often silenced. Thirdly, without this being part of the initial idea, COiNVITE also provides a toolkit for using storytelling as an instrument for urban learning. These are the key elements of this project (Figure 14.2).

Now, going back to housing and how we can relate it to *convite*, in my opinion, we need to understand housing as a verb. As an urbanist, I cannot detach housing from the general interrelatedness and complexity of urban systems. Further, and propelled by this pandemic, I think that we need to understand this crisis (the pandemic) as a crisis of infrastructure of care. Central to *convite* are the ideas of empathy, solidarity and creating, bonding, the affect and reading housing (also) through the lens of affection. These are central components of care, if you will. So, part of what we have developed in our methodological toolkit is a set of bonding strategies. When addressing *convite*, you are bringing up a participatory practice, with its participants are located in very asymmetrical positions in the constellation of power. For instance, we brought together to work with us in a horizontal manner

Figure 14.2 COiNVITE project, Medellin (Illustration by Alejandra Congote for the project COiNVITE – Activating Learning for Slum Upgrading through Transmedia Storytelling led by Catalina Ortiz.)

the regional director of UN-Habitat and community leaders from different neighbourhoods of Medellin. [We did this] because we think that we need to be more innovative: not working in the comfort zone of community-led-only, or elite-only [practices], but trying to bring together antagonistic perspectives in order to change [the way problems are viewed] and reframe strategies for addressing these problems. Bonding and the affective element, as constituents of care, were part of what we did in our project. The centrepiece of the project was trying to understand how to learn about the 'slum upgrading' strategies in Medellin and, also, how we can [come] together to envision ways of making [this strategy] more inclusive, and to bring in the perspectives of the inhabitants as well. For us, housing is the core axis of slum upgrading. Even though housing itself, and the conditions of habitability, are just two of the ten dimensions of slum upgrading, housing, as a verb and as an infrastructure of care, is fully embedded in the strategies of slum upgrading.

PT: Could *convite* be relevant to '*Buen Vivir*'[4] (common well-being) and, more generally, to the commons in relation to housing, that is, the theme of this book?

4 The Latin American concept of *Buen Vivir*, which translates to English as 'good living', well-being refers to a world view of harmonious cohabitation between humans, more-than-humans and nature. *Buen Vivir* is directly derived from what Quechua people of Ecuador call *Sumak Kawsay*: 'knowing how to live well'. *Sumak Kawsay* is a set of principles on how to live a good life, informed by the notions of measure and harmony with nature's cycles. *Buen Vivir* is thus a contemporary interpretation of the ancestral cosmovision of *Sumak Kawsay*. In recent years, *Buen Vivir* has been linked to the commons referring to common goods and/or common well-being. What seems to

CO: I think that, in terms of building strategies for effecting collective action, what we are [putting together] now is a decalogue on slum upgrading. This is an evolution of the 'COiNVITE' project: an expanded network, a coalition of very different organizations, trying to articulate, as commoners, the public [realm] that could be consider as a common. These key principles – a sort of manifesto of slum upgrading – need to become the key avenue for recovery from the pandemic and for placing informal settlements at the centre of public investment in the following [post-pandemic] phase. I could see urban learning and coalition building as ways to create and cultivate the commons. This is where the COiNVITE crowd has been moving [towards]. Therefore, you cannot talk about housing without [talking about] urbanism. We think of housing as urbanism; [as such], it needs to be addressed holistically, in all its dimensions. You cannot decouple housing from collective memory, climate justice, political recognition, solidarity economy, social diversity. I think that these intersections are absolutely essential. I [am finding it increasingly difficult] to just talk about housing per se; instead, by thinking of the city as a complex whole, I see [housing as part of] this mesh.

References

Acosta, A. (2012). Buen Vivir: An Opportunity to Imagine Another World. In *Inside a Champion: An Analysis of the Brazilian Development Model*. Heinrich Böll Foundation. pp. 192–210. Available at: https://www.boell.de/sites/default/files/Inside_A_Champion_Democracy.pdf#page=194

Boff, L. (2009). *¿Vivir mejor o "l Buen Vivir"?' Revista Fusión. Abril.* Available at: http://www.revistafusion.com/20090403817/Firmas/Leonardo-Boff/ivivir-mejor-o-el-buen-vivir.htm

De Sousa Santos, B. (2014). *Epistemologies of the South: Justice against Epistemicide*. London: Routledge.

Escobar, A. (2020). *Pluriversal Politics: The Real and the Possible*. Durham: Duke University Press.

Gerlach, M. (2019) The Concept of 'Buen Vivir' and the Social Work Profession. *Journal of Human Rights and Social Work*, 4: 116–118. Available at: https://link.springer.com/article/10.1007/s41134-018-0081-4

quite well aligned with *Buen Vivir*, nevertheless, is 'commoning': the notion of making/becoming a common. (See Boff 2009; Acosta 2012; Santiesteban and Helfrich 2014; de Sousa Santos 2014; Gerlach 2019; Escobar 2020.)

Soto Santiesteban, G. and Helfrich, S. (2014) El Buen Vivir and the Commons: A Conversation Between Gustavo Soto Santiesteban and Silke Helfrich. In D. Bollier and S. Helfrich (Eds) *The Wealth of the Commons: A World Beyond Market & State*. Heinrich Böll Foundation. Available at: http:// wealthofthecommons.org/essay/el-buen-vivir-and-commons-conversation -between-gustavo-soto-santiesteban-and-silke-helfrich

15

Housing policy as a form of urban governance

The Barbican Estate and the enclosure of the urban commons

Ioanna Piniara

From the welfare city to the neoliberal city

The rise of urban governance in Western European cities became a key mechanism in the rescaling of state and central (state) planning already in the late 1950s (Brenner, 2004: 449). This process involved a downscaling of the state and an upscaling of welfare projects (such as housing) to underwrite urban and regional growth (Brenner, 2004: 457). The shift from austerity to growth captured the promise of the new urban order which did not address the housing project as what it should be (a minimum welfare provision to all), but as what it *could* be. This state-led 'scale-making project' crystallizing in the 1960s (Brenner, 2004: 458) involved political strategies to embed large-scale city areas (urban commons) within local circuits of capital accumulation which dictated radically different regulatory frameworks of social reproduction. As these policies were targeted to underdeveloped areas and peripheral zones with minor (or zero) land revenue, political opposition could not counteract the argument on financial necessity for a sort of housing development that could attract market interest to compensate for its expenditure. The regulatory frameworks for planning and housing were aimed at raising the place-bound reputation and market value of these newly constituted metropolitan areas as residential areas. This form of urban governance, which was an essential pillar of the Keynesian welfare state, became the stepping-stone towards the full-fledged neoliberal 'global order' of the 1980s, when speculation made housing all the more unaffordable. Neoliberalism ultimately mastered the construction of a narrative for domesticity with a utopian promise of security encrypted in its image.

This dictated an approach to urban planning that mobilized historically established architectural references and social hierarchies to express the values of domesticity; it signalled a shift in the conception of community autonomy from the inclusivity of public space to the exclusivity of private space, from sharing to individualism and, ultimately, from urban openness to enclosure.

What marks neoliberalism as a phenomenon beyond liberalism in the second half of the twentieth century is the professionalization of commodity exchange in the market economy. Neoliberalism was unique in promoting a narrative of private living as the luxury of *the middle classes*, which were seen as the main consumerist force that would boost the post-war urban economies. The promotion of personal freedom in the ability to acquire domestic privacy, as the luxury of space in the dense city, exemplified the exchange value over the use value of housing. In terms of planning, the enclosure of urban land marked the private as an exclusive luxurious interior and the public as a shared undesirable exterior. In terms of housing design, the liberation from central (state) planning, which suppressed individual identity, was pursued through the neoliberal principles of 'differentiation' and 'freedom of choice' (Hayek, 1944). The formal language became not only a reflection of the different qualities and organizations of private space but also an invitation to this process of social upgrade. Since the symbolic capital of the private and the city became inextricably linked, this entailed processes of alienation, gentrification and displacement, which led to inaccessibility to urban housing for a growing part of society.

Therefore, the insistence to problematize the neoliberal housing crisis affecting the European capital cities as an economic and not an institutional and spatial issue is, I believe, the most critical negligence of duty of contemporary architecture. So far, neoliberal critique in the field of urban planning and architecture has notably focused either on the production of policies (Madden and Marcuse, 2016) or on the language of formal production (Spencer, 2016), missing the opportunity to address these two as inseparable and methodologically linked. To draw the link between housing policy and architecture is quintessential in framing neoliberalism as a paradigm of urban order that appropriated housing as an 'enabling framework' to deal with the post-war crisis of state planning. In order to do so, this chapter engages in a close reading of the Barbican Estate in London (1954–82), a celebrated and emblematic housing model that was strategically devised in a critical moment for the future of the post-war devastated London. The selection of the Barbican as a case study is instrumental in expanding the operational framework of neoliberalism as an ideology beyond specific political programmes and understanding it as a broader cultural project to change the ethos, culture and organization of urban domesticity.

Since the turn of the century, the Barbican has enjoyed recognition as one of the most remarkable post-war redevelopment schemes in Britain that has incarnated a utopian ideal of inner-city living (Figure 15.1). It is a special case of a 1950s' council estate in the City of London's east end designed by a partnership of three ambitious young architects, Peter Chamberlin, Geoffry Powell and Christoph Bon. The history of the Barbican has been a tale of both idealism and criticism. The almost-thirty-year span from conception (1954) to inauguration (1982) is indicative of the controversy that the Barbican, as a bold housing statement, has sparked to the public. It has been praised and dismissed for the exact same reasons: admired as a 'social condenser' for its scale, fancy accommodation and extraordinary urban landscaping in times of economic prosperity and reviled as socially unsustainable for its exclusive style, high maintenance fees and rental rates in times of economic crisis. Despite the mixed feelings it evoked, the Barbican as an urban artefact always had an appeal to the popular imagination. The complex's award of Grade II listed status in 2001 officially marked the period of its revival as the par excellence place for living of new generations, especially people working in the cultural and creative industries.

Figure 15.1 Interior view of the Barbican showing the monumental staircase connecting the podium to the lakeside entrance to the recreation and arts complex. (Photograph by/Copyright: author/Ioanna Piniara.)

However, the Barbican was never meant to be just a housing estate. Monolithic yet diverse, modern yet historically suggestive, domestic yet grand, urban yet secluded, it embodied a recapitalization of tropes in the placemaking for urban development. What marked the Barbican out as exceptional from the outset was the local government's investment in such a large-scale housing scheme in the City of London. This area is one of the oldest boroughs of London traditionally containing the Historic Centre, marked by the medieval walled settlement constituted by the Romans in the first century AD, and the primary central business district. In a time when the Greater London Plan continued efforts to designate Inner London as an industrial and corporate zone and to create a metropolis of suburbs for living (Hall, 1980), the proposal of a housing scheme in the central business district was revolutionary. What is more, elsewhere in Britain at that time local authority capital expenditure was eliminated due to the Suez Crisis and housing was limited to slum clearance programmes. The housing policy and investment capital of the Barbican were not just meant to address a housing shortage in the City, but to embody a vision of urban growth, social progress and future living in London.

This chapter chronicles the formation of the Barbican policy by the local government starting in 1952 and putting forward an aspiration of living which was way beyond the typical objectives of council housing. It highlights its premises in terms of scale, grandiosity and exclusivity and analyse the urban gestures and architectural vocabulary in which these were translated and enacted. The aim is to illuminate the emergence of housing policy as a form of urban governance for successful development, which pioneered a process of distribution of spatial planning from central to metropolitan and local states. This process, which began to unfold in Western Europe in the late 1950s (Brenner, 2004), is considered a proto-neoliberal planning instruction for the privatization of living as a form of new enclosure (Piniara, 2020). The architectural critique aims to show how this new paradigm of enclosure was enabled by a carefully designed pedagogy of domestic privacy that set urban housing at the epicentre of social and economic antagonism. The Barbican is assessed here not as the outcome but rather as the introduction to the principles of this new spatial order that distanced itself from the reality of affordable housing in a welfare state and literally constructed the narrative of urban living in a market economy. A discussion of the critical fortune of the Barbican is necessary for an understanding of the agenda that inspired a generation of housing projects in Britain and in Europe and was only identified as neoliberal after the implementation of the Thatcherite policies in the 1980s.

The Barbican policy as a new form of urban governance

To understand the Barbican, it should be considered a monument to the ideals and efforts to modernize and, at the same time, revive a glorious image of London. The conception of a comprehensive plan was necessitated by the dramatic situation in Inner London. Large-scale suburbanization, stimulated by the growth of transport networks under the Greater London Plan (1943–4), and the Blitz (1945), which had decimated large areas of the City, had intensified the shrinking of its residential population to a critical limit by 1951 (The Architects' Journal, 1968: 704). The Barbican area was part of a larger area of the post-war redevelopment plan for London, the Ward of Cripplegate, which was the epicentre of economic and business activity (including the Smithfield Market – the oldest market in London – the Bank of England, and the stock market). To the South, the area shared the status of St Paul's Cathedral, but to the Northeast the site was on the verge of the dodgy area of Moorland suburbs. In particular, the Barbican site had become a commercial and transportation hub dominated by the Midland and Metropolitan railway companies. Adding to this were the pollution and the traffic congestion; hence, the image of the inner city at the time was that of a highly undesirable place to live, which caused property values in London to plummet.

Although the immediate implementation of a post-war reconstruction plan for London was a clear expectation on the part of the population, the command economy maintained since the war had been slow. It was, to some extent, frustration over this lack of direct governmental initiative that led to the first plans for the Barbican development to be undertaken by the local authority, the City of London Corporation. The strategic tools that were mobilized to prevent 'uncontrolled piecemeal development with no aesthetic coherence' (Heathcote, 2004: 73) were the compulsory purchase of large areas of land and comprehensive planning by the local authorities. While the development of these areas would fall under local control, the central government could still inflict 'national priorities' regarding social and programmatic criteria and apply restrictions through the building-licence bureaucracy. The City was a focal area of interests for the government, the local authority and the business establishment.

While the policy for reconstruction in the area was decided at the highest offices (Town and Country Planning Act, 1947), the term 'comprehensive planning' was mobilized by each of the involved parties as a way to regulate the form and style of the new scheme over a large area. Planning authorities, such as the London County Council (LCC), saw it as a tool for enforcing a degree of aesthetic proscription and regularity on the planning applications submitted for each site. According to this model, the local authority had to devise a plan for the general character of an area, and the developers would, then, put forward proposals to fit in with this overview. The architectural profession, on the other hand, saw comprehensive planning as a disciplinary tool, which upgraded their involvement on a programmatic and urban scale. It was also seen as a design exercise to devise three-dimensional models for areas of large-scale redevelopment. Once a planning proposal of massing and general appearance met the authority's approval, then there would be room for more detailed programmatic and design proposals to be negotiated. In cases where the local authority was against overregulation in the first round, such as the City of London Corporation, the architects played a decisive role in the formulation of not just a planning scheme but an ambitious vision of urbanity.

The period between 1952 and 1954 was crucial for the radical introduction of a housing policy instead of a business plan as the driving force for the redevelopment of the City. Having compulsorily purchased much of the ruined land of the Barbican site, it was costing the Corporation a fortune to leave the area undeveloped. This financial argument in combination with its huge size (40 acres) and position in the historical centre made it a field of symbolic status and conflicting interests. Initially, ideas for zoning according to its pre-war use of corporate development were propagated by planning consultant firms, echoing the designation of the City as a business district. However, by 1952 there was an increasing challenge to the policy of no housing in the City due to a general shortage of accommodation affecting not only industrial workers but also the middle and professional classes. Therefore, 'national priorities' changed with discussions about a new local government legislation proposing that the power of an authority depend on the size of its resident electorate. What this meant for the City of London Corporation as the local authority was that if it was to maintain local autonomy, it would have to incentivize people to take up residency in the City. By 1954, the Corporation was already working together with the LCC on some type of residential accommodation in the Barbican for the new profile of council tenant; anyone employed in the City with preference given to families and young professionals. As the 1950s were the first years of affluence after the war, this profile was meant to address a more sophisticated type than the industrial worker. Unlike other local authorities, the Corporation decided to endorse the aspirations of an emerging young generation in 'a self-consciously elitist pursuit of quality' (Heathcote, 2004: 34) in urban living as a means of escaping austerity and the crippled City.

Programmatically, it took the dedication of the architects and many advocates within the Corporation to gain a residential rather than a commercial scheme for the Barbican. Although the 1954 campaign for housing in the City had already gained considerable support, opposition still persisted among members of the Corporation who favoured an allegedly more lucrative office development. Signalling the beginning of a war among the administrative bodies, the promotion of the housing scheme was finally transferred from the Improvements and Town Planning Committee to the Public Health Committee. The latter advocated for high-standard housing for more residents against the substandard homes that millions had been living in throughout the towns and cities of the country. The fight for a high-standard residential development, or, more precisely, a development that would boost the place-bound value of Cripplegate and the City as a residential area gained support within the Corporation by members of parliament and prominent figures of Britain's corporate culture. The silencing of opposition voices led to the total separation of planning from housing under different administrations, which caused many problems in the completion of the Barbican and became a key strategy of housing development in the years that followed. In order to isolate entirely the Planning Committee, the Barbican Committee was founded to oversee the development. The new Barbican Committee firmly supported the development of *a proper residential community* in the City based on the adjacent Golden Lane estate. Thus, the Corporation commissioned from its architects, Chamberlin, Powell & Bon (CPB), a viability study on the new Barbican residential development (Chamberlin Powell & Bon Architects, 1956).

A new formal language for 'a sense of community'

The establishment of the idea of a high-density elite quarter in the proposal underpinned the Barbican's unique character as a council estate for the 'more than moderately well-off' (Banham, 1974: 222). CPB's material for the Barbican Committee's campaign to get planning permission in 1958 was quite sophisticated in the portrayal of this vision of urban and social upgrade. It ought to be convincing, as the Corporation had no financial means of building the scheme itself. Therefore, the promotion of the Barbican flats mobilized symbolic images of a traditional upper-class family and views of the City monuments that stressed the historical status of the area. The final 1959 Barbican Development Plan suggested that the Corporation act as developer and landlord, taking on a huge investment (£55 million) and aspiring to long-term returns, while it set the key objectives of the development (Chamberlin Powell & Bon Architects, 1959). The first regarded the concern that the residential development should be large and dense enough to provide the City with a genuine electorate able to maintain the autonomy of the local authority. The second regarded the discourse that could justify such a controversial project; the Barbican as a residential investment had to compensate for (and hopefully exceed) the commercial value of the site in order to counteract the arguments of its opponents. These requirements from the architects and the Barbican Committee express the struggle to win the competition with local authority partners, who kept scanning the horizon for investment opportunities. As local authorities were concerned with the affordability of housing, CPB were required to ensure the viability of 'providing living accommodation for a large number of people, who could be expected to pay an economic rent' (Chamberlin Powell & Bon Architects, 1959: 2). However, the architects were convinced that it would give the financial return required by the Corporation, if it was built at an exceptionally high density – 330 persons per acre – and if it was aimed at a middle- and high-income bracket. Hence, the Corporation set CPB the task of suggesting ways in which the development would ensure 'continuing demand' among wealthy tenants, 'have some characteristics that are outstanding and unique', 'reflect the prestige of the City', and achieve 'a definite formality in the layout' (Chamberlin Powell & Bon Architects, 1959: 2).

The aspiration to produce a statement housing project also defined the planning principles and the architectural language. In this statement, the architects tried to combine policy requirements, historical referencing and personal taste into their own theoretical and design discourse. The idea of the City of London Plan for *a new inner-city suburb*, which had been inaugurated at the Golden Lane estate by CPB in 1954, was set as the prototype of a social condenser for the Barbican. The combination of courts and terraces to create internal private spaces and a high-rise structure were the precursors of the strategy to reduce ground density employed and reinterpreted in a grand scale at the Barbican. The popularity of the Golden Lane among young professionals in the City, once the Corporation had increased the eligibility criteria for tenants, gave the Public Health Committee the confidence to propose a larger development for wealthier tenants for the Barbican. The Ministry of Housing and Local Government suggested that certain qualities of living in the suburbs be reconfigured in the new urban model, prioritizing 'the quiet sense of seclusion which should be characteristic of a residential neighbourhood' (Chamberlin Powell & Bon Architects, 1959: 4). Therefore, in 1958 CPB formed a theoretical community project, the 'Living Suburb', in order to 'make the case for a new type of urban life' (Gold, 2007: 93–104). Proposing a podium to isolate the underground tracks, it included tower blocks and medium-rise terraces set around courtyards, as well as offices and neighbourhood shops. Chamberlin described this vision, which finally led to the Barbican scheme, as 'a suburban community within the city' (Chamberlin, 1958: 347). Urban aspects were underlined by planning requirements for 'respect for the historical associations, traditions and monuments of the City' and 'buildings in a form worthy of the finest City monuments in contemporary material and in the service of contemporary necessities'. Suburban aspects were stressed by requirements for 'gardens and open spaces' and 'a sense of community' (The Architects' Journal, 1954: 458–9).

The formal take on the layout was described by Chamberlin as 'a landscaped environment with community facilities' that would 'turn this desert [Barbican site] into a garden' (Chamberlin Powell & Bon Architects, 1956). The basic principles of the design were the provision of housing in compact blocks and towers structured around a system of courts, the incorporation of an in-site surviving monument – the twelfth-century St Giles Church – and the inclusion of modern community facilities. 'The sense of community' was conditioned by the architects' aspect that people prepared to pay a large part of their income for the rent would expect their money to purchase, indirectly, certain amenities not confined within the actual walls of their home (Chamberlin Powell & Bon Architects, 1955). A study of the Barbican programme reveals that it aspired to provide not just the ordinary council housing amenities. It was an 'all-inclusive' community with neighbourhood services (schools, cafeterias, restaurants and car parks), cultural facilities (arts centre, concert hall and cinema) and recreation facilities with overtones of exoticism – from the central 2 acre water garden with fountains to the glass conservatory with rare tropical plants. At the same time, the three towers rising up into the sky would give dramatic contrast to the horizontal treatment of the development and, by their distinctive form and relationship to each other, would give identity to the neighbourhood from afar (Chamberlin Powell & Bon Architects, 1955). Indeed, Cromwell, Lauderdale and Shakespeare Towers, completed in the mid-1970s and reaching 123 metres (404 feet), remained London's tallest residential buildings until the turn of the twenty-first century. The overall concept was the establishment of the Barbican as a landmark in the City that was a cross between London's traditional inner suburbs and modern 'loft' developments, between Englishness and International Style.

Thus, the attempt was a connection with London's most exquisite and high-end environments with architectural references stretching from the 1930s back to the medieval times. At the same time, it was a very tentative speculation of the physical and 'mental' leisure of the tenants. The sixteenth-century Inns of Court of London were a main reference in terms of their important role in the intellectual history of the English Renaissance by offering outdoor courts and indoor halls to notable literary figures and playwrights. The Inns inspired ideas on the configuration of enclosures with focal points of interest, thus breaking down the vast Barbican site into more intimate platforms and conceptualizing a navigation through them designed as a theatrical experience. The architects were also fascinated by Dolphin Square, a 1930s' high-density private estate in Pimlico, for its successful isolation from the surroundings and its lavish landscaping including gardens, ponds and squash courts. Similarly, the Barbican key, known as the 'Magic Key', reflects the exclusive privilege of the residents to be granted access into certain areas of the complex where their daily lives could 'unwind in private' (Rodriguez, 2016: Foreword). In terms of exclusivity and individuation of living, the architects drew references from the secluded, almost-sanctuary-like ambience of the Albany at Piccadilly, a nineteenth-century prestigious set of bachelor apartments. Inspired by the 'ropewalk', the covered walkway serving individual access to the bachelor 'sets', the architects imagined that the Barbican flats would be approached through arcaded ways opening onto small enclosured courtyards (Chamberlin Powell & Bon Architects, 1955). The final composition was compromised by the requirement to be included to the London's urban plan of aerial pedways separating pedestrian from motor traffic in the city. For the Barbican's podium of elevated walkways, references were drawn from the elevated terraces of the Carlton House Terrace. This was a nineteenth-century neoclassical residential development facing St James's Park in Westminster. The requirement of the podium suggested that some of the housing blocks be elevated 6 metres above street level, and this led to a monumental exaggeration of the piloti.

The architects also tried to evoke international housing culture into a luxurious residential architecture, by also citing historical types and contemporary examples of their preferred travel destinations. In October 1958, the partnership took the Barbican Committee on a tour of new European architecture. This was meant to be didactic not only of contemporary design in Germany, Sweden and Italy but also of the delights of travelling in the Mediterranean. These references inspired a scheme that offered an unprecedented variety of residential forms: three 44-storey tower blocks, thirteen 8-storey terrace blocks, a row of townhouses (a type of terraced housing with a small footprint on multiple floors), a cluster of fourteen 'mews' (terraces of small two-story houses) and a crescent block. The Barbican towers were influenced by the medieval Mannerism of Torre Velasca in Milan. They adopted the monolithic appearance, which was extrapolated into a triangular footprint at the Barbican, and the imposing massing, which was stressed by the pre-cast concrete panelling. The stylistic intention was a medieval character of 'permanence' pursued at the Barbican as the new 'City

Monument'. To this attests another medieval reference of the top features and jagged balconies that dramatize the external framing of the towers (Pevsner and Bradley, 1997), which were inspired by the meanderings of the medieval St Giles Church in the site. In fact, what remains largely unknown is that the original intention for monumentality was to be incarnated in the white marble cladding of the entire complex. Eventually, this idea was abandoned due to its outrageous cost and was compromised to the weightiness of rough pick-hammered concrete.

The material treatment extended to the terrace blocks, which were architecturally informed by Le Corbusier's Unite d'Habitation of Berlin and followed his vision of a 'vertical garden city' that would be 'the perfect receptacle for the family' (Blake, 1964: 124). However, a special crowning was devised here too in order to dramatize the underlying regularity. This adopted Le Corbusier's interest in the Mediterranean uses of the barrel vault as featured in the dome of the Notre-Dame du Haut in Ronchamp, which was included in the 1958 tour. At the Barbican terrace blocks, this resulted into a geometric interpretation of a roofline accommodating a two-and-a-half-storey penthouse type. The white vaulted rooftops were employed also in the synthetic language of the Frobisher crescent block. The crescent is a Roman-inspired semicircle typical British urban form, which revived in the nineteenth century as a part of architect John Nash's imperial town-planning approach. In particular, it was featured in the development of the Park crescent by the Regent's Park. A mix of exceptional metaphors was also devised in the townhouses, which were situated in a rather disadvantageous spot below the podium. Therefore, stress was placed in creating a spectacular surrounding landscape to which these houses could offer luxurious views. The configuration of walk-in gardens in the central lake referenced the formality and conception of a garden of a Tuscan villa offering at the same time serenity and dignity. The large windows of the townhouse ground floors featured a reversed arch in the bottom as a reflection of the barrel vaults at the top of the superstructure. Finally, the ultimate suburban dream of seclusion was captured in the mews. These small terraced houses with the individual access and parking space were situated on the west side of a private garden for the Barbican residents only. They were submerged at the level below the podium to the extent that they were almost invisible as approaching from the west, street-level point of entrance to the complex.

Besides housing, the notion that the City could accommodate a high-culture community was highlighted in the Barbican arts centre, which was aimed at attracting a wide audience as a world-class cultural establishment. The final plan submitted by CPB in 1968 included an art gallery, a theatre, a concert hall also serving as a conference auditorium, a lending library, three cinemas and the Guildhall School of Music and Drama Theatre. It was the suggestion of the architects that a significantly sized theatre, seating 1,500, and concert hall, seating 2,000, could achieve a financial return by being let to professional companies. At the same time, a leading arts complex addressing the chronic shortage of performance venues in London would enhance the image of the then corporate City. In the built estate, considerable effort was made to downplay the presence of the arts venues since significant political power, which was necessary to support the scheme, had been invested in the character of a quiet residential quarter. This led to the architects' decision to submerge the concert hall underground to reduce its impact on residents. Its primary pedestrian lakeside entrance, framed by the restaurant, the cafeteria and the library, was meant to minimize intrusion into the views of the surrounding flats. At the same time, this placing of the entrance encouraged the assumption of pedestrian circulation in the estate from the west leading to the monumental staircase connecting the podium to the lakeside. Thus, visitors to the arts and recreation complex would mingle with the local community, resulting in a highly sophisticated mix.

The architects' conception of exclusivity was completed by the estate's overall isolation from its surroundings by turning its back on the industrial grimness of the City. The Barbican, literally meaning a fortified outpost or defensive tower, aimed at being a safe haven that encompassed anything the inhabitants would need. Its formal layout took on the self-referential character of a palace which was translated in urban terms into *a precinct* that had everything within or close at hand. The chief difference between the idea of the Golden Lane square and the Barbican precinct lay precisely in the intended autonomy of the latter as opposed to the urban inclusivity of the former. While the Golden Lane complex maintained an openness of communal spaces that were essentially part of the public realm, the Barbican attempted to enclose its precious provisions into a well-protected envelope that disrupted visual continuity with the City. The precinct became the new urban *enclosure* of the reconstructed city. The main theme of suburban luxury is captured here in a sense of privacy and personal character that expands beyond the domestic interior to include a lush landscape within the boundaries of its medieval and massive far beyond utility beached liner. By incorporating unintuitive thresholds, imposing walls and hidden entrances, the architecture discouraged passers-by from wandering in. The contradiction between the exterior impenetrable impression and the interior oasis enhanced the idea of an exclusive experience that the traditional council housing was lacking. The view from most of the flats, except those in the towers, almost obliterated any sense of being in the City. On the contrary, they induced a sense of naturalness and serenity similar to that experienced in the countryside. Thus, the overall effect would be one of dislocation from the London of car-congested streets, blackened buildings and rush-hour crowds to a beautiful, spacious, quiet piece of urban land. Domestic privacy was encapsulated in this experiential framework of the modern 'living suburb' as a quality that should be as much proximate to the City as secluded and exclusive, or, as architectural critic Reyner Bahnam put it, 'a voluntary ghetto'.

The attempt to demonstrate the individual character of private living, or dare I say, 'bespoke design', was also employed in the extreme diversification of dwelling types. By this, the Barbican aspired to achieve the maximum appeal to the market by capturing all aspects of possible clientele. Over a hundred different flat types were created throughout the estate, and each signified luxury in an exclusive manner. The top flats of the towers set literally a new high in the city while they are still today among the most sought-after properties on the London market. If tower flats symbolized the idea of living at the top of the City with breathtaking views, the barrel-vaulted penthouses attracted the attention to the medium-rise blocks. Emblematic of the avant-garde and luxurious designs, both tower flats and penthouses instigated class difference by creating vectors pointing at the top. To induce grand life dreams of climbing up the social and economic ladder was the goal as well as the point of departure for the architects of the Barbican. In describing the social outlook of a generation of young professionals likely to be familiar with the attractions of Mediterranean resorts, French modernism and German design, they were most probably drawing their self-portraits. The design of the estate set the stage for a new international lifestyle combining elements of baroque formality, Mediterranean leitmotifs, penthouse Americanism and Corbusian avant-gardism. No matter how incongruous, this combination underlined the intention to build a narrative around the rather technical term 'reconstruction'. This narrative expressed the fetish of a sociality that takes over and reinvents the centre and, at the same time, the idea of differentiation that removes the stigma of standardized housing and supports the claim for a better life. The Barbican was created for those who had who had 'earned' it, and, thus, access to this kind of urban privacy became a matter of entitlement.

Housing and the new urban enclosures

The tropes of the Barbican anticipated so much as they tested a currently familiar cocktail of urban policies, place-marketing and social restructuring, which became the role model for housing development. By using all these metaphors in the design, it actually intended to improvise the urban living of the future, and, in that sense, the Barbican plan was more a coherent exercise in brainstorming than an implementation design; it was more *a story* than a plan. Thus, it introduced an approach to housing development which became the norm in the neoliberal years: the design proposition of a narrative of private living to attract market interest as the indicator for subsequent support by planning authorities. In this respect, it introduced innovations in policy and design. On the one hand, it employed suggestive forms to symbolize status and quality. On the other hand, it created dramatic effects out of the mundane in order to create place value. Even the integration of a cosmopolitan cultural aspect into the local living experience served the imperative to value the originality of the Barbican as more than a housing scheme and the social status of the residents as above the average. By flaunting its programmatic and spatial autonomy, the Barbican draw a clear boundary between housing and the city and raised the symbolic capital of the City through the aspirational apparatus of getting inside; of *being private in the heart of the city*.

In the Barbican, more than any of their projects, CPB acted as proponents for the reversal of decentralization, by reinstating the idea of domestic privacy in a city centre worth living in. However, this cordial invite did not extend to those of modest means in any stage of the urban regeneration process. The 'return to the centre' rhetoric employed by the Barbican Committee leaders obscures the brutal class politics involved in the re-ordering of the urban space of the City. The idea that the Barbican was a 'ghetto' of high culture, of a 'private' character assigned to the public experience of the development, could be seen as the first instance of *gentrification*. Urban sociologist Ruth Glass coined the term in 1964 to express changes in the social character of the city voiced by architects, planners and politicians of the time (Glass, 1964). She identified the demographic replacement of many of the working-class quarters of London by the middle classes – both upper and lower. The phenomenon witnessed the upgrade of modest mews, cottages and old Victorian houses into 'elegant, expensive residences' becoming accessible to only 'the financially fittest, who can still afford to live and work there' (Glass, 1964: 17). Although at the Barbican there was no pre-existing displaced community, architectural gestures of seclusion, difficulty of access for the uninitiated and well-hidden extravagances were emphatically built in the idea of privacy and exclusivity of the new community. In addition, the high demand demonstrated in the waiting list for the 2,100 Barbican units in 1968 led to the cancellation of plans for small subsidized flats in the North Barbican, and all dwellings were to be leased at market rents. This kind of welfare did not address minimum needs; it picked up on emerging trends that matched its desired profile of council tenant and constructed the image of society it aspired to serve.

Deeming the Barbican a successful development from the market point of view internalizes the neoliberal logic 'that views mega-projects and place-marketing as a means for generating future growth and for waging a competitive struggle to attract investment capital' (Brenner and Theodore, 2002: 199). At the Barbican, competition was primarily placed in the architecture as the struggle to address (urban) privacy as a luxury. That is, to induce a pattern of social reproduction in order to ensure market demand and, thus, capital accumulation. While council housing was intended to provide a safety net for the most deprived, the transformation from standard to 'good-class' housing asserted that a market economy can function only once a market society has been established. The neoliberal vision was not fully realized until the election of Thatcher's conservative government in 1980. As the Barbican was near completion and almost half of the population lived in council housing, that year officially marked a turning point. Barbican flats began to be sold on the market or to the tenants at a discount following the Right-to-Buy legislation in 1981. While the crucial idea that no one can abstain from the market network within capitalism is not new, what differentiates neoliberalism as a discourse on the enclosure of urban commons is mainly the displacement of antagonism and the reproduction of inequalities at the most intimate level of everyday life. The policy and design of the Barbican had already provided the ideal of a stratified urban society and of domestic privacy as a commodity, and, therefore, the full-fledged neoliberalism of the Thatcherite policy was simply a fate fulfilled.

References

Banham, R. (1974) 'A Walled City: The Barbican in the City of London', *New Society*, 30(629), 222–3.

Blake, P. (1964) *Le Corbusier: Architecture and Form*. London: Penguin Books.

Brenner, N. (August 2004) 'Urban Governance and the Production of New State Spaces in Western Europe, 1960–2000', *Review of International Political Economy*, 11(3), 449–62.

Brenner, N. and Theodore, N. (2002) *Spaces of Neoliberalism: Urban restructuring in North America and Western Europe*. Oxford: Blackwell Publishing.

Chamberlin, P. (September 1958) 'The Living Suburb', *Architecture and Building*, 33(9), 347.

Chamberlin Powell & Bon Architects (3 June 1955) *Confidential Report to the Town Clerk on Proposed City Housing*. Available at: https://www.barbicanliving.co.uk/1955-scheme.

Chamberlin Powell & Bon Architects (May 31, 1956) *Barbican Development: Report to the Court of Common Council of the Corporation of the City of London on residential development within the Barbican Area.* Available at: https://www.barbicanliving.co.uk/1956-scheme.

Chamberlin Powell & Bon Architects (1959) *Barbican Redevelopment: Report to the Court of Common Council of the Corporation of the City of London on Residential Redevelopment within the Barbican Area.* Bolton and London: Tillotsons Bolton Ltd.

Glass, R. (1964) *London: Aspects of Change.* London: MacGibbon & Kee Ltd.

Gold, J. R. (2007) *The Practice of Modernism: Modern Architects and Urban Transformation, 1954–1972.* London: Routledge.

Hall, P. (1980) *Great Planning Disasters.* Berkeley and LA: California University Press.

Hayek, F. A. (1944) *The Road to Serfdom.* Chicago, IL: University of Chicago Press,

Heathcote, D. (2004) *Barbican: Penthouse over the City.* Chichester: Wiley-Blackwell Publishing.

Madden, D. and Marcuse, P. (2016) *In Defense of Housing: The Politics of Crisis.* London: Verso Books.

October (1954) 'New Barbican', *The Architects' Journal,* 120, 458–9.

October (1968) 'London: Living in the City', *The Architects' Journal,* 148(40), 704.

Pevsner, N. and Bradley, S. (1997) *The Buildings of England, London: The City Of London.* Volume 1. London: Penguin Books.

Piniara, I. (2020) *We Have Never Been Private: The Housing Project in Neoliberal Europe.* PhD dissertation. Architectural Association/Open University.

Rodriguez, A. (2016) *Residents: Inside the Iconic Barbican Estate.* London: Barbican Centre.

Spencer, D. (2016) *The Architecture of Neoliberalism: How Contemporary Architecture Became an Instrument of Control and Compliance.* London: Bloomsbury Academic.

Epilogue

Congregations: On the inhabitation of urban humans

AbduMaliq Simone

Congregations: On the inhabitation of urban humans

Part 1: The 'all-together'

Today, humans are perhaps the least-adept inhabitants of the urban. Despite all of the grand works, and despite all of the ways in which the urban may appear to be engineered by human aspirations and conceits, human inhabitants seem increasingly unaware of the extent to which urbanization is the interweaving, the entanglements of continuously mutating materiality. Far from cities being for 'us', and far from being the concretization of the extension of human capacity, cities are rapidly shifting entities that consolidate and disperse force, assume the illusion of stalwart, fractally replicating identities, and also fragment into unframeable details.

Each attainment, in terms of institutions and infrastructures, is haunted not only by the prospects of their possible failures or unanticipated dispositions but also by the brutal ways in which lives were put to work as the substrate of their construction. These include all of the enslavements, expulsions and exclusions that were necessary in order to secure the differentiation of the human inhabitant from their embeddedness in the 'thick of things', in ineluctable relations of interdependency with forces impervious to human control. Here, the human constitutes a cruel trick, a legacy of false advertising that attributes its defining capacity to the exercise of a self-conscious subject, thus occluding the banal, repetitive and toxic labour of those denied the status of human. For it was those whose ability to extend themselves in and through the forests, waters, swamplands, mountains, deserts, muddy rivers and wastelands that cleared the way for the enclosures and spectacles that have become the primary feature of urban life. As an abstraction from the systemic relationalities among matter, the human entity, in positing its own self-sufficiency, remains something that offers both promise and incessant disappointment. Because its nurturance and protection have been deployed as the basis from which to disqualify other forms of liveliness, to render inert, useless or dead those ways of living that never aspired to be human, the urban subject seizes itself as the most important form of life worth living.

Yet, in cities across the world, it is impossible to sort out, separate one life from another. What is important are not the accounts of individual projects, the trajectory of careers or the moral economies of social interchange, but all of the 'work-arounds' that take place every day as inhabitants move, talk, retrieve, extend, withdraw and circle. For individuals live among a plethora of actions – eating, sleeping, fucking, working, travelling, exchanging and making. These actions leave a multitude of traces and implications that have to be worked around, whether this entails their use, avoidance, deflection, acceleration or integration. Through these workarounds, spaces of operation come and go, things are opened up and closed down, with and without anticipation.

On Rue des Longues Capucins in Marseille, an elderly man in a wheelchair appears around 14.30 each day, and within thirty minutes the entire area is crowded with men selling found or stolen goods, both useful and useless. Each assumes his spot, but the order of appearance is never the same, nor is the price or the stories told about where the goods come from or even who these 'traders' are. It is a machine involving hundreds that have both everything and nothing to do with each other in that each works around the other for their limited space and opportunities, while each knows that they are easily substitutable and, therefore, need to perform a singular presence often marked by having the most useless thing to offer. But in making the offer, in announcing their presence with their own style of speech and dress, they attempt to lure a quick look from a passer-by, a brief conversation, an irreverent remark that is an invitation for them to show something else, to point down the street to a rumoured transaction that is set to make a lot of money for those who appear at the right time.

In one sense, these are the discarded collecting the detritus of the market, yet they are also flashpoints for rapid and short-lived congregations of those in a hurry to 'spill the beans', to point to things happening beyond the conventional imagination. Bootleg cigarettes and alcohol as well as fake identification cards mix with expired entry tickets and memorabilia in a vernacular where each seller's particular assemblage of goods constitutes a working map of lifetimes of circulation. It may seem like these traders are selling themselves (short), but they are publicizing a series of entries and exits, a world of manoeuvres that otherwise remains largely invisible. It is these workarounds that are the urban equivalent of indigenous walkabouts –

ways of designing a multitude of spaces that enfold and gather up congregants of all kinds.

Much of urban life has devolved into the repetition of complaint, of the exigency of residents to announce themselves, to display their anxieties and fever dreams and thus turn themselves in a vast substrate of extraction. The compulsion to speak and to impress combines with a more intricate architecture of monitoring and surveillance that attenuates the impact of any speech or performance, and thus, in turn, powering up the need to speak all the more. The long-honed cultures of mutual witnessing and attunement seem to increasingly dissipate into urban worlds of parallel play as residents parade out the well-worn stories of their relative successes and failures, or amplify that their neediness is more eligible to take up space than that of others. All of the props that have been constructed to prop up the well-individuated inhabitant insulated from the secretions of foreign bodies seem only to amplify a sense of insecurity compensated by an exaggerated self-confidence that 'everything will be alright'. White privilege was always based on this promise, a promise that entailed ignoring the empirical details in favour of an image of sufficiency propped up by the enforced precarity and expendability of others. In urban conditions where now everyone is potentially expandable, where there is no conceivable way of working around the costs that the abstraction of humanity has wrought, the right to be human is either buttressed at all costs or abandoned *all, together*. For only in an abandonment of the 'all, together' might it be possible to conceive of an enduring life worth living.

The 'all, together' may be simply another vain abstraction, but it does point out something inherent to urban conditions today: that the urban cannot pick and choose its own exemplary definitions; that it cannot be located in one place to the exclusion of others; and that it cannot manifest itself as something more or less, as all the old 'trademarks' of density, locational advantage and proximity are no longer the arbiters of what is urban or not. The lines of implication, circulation, logistics, inputs and outputs continuously establish and erase makeshift boundaries, depreciating any privileged linkage between the techniques of differentiation – of the 'here' and the 'there' – with some natural history of place or origin.

In a time of quantum physics, where locality does not entail physical proximity, the urban congregation is necessarily diffuse and shape-shifting. Power differentials of course remain, certain lives can be wasted at will, yet the 'all, together', far from connoting a human nature in the last instance, reflects the fundamental indeterminacy of what counts and what doesn't, even in the midst of an unprecedented machinery of accounting. For there is nothing not there. Despite all of the histories of getting rid of things, of eliminating dangers, of expelling the apparently useless and of deciding what lives, what dies and what simply is as lifeless form, urbanization's lines of implications and its extensions across time and space and enfolding of diverse of logics and practices of making, posits a world where nothing can be counted out, as the 'out there' becomes something more intimate, as compensation, possibility and remainder.

So, in considerations of marginality, of where and how urban residents may dwell, it is technically and often politically possible to define and operationalize more finite and discrete territories. Certainly, gated communities and increasingly segregated cities point to this. But this movement inward simply amplifies the salience and forcefulness of an 'out there' that must be either extracted from or defended against. Such immunization, such amplification of the 'settlement', relies upon the capitalization of new horizons, an expansive beyond. For what is 'subtracted' from cities in terms of protected realms necessitates the addition of the 'open-ended', of new frontiers of exploitation in a seemingly zero-sum game.

Yet, in-between this calculus, there are all the Rue des Longues Capucins, all of the unruly markets and dwelling places of unruly populations whose wanton sentiments, exaggerated claims, modest generosities and wilful dissimulations depend upon forms of inhabitation that continuously work around each other, both engaging and staying out of each other's way, and, in the process, making room for something no one has seen coming and don't know quite what to do with. So, there are no rules in advance, no fixed measures of efficacy. What works is to be worked out, and the working out will have to entail bits and pieces of everything that different actors bring the process.

For we must take what has long been considered marginal and render it an integral aspect of the 'all, together', as that which in fact enables a process of coming together, and not simply a supplement, an adding on to some firmly established sense of normality or propriety. The 'all, together' is not an advocacy of universality, it is not one big happy family, but urbanization's very horizon as a positing of gatherings among the disparate. It is the eventual coupling of that which does not belong, as in the Islamic notion of *tawhid*, where everything that exists as different has something fundamental and unique to say about everything else, so that the ontological completion of any event or existence is only possible in a gathering 'all, together'.

We can cite so many events and scenarios that reiterate a sense of fragility and oppression, of people denied and in sorrow. But there is more than this if we place the human at the centre of a precarious suturing of materials and other forms of life and non-life. Not as the engineer, but as the stitch and weave itself, the circuit breakers, the rivers and dams, the high wires and

Epilogue 299

fibre cables – the fleshy underpinnings of an urban liveliness that does not represent accumulation or human imagination but the tentative outcomes of all kinds of things rubbing up against the other.

All are liminal spaces where erasure mixes with spectral endurance, where the traces of struggles and improvisations constitute an obdurate turbulence to any definitive consolidation. These are spaces that keep things moving along in a circuitry that gathers up other traces and spaces in an urban extensionality that is more and less than capitalist expansionism. For the 'all, together' subsumes nothing, it explains nothing. Inhabitation here is less emplacement than an abiding, a way of carrying on, stealing away in the cover of night and finding oneself after a long journey back to the place from which one left, only now unrecognizable, detached from any familiarity or apparent use. Liminality is not that of a stranger in a strange land but a refrain, a call, not to arms only, but a call to everything out there, a beckoning home.

Part 2: Unravelling and detachment

What is it that we have in common? When do the congregations discussed earlier turn into a hardened grip that enforces particular ways of relating? A current conundrum in urban work is the seemingly irreconcilable incompatibility and applicability of relationality and detachment. Each notion simultaneously confirms and negates the other. As concepts, each is in an obvious relationship with the other, as they are simultaneously detached. But far from being a 'both-and' situation, with the convenience that such a formulation might provide, there is something that refuses to be worked out, where the terms might be conjoined as a simultaneity. For each posits implications that would 'wipe out' the other, undermine dialectical possibilities and, instead, point to a vast interstitial space for which there is no ready vernacular to provide a positive identity of any kind.

Both 'relationality' and 'detachment' point to empirical and political aspirations in contemporary urban thought and how the urban may be inhabited in face of climate exigencies. On the one hand, arguments for a pluriverse foreground an essential relationality of all things, of how the very materiality of distinct entities constitutes a force that incessantly shapes the capacities of each, and of how apparent differences operate as guarantors for an overarching commons that is continuously self-constituted from the oscillating proportionalities of affordances each provides. Instead of identifying vectors of control-command systems, where the human inhabitant operates as a kind of meta-governor, the pluriversal (Escobar

2020) points to the specificities of force fields, metabolisms, intellection, crystallization, photosynthesis, infection, leeching, decay, carbonization, atmospheric pressure and affect – to name a few critical processes – and how they reciprocally shape the operational capacities of material and immaterial entities. In a convergence of decolonial, quantum, feminist and post-humanist logics, this is a phenomenon of trans*mattering – to use Karen Barad's (2011) term – all of the way down as entities and processes 'reach' for each other, are gathered up in specific dispositions of sense. In-forming becomes an ongoing mode of working out mutual accommodations, a means of grasping how things 'lead' to each other, and assume reciprocal emplacement as an aesthetics of rendering each entity relevant to one another.

In contemporary epistemology, relationality becomes a demand, an urgent call to recognize the salience of long-suppressed knowledges that valorize the ways in which humans, plants, animals, soils and minerals – 'processed' in various forms – co-inhabit the earth and require the curation of forms of mutual care. It is matter of how each 'tends' to the other, both in the sense of bearing witness and in practices of affecting and being affected (De La Cadena 2016; Puig de la Bellacasa 2017). Sustainable urban development and climate mitigation would seem to demand recognition of these fundamental interdependencies and attention to recalibrating the purported needs of urban human inhabitants to actions capable of sustaining nurturing intersections of various forms of life and non-life. Particularly as media ecologies assume a life of their own, capable of measuring and adjusting the interactive impacts of diverse materiality, the urban is foreseen as increasingly a topological process, folding and unfolding various formats given the specificities of how the diverse materials are present to each other (Hui 2017). Parametrics, interoperability, feedback loops and machine learning become technicities capable of amplifying and operating the essential relationality of things, rendering dwelling as something 'optimally resilient'. Attention to anti-blackness, settler logics and imperialism, which function to petrify the fleshy interfaces among things and calcify the 'human' as the node through which all causative explanations take place, attempts to open up long-suppressed capacities *to dwell* and move with the earth in all of its unsettled volatility.

Much attention has been paid to reworking notions of the commons, with particular emphasis on the interrelationships among wage and reproductive labour, the production of material sustenance and the elaboration of collective responsibilities (popular economy), as well as the social ecology of human-machinic relations (Brancaccio and Vercellone 2019; Mattei and Mancall 2019; Stavrides 2019). These figurations of imagination are efforts to derive workable territories of recognition and governance. Here territory is less a demarcation of physical or volumetric space than pragmatic collections of ethical practices and technical instruments that might be intersected to conceive and administer zones of mutual implication and of people residing and working together and with their environments to provide the basics of a life worth living. They configure porous boundaries that less operate as markers of definition or defence, but measured platforms for accessing a larger world, while curating an experience of coherence for those who live within them.

But the question is on what basis do things necessarily relate. Certainly, much of urban experience today demonstrates that the proximity of different ways of life and built environments do not guarantee that they will have anything to do with each other. In a world where relationality entails an ever-prolific expansion of the ways in which things are at least potentially connected to each other, aspirations to enhance our ability to tend to things, to be attentive to the operations of the earth we inhabit, would seem to be undermined by the sheer excess of things to pay attention to. If our capacity to alter our behaviours is motivated by paying attention to our surroundings and our actions in new ways, how do we decide what is most relevant to pay attention to, which things are construed as most relevant to how we feel and act, and how do we draw the line at what kinds of events in our surrounds have something most immediately to do with us and our capacities to act? The apparent demise of political liberalism, with its faux celebrations of diversity and tolerance of differences, as well as its implicit 'request' that citizens take mind of each other's needs and realities, occurs in part because it instils a sense of incessant comparison, of diminishing entitlements and of heightened anxiety that the self and place one occupies is permanently insufficient (Brown 2015).

Cities rushed to stake their future economic viability on maximizing their relatability to a larger world, operationalized by availing all kinds of opportunities to enable that larger world to 'show up' within city jurisdictions – and in ways in which such jurisdictions were inevitably diminished by that very availing. As a result, their capacity to shape anything like a common municipal identify increasingly became impossible. Of course, cities were never spaces of overarching cohesion and were always fraught with inequities and spatial fission (Holston and Appadurai 1996). But the very amplification of urbanity as a territorialization of relationality, as an arena of a circulation of materiality that exceeded a city-form accelerated the dissolution of 'municipality' as the primary referent of dwelling. Residents experientially saw their worlds both narrow into increasingly individuated modules of itineraries and expand into an increasing nebulous space of financial flows, speculations and global growth machines (Sassen 2000; Adams 2018). Now even the most seemingly marginal locations of the world, subject to an enforced remoteness but never empirically remote, demand attention to their applicability to fundamental decisions at the heart of urban power – for example, the emerging centres of low carbon extraction whose rare earth materials are the fuels for the smart city (Walker et al. 2015; Silver and Marvin 2017; Bouzarovski and Haarstad 2019).

The question is whether things need to relate. To what extent is relationality at the heart of an emerging sustainable economy of care, and to what extent is it the ruse of making everything fit or fixed, where every aspect of life is subsumed within an implicit calculus of mutual implication? Do the physics of locality, which upend our conventional notions of how things impact upon each other, that rework the spatialization of intimacy and cause and effect translate into workable apparatuses of administration and provisions of basic needs? If what operates at a distance is more salient to the terms of my life than what I find right next to me, what then do I do with my proximity to others? Clearly, as what is near moves further away, and what is 'out there' assumes a position of greater intimacy, there is room for all kinds of inversions not bound to linear conventions. But in this 'crossfire', relationality is something that spreads out, almost virally, rather than assumes images of concentration. Here, I have the experiential sense of convening my life with multiple others, right here, right now. Here, precarity operates as a kind of 'architectural design', pushing residents into new arrangements of residence, income generation and interdependency, but with the tacit presumption that nothing will last for very long. Institutions are not being built, but rather temporary arrangements, even autonomous zones, whose experimental nature is driven more by the inability to assume a normal life than a progressive social imagination. The ability to jump scale, to suture together innovative connections among media, materials, cultural norms, physical settings and money is less the curation of a new collective sensibility than a series of tactical improvisations in the midst of sociality falling apart, being dissolved into an expanding archive of details strewn across vast distances not really distant given the reach of social media (Stiegler 2019).

The configuration of urban spaces appears increasingly as serialized detachments. Even as residents of all backgrounds appear to intensify and extend the scope of their mobilities, as urban transport options increase in terms of modalities, settlements themselves seem increasingly separate. In part, despite the homogenization of specific metropolitan zones, with their standardized suite of built environments and services, this separateness is a function of the individuating forces of modern urban life, its valorization of individual attainment and consumption, the time demands of income generation and the desire to attenuate the labour-intensive demands of social integration and neighbourhood life (Rose 2017). In part, the tendency towards detachment emanates from the very expansiveness of relationality, a concretization of a desire to narrow the confines of what one pays attention to, of compartmentalizing the control over one's surrounds (Strathern 1995; Kohn 2013). The genealogy of detachments, however, can be quite varied (Candea et al. 2015).

Some emanate from the singularities of locatedness – the ways in which infrastructural layouts, toxicities, natural elements configure highly specific definitions and boundaries. Others are generated from collectively deliberated decisions to operate at a remove, to engineer specific visibilities of internal dynamics, to protect specific economies and ways of life from the pressures of encroachment. Still others proceed from the specific designs of new residential situations in a panoply of developments, such as new towns, housing projects, gated communities and development zones. As urban spaces extend outwards away from urban cores, and 'inwards' from towns in the hinterlands, built environments are produced by a wide array of finance, speculative projects, auto-constructed settlements and industrial developments that work their way around and through each other often without any overarching spatial development planning or clear jurisdictional frameworks (Halbert and Rouanet 2013; Keil 2018).

So, while all of these spatial products may sit next to each other, there is no basis for them to necessarily relate, even if a series of backward and forward linkages can be identified on paper. Even in settings that seem to be consolidated, such as an area of thousands of migrant dormitories on the outskirts of Jakarta, residents living on one 'row' may have little to do with those on the next. Detachment is a metaphor for 'keeping one's head down' or 'keeping indebtedness at bay'.

At times, detachment becomes an implicit form of neighbourhood solidarity. Instead of co-residents abiding by an overarching series of norms or reciprocal responsibilities to each other, or managing local affairs through consensus or attributing management to agreed upon 'authority figures', they are 'let go' to pursue their own ways of doing things along their own conduits through the larger city so that new inputs, sources of income or political power can be resourced. Here, detachment becomes a modus operandi not only for individuals and households but also for larger aggregates of residents who stake their long-term prospects on attaining proximity to an intensified heterogeneity of how their neighbourhoods are networked to something 'out there'.

This is less the curation of the commons than it is a process of leveraging disconnected details, itineraries and personal projects whose implications always remain difficult to pinpoint but nevertheless remain objects of vague hopefulness. Even under conditions of high residential and commercial density, where people are literally running into each other all of the time, where streets may be intensely jammed with all kinds of activities, and where multiple vectors of servicing across disparate occupations and trades exist, an atmosphere of detachment prevails lane by lane with their increasingly singular compositions (Murray 2017; McFarlane 2020). While this diversity may indeed have been there all along, it now assumes a heightened visibility where singularities matter more than convergences, as these singularities operate as specific ways of interpreting what is going on, managing the small differences as a matter of capturing value, as indeed small particularities – in the ways things are made, consumed, distributed (even relationships) – come to matter more in urban economies (Brenner 2019).

Relationalities among specific sectors of urban residents also are made to depreciate in value. As the relations among the 'dangerous classes' have long been matters of concern to the elites that administered cities, these administrators have become increasingly brazen and adept at mitigating the dangerous atmospheres that hang over large metropolitan areas and which are seen as impeding more profitable engagements with the larger world. The 'popular classes' have themselves become more skilled at urban politics and appropriating medias and technologies to buttress the growth of the affiliative economies both licit and illicit. Still, they remain easy and available targets for the self-aggrandizing manoeuvres of aspirant political assemblages, who reiterate old stories about cleaning up the city.

What is perhaps new is the shift in emphasis from negotiating favourable relationships with the poor, of repeating the tried-and-true strategies of vote banks and gestures of provisioning, to pursuing models of financialization where the lives of the poor are 'securitized', managed as an aggregate mass in order to demonstrate the creditworthiness of the 'nation', to displaying its capacities to move bodies around, and extract from them specific energies and flexibilities outside of their familiar contexts (Tadiar 2022). Here the specific relationalities of the popular classes are rendered expendable, as the very intimacies of household and neighbourhood connections become the targets of police intervention. As a result, neighbours lose faith in other, and thus their ability to operate in concert. The poor are detached from the specifics of everyday social relationships. They are overseen as small enterprises worthy of conditional cash transfers, eliminated or incarcerated for their criminality, left alone in highly volatile situations engineered by the state through threats of eviction or service cuts to implode, or resituated in highly managed relations of dependency across part-time, provisional jobs and residences whose prices almost immediately place them in interminable debt (Abourahme 2018.)

In situations of engineered detachment, detachment also becomes a modality of resistance. Here, residents may refuse all procedures of normalization and development, where marginalized youth in particular may sometimes embrace the very negative images attributed to them. Here detachment is from the game of trying to prove oneself as human, of being as good or worthy as anyone else. Regardless of the exigency to make a living, to put bread on the table, there is substantive detachment from trying to anchor one's life in a specific place or territory. Circulation and movement become the practices of everyday inhabitation, and while residents may not move very far, it is imperative to keep moving – as a means of deflecting being the target of police, familiar judgements, restrictions or obligations – which effects a kind of detachment from a discernible relationship with a place or occupation. It can be argued that such practices of movement are a means of maintaining a relationship with the larger city or urban setting, to keep from being immobilized. Yet, the focus of investment is to maintain the possibility of moving on, just out of reach of the constraints of a past life even if the nature of such transitions is small and seemingly insignificant. The aim is that of detachment, to not be readily identifiable, but, at the same time, to be known as someone beyond the possibilities implied by a specific background. Witness the massive popularity of *TikTok* among the popular classes, wherein these short videos, residents portray a multiplicity of identities all detached from each other – a constantly mutating body with no discernible connection to a past or future.

There are of course instances where relationality and detachment come together and operate in tandem. Logistics is perhaps the most powerful instance of this, where places are dis-embedded from an 'organic' or historical relationship with their surrounds in order to become a component in an elongated string of relationalities aimed at facilitating the circulation and transshipment of specific commodities, information and services (Cowen 2014; Chua 2018). Here places are detached in order to be sutured in ways that lock them in to servicing an overarching infrastructure of connectivity that may have little relevance or benefit to the specific territory to which they are now only nominally a part (Martin 2012). Here, too, the notion of movement and circulation dominates, with all of its attendant violence on the sensibilities and concretization of belonging among specific residents.

In contrast to the tropes of settler colonialism, logistics prolongs the colonial apparatus by settling specific resources, infrastructures, land and labour within circuits of exchange to which there is no belonging, only interoperability, that is, to be a component that is replaceable, circumnavigable. Places are detached not to find new modalities of belonging but to remain detached, available to shifting circuits of throughflows, whose futures may be short-lived. Yet, the impetus here remains the cultivation of infrastructures of relationality and of the ability to concretize specific relationships between land, plantations, shipping, production, financialization, local development, political control and capital accumulation. The logistical relationship aims to skip over history and overcome the blockages of distance, culture and nature to forge connections that are abstracted from local sentiment or practice (Gregson et al. 2017).

This is a long way from the political sentiments of a particularly Latin American strand of collective becoming that emphasizes the importance of working out new values of living life in place, of the importance of the way in which territory might be configured as a means of operationalizing awareness and practices of mutual tending, and of sensing and living with the essential relationships of earth, things, critters, waterways, atmospheres, forests and humans. In a recent article, Arturo Escobar (2019) calls for the experimental design of urban space so that long-honed knowledges of 'non-urbans' might find applicability on new terrain. While these pluriversal notions remain important, there is also something to be gleaned from logistics as well, in its particular and peculiar conflations of relationality and detachment. There is something about the ways in which many young people, particularly from the popular classes, live their lives as logistics that may prove as generative as the now conventional decolonial designs.

While it is true that in their displacement youth become objects of extraction – their efforts to keep in motion rendering them temporary and cheapened labour of all kinds outside of any long-term investment. Yet, their sometime capacity to harvest their surrounds for bits and pieces of opportunity, hacking and information become the resources that enable them to prolong circulations across urban space. Even if they profess that their provisionality can only be a temporary thing, they aim to work around apparent stabilities, often perceiving them as a dead end or too costly. This does not obviate the fact that social control too has shifted from efforts to keep people in place, to restrict mobility, to conceding that even the most dangerous elements will move and move widely. As such, policing is aimed at targeting threats in motion, and of discerning the advantages and concrete opportunities entailed in bodies being shifted around, without long-term attachments to any given space. As political recalcitrance also shifts from mobilizations in place to 'hit and run and hack', tracking these operations on the move becomes more proficient, which in terms prompts even greater levels of dissimulation, and attachment to specific identities, on the part of the targeted (Valayden 2016).

At the same time, it may be necessary to work with these movements towards detachment. Subsidiary, localized branding, extensive residential mobility, restructuration, land value capture, gentrification, re-densification and urban renewal have all conspired to atomize urban space. Additionally, cross-district solidarities have diminished in face of more intricate targeting of resource allocations and capital investments. To what extent is it possible to consider urban regions as a multiplicity of centres or settlements or municipalities? In some way, this repeats the American model of individualized municipalities within single urban regions that were largely motivated by real estate covenants, racial segregation, differential tax preferences and development coalitions. Such detachments proved costly in terms of spatial planning, infrastructure development and fiscal viability. But the reality is that an off-grid existence may be the only medium-term viable disposition in terms of encouraging and even mandating greater resident participation in the care of environments and the management of low carbon technologies applied to urban services. Experiments in dwelling may need to be sufficiently detached from overarching metropolitan exigencies and development agendas in order to accrue the space necessary in order to go through what will likely be many renditions of experiments and many instances of failure.

Across many regions of the South, it is precisely the peripheries of large urban areas where experiments in residing and producing are taking place. The impetus is to draw them in under overarching regional development authorities and development commissions, and this is legitimated in terms of economic viability and administrative efficacy. Nonetheless, the relative detachment of projects and settlements and their combined incongruities and contradictions are also incentives to find ways of articulation that are 'off the grid' in terms of the conventional designs of zoning and so forth. What kinds of planning mechanisms could be generated from finding ways to systematize provisionally those kinds of articulations that are being engineered by different kinds of actors in these spaces? Again, how do we form bands of investigators, relaying among ourselves to engage the relays of always emerging urban congregations?

References

Abourahme, N. (2018). Of monsters and boomerangs: Colonial returns in the late liberal city. *City* 22(1): 106–15.

Adams, R. E. (2018). *Circulation and Urbanization*. London: Sage.

Barad, K. (2011). Nature's queer performativity. *Qui Parle* 19(2): 121–58.

Bouzarovski, S. and Haarsta, H. (2019). Rescaling low-carbon transformations: Towards a relational ontology. *Transactions of the Institute of British Geographers* 44(2): 256–69.

Brancaccio, F. and Vercellone, C. (2019). Birth, death, and resurrection of the issue of the common: A historical and theoretical perspective. *South Atlantic Quarterly* 118(4): 699–709.

Brenner, N. (2019). *New Urban Spaces: Urban Theory and the Scale Question.* New York: Oxford University Press.

Brown, W. (2015). *Undoing the Demos: Neoliberalism's Stealth Revolution.* New York: Zone Books.

Candea, C., Cook, J., Trundle, C. and Yarrow, T. (2015). Introduction: reconsidering detachment. In *Detachment: essays on the limits of relational thinking.* Manchester: Manchester University Press, pp. 1–34.

Chua, C. (2018). Logistical violence, logistical vulnerabilities. *Historical Materialism* 24(4): 167–82.

Cowen, D. (2014). *The Deadly Life of Logistics: Mapping Violence in Global Trade.* Minneapolis, MN; London: University of Minnesota Press.

De La Cadena, M. (2016). *Earth Beings: Ecologies of Practice across Andean Worlds.* Durham NC; London: Duke University Press.

Escobar, A. (2019). Habitability and design: radical interdependence and the re-earthing of cities. *Geoforum* 101: 132–140.

Escobar, A. (2020). *Pluriversal Politics: The Real and the Possible.* Durham, NC: Duke University of Press.

Gregson, N., Crang, M. and Antonopoulos, C. (2017). Holding together logistical worlds: Friction, seams and circulation in the emerging 'global warehouse'. *Environment & Planning D: Society and Space* 35(3): 381–98.

Halbert, L. and Rouanet, H. (2013). Filtering risk away: global finance capital, transcalar territorial networks and the (un)making of city-regions: An analysis of commercial property development in Bangalore, India. *Regional Studies* 48(3): 471–84.

Holston, J. and Appadurai, A. (1996). Cities and citizenship. *Public Culture* 8(2): 187–204.

Hui, Y. (2017). On cosmotechnics: For a renewed relation between technology and nature in the anthropocene. *Techné: Research in Philosophy and Technology* 21(2–3): 1–23.

Keil, R. (2018). Extended urbanization, "disjunct fragments" and global suburbanisms. *Environmental and Planning D; Society and Space* 36(3): 494–511.

Kohn, E. (2013). *How Forests Think: Toward an Anthropology beyond the Human.* Berkeley: University of California Press.

Martin, C. (2012). Desperate mobilities: Logistics, security and the extra-logistical knowledge of "appropriation." *Geopolitics* 17(2): 355–76.

Mattei, U. and Mancall, M. (2019). Communology: The emergence of a social theory of the commons. *South Atlantic Quarterly* 118(4): 725–46.

McFarlane (2020). De/re-densification. *City.* DOI: 10.1080/13604813.2020.1739911

Murray, M. (2017). *The Urbanism of Exception: The Dynamics of Global City Building in the 21ˢᵗ Century.* New York: Cambridge University Press.

Puig de la Bellacasa, M. (2017). *Matters of Care: Speculative Ethics in More Than Human Worlds*. Minneapolis, MN: University of Minnesota Press.

Rose, G. (2017). Posthuman agency in the digitally mediated city: Exteriorization, individuation, reinvention. *Annals of the American Association of Geographers* 107(4): 779–93.

Sassen, S. (2000). Territory and territoriality in the global economy. *International Sociology* 15(2): 372–393.

Silver, J. and Marvin, S. (2017). Powering sub-Saharan Africa's urban revolution: An energy transitions approach. *Urban Studies* 54(4): 847–61.

Stavrides, S. (2019). *Common Spaces of Urban Emancipation*. Manchester: University of Manchester Press.

Stiegler, B. (2019). *The Age of Disruption: Technology and Madness in Computational Capitalism*. London; New York: Polity.

Strathern, M. (1995). *The Relation: Issues in Complexity and Scale*. Chicago: Prickly Pear Press.

Tadiar, N. (2022). *Remaindered Life*. Durham, NC: Duke University Press.

Valayden, D. (2016). Racial feralization: targeting race in the age of 'planetary urbanization.' *Theory, Culture & Society* 33(7–8): 159–82.

Walker, G., Karvonen, A. and Guy, S. (2015). Zero carbon homes and zero carbon living: Sociomaterial interdependencies in carbon governance. *Transactions of the Institute of British Geographers* 40(4): 494–506.

Index